THE CULTURE OF INTERNATIONAL ARBITRATION AND THE EVOLUTION OF CONTRACT LAW

The Culture of International Arbitration and the Evolution of Contract Law

JOSHUA KARTON

OXFORD
UNIVERSITY PRESS

OXFORD
UNIVERSITY PRESS

Great Clarendon Street, Oxford, OX2 6DP,
United Kingdom

Oxford University Press is a department of the University of Oxford.
It furthers the University's objective of excellence in research, scholarship,
and education by publishing worldwide. Oxford is a registered trade mark of
Oxford University Press in the UK and in certain other countries

First Edition published in 2013

British Library Cataloguing in Publication Data
Data available

ISBN 978–0–19–965800–8

For Asher

Preface

When I entered law school, my sole intention was to study public international law. I had studied international relations as an undergraduate and nearly joined the Canadian foreign service before deciding to go to law school first. But then I was randomly assigned to the first-year Contracts class of Allan Farnsworth, a first-rate scholar and an inspiring teacher. He kindled my abiding interest in contract law. This development put me into a quandary: how could I be both an international lawyer and a contract lawyer? The next year, when I had a chance encounter with the field of international commercial arbitration, I knew that I had found my niche. Where else do international politics, business, and law so closely intersect?

After a brief turn in private practice, that interest took me to Pembroke College, Cambridge, where I conduct the doctoral research that lay the foundations for this book. Both my PhD thesis and this book could not have been completed without the friendly but firm guidance of my PhD supervisors, James Crawford and Louise Merrett. They stood by me through years of missed deadlines and uneven drafts. Their patience, good advice, and thorough (and fast!) edits have improved my thinking and this text immensely.

I am grateful to the many expert practitioners who generously agreed to my request for an interview and who freely gave of their time and their insights. This book has been greatly enhanced by their contributions.

I also owe a debt of gratitude to the many people who have provided useful comments, in particular colleagues and friends at the Queen's University Faculty of Law and my fellow members of the Cambridge International Law PhD Roundtable and the Cambridge Comparative Law Discussion Group. Thanks are also due to my PhD examiners, John Bell and Loukas Mistelis, who were rigorous in their examination of my work but also unfailingly supportive and encouraging, and who also introduced me to the fine editors at OUP. John was also a true mentor in his capacities as fellow of Pembroke College and convener of the first year PhD programme.

I was aided in the preparation of this text by the energetic and thorough research assistance of Daniel Dawalibi, Ian Iatzko, and especially Andrew Reid-Workman, all JD students at Queen's University.

Parts of this book that have previously been published in academic journals have benefited from the attentions of anonymous referees and staff editors. I would like to thank the referees and editors at International and Comparative Law Quarterly and the International Business Law Journal for their conscientious and constructive criticisms. I am also grateful to OUP for permitting me to publish earlier versions of two chapters as separate articles.

My parents, Michael Karton and Barbara Heller, have been my best teachers for longer than I can remember. Their patience, love, and wisdom made me a man and made it possible for me to write this book.

More than mere thanks are due to my partner in every way, Dr Ann Shih-yi Chen. She has loved me and taken care of me for ten years now, and I can't wait for the next ten.

Finally, this book completed its long gestation around the same time as Asher, my firstborn son and darling baby. It is dedicated to him.

Table of Contents

II. INTERNATIONAL ARBITRATION CULTURE AND CONTRACT LAW

Table of Cases

Tables of Legislation

NATIONAL PRIMARY LEGISLATION

France

Code civil
- art 1134 210
- art 1135 209
- art 1156 208
- art 1184 168
- art 1341 209
- art 1612 169
- art 1653 169
- art 1704 169
- art 1948 169

Code de la consummation, Art 132-1 6
Code de procédure civile 163
- art 1502(5) 134
- art 1522 69

Ecuador

Civil Code, art 1568 188

Germany

BGB
- s 133 . . . . . 197, 208
- s 157 210
- ss 305–10 6
- s 320 167
- s 320(1) 167
- s 320(2) 168

Denmark

Arbitration Act, s 27(2) 155

Egypt

Civil Code, art 161 182

Netherlands

Code of Civil Procedure, art 1044(1) 155

Spain

Civil Code
- art 1281 224
- art 1282 224
- art 1285 224

Personal Data Protection Act 99

Switzerland

Arbitral Rules of Procedure, art 33(1) 148
Code of Obligations, art 82 . . . . . 168, 179, 180
Federal Code of Private International Law, art 187(1) 98
Private International Law Statute
- art 16 158
- art 33(1) 148
- art 187(1) 148

United Kingdom

Arbitration Acts 1889–1950 81
Arbitration Act 1979 . . . . . 68, 82
Arbitration Act 1996 . . . . . 68, 133
- s 1 83
- s 4(1) 84
- s 33(1)(a) 45
- s 34 154
- s 46(3) 148
- s 68(2)(a) 45
- s 69 . . . . . 81, 82
- s 82(1) 82
- Sch 1 84

Civil Evidence Act 1995, s 4 200
Sale of Goods Act 1893 172
Sale of Goods Act 1979
- s 11 173
- s 12 173
- s 14 173
- s 28 165
- s 31(2) 175

Statutory Instruments

Civil Procedure Rules 1998 (SI 1998/3132) 105
Sale and Supply of Goods to Consumers Regulations 2002 (SI 2002/3045) . . . 166
Unfair Terms in Consumer Contracts Regulations 1999 (SI 1999/ 2083) 6

United States

Arbitration Fairness Act, HR 1020, 111th Cong (2009) 6
Federal Arbitration Act 1925 (FAA) 70, 81
Federal Rules of Civil Procedure 200
Federal Securities Act 83
Restatement (2d) of Contracts
- s 209 202
- s 209(3) 202
- s 210(2) 203
- s 215 203
- s 216(1) 203
- s 231 173
- s 234 171
- s 237 174
- s 241 174
- s 259 173

EUROPEAN SECONDARY LEGISLATION

ARBITRAL RULES OF PROCEDURE

TRANSNATIONAL LEGAL INSTRUMENTS

TREATIES

Judicial and Arbitral Decisions Cited

DECISIONS OF NATIONAL COURTS

Australia

Austria

Belgium

France

Germany

Italy

The Netherlands

Portugal

Sweden

Switzerland

United Kingdom

United States

DECISIONS OF INTERNATIONAL JUDICIAL TRIBUNALS

Permanent Court of International Justice

International Court of Justice

European Court of Justice

INTERNATIONAL ARBITRAL AWARDS

Ad hoc Awards

ICC Awards

Other Institutional Awards

Table of Abbreviations

AAA	American Arbitration Association
ACICA	Australian Centre for International Commercial Arbitration
ADR	Alternative Dispute Resolution
AED	United Arab Emirates Dirhams
aff'd	Affirmed
AJIL	American Journal of International Law
Am	American
Arb	Arbitration
Art	Article
ASA	Swiss Arbitration Association
Ass	Association
AUD	Australian Dollars
BGB	Bundesgesetzbuch [German Civil Code]
Bull	Bulletin
Bus	Business
Cal	California
Can	Canada/Canadian
CAS	Court of Arbitration for Sport
Cf	Compare Favourably
CIArb	Chartered Institute of Arbitrators (UK)
CIETAC	Chinese International Economic and Trade Arbitration Commission
CISG	UN Convention on Contracts for the International Sale of Goods (1980)
CLJ	Cambridge Law Journal
CO	Swiss Code of Obligations (*Obligationenrecht/Code des obligations*)
CUP	Cambridge University Press
cmt	Comment
Co	Company
Comm	Commerce/Commercial
Comp	Comparative
Corp	Corporation/Corporate
Ct	Court
DIAC	Dubai International Arbitration Centre
Disp	Dispute
Doc	Document
ECJ	European Court of Justice
Econ	Economics
ed	Editor
edn	Edition
EJIL	European Journal of International Law
Eur	European
Fla	Florida

fn	Footnote
Harv	Harvard
HK	Hong Kong
HKIAC	Hong Kong International Arbitration Centre
IBA	International Bar Association
ICA	International Commercial Arbitration
ICC	International Chamber of Commerce
ICC Rules	Rules of Arbitration of the ICC (2012)
ICCA	International Council for Commercial Arbitration
ICDR	International Center for Dispute Resolution (a division of the AAA)
ICDR Rules	ICDR International Dispute Resolution Procedures (2009)
ICJ	International Court of Justice
ICLQ	International and Comparative Law Quarterly
ICSID	International Centre for the Settlement of Investment Disputes
ILA	International Law Association
ILSA	International Law Students Association
Int'l	International
Invs	Investment
J	Journal
JDI	Journal de droit international
L	Law
La	Louisiana
Lab	Labour
LCIA	London Court of International Arbitration
LCIA Rules	LCIA Arbitration Rules (1998)
Leg	Legal
Med	Mediation
Mich	Michigan
Minn	Minnesota
MLR	Modern Law Review
NC	North Carolina
New York Convention	UN Convention on the Recognition and Enforcement of Foreign Arbitral Awards (1958)
No	Number
Nw	Northwestern
NY	New York
NZ	New Zealand
obs	Observations
OJLS	Oxford Journal of Legal Studies
OUP	Oxford University Press
P	Press
para	Paragraph
PECL	Principles of European Contract Law

Penn	Pennsylvania
PCIJ	Permanent Court of International Justice
Pol	Politics/Political
Pol'y	Policy
Prob	Problems
Proc	Proceedings
Pub	Public
Q	Quarterly
R	Review
Reh'g	Rehearing
Rep	Report
Resol	Resolution
rev'd	Reversed
Rev arb	*Revue de l'arbitrage*
s	Section
SCC	Arbitration Institute of the Stockholm Chamber of Commerce
Sci	Science
SIAC	Singapore International Arbitration Centre
So	South/Southern
Soc	Social
Soc'y	Society
St	State
Stud	Studies
Tex	Texas
tr	Translator/Translation
Transnat'l	Transnational
Trav	Travaux
U	University
UCC	Uniform Commercial Code (US)
UCP	Uniform Customs and Practices on Documentary Credits
UK	United Kingdom
ULIS	Uniform Law on the International Sale of Goods
UN	United Nations
UNIDROIT	International Institute for the Unification of Private Law
UNIDROIT Principles	UNIDROIT Principles of International Commercial Contracts (2006)
UNCITRAL	UN Commission on International Trade Law
UNCITRAL Model Law	The UNCITRAL Model Law on International Commercial Arbitration (1985, with amendments adopted in 2006)
UNCITRAL Rules	UNCITRAL Rules of Arbitration (2010)
UNTS UN Treaty Service	
US	United States
Va	Virginia

Vol	Volume
VCLT	Vienna Convention on the Law of Treaties
VDMA Conditions	General Conditions of the Association of German Mechanical Construction Firms
Wash	Washington (state)
Ybk	Yearbook

1

Introduction

> International law ... clearly manifests a desire for unity and universality, based on the common needs and interests of the international economic community. As such, it does not accord with a fragmentation of the international legal framework and encourages the use of unifying legal notions, such as ... general principles of law, or truly international public policy.[1]

This book explores two discrete subjects, subjects whose relationship is acknowledged but often underappreciated: contract law and international commercial arbitration (ICA). One cannot have a commercial arbitration without a dispute involving a contract, so the two go together naturally. And yet the common belief is that they have a one-way relationship: the applicable contract law affects outcomes in international arbitrations, but the dispute resolution mechanism—arbitration—has no effect on the content of the law or its application to the facts. After all, international arbitrators undoubtedly have a duty to apply the law, although the precise scope of the duty is contested.[2] To put the matter another way, most commentators seem to assume that when international commercial arbitrators apply national contract laws (which occurs in the vast majority of cases), they do so in fundamentally the same manner as national court judges of the jurisdictions whose laws are being applied.

An English independent arbitrator interviewed for this book, who specializes in construction and engineering disputes, endorsed this point of view. When asked whether litigation and arbitration differ in the way they resolve matters of substantive law, he replied:

> Very similar. People come to you and arbitrate because that's what's in the contract. The people that come to you to arbitrate are the sort of people, i.e., specialist solicitors in the field, that if it weren't in the contract, the dispute would be going to the court. So they're familiar with the court system. And they trust the court system and they trust you, because they think you know what the court system is.

This book challenges that belief. It contends that a legal culture specific to ICA may lead arbitrators to decide issues governed by national contract laws differently from the way that national courts do. Moreover, they do so in ways that are predictable based on various aspects of the ICA culture.

[1] B Oppetit, *Philosophie du droit* (Dalloz, Paris 1999) 119, quoted and translated in Gaillard 2010a, 42. All footnotes citing secondary sources give the name of the author, the year of publication and, if appropriate, the relevant page or paragraph number in the cited source. For complete citations, see the list of Works Cited.

[2] See, eg, ILA Report on the Applicable Law 2008: 'aside from exceptional cases where they act as *amiable compositeurs*, arbitrators are duty bound to apply the relevant law and rules. They are not free simply to ignore them in favour of facts and equities'. On the scope of this duty, see Chapter 5, Section III.

At one level, it may seem obvious or natural that a system of dispute resolution, largely autonomous from national court systems and with no appeals on matters of substantive law, would over time diverge from domestic approaches. But it is altogether more tenuous to conclude that ICA is developing its own contract law doctrines. Individual arbitrations involve not only different contracts, but a variety of substantive laws, and endless combinations of different arbitrators, parties, national arbitration laws, and rules of procedure—all with no supreme court to ensure uniformity of approaches. And since almost all international commercial arbitration awards remain confidential, how could we know if a uniform approach is evolving?

Different international arbitrations may not share the same substantive law or the same arbitrators, but they do take place within the same professional and cultural context. Within the small, notoriously close-knit international arbitration community, a distinct and cohesive legal culture is developing. In the absence of reliable, direct data on outcomes in ICA, this culture is the key to understanding the decision-making processes of international commercial arbitrators. In turn, the culture of ICA helps us to predict how contract law will evolve through the decisions of international arbitrators.

I. Background

Harmonization or unification of commercial law has always been a goal of the international commercial community. A well-functioning commercial system requires a high degree of legal certainty, and doubts about the applicability and interpretation of laws that may apply to a given international dispute detract from that certainty. The various uniform law projects, going back at least to the drafting of the Franco–Italian Code of Obligations in 1913, 'provide ample evidence ... that there has always been a substantial need for the transnationalization of the legal relationships of international commerce'.[3]

And yet, despite a century of effort during which international commerce has expanded exponentially, commercial law remains stubbornly un-unified. The only supranational instrument of substantive commercial law that has enjoyed any real measure of international acceptance is the UN Convention on Contracts for the International Sale of Goods ('CISG').[4] The CISG deals only with contracts for the sale of goods,[5] for the most part only with contracts between nationals of contracting states,[6] and deals with even this subset of international transactions in an incomplete way.[7] While the CISG has

[3] Berger 2010, 34.

[4] United Nations Convention on Contracts for the International Sale of Goods (adopted 11 April 1980, entered into force 1 January 1988) 1489 UNTS 3.

[5] Article 1(1). Under art 3, the CISG applies to contracts for the manufacture and sale of goods unless the buyer furnishes the preponderant part of the materials, and to contracts for goods and services unless the services form the preponderant part of the seller's obligations.

[6] Article 1(1)(a). Under art 1(1)(b), the CISG may also apply when 'the rules of private international law lead to the application of the law of a Contracting State'. However, several states made reservations with respect to art (1)(b); if the law of one of those states applies, and the parties are not both nationals of contracting states, then the CISG does not displace the otherwise applicable law.

[7] By its own terms, the CISG applies only to 'the formation of the contract of sale and the rights and obligations of the seller and the buyer arising from such a contract' (art 4). Accordingly, it provides no rules on such core issues as contractual validity (including incapacity, lack of agency authority, misrepresentation, duress, mistake, unconscionability, and illegality), the rights of third parties, and the effects of the contract on title to the goods. On the issues not resolved by the CISG, see Mather 2001.

been a dramatic success when compared with earlier efforts at drafting an international sales code,[8] its ratification rate surely does not demonstrate a global commitment to unify sales law; only seventy-eight states are signatories, and the abstainers include such economically important polities as the UK and Brazil.[9] The CISG took years to negotiate and has not been amended since its drafting was completed in 1980.

'Soft law' attempts at harmonization—those not adopted into national laws in the manner of treaties and model laws—have fared no better. The best-known examples of such instruments are compilations drafted by academics and international civil servants, such as the UNIDROIT Principles of International Commercial Contracts ('UNIDROIT Principles')[10] and the Principles of European Contract Law (PECL).[11] These have received a great deal of academic attention[12] and have influenced revisions to the contract codes of a few countries,[13] but have not had a broad impact on the harmonization of law.[14]

Thus, if harmonization of commercial law on a global scale is to be achieved, it seems that it will have to develop organically, and not through negotiations at international conferences or scholarly drafting committees.[15] Economic globalization may already be engendering just such a legal globalization. Scholars now regularly speak of declining legal nationalism and greater acceptance of supranational and transnational decision-making bodies.[16] The result of this phenomenon is 'a kind of internationalized law, or globalized law, which exists side by side of, or on top of, the national or local

[8] The CISG's immediate predecessor, the 1964 Convention Relating to a Uniform Law on the International Sale of Goods (ULIS), was only ratified by nine countries. See Stoffel 2001, 1201, calling the CISG the first 'lasting effort to bridge the common law-civil law divide'.

[9] <http://www.uncitral.org/uncitral/en/uncitral_texts/sale_goods/1980CISG_status.html> accessed 20 July 2012.

[10] <http://www.unidroit.org/english/principles/contracts/principles2010/integralversionprinciples2010-e.pdf> accessed 18 July 2012. The International Institute for the Unification of Private Law (UNIDROIT) is an independent intergovernmental organization headquartered in Rome. It is charged, inter alia, with developing uniform private law instruments. <http://www.unidroit.org/dynasite.cfm?dsmid=103284> accessed 17 August 2012.

[11] The PECL were drafted by the Commission on European Contract Law, sometimes called the Lando Commission after its Chair, Dutch professor Ole Lando. The Commission is a private initiative but has been supported by the European Parliament. <http://webh01.ua.ac.be/storme/CECL_Resolution.html> accessed 20 July 2012.

[12] For example, searches on the Westlaw and Kluwer Online databases turned up more than 120 articles published in English with 'UNIDROIT Principles' in the title and over 300 articles published in English in the last three years alone that mention the Principles.

[13] For example, the 2001 civil code of Lithuania contains 'many clauses [that] repeat almost word for word sections of the [PECL] or UNIDROIT Principles' Klimas 2006, xxvi. This phenomenon is not limited to small, newly independent states like Lithuania; the 2002 amendments to the German Obligations Law included provisions translated from or inspired by the UNIDROIT Principles and PECL. Reimann 2009, 884, characterizing the promulg of the PECL and UNIDROIT Principles as among the important developments that had occurred since the publication of a 1992 report on reform of the German Obligations Law. See also Heldrich and Rehm 2005.

[14] By contrast, some sets of internationally standardized contract terms, like the INCOTERMS and the Uniform Customs and Practices for Documentary Credits (UCP), both drafted by the International Chamber of Commerce (ICC), have attained wide acceptance in their respective commercial sectors. To the extent that parties refer to these standardized terms in their contracts, they too promote harmonization.

[15] The process by which transnational law is developing 'matches the one experienced in the first stages of judicial development described by legal historians and anthropologists.... law percolates up from the bottom' Grizel 2006, 168.

[16] See, eg, Andersen 2009; Michaels 2006; Ahdieh 2004; Koch 2003; Menyhart 2003; Ramos 2002; Havel 2000; McGinnis and Movsesian 2000; Slaughter 2000; Sweet and Brunell 1998; Koopmans 1991.

sector. It may well represent a minority, even a small minority, of lawyers' work, but its importance is clearly on the rise.'[17]

The most fertile ground for the growth of an internationalized commercial law is ICA, a system of dispute resolution that exists outside the legal system of any state and is structured for the resolution of international commercial disputes. It is often described as the primary means for resolving such disputes.[18]

The extent to which arbitration does in fact dominate international commercial dispute resolution is contested, but it is undeniable that arbitration now accounts for a significant share of international commercial disputes and that it has increased greatly in importance since the beginnings of the modern commercial arbitration era in the mid-20th century. Caseloads for the major arbitral institutions have increased dramatically, new institutions have been founded that now attract their own significant clienteles, more lawyers now work in ICA than ever before, and multinational firms increasingly tout their expertise in the field.[19]

Despite its increasing importance, international arbitration continues to be seen by both participants and commentators primarily as an alternative to the default option of litigation in national courts. In other words, parties in international commerce choose arbitration because they do not (or at the time they concluded their contract did not) want their dispute decided by a court: 'Arbitration is, more or less, liberation from ... court jurisdiction.'[20] A prominent Swiss arbitrator, interviewed for this book, was blunt:

> Parties go to arbitration not because they think arbitration is better than court, but because they don't have a real other choice in many cases. Obviously it depends on the types of courts you have in mind, but often one party won't go to the courts of the other and vice versa as a matter of principle. That is the end of the discussion *about courts*. In addition, there are many places in the world where courts are not good; they are incompetent; they are corrupt.... and often, even where they are good and honest, they may not be equipped to deal with large international disputes, in terms of resources.

Surveys confirm that parties' specific reasons for choosing arbitration are generally procedural—matters such as the enforceability of arbitral awards, the neutrality of the forum, the ability to choose one's arbitrator, the speed and cost of the proceedings, confidentiality, and the flexibility of evidentiary rules.[21] As Ogus observes: 'Procedural reasons, rather than substantive reasons, seem to predominate when parties to international contracts choose between arbitration and litigation.'[22]

Indeed, arbitration is seen primarily as a procedural—and not a substantive—alternative to litigation. The US Supreme Court has described the difference between litigation and arbitration as purely 'procedural'[23] and arbitration agreements as simply 'a specialized kind of forum-selection clause'.[24] Ridgway writes that users of international

[17] Friedman 2001, 355.
[18] See Chapter 4, Section III.2.
[19] This trend is described in detail in Born 2009, 67–70.
[20] Kitagawa 1967, 135.
[21] See, eg, Drahozal and Ware 2010; Naimark and Keer 2002; Bühring-Uhle 1996, 129–34.
[22] Ogus 2002, 430. Drahozal's meta-study of party preferences supports the proposition that parties choose arbitration predominantly for procedural reasons: Drahozal 2011.
[23] *Shearson/American Express, Inc v McMahon*, 482 US 220, 232 (1987), reasoning that 'the streamlined procedures of arbitration do not entail any consequential restriction on substantive rights'.
[24] *Scherk v Alberto-Culver Co*, 417 US 506, 519 (1974). See also *Mitsubishi Motors Corp v Soler Chrysler-Plymouth, Inc*, 473 US 614, 628 (1985): 'By agreeing to arbitrate a statutory claim, a party does not forgo the substantive rights afforded by the statute; it only submits to their resolution in an arbitral, rather than a judicial, forum.'

arbitration are seeking only 'a ... degree of detachment from local procedural law'—not local substantive law.[25] In the vast majority of cases—97.7 per cent, according to one study[26]—international disputes resolved by arbitration are governed by the substantive law of a state.[27] In such cases, most people would expect the tribunal to decide issues of substantive law in the same way that a court from the country whose law governs the dispute would decide them. That expectation is somewhat misplaced.

To the extent that parties actively consider the dispute resolution clause when they negotiate a contract (as opposed to relying on the dispute resolution clause in a standard form),[28] they probably believe that providing for arbitration of any eventual disputes is purely a procedural choice. In theory, so long as the parties choose a national law—any national law—to govern the contract, it ought to make no difference to the substantive legal determinations whether a dispute is resolved by litigation or arbitration.[29] Yet the procedure adopted by a tribunal necessarily affects the tribunal's determinations on the merits, and having arbitrators (as opposed to judges) decide the merits also affects the outcome. As Park puts it: 'Since contracts do not enforce themselves, but need flesh-and-blood adjudicators, who interprets an international agreement has often been more significant than what the applicable law says about its construction.'[30]

The academic literature does recognize that arbitrators might choose different substantive law or interpret that law differently from national court judges. For example, as Craig, Park, and Paulsson note, when parties select an arbitrator, they do so in part based on 'the normative standards' they want to be applied to the dispute.[31] More comprehensively, Brower and Sharpe give three reasons why arbitrators and national court judges might reach divergent outcomes: where the governing substantive law is unclear or incomplete, where arbitrators seek to reach a compromise award (the purported tendency of arbitrators to 'split the baby'[32]), or where a 'rogue tribunal' issues an award in disregard of the governing law.[33] Most important—in the literature, although not in practice—is the so-called *lex mercatoria*, the autonomous global law of international commerce that has been developed by international arbitrators and academics associated with international arbitration.[34]

However, no general or overarching theory of arbitral decision-making has been proposed that might explain whether or in what ways arbitrators decide substantive law issues differently from national courts. This book proposes such a theory. It argues that there exist legal and social norms in ICA, norms that are distinct from those prevailing in any national legal system, and that collectively constitute a legal culture specific to ICA. Moreover, it proposes that these norms affect the way that arbitrators approach matters of substantive law, which in turn affects the outcomes. In other words, this

25 Ridgway 1999, 52. 26 Dasser 2008, 140.

27 This figure includes cases where the choice of law rules of the state whose law governs the dispute lead to the application of a treaty as the governing law of the contract, eg, jurisdiction under art 1(1)(b) of the CISG.

28 It is often observed that: 'Parties negotiating a contract usually deal with the dispute resolution clause as a type of necessary evil that serves only to dampen an otherwise optimistic atmosphere of cooperation' (Webster 2003, 120). Corporate counsel interviewed for a study of corporations' dispute resolution policies reported that they are 'often ... brought into negotiations late and expected to conclude dispute resolution clauses with minimal negotiation because the commercial terms are settled' W&C/QMUL 2010, 10.

29 Except to the extent that procedural decisions, such as on the scope of document production, are determinative of outcomes on the merits.

30 Park 2003, 1257–8. 31 Craig, Park, and Paulsson 2001, 296.

32 See Chapter 2, Section IV.2. 33 Brower and Sharpe 2004, 200 (citations omitted).

34 The *lex mercatoria* is discussed in more detail in Chapter 2.

book proposes that norms specific to ICA often lead arbitrators to reach different outcomes from national court judges on the merits of disputes, even when they are applying the same laws.

The term 'norm' is used here in a broad and non-technical sense to describe any standard that does or is supposed to guide conduct and may serve as a basis for the assessment of conduct.[35] Rules, presumptions, principles, guidelines, maxims, perspectives, standard practices, and customs may all be described as norms. They are 'normative' in that they do not determine what the people influenced by them are able or unable to do, but rather what such people feel they are entitled or ought to do. Norms are often characterized as obligations backed by a sanction and are categorized according to the source of the sanction: violation of a legal norm results in a legal sanction imposed by a court, such as a fine or jail sentence; violation of a religious norm results in a religious sanction imposed by a cleric, such as excommunication; violation of a commercial norm results in a commercial sanction imposed by a boss or business partner, such as demotion within a company or exclusion from a business opportunity; violation of a social norm results in a social sanction imposed by fellow members of an identifiable social group or community, such as shunning or loss of respect. In ICA, legal and social norms interact in the formation of a distinct culture.

It may be difficult to see why the decisions of international commercial arbitrators would be of interest to anyone beyond the parties to those disputes. After all, except where states or state agencies are themselves parties to commercial contracts (a well-recognized exception to state immunity[36]), the protection of vital national interests has little relevance in ICA. The morality of crime and punishment is not implicated. Inequalities among social classes, races, or religious groups are seldom germane. National mores do not have as great an impact as in other areas of law. ICA does not involve fraught issues of regulation; workplace safety, environmental and consumer protection, labour relations, and corporate governance are rarely relevant to international commercial disputes. Questions of social justice and the greater good are seldom directly implicated in disputes between commercial entities, still less in cross-border commercial disputes. ICA deals only with ad hoc transactions between equals (contractual, not necessarily economic) entering into voluntary arrangements limited in time, scope, and duties. In short, except in limited ways, issues of concern to political leaders or the general public rarely arise in ICA.

Moreover, the parties that typically enter into international commercial contracts of the type that contain arbitration clauses have relatively equal bargaining power. As a result, international arbitral tribunals are unlikely to concern themselves with contract law doctrines intended to protect the interests of weaker parties.[37] Each international arbitration is also self-contained. Since there is no system of binding precedent within arbitration, and arbitral awards do not establish new legal rules

[35] This definition of 'norm' is derived from the definition set forth in Shapiro 2010, 42. See also Ellickson 1998.

[36] See, eg, Dicey and Morris 2000, 246–8 (Rule 19, Exception 2).

[37] In domestic arbitrations, it is common for arbitration clauses to be included in employment and consumer contracts, which are often adhesive. Various consumer protection statutes restrict or prohibit pre-dispute arbitration agreements in consumer contracts. See, eg, in the US, the proposed Arbitration Fairness Act, HR 1020, 111th Cong (2009) (introduced on 12 February 2009 by Representative Henry Johnson with 108 co-sponsors and referred to the Subcommittee on Commercial and Administrative Law on 16 March 2009); in the UK, the Unfair Terms in Consumer Contracts Regulations 1999, SI 1999 No 2083; in France, *Code de la consommation*, art 132-1; in Germany, BGB, ss 305–10. The British, French, and German rules were laid down in compliance with an EU Directive, Council Directive 93/10/EEC of 5 April 1993 on unfair terms in consumer

outside the ICA system,[38] arbitral tribunals need not consider the effects of their rulings beyond the parties.

Nevertheless, understanding the way that international arbitrators decide substantive law issues matters because ICA has become a significant generator of law. Despite the lack of a formal system of precedent, arbitrators do cite each other on matters of law.[39] Development of law through arbitral awards is hampered (as is research on ICA) by a lack of systematic publication of awards; however, the awards that are published are regularly cited by subsequent tribunals, even on points of substantive national law.[40] Perhaps more importantly, international commercial arbitrators are relatively few in number and tend to be closely connected, both professionally and personally. The same arbitrators are appointed repeatedly in the most important cases, and may also appear as counsel or expert witnesses in front of each other. There are frequent academic- and practitioner-focused conferences and many of the top arbitrators and arbitration counsel publish in scholarly journals. Thus, several channels exist by which principles and perspectives diffuse between arbitrators. An American interviewee concluded that the harmonization of procedural approaches in ICA is due to 'the fact that a lot of arbitrators have sat with a lot of other arbitrators.... A lot of other arbitrators from other parts of the world and other backgrounds have grown comfortable with each other's procedures'.

Accordingly, what arbitrators do when making decisions on issues of substantive law is of both practical and academic interest. At minimum, a theory of arbitral decision-making that can be tested against the available awards is needed. Such a theory would help parties to make more informed decisions regarding arbitration: whether to arbitrate, which arbitral institution or procedural rules to select, which arbitrators to select, whether to conclude a choice of law agreement (and, if so, which law to choose), and whether to include in their arbitration agreements provisions that alter or restrict the scope of their arbitrators' authority.

Parties and their counsel would be the primary beneficiaries of an improved understanding of arbitral decision-making, but providers of arbitration services—arbitrators, arbitral institutions, and counsel—would also benefit. Predictability of outcomes is regularly cited as one of the most important interests of the business community, yet predictability has long been described as the 'principal challenge' facing ICA.[41] The close professional relationships between arbitrators and counsel,[42] the informality of arbitration proceedings, the confidentiality of both the proceedings and the ensuing

contracts, [1993] OJ L 95/29, which in effect sets up a rebuttable presumption that mandatory arbitration clauses in consumer contracts constitute unfair terms. Courts remain divided on the circumstances in which they will invalidate mandatory arbitration clauses in consumer contracts. See generally Rutledge and Howard 2010; McGill 2010.

[38] With the exception of international investment law.

[39] For example, Fauchald surveyed ninety-eight ICSID awards with respect to the interpretive arguments adopted by tribunals. Ninety of the ninety-eight awards contained arguments based on prior ICSID case law, thirty awards relied on UNCITRAL case law, and twenty-two relied on case law from the Iran–US Claims Tribunal. Fauchald 2008, 356. See also Cheng 2007.

[40] Primarily for this reason, Carbonneau refers to international arbitral tribunals, even in private commercial disputes, as 'law-makers': Carbonneau 2004. To be sure, most citations to other arbitral awards relate to matters of arbitral jurisdiction and procedure. Except in investment treaty arbitrations and those administered by the Court of Arbitration for Sport, arbitral tribunals are likely to cite national court judgments on matters of national substantive law. On whether arbitral awards create 'precedents', see generally Weidemeier 2010, arguing that international arbitral awards are capable of constituting precedents, but that ICA has not yet evolved a true system of precedent.

[41] Domke 1965, 14. [42] See Chapter 3, Section III.1.

awards, and the absence of an appeals process, all conspire to make arbitration a gamble. Arbitrators and arbitral institutions should also favour greater elucidation of the likely outcomes in arbitration; parties must actively choose to have their disputes resolved by arbitration and 'unrealistic expectations are resentments waiting to happen'.[43] Resentful parties will turn their backs on arbitration.[44]

More generally, a better understanding of arbitral decision-making will yield insights into the ways that international commercial law is evolving through the jurisprudence of ICA. In particular, it will help to explain how principles of law can develop outside of national legal systems. Transnational contract law (also characterized as a-national law, non-national law, the *lex mercatoria*, or general principles of international private law) is a controversial subject.[45] Disagreements remain over whether a body of transnational laws does in fact exist or is developing and, if so, what rules compose it and in what directions it is likely to evolve. Most national choice of law regimes prevent national court judges from applying transnational rules, so ICA is the most important forum in which transnational or uniform rules are applied.[46] Arbitrators have also taken the lead in developing and promoting transnational rules of law, both in using those rules to decide disputes and in drafting codified sets of rules such as the UNIDROIT Principles.

This book will not attempt to identify specific general principles of international contract law, as has been done by a variety of scholars.[47] The UNDIROIT Principles, which attempt to codify general principles of international commercial law, are a prime example, as are non-codified compilations of principles such as that maintained by the Center for Transnational Law at the University of Cologne.[48] Instead, this book seeks to identify the legal and social norms that inform arbitral decision-making, and thus to explain why the transnational principles that have so far been identified and applied came to be recognized and to predict the principles that are likely to develop in the future.

II. Methodology and Structure

The questions this book seeks to answer are empirical; its goals are descriptive rather than prescriptive. The most straightforward way to answer such empirical questions about arbitrators' decision-making would simply be to read a sufficient number of arbitral awards, then catalogue and characterize the decisions. This is how traditional legal scholarship proceeds, at least within the common law world. However, it is impossible in international arbitration because only a tiny percentage of arbitral awards is published. Access to the raw data necessary to implement this 'brute force' approach does not exist.

43 Park 2002, 283.

44 The interests of the international arbitration system as a whole would be served by anything that improves the predictability of outcomes in ICA. See generally Karton 2012.

45 Of these terms, this book will generally employ 'transnational law'. As Gaillard points out, 'transnational' is preferable to terms like 'a-national' or 'non-national' because the latter do not 'convey the notion that the rules thus identified often find their roots in national laws' Gaillard 2010a.

46 See, eg, Drahozal 2009a, 1036, referring to ICA as the 'source' of the *lex mercatoria*; Rogers 2002, 351–2, describing the *lex mercatoria* as 'developed by academics, who were also actively involved in arbitrations, as a means to permit arbitrators to tailor decisions to customary trade usages'; Benson 1989, calling *lex mercatoria* 'the law that dominates international trade through the use of arbitration'. An early example is Goldstajn 1961.

47 The most ambitious such attempt in print is Berger 2010.

48 <http://www.trans-lex.org/principles> accessed 20 July 2012.

Accordingly, any researcher attempting to describe international arbitral decision-making must resort to some kind of interpretive paradigm. In traditional legal scholarship, this would involve an investigation of the relevant legal norms, in particular the rules of law applicable to international commercial disputes decided by arbitration. In international arbitration, however, this approach, too, confronts serious limitations. ICA does not have its own, unified substantive law;[49] arbitrators apply different substantive laws in different disputes. Accordingly, there is no substantive law *of* arbitration, no unified, integrated set of substantive law rules that apply in ICA.[50]

Rules specific to ICA that pertain to substantive law do exist, in particular with respect to the choice of that law.[51] However, the rules do not—cannot—tell the entire story of how adjudicators make decisions. This proposition is supported by the two case studies presented in Part II, which provide evidence that the outcomes in ICA and national court litigation may differ, even when the same substantive law applies.

To understand the new procedural and substantive norms that are developing in ICA, it is vital to go beyond the legal rules. This principle is well established when it comes to national laws. As Legrand writes, 'the notion of "French law" cannot be reduced to that of "binding law in France". French law is much more than a compendium of rules and precepts. Accordingly, to assert that the study of French law consists in the study of French legislative texts and judicial decisions is plainly inadequate.'[52] Comparativists similarly agree that 'one must take account not only of legislative rules, judicial decisions, the "law in the books", and also of general conditions of business, customs, and practices, but in fact of everything whatever which helps to mould human conduct in the situation under consideration'.[53]

However, the same insight has not been so readily applied in the international sphere. Notes Hirsch:

> The idea that international law and other societal processes are profoundly interlinked is not new, but sociological theories are seldom employed in mainstream international law scholarship.... Only recently [have] international law scholars ... turned their attention to modern sociology and employed its tools to study international legal concepts and problems.[54]

Existing research on ICA is primarily doctrinal, focused on explicating the multiple and overlapping sets of rules that govern the field. The empirical research that exists in the literature similarly does not focus on arbitrators themselves, but on the attitudes of the consumers of arbitration services: parties engaged in international commerce and their counsel.[55] However, as Friedman argues, transnational law 'is as much a product of its times and its social context as national or local law'.[56] There is no reason in principle why the ICA field could not possess its own, distinct culture. Indeed, there is reason to believe that such a culture is already developing. Globalization places pressure on national legal cultures; where once these were autonomous, now they must interact

[49] ICA also does not have a single, unified procedural law. However, there is a far greater degree of convergence in procedure than in substance. See Newman 2009; Del Duca 2007; Kaufman-Kohler 2003; Elsing and Townsend 2002.

[50] Such substantive law rules as do exist specific to ICA are discussed in Chapter 5.

[51] The rules are outlined in Chapter 5.

[52] Legrand 1999, 5.

[53] Zweigert and Kötz 1998, 11.

[54] Hirsch 2005, 891, noting that 'the sociological perspective was not included in the seven major methods of international legal scholarship that were presented in the 1999 Symposium on Methods in International Law published as a special issue of the American Journal of International Law'.

[55] For a summary of the empirical research that has been performed on ICA, see Chapter 2, Section IV.2.

[56] Friedman 1996, 90.

(and, at times, compete) with other national legal cultures. This same cross-cultural interaction may be leading to the generation of a coherent set of norms outside of any national culture, in the discrete, international space inhabited by ICA.

Commentators have begun to identify a culture of international arbitration; however, thus far, such commentaries have focused on the generation of a common set of standardized procedures within ICA.[57] These procedures are a hybrid; they borrow from both common law and civil law and are specifically adapted to the needs of commercial parties. More importantly, the harmonized procedures developed 'less through formal exchange of published opinions than through the cross-pollination that comes with the overlapping experiences of those in the international arbitration community'.[58] Such procedural convergence is outside the scope of this book, but it does demonstrate that ICA is sufficiently coherent as a field to develop shared norms that organically generate legal rules.

To study the extra-legal features of international arbitrators' decision-making, this book adopts the vocabulary and methods of sociology, a field of inquiry intimately connected with questions of culture. In particular, the method adopted here is that of 'grounded theory', an inductive method employed in socio-legal research, according to which a broad theory is allowed to emerge from repeated comparisons between individual items of data. The theory is grounded in the data, rather than being posited a priori and verified by the data, as in traditional sociological research.

The data analysed here come from three main sources: original interviews with twenty international commercial arbitrators, the academic writings and conference presentations of arbitrators and other participants in ICA, and the few published arbitral awards. Consideration of these data led to the identification of a set of social norms specific to ICA that collectively constitute an emerging culture of international arbitration. The social norms that compose this culture explain the divergence in outcomes between arbitration and litigation that is depicted in the two case studies.

Readers may be most interested in the interviews, which were conducted specifically for this book. Interviewees were selected to represent as wide as possible a range of backgrounds among the group of international arbitrators. They are all active as arbitrators, but some work primarily as counsel or as academics. They come from or currently practice in thirteen different countries[59] and were trained in a variety of legal systems; nearly every major region of the globe is represented.[60] They range in age from their early forties to their late seventies. Some have a primarily academic background, while others spent their entire professional lives in law firms. Some worked for several years in arbitral institutions or in government. All of them work mostly or exclusively on international arbitration, but some are generalists and some specialize in particular types of disputes. Approximately two thirds are on lists of the world's most in-demand arbitrators, while others sit as an arbitrator less frequently or began to receive appointments as an arbitrator only within the last few years. Only three are women, but this was not for lack of effort to secure the participation of female interviewees; women were more likely than men to decline requests for an interview.[61]

[57] Ginsburg 2003, 1337–8. [58] Rogers 2005, 1001.

[59] Some interviewees requested that their home states not be named because they come from states that have produced only a small number of high-profile international arbitrators.

[60] There were no interviewees from Eastern Europe, Sub-Saharan Africa, or South Asia; however, several interviewees have extensive experience with disputes relating to those regions.

[61] Since there is a relatively small number of elite female arbitrators, it is possible that they receive a large number of similar requests and are therefore more likely to decline to participate.

The interviews give readers insight into the perspectives of a range of leading and up-and-coming international commercial arbitrators, in their own words, on several matters of central importance in ICA. The interviews covered such topics as the proper role of the international arbitrator, the nature of arbitrators' relationships with the parties, counsel, and other members of the tribunal, the convergence of different national legal systems and cultures in ICA, characteristics necessary to be successful as an arbitrator, and arbitrators' adjudicative philosophy as it pertains to substantive law matters (for example, how arbitrators go about determining the content of the applicable law, their sense of the impact of the governing law in the resolution of contractual questions, and the place of non-national principles of substantive law).

It was important that the interviewees feel they could speak freely, so all interviews are presented in an anonymized fashion. Where appropriate, interviewees are described in a general way so that the reader can put the interviewee's comments in context. No details about the interviewees' lives and careers have been changed, but information about them has been omitted to protect their anonymity.

While this book focuses on arbitration and arbitrators, it is ultimately concerned with the evolution of contract law. As such, it deals only with ICA narrowly defined. That is, it considers only arbitrations of disputes arising from cross-border contractual relationships between commercial entities (including state entities engaged in commerce). It excludes from consideration arbitrations of disputes between employers and employees or between commercial entities and consumers, which implicate public policy considerations that vary widely from jurisdiction to jurisdiction and are quite different from those raised by relationships between commercial entities.

In addition, this book excludes from consideration a class of arbitrations that is often joined with contractual disputes under the umbrella of 'international arbitration'—those arising out of investment treaties. Investment arbitrations directly implicate public interests and state actors, and therefore are governed in part by public international law, which possesses doctrines and mores distinct from (although related to) those involved in international commercial relationships. Accordingly, investment arbitrations will not be discussed here, except to the extent that a given investment arbitration also involves the interpretation of private contracts or matters of arbitral practice common to both investment and commercial arbitrations.

One must also distinguish the international commercial arbitrations studied in this book from trade association arbitrations (usually involving disputes over the characteristics or qualities of commodities), where merchants entirely contract out of any national or transnational legal system—so-called 'look–sniff' arbitrations. In trade association arbitrations, the arbitrators are usually industry experts (as opposed to lawyers); they are expected to apply industry usages and impose extra-legal sanctions. Such arbitrations typically do not require legal reasoning from the arbitrators.[62] A significant body of empirical literature exists analysing trade association arbitrations, some of which assesses the social context of these arbitrations.[63] However, while such specialized

[62] Cf Bingham 1988, 145, commenting that: 'There are some arbitrations ... where there is really no room for the giving of reasons: tapioca pellets either are, in the experienced judgment of a trade arbitrator, of fair average quality or they are not; whichever way his opinion goes there is probably not much that he can usefully add by way of exegesis.'

[63] See, eg, four articles by Lisa Bernstein: 'Private Commercial Law in the Cotton Industry: Creating Cooperation Through Rules, Norms and Institutions' (2004) 99 Mich L R 1724; 'The Questionable Empirical Basis of Article 2's Incorporation Strategy: A Preliminary Study' (1999) 66 U Chicago L R 710; 'Merchant Law in a Merchant Court: Rethinking the Code's Search for Immanent Business Norms' (1996) 144 U Penn L R 1765; 'Opting Out of the Legal System: Extralegal Contractual Relations in the Diamond Industry' (1992) 21 J Leg Stud 115.

arbitrations may be international and commercial, they 'are commonly not covered by the general literature on international commercial arbitration'.[64] Accordingly, they are excluded from the analysis presented here.

It is also important to note that, for the purposes of identifying the substantive law principles preferred by international commercial arbitrators, this book will not consider submission agreements (contracts to submit a pre-existing dispute to arbitration), nor will it consider the interpretation of arbitration clauses within contracts. Agreements to arbitrate are treated differently from other contractual provisions by arbitral tribunals and by the courts of most countries. In particular, different laws may apply to them than to the underlying contracts, and they may be interpreted according to different principles.[65] This book restricts its analysis and predictions to the law that governs commercial relationships, excluding arbitration agreements and forum selection agreements.

This book proceeds in two parts, which can be read in either order, depending on the reader's interests. Part I develops a theory of international arbitral culture that helps to explain the decision-making of international arbitrators. Part II then applies that theory to determinations of substantive contract law. It demonstrates, by means of case study, that the legal rules that apply in international arbitrations are insufficient to explain the outcomes reached in international arbitrations. The same case studies show that these outcomes are explicable as motivated by the various norms of international arbitral culture. An understanding of the culture of international arbitration makes possible specific predictions about the contract law doctrines that arbitrators are likely to prefer, with direct implications for advocacy, arbitral practice, and arbitration scholarship.

Part I proposes and describes a cultural theory of arbitral decision-making that is grounded in the words of international arbitrators and arbitration scholars. Students and lawyers new to ICA may gain some insights into a field that 'remains rather mysterious, especially for those not fully initiated into it'.[66] But the description of arbitral culture in Part I will also enable experienced practitioners and academics to better understand the character of the international arbitration system and their role within it. Readers who are primarily interested in this theory, or are more interested in arbitral decision-making in general than in substantive law determinations, should begin with Part I. Indeed, it can stand on its own as a monograph on the culture of international arbitration.

Part I is divided into three chapters. Chapter 2 provides some background; it explains why we ought to study ICA culture and introduces the methodology used to develop the theory of international arbitral culture: a sociological approach based on the grounded theory method.[67] The cultural theory of arbitral decision-making proposes that a unified culture of international arbitration is in the process of coalescing, a culture that affects the way international commercial arbitrators make decisions. This culture is defined by various social norms that can be identified in the words and actions of international arbitrators.

The remainder of Part I develops the theory. It describes the social norms that exist in ICA and their effects. These norms may lead arbitrators both to choose different laws

[64] Bühring-Uhle 1996, 45.
[65] See generally Born 2009, 411–21.
[66] Dezalay and Garth 1996, 4.
[67] The foundational text of grounded theory is Glaser and Strauss 1967.

than national court judges (to the extent that the relevant rules give them discretion) and also to apply any given law differently than would national court judges. These norms may also influence the content of transnational substantive law principles recognized by international arbitrators.

The aspects of ICA culture identified in Part I are divided for analytical purposes into those arising from the structure of the ICA system and those arising from arbitrators' values; these are considered in Chapters 3 and 4, respectively. Chapter 3 describes the sources of arbitral authority, arbitrators' relationships with the disputing parties, and the role of competitive forces in ICA. Chapter 4 considers the ideological values prevalent among international commercial arbitrators. In particular, it describes arbitrators' dedication to the normative values of party autonomy, the service of business, neutrality, and internationalism.

Part II considers international arbitral decision-making in action. It takes the theory developed in Part I and applies it to the determinations of arbitrators on the merits of international commercial disputes and, in particular, on matters of contract law. The process of applying the theory to a concrete set of arbitral decisions illuminates both the theory and the decisions. It tests the theory against the available data on the actual outcomes in ICA (ie, published awards) and it provides a means by which to explain those outcomes.

The field of contract law is too broad to conduct a full comparison between the approach of international arbitrators and the approach of national court judges from every jurisdiction. Accordingly, Part II proceeds by means of a pair of case studies. The case studies are useful in themselves, if for no other reason than that they help parties and counsel to understand the legal arguments that are likely to appeal to tribunals confronted with the specific issues discussed in the two case studies. But they also have a broader theoretical purpose; they provide evidence that arbitrators do in fact reach different outcomes from national court judges on issues of substantive contract law. Readers who are sceptical that this could be the case may want to read Part II first.

Part II begins by setting out the legal rules specific to ICA that are relevant to substantive law determinations. Next, it presents two case studies, each of which considers a discrete area of contract law: first, in Chapter 6, suspension of performance in response to non-performance, and second, in Chapter 7, the admissibility and use of extrinsic evidence to interpret contracts.

These topics were selected based on two characteristics that they share: both arise with enough frequency to provide a number of published awards sufficient to discern trends in arbitral decision-making, and both involve areas of law where the common law and civil law differ markedly. The latter is important because there would be little point in considering how arbitrators approach contract law issues on which there is a broad international consensus. It would be of little use to conduct a detailed study in order to demonstrate that international arbitrators believe that those who breach contracts should generally be sanctioned, but that certain exceptions exist. Such a conclusion is neither of intrinsic interest nor is it likely to provide much insight into which doctrines international arbitrators tend to prefer. In those areas where there is no international consensus—that are still 'up for grabs'—the particular influence of ICA on contract law's evolution can best be seen.

Each of the case studies explains and compares the prevailing doctrines in a representative sample of common law and civil law jurisdictions, in order to set out the way judges decide disputes involving these two issues. Next, the case studies examine the available arbitral awards and compare the results reached by arbitrators with the various national approaches. In the process, the case studies demonstrate that the applicable substantive legal norms set out in Chapter 5 do not adequately explain the outcomes reached, but that the cultural theory set out in Part I provides a better explanation.

Finally, Chapter 8 discusses the implications of ICA culture for the future of contract law. In particular, it identifies the substantive law doctrines that arbitrators are likely to prefer and predicts the directions in which international commercial law is likely to evolve. Without a sufficient sample of arbitrators' decisions on substantive law matters, definitive predictions of how arbitrators will decide such issues are impossible. However, a sociological analysis of ICA culture makes possible more accurate predictions than could otherwise be made.

PART I

A CULTURAL THEORY OF INTERNATIONAL ARBITRAL DECISION-MAKING

2

Studying International Arbitral Culture

> The concept of legal culture is at the same time stimulating and disappointing. It is stimulating because it raises the expectation that it will lead us directly to the root of the differences between legal systems, but disappointing because claims about legal culture are so often forced to remain impressionistic. One cannot talk 'scientifically' because so little that is important is quantifiable, and the use of numbers only serves to reassure the researcher.[1]

I. Introduction

Scholarly attention to ICA has thus far been dominated by traditional, doctrinal analysis that focuses on codified rules and published decisions.[2] However, 'pure legal analysis' is a highly problematic concept: 'The analysis of legal doctrine ... involves numerous decisions as to how far and in what manner logical analysis can be developed. Considerations of policy cannot be excluded ... since legal doctrine is continually being shaped in the practice of courts and other agencies of interpretation by reference to assumed social purposes of law.'[3] In any legal system, an understanding of the rules alone is insufficient to explain the outcomes reached in adjudication—the entire field of socio-legal studies is premised on this notion.[4]

As incomplete as traditional methods of legal scholarship are when applied to domestic legal systems, they are even more problematic when used to describe substantive law determinations in ICA because the researcher does not have access to the raw data of standard doctrinal research—the decisions themselves. More broadly, interdisciplinary research is well suited to a field, like ICA, where the sources of law are varied and multiple legal orders converge in every dispute.

Most would agree that there is no such thing as a substantive law *of* ICA. The relevant rules that do exist barely constrain arbitrators' decision-making. The choice of law rules pertaining in ICA empower arbitrators (in the absence of a choice by the parties) to choose an appropriate choice of law rule or to choose directly the substantive law governing the dispute, but the rules do not direct the use of that power. Most arbitral rules of procedure endow arbitrators with the authority to recognize and apply general principles of international contract law, but give no direction as to what those principles are or how to apply them. They permit arbitrators (with the express consent of the parties) to act as *amiables compositeurs* (ie to decide based on their own sense of fairness

[1] Garapon 1995, 495.

[2] A small but increasing number of quantitative, empirical studies has been conducted. Many of these also focus on published awards, and so are either limited to investment arbitration (where most awards are publicly available) or of limited value because of the lack of a statistically valid sample of the total body of arbitral awards. The surveys conducted by Queen Mary, University of London, with a variety of research partners are a notable exception. See also Schultz and Kovacs 2012.

[3] Cotterrell 1992, 2.

[4] Also called 'law and society' or 'sociology of law'.

without any reference to law), but the exercise of the amiable composition power is by definition unconstrained. In the great majority of cases governed by the substantive law of a state, nothing actually requires arbitrators to apply state laws in the same way that courts of the relevant jurisdiction would. Due to the absence of any hierarchy of tribunals or *stare decisis* doctrine, arbitral tribunals also need not decide consistently with each other.[5]

Nevertheless, there is good reason to believe that arbitrators do in fact decide legal matters in ways that are consistent with each other.[6] The case studies presented in Part II provide evidence that arbitrators may not always interpret the applicable substantive law in the same way that courts would, but that their decisions do converge with those of other arbitral tribunals. Given how little the rules constrain arbitrators' decision-making, some factors beyond the applicable law must be at work. A shared culture may well be the most important of these factors.

While the existing literature does discuss the interaction of multiple legal cultures in the ICA system, it largely fails to account for the effects that cultural factors may have on the outcomes reached in arbitrations. This is not surprising; lawyers—who, after all, make their living by working with legal rules—often resist explanations for adjudicative outcomes that discount the rules. Indeed, for most lawyers, 'culture' makes for an unsatisfying account of observed behaviour. It is simultaneously broad enough to be vague and narrow enough to be reductionist.

Yet some concept of culture is required, as researchers studying international law and international legal practice have begun to discover. When Flood conducted a series of interviews for a study of international law firm business, he discovered to his surprise that 'the concept of culture was continuously invoked as a means of explaining many things. I rarely raised the subject myself, but others found it inescapable.'[7] This author's experience in researching this book was similar; the book focuses on the role of culture not because it is the only or even necessarily the dominant extra-legal factor in arbitral decision-making, but because culture emerged as a unifying theme during the process of data gathering and analysis.

An explanation of arbitral decision-making that does not at least acknowledge cultural realities cannot hope to be complete. Despite the analytical baggage the word 'culture' carries, it is the best word to encompass both the specific instances of arbitral decision-making and the overall subject of this enquiry—the social context within which arbitrators decide disputes. Culture is the only word that adequately encompasses the various social factors that affect decision-making: standard practices, interests, values, goals, and attitudes.

It may be objected that, even if cultural factors have some relevance, there is not 'a culture' of ICA. This objection will be discussed in detail below.[8] However, the key point is that even if there is not decisive evidence that a fully-formed culture now exists, the norms that prevail in ICA can be identified and their impact assessed. Collectively, these norms form, at minimum, an incipient culture specific to ICA that is solidifying and maturing.

[5] The substantive law rules that do apply in ICA and the minimal constraints that they impose on arbitrators are discussed in detail in Chapter 5.

[6] This is especially the case in investor-state arbitrations, where a relatively small number of discrete legal issues arise in a wide range of disputes. See, eg, Bjorklund 2008, Schreuer and Weiniger 2008; Commission 2007; Kaufmann-Kohler 2007; Franck 2005; Afilalo 2005. On consistency of international arbitral decision-making outside the investment arbitration context, see, eg, Weidemeier 2010; Jacquet 2010.

[7] Flood 1996, 175.

[8] See Section III of this chapter.

Research was conducted in accordance with 'grounded theory', an inductive sociological method developed by Glaser and Strauss in the 1960s. This book uses grounded theory to understand the factors—other than the applicable law itself—that affect the decisions that international commercial arbitrators make. The data analysed are comprised primarily of statements by arbitrators and commentators, expressed in interviews or written down in awards and publications. Once research began, it became apparent that these statements could be characterized as relating to a set of social norms specific to ICA. These, in turn, share the characteristic of being cultural, in that they are driven by unwritten social forces pervasive in ICA that both express and shape arbitrators' preferences and ways of making decisions.

This chapter provides the background for the cultural theory developed in Chapters 3 and 4. It sets out a definition of culture as the term is used in this book, explains culture's importance as a tool for analyzing legal determinations, and describes the methodology used here to generate a theory of ICA culture. In the chapters that follow, the various social norms that emerged in the course of research are identified and discussed.

II. The Nature and Importance of Culture

References to an international arbitration culture do appear in the existing literature. However, previous explorations of a putative arbitral culture have focused on procedural matters, and in particular on the growing acceptance of a set of standard ICA procedures.[9] While standardized procedures are related to culture, they do not themselves constitute culture—they are instead a product of it. Consequently, catalogues of harmonized practices constitute illustrations of specific manifestations of ICA culture, not analyses of the culture itself.

It sometimes seems that as many definitions of culture exist as there are researchers in the field. A fairly standard definition is given by Cotterrell: 'the complex of beliefs, attitudes, cognitive ideas, values and modes of reasoning and perception typical of a particular society or social group'.[10] Culture develops from the repeated interactions of actors in a social group.[11] Over time, the norms that this process produces gain the force of tradition and habituate the members of the social group, forming a community with a common identity. Culture is a process by which the interactions between members of a community become self-reinforcing and determine the contours of future interactions. When these interactions reach a critical mass, the various norms of the culture create a harmonious whole that 'gives people a sense of who they are, of belonging, of how they should behave and what they should be doing'.[12]

In sum, culture exists where members of a community share a set of norms that produce reflexive behaviour conditioned by tradition or community approbation. Culture forms a feedback loop with behaviour; it both shapes and is shaped by the conduct of the community's members. In other words, culture consists of a complex of norms that condition behaviour both by shaping the thinking of individual members of the community and by creating a community consensus or peer pressure that discourages

[9] See, eg, Bjorklund 2009; Carbonneau 2009a; Drahozal 2009a; Trakman 2006; Alford 2003; Kaufmann-Kohler 2003; Ginsburg 2003; Elsing and Townsend 2002; Lazareff 1999. But see Commission 2007, arguing that *esprit de corps* among international arbitrators is a unifying force in substantive determinations in investment treaty arbitrations.

[10] Cotterrell 1992, 23 (citation omitted). See generally Kroeber and Kluckhohn 1952.

[11] Ginsburg 2003, 1337 (citation omitted).

[12] Harris and Moran 1991, 12.

deviation from those norms. The key aspect of culture that differentiates it from other factors that shape behaviour is that it is reflexive. It operates prior to—and therefore frequently obviates—deliberate decision-making. Cultural factors 'make it unnecessary to think out afresh our reactions to situations. The situations become standardized. Their meaning and the appropriate way to act in relation to them become taken for granted'.[13]

For analytical purposes, cultures are often broken down into their constituent social norms. The literature indicates that social norms have the same effects on specific behaviours as culture does on behavio ur generally: they both condition and are conditioned by the interactions between members of the community. To put it differently, social norms and cultures are micro-level and macro-level equivalents. In the legal context, the socio-legal scholar Robert Cooter has identified three effects of social norms on law: expression, internalization, and deterrence. That is, norms express the customs and values of a given community, inculcate those customs and values into members of the community and deter violations of the norms by sanctions.[14]

Social norms are obligations backed by social sanctions, which are 'punishments' meted out by fellow members of one's community, as when a dog-owner who does not clean up after their dog is shunned by their neighbours.[15] In practice, sanctions such as shunning are rarely imposed because they are not necessary; members of the community will likely have internalized the norm, and thus feel that they ought to clean up after their dogs. It is important to remember that social norms are enforced not only from the threat of legal punishment, but also from social disapprobation. In economic terms, as Eric Posner puts it, behaviour in conformity with social norms represents the equilibrium position:

> ... the social norm describes the behaviour that arises in equilibrium. It is not that X punishes Y for violating a social norm; rather, X (and many other people) avoids Y because Y's behaviour reveals to X that association with Y will not serve X's interests. Although in common speech we say that Y's behaviour violates a social norm, the punishment is endogenous, not imposed by an external force.[16]

Moreover, legal rules are themselves often crystallizations of social norms. For example, municipal ordinances requiring dog-owners to clean up after their dogs express a broader social norm about keeping common spaces clean for all members of the community. However, the imposition of a rule can in turn reinforce the norm. Cooter gives the example of a dog ordinance enacted in Berkeley, California. It highlights a fundamental aspect of culture, that it both conditions and is conditioned by the behaviour of individuals:

> After the Berkeley town council enacted an ordinance requiring owners to clean up after their dogs the sidewalks became much cleaner, even though officials never issued citations for breaking the law. The law apparently tipped the balance in favour of informal enforcement. Citizens became more aggressive about complaining to inconsiderate dog owners, and, anticipating this fact, dog owners became more considerate.[17]

Using norms (on the micro level) or culture (on the macro level) to explain observed behaviour is a necessarily uncertain proposition. Culture is 'indeterminate'—it amalgamates a 'variety of activities and attributes into one common bundle' and thereby

[13] Cotterrell 1992, 146–7. [14] Cooter 2000, 3.
[15] Ibid, 5. [16] EA Posner 1998, 797. See also Ellickson 2001.
[17] Cooter 2000, 10–1.

may confuse different factors affecting behaviour or disguise the differences between them.[18] Culture is also 'impressionistic'[19]—it lacks 'sufficient analytical precision ... to allow it to indicate a significant explanatory variable in empirical research'.[20] For these reasons, it is impossible to identify direct causal relationships between specific social norms and corresponding behaviours; specific behaviours cannot be ascribed with certainty to the effects of culture generally, let alone to any one norm. Similarly, it is impossible to separate entirely the effects of culture from the effects of other factors, such as the threat of punishment or economic self-interest. Nevertheless, so long as the researcher is careful not to indulge in false determinism, 'the malleability surrounding the notion of "culture" does not prevent the ascription of determinative efficacy and the articulation of various characteristics which can prove of direct relevance'.[21] Cultural theories can never provide the kinds of deterministic explanations that science offers, but an impressionistic account of ICA that includes the essential variable of culture is preferable to a concrete-seeming account without it.[22]

III. The Current State of International Arbitral Culture

Arbitrators are a heterogeneous group, in that they come from widely varied backgrounds. They will continue to bring into ICA the 'bag and baggage' of the various national cultures in which they were trained. This book proposes that, as the legal culture specific to ICA matures, what arbitrators have in common will increasingly overshadow their disparate backgrounds and legal traditions. The elite transnational community that presides over the majority of international arbitrations may already share a common legal and professional culture.

Scholars have for some time written about the distinct cultures of the legal professions in different jurisdictions.[23] While disagreements persist as to the particular characteristics of a given state's legal culture, the concept of a culture shared by the legal professionals of a state (or province, or municipality) is uncontroversial.[24] However, it is altogether more problematic to claim that a legal culture now exists in ICA, where practitioners do not share a common nationality, language, or training. In fact, most of the studies of culture in ICA that have been published focus on the divergent effects of the multiplicity national legal cultures in which arbitrators and counsel were trained.[25]

[18] Legrand 1999, 27, quoting EP Thompson, *Customs in Common* (Penguin, London 1991) 13.

[19] Cotterrell 1997, 21. [20] Ibid, 14.

[21] Legrand 1999, 28–9, calling the indeterminacy of culture 'a handicap only for the positivist'.

[22] Cf Friedman 1997, 34.

[23] See, eg, the studies collected in Bruinsma and Nelken 2007 and Gessner et al 1996; recent examples of these kinds of studies include Kurkchiyan 2009, describing 'Russian legal culture'; Cooper 2008, describing competing cultures within the Chilean legal profession; Smits 2007, describing the effects of divergent national legal cultures on EU law-making; Arold 2007, describing the 'legal culture of the European Court of Human Rights'; Sellers 2006, 68–9, asserting that: 'The practice of precedent may differ slightly as applied to the common law, constitutions, and legislation ... but all depend ultimately on the culture of American lawyers.'; Bell 2001, describing multiple, distinct legal cultures within the French bar, judiciary and legal academy; Haskell 1998, elucidating various aspects of US professional legal culture to explain 'why lawyers behave as they do'.

[24] Cotterrell 1997, 17; Gessner et al 1996, xvii.

[25] See, eg, de Vera 2004; Slate 2004; Pair 2002; Stallard 2002; Borris 1999; Cremades 1999; Grigera Naón 1999; Lazareff 1999; Wilkey 1999.

However, the notion that so varied a group as international arbitrators might possess a common culture is consistent with the growing importance and autonomy of transnational commercial legal practice and private governance regimes. Commerce is always embedded in a mixture of public and private governance mechanisms. In ordinary domestic commercial dealings, private governance mechanisms—including not only arbitration and other alternative dispute resolution (ADR) processes, but also negotiation and trade practices—take place in the shadow of the national legal system. By contrast, in international commerce, 'the relative weight of public governance mechanisms decreases while the importance of private governance mechanisms increases as compared to commerce within the territorial limits of the nation state'.[26] The globalization of commerce has boosted cross-border economic activity and its importance relative to domestic transacting. Scholars have identified a related trend: 'as governance mechanisms become increasingly decoupled from state legal systems they are at the same time internationalized and privatized'.[27]

It is only natural that internationalized legal regimes would lead to internationalized legal practice. Modern commercial law practice has become sufficiently complex that specialization is necessary to attract clients,[28] and law firms increasingly market their international arbitration groups as specialist practices.[29] This trend has been abetted by the decoupling of legal practice from citizenship requirements, such as the elimination of educational and citizenship requirements as a bar to transborder mobility within the EU.[30] In a modern commercial practice, a lawyer of one nationality might work in a second country on a transaction governed by a third country's law, and the dispute is referred to arbitration in a fourth country. In such situations, practitioners effectively operate in a geographic limbo.[31]

When actors are placed outside existing systems of governance and interact repeatedly with each other, it is not surprising that new regimes specific to the new field of interaction might develop. This is a process that Teubner has called 'auto-constitutionalization'—the tendency of private governance regimes operating outside the state to develop their own sets of norms.[32] In other words, where economic globalization has given rise to the establishment of a corpus of specialist transnational legal practitioners who work primarily with each other and outside the governance of any one state, autonomous professional norms will coalesce—into a culture of ICA.

A number of commentators have posited an existing or emerging international arbitration culture, so the proposition underlying Part I of this book is not entirely without precedent.[33] However, it may be contended that ICA cannot possess a culture for two reasons: first, arbitrators are too heterogeneous to constitute a unified community, and second, arbitrators' actions are not reflexively conditioned by a common tradition.

A culture is a characteristic of an identifiable group; although definitions of culture vary, they all share this aspect.[34] Yet international arbitrators speak a variety of

[26] Calliess and Renner 2009, 1342.

[27] Calliess and Hoffmann 2009, 119 (citation omitted).

[28] Faulconbridge and Muzio 2009, 1352.

[29] See, eg, Wittinghofer 2007, 5.

[30] Glenn 2001, 981.

[31] Cf Faulconbridge and Muzio 2009, 1347.

[32] Teubner 2004.

[33] Trakman 2006; Petsche 2005; Ginsburg 2003; Koch 2003; Kaufmann-Kohler 2003; Elsing and Townsend 2002; Pair 2002; Reed and Sutcliffe 2001; Gélinas 2000; Dezalay and Garth 1996; Cremades 1999; Lazareff 1999; Grigera Naón 1999. In addition, the theme of the 1996 Congress of the International Council for Commercial Arbitration was 'Towards an International Arbitration Culture'.

[34] For a summary of different definitions of culture as the term is used in socio-legal research, see Cotterrell 1992, 23–4.

languages, come from different national cultures and adhere to diverse religions and ethical traditions. They were trained in different legal systems or may have no legal training whatsoever.[35] They are practising lawyers, academics, former judges, and (though less frequently than in the past) diplomats, politicians, or industry experts such as accountants or engineers. While the most prominent arbitrators tend to be specialists in arbitration law who have built their careers around ICA, others may act as arbitrator only once or twice.[36]

However, the same objections can be made about lawyers working within a single domestic legal system. As Cotterrell points out, 'the distance between the work environment, career pattern and outlook of the high prestige corporation lawyer and the sole practitioner in a large American urban centre is so great as to make it difficult to see any significant bonds of common experience and interest between them within a single professional community'.[37] In many ways, international arbitration practitioners have more in common than the body of legal practitioners within any one country. ICA practitioners, especially arbitrators, tend to have elite educational (if no longer socioeconomic) credentials, to have developed their careers in large, corporate, usually Anglo-American firms or major universities, and to travel in business and academic circles. They tend to share cosmopolitan, multinational backgrounds and speak multiple languages.[38] They work repeatedly with each other and on disputes within a relatively narrow band of commercial subjects. Therefore, it actually makes more sense to speak of an ICA community than to speak of a legal community within a country.

Social scientists have coined such terms as 'epistemic communities' and 'transnational issue networks' to describe transnational groups that are less cohesive than 'communities'. Commentators, apparently reluctant to use the term 'community', have applied these terms to the body of ICA practitioners.[39] ICA practitioners from around the world deal with each other regularly on the same issues; they thus constitute a network. In addition, as will be discussed below,[40] arbitration practitioners tend to share similar epistemic conceptions of an ideal of international private justice.

However, the distinctions between communities on the one hand, and epistemic communities or transnational issue networks on the other, are not relevant for current purposes. The groups defined by these different terms all share the property of being sufficiently cohesive to be capable of evolving a culture. Accordingly, when this book describes ICA practitioners as forming a 'community', the word is used in a colloquial sense; it is not intended to argue that ICA practitioners constitute something different from—or more robust than—an epistemic community or transnational issue network.

The second reason to doubt whether ICA possesses a culture is that arbitrators' shared values and standard practices are not reflexively conditioned by one common tradition. Some commentators who support the notion that an ICA culture exists have argued that arbitration is differentiated from national processes by its 'traditions'. For example, Trakman emphasizes the influence on ICA of the public and private interna-

[35] See Bisom-Rapp 2004, 299–300.

[36] For a contrary view, see Kerr 1997, 124, referring to the 'community of lawyers specializing in international arbitrations'; Teubner 1997, 158, calling the international arbitral legal order a 'global society'.

[37] Cotterrell 1992, 186 (citation omitted).

[38] See Chapter 4, Section V.2.

[39] Most notably Dezalay and Garth 1996, 16. However, even these two agree that ICA is only 'partly' an epistemic community or issue network. Ibid.

[40] These themes are addressed in Chapter 4.

tional law traditions,[41] while several commentators have described the integration in ICA of common law and civil law traditions.[42]

It is true that private and public international law traditions have both influenced ICA and that modern arbitral procedures draw from both civil and common law practices. However, while these arguments describe the sources of a purported common arbitral tradition, they do not demonstrate that ICA has developed its own, autonomous traditions—traditions the internalization of which have created a 'conventional and unreflective consensus'.[43]

Culture shapes the identity of a community through repeated interactions 'over the *longue durée*'.[44] But ICA in its modern incarnation has existed for scarcely three generations; it is still an emerging field. As Dezalay and Garth point out, the first generation of prominent arbitrators, whom they called the 'grand old men', was succeeded by a generation of 'technocrats', specialists in the law of arbitration.[45] Schultz and Kovacs argue that a third generation of international arbitrators, whom they dub the 'managers', may now be ascendant.[46] The field is arguably still too young for a culture to have solidified.

In addition, many of the practices and norms now widespread among international arbitrators result from conscious choices among competing options. Some are pragmatic and others ideologically motivated, but they are all deliberate; they therefore stand in contrast to cultural norms, which are by definition reflexive. As Hirsch points out, 'the readiness to abide by norms depends largely on the internalization of the relevant social norm, and not on rational calculation of whether the behaviour is profitable'.[47]

In short, there is good reason to doubt that an international commercial arbitration culture already exists. However, this misses the point. The important question is not whether something that can properly be labelled 'a culture' exists, but whether social norms are affecting arbitral decision-making. As the remainder of Part I demonstrates, it is possible to identify specific social norms that international arbitrators share, and to draw correspondences between those norms and the outcomes reached in international arbitrations.

IV. Methodology

This book adopts a sociological perspective. While sociology is not the only field in which cultural phenomena are analyzed, it provides a rich vein of theoretical models on which to draw that are specifically adapted to explaining the behaviour of defined groups. Sociology also deals as a matter of course in the language of norms: 'Social inquiry generally emphasizes that norms and roles constrain human behaviour.'[48] Durkheim describes sociological analysis as focusing on 'social facts', which he defines as 'every way of acting, fixed or not, capable of exercising on the individual an external constraint; or again, every way of acting which is general throughout a given

[41] Trakman 2006, 26. [42] See, eg, Elsing and Townsend 2002.

[43] Legrand 1999, 29. [44] Ibid, 27.

[45] This process has been called the 'professionalization' or 'judicialization' of ICA. See Chapter 4, Section II.4.

[46] Schultz and Kovacs 2012. See also Langer 2005. [47] Hirsch 2008, 280 (citations omitted).

[48] Hirsch 2008, 280. Writing specifically of international law, Hirsch writes that sociological analysis 'begins from the premise that individuals' behaviour and normative choices are significantly affected by social factors'. Hirsch 2005, 893.

society, while at the same time existing in its own right independent of its individual manifestations'.[49]

A distinct culture is not, of course, the only thing that distinguishes arbitral from judicial decision-making, nor is a sociologically-influenced method the only means by which to consider arbitral awards within their broader context. Two other fields, psychology and economics, have proven particularly useful in understanding the decision-making of national court judges, although scholars of international law have been slower to adopt interdisciplinary methods. Psychological studies of judging—that is, studies of judges' moral and political preferences—abound in the literature on domestic litigation.[50] Similarly, many studies have been carried out that apply economic models to construct what might be called materialistic accounts of judicial decision-making.[51] No similar studies have been conducted on ICA,[52] but in any event, for this research, the sociological approach was preferable to both economic and psychological methods.

The psychological makeup and political predilections of both judges and arbitrators undoubtedly affect the way they make decisions, including their application of substantive law. However, international commercial arbitrations rarely involve the kinds of politically-charged issues where differences in adjudicators' political orientations are likely to play a role. Such factors are therefore unlikely to create divergences between the ways that judges and arbitrators make decisions on the kinds of disputes that are referred to ICA. Consequently, psychological data are, on their own, unlikely to explain whether and how arbitrators and judges will reach different decisions on the merits of international commercial disputes.

In addition, as Tamanaha notes in his meta-study of psychological studies of judicial decision-making, the personal idiosyncrasies of judges are likely to be overshadowed by the 'significant, predictable, social determinants that govern the course of judicial decision-making'.[53] The 'social determinants' to which Tamanaha refers include such factors as shared professional formation, mindset, practices, and values—the kind of social norms that will be discussed below.[54] Sociological studies are thus more likely than psychological studies to produce the kind of insights that will better inform predictions about the outcomes reached in ICA.

Economic analysis, too, has its limitations when applied to study ICA. As will be discussed below, economic competition between arbitrators and between arbitral fora is one of the core institutional differences between arbitration and litigation.[55] Indeed, some commentators have argued that the global convergence in arbitral rules and practices is best explained by economic factors. For example, Ginsburg writes that convergence is simply a case of network effects in action—like Facebook or LinkedIn, the more members a legal network has, the more valuable it is to each of its members. Accordingly, practices will tend toward convergence and newcomers will have an incentive to align themselves with existing norms.[56] However, pure economic analysis

[49] Cited in ibid, 898.

[50] The field has a long history, especially in the US. An early text is Haines 1922 (characterized by Maveety as 'the origins of what was to become behavioralism in public law' (Maveety 2003, 8)). Recent examples include Staudt et al 2006; Sunstein et al 2006; Abel 2003; Segal and Spaeth 2002; Epstein and Knight 1998; McNollgast 1995; M Shapiro 1981; Epstein and others 2007. This line of scholarship, associated at first with political scientists and later with legal scholars, is anthologized and reviewed in Maveety 2003.

[51] See, eg, Brennan et al 2009; Foxall 2005; R Posner 1993; Spiller and Gely 1992.

[52] See Drahozal 2003, 33.

[53] Tamanaha 2009, 697, quoting F Cohen, '"Transcendental Nonsense" and the Functional Approach' (1935) 35 Columbia L R 809, 849.

[54] Personal characteristics that arbitrators tend to share as a group will be discussed in Chapter 7.

[55] See Chapter 3, Section IV.

[56] Ginsburg 2003, 1342.

often fails to account for the influence of social norms, which constrain behaviour in ways that are difficult to model in terms of economic value. For this reason, sociologists who explore economic behaviour often criticize economists for ignoring the social dimension of human actions.[57]

While economic analyses often disregard the impact of social forces, the reverse is less true—sociological analyses often account for the impact of economic forces. We usually associate the word 'culture' with religious, philosophical, or historical influences, but a culture may also develop out of economic forces or business practices.[58] Ogus argues that many of the characteristics of national legal cultures are explicable according to the economic value of networks.[59] As an example of legal culture developing from routine business practices, Trakman cites the informal practice of making deals over the phone, rather than relying on written contracts negotiated with the assistance of lawyers.[60] Thus, when commercial lawyers speak of 'trade usages', 'industry custom', or 'commercial practice', they are referring to business culture. Since aspects of a culture are no less cultural for the fact that they evolved from economically determined behaviours, a sociological analysis will highlight many of the same factors as a purely economic analysis, but will also provide insights that cannot be expressed in economic models.

1. Selection of grounded theory

Once a sociological perspective emerged as the best means of analyzing international arbitrators' decisions on matters of substantive law, it became necessary to choose the most appropriate sociological methodology. As the pioneering sociologist Émile Durkheim writes, sociological researchers should 'treat social facts as things'.[61] This means that 'social phenomena should be measured and analysed in basically the same manner as the natural scientist would measure and analyze substances and processes in laboratory experiments'.[62] Social phenomena are intangible and cannot be measured directly; however, it is possible to discern them by their effects, just as physicists might identify subatomic particles by the trails they leave in a cloud chamber. Here, the chamber is the field of ICA and the trails are the statements and pronouncements of arbitrators.

Sociologists are concerned not just with identifying and describing social phenomena, but also with developing theories to provide comprehensive explanations for social behaviours. Classical sociological analysis is deductive; the researcher begins with one of the prevailing sociological theories and applies it to the social phenomena under consideration.[63] These theories not only describe these phenomena differently, but also differ as to which phenomena ought to be the focus of social research.[64]

The adoption of a sociological perspective was inspired partly by the only previous large-scale sociological study of ICA, Dezalay and Garth's *Dealing in Virtue*.[65] This 1996 study, based primarily on interviews with arbitration practitioners and academics,

[57] Hirsch 2008, 280, citing M Granovetter, 'Economic Action and Social Structure: The Problem of Embeddedness' in R Swedberg (ed), *Economic Sociology* (Edward Elgar, Cheltenham 1996) 245.

[58] Sociologists often cite market forces as underappreciated contributors to culture. See, eg, Blankenburg 1998.

[59] Ogus 2002.

[60] Trakman 2006, 3.

[61] Durkheim 1988, 60, 161–2.

[62] Cotterrell 1992, 11.

[63] Glaser and Strauss describe such research as involving merely the 'verification' of theory. Glaser and Strauss 1967, 2.

[64] Hirsch 2005, 892–3 (citations omitted).

[65] Dezalay and Garth 1996.

is well known in arbitration circles and has justly been described as 'enormously successful'.[66] However, *Dealing in Virtue* has its limitations. Dezalay and Garth focused their efforts on the question of what kinds of people become successful international arbitrators. They never addressed the question of how arbitrators make decisions, so their conclusions are of limited usefulness for explaining and predicting outcomes in international arbitrations.

Dealing in Virtue's focus on arbitrators themselves was influenced by the theory of social fields advanced by the French sociologist Pierre Bourdieu (who was Dezalay's mentor).[67] Since this book is concerned with outcomes more than with the personalities of arbitrators, it does not adopt Bourdieu's theory *in toto*. However, it does adopt some of his vocabulary, especially in relation to the role of competition among members of a social field. As will be discussed below, competition for arbitration business—between individual arbitrators and between arbitral fora—plays an important role in shaping arbitral decision-making.[68]

It is well recognized in the sociological literature that the competition for pre-eminence in a social group plays an important part in shaping, disseminating and preserving the values and practices of the group. For Bourdieu, competition is the process by which a social field defines itself, generates and spreads its values, ensures conformity by new entrants, and propels the field to evolve—in short, competition is one of the primary forces that constructs culture.[69] Thus, for Bourdieu, a term like 'profession' or 'field' is itself the social product of the construction of the group through the medium of competition.[70]

Success as an arbitrator, as in any field, is defined according to achievement in the areas which the field considers important. Arbitrators and would-be arbitrators seek to accumulate the indicia of such success, which Bourdieu called 'symbolic capital'. The key to symbolic capital is 'recognized power'; it constitutes the recognition, institutionalized or not, that successful members of a community receive from the rest of the group.[71] The forms of symbolic capital which members of the field try to accumulate are closely related to social norms of the field. Leaders in the field have become leaders because of their stores of symbolic capital, while those seeking entrance to the field must conform to accepted norms and practices, thus reinforcing prevailing orthodoxies.

Symbolic capital is not necessarily stable within a given community; different kinds of symbolic capital may gain or lose in value over time.[72] Indeed, Dezalay and Garth's primary conclusion in *Dealing in Virtue* was that the predominant forms of social capital in ICA shifted from the 1970s to the 1990s, as the generation of the grand old men gave way to the generation of the technocrats.

Today, symbolic capital in ICA includes (in no particular order) such attributes as degrees from prestigious universities, partnerships at major law firms, professorships, academic publications, invitations to speak at conferences, proficiency in technical aspects of arbitration practice, experience as an arbitrator, counsel, or expert witness, connections to political or business power centres, and facility with multiple languages and legal systems.[73] These indicia might seem to depend on a circular argument: those

[66] Schultz and Kovacs 2012, 161.

[67] Dezalay and Garth 1996, 17–19.

[68] See Chapter 3, Section IV.

[69] Trubek et al 1994, 414, observing that: 'Conflict within the field gives it its dynamism, but also maintains it as a field: the contending players challenge each other, but not the field itself, so the struggle reaffirms and even strengthens the field.'

[70] Bourdieu and Wacquant 1992, 243. For an application of social fields to the legal profession, see Bourdieu 1987.

[71] Dezalay and Garth 1996, 18, quoting Bourdieu and Wacquant 1991, 72.

[72] Dezalay and Garth 1996, 19.

[73] Ibid.

who think these kinds of qualifications are important will find these kinds of qualifications important. However, it remains that the definition of arbitral excellence that tends to inform parties' choice of arbitrators includes the prevailing forms of symbolic capital.[74]

The importance of these forms of symbolic capital is highlighted by the other types of potentially relevant experience that do not tend to be important in appointments of arbitrators. For example, as Dezalay and Garth observed, background in high-level government and community service (such as ambassadorships or presidencies of chambers of commerce) were once highly valued but are no longer vital.[75] Similarly, personal experience as a business executive or technical subject area expertise (eg, training as a programmer if the appointment concerns computer software or a background in accounting if the dispute concerns financial products), do not seem to be influential.[76] This pattern fits with the so-called 'judicialization' or 'professionalization' trend in ICA, in which arbitration awards have displayed increasingly rigorous legal analysis.[77]

This book draws on the concept of symbolic capital and will highlight the correspondences between social norms of ICA and the types of symbolic capital sought by arbitrators. However, it does not adopt the theory of social fields more generally. A priori sociological models such as Bourdieu's appear to increase analytical rigour, but that rigour is often illusory; the international arbitration community is sufficiently heterogeneous that an attempt to fit all international arbitrators or all international arbitrations into a single model will necessarily distort the description. Instead, this book adopts the methodology of 'grounded theory' introduced by Glaser and Strauss in their landmark 1967 work, *The Discovery of Grounded Theory*.

Glaser and Strauss challenged the prevailing, 'hypothetico-deductive' mode of sociological research,[78] in which 'theories were first dreamed up ... and then subsequently "tested" against evidence through field research'.[79] They criticize 'the overemphasis in [then-] current sociology on the verification of theory, and a resultant de-emphasis on the prior step of discovering what concepts and hypotheses are relevant for the area that one wishes to research'.[80]

In place of such an approach, Glaser and Strauss urged researchers to develop theories from the data that they collect. The term 'grounded theory' is something of a misnomer, because it refers to a method for generating theories of human interaction, not a theory in itself.[81] When working under grounded theory, the researcher 'does not begin

[74] See W&C 2010, 25–8, surveying commercial parties as to the factors they consider when choosing an arbitrator. Prior experience as an arbitrator, reputation, knowledge of arbitration law, language skills, and experience of different legal cultures are all among the factors considered most important by parties.

[75] Dezalay and Garth 1996, 18–29

[76] The Chambers and Partners 2012 list of the thirty-two 'most in demand arbitrators global-wide' lists no individuals with significant education or professional experience in areas other than law or politics (including diplomacy). <http://www.chambersandpartners.com/Global/Editorial/46313> accessed 23 August 2012. It is worth noting, however, that subject matter expertise is more important in certain sectors, such as engineering/construction disputes. Often, lawyers with engineering backgrounds will be appointed by the parties, although tribunal chairs appear to be chosen more for their expertise in case management than for their technical knowledge. For example, one interviewee, who sits mostly as chair, described the value of having technical experts on the tribunal: 'We were lucky we had on the tribunal one person, a QC, who was an expert in that area. I was the chairman, but on the details of the construction of ships, flanges and the like, he was very good. And that was helpful—a mix on the tribunal. I couldn't have done it without him.'

[77] See Chapter 4, Section II.4.

[78] Kelle 2010, 2.

[79] Dey 1999, 12.

[80] Glaser and Strauss 1967, 1.

[81] Strauss and Corbin 1994, 275.

a project with a preconceived theory in mind.... Rather, the researcher begins with an area of study and allows the theory to emerge from the data'.[82] Theories generated by this method are therefore said to be 'grounded in the data'. In sum, grounded theory research leads to the development of theories of human interaction that are derived from data that have been systematically gathered and analyzed.[83]

Grounded theory may be employed for any study involving human interactions, and is considered particularly appropriate for research into phenomena that have not been adequately described or for which no or few widely accepted theories have been advanced.[84] It is now considered to be one of the core techniques of socio-legal studies,[85] although socio-legal scholars have taken to grounded theory only recently. A search of the Westlaw database identified over two hundred empirical studies published in English-language legal journals that employ grounded theory; the earliest was published in 1994 and only sixteen pre-date 2000.

Many of these are what might be called purely sociological inquiries; they examine the feelings of members of the general public about their interactions with the legal system. For example, researchers have studied parents' experiences with the Canadian legal system in cases of child sexual abuse,[86] the reactions of traumatized victims of violent crime to the prospect of victim–offender mediation,[87] feelings of stress and workplace burnout among US immigration judges,[88] and the perspectives of Latin American government agency employees on government transparency initiatives.[89]

More relevant are explorations of the norms prevailing in specific (thematic or geographic) areas of legal practice. There are several such studies in the existing literature. They consider the rationales given by Canadian judges in deciding wrongful dismissal suits,[90] American judges' assessments of the credibility of complainants alleging child sexual abuse in the distant past,[91] the effects of culture and politics on procedural rules in the California juvenile justice system,[92] the degree of importance that American mediators place on achieving consensus,[93] and jurors' evaluations of the credibility of expert witnesses in American civil trials.[94] However, there appears to be no study of international arbitration that makes use of grounded theory.

[82] Strauss and Corbin 1998, 12.

[83] L Cohen et al 2007, 491 (emphasis in original).

[84] Ibid. Grounded theory has been particularly popular among researchers studying the health care professions, especially nursing, in part because the first two grounded theory monographs concerned the culture surrounding death in hospitals. Strauss and Corbin 1994, 275.

[85] For example, the web page of the University of Bristol School of Law's MSc programme in socio-legal studies lists one of the core activities of socio-legal studies as 'empirical work which leads to the development of grounded theory' <http://www.bristol.ac.uk/law/pgdegrees/taughtdegrees/msc-socio-legal-studies.html> accessed 20 July 2012. On the appropriateness of grounded theory for socio-legal research projects generally, see Outhwaite et al 2007.

[86] Alaggia et al 2009. [87] Madeira 2009. [88] Lustig et al 2008.

[89] Pinto 2009. Similar studies have been conducted on the tasks assigned to skilled contractors and regular employees in different workplaces (Bidwell 2009), sexual harassment victims' awareness of the available legal remedies (Blackstone et al 2009), the process of defining the crime of aggression under public international law (Weisbord 2009), the attitudes of deaf and hard-of-hearing victims of institutional sexual abuse toward legal redress (Battersby et al 2008), the purposes and goals of plaintiffs in medical injury suits in the US (Relis 2007), and peacebuilding professionals' perspectives on the use of facilitative alternative dispute resolution techniques in conflict-torn regions (Erbe 2004).

[90] Nierobisz 2010. [91] Connolly et al 2009. [92] Harris 2007.

[93] Della Noce 2004.

[94] Ivkovic and Hans 2003. Similar studies have been carried out on small businesses' use of cash transactions to evade taxes (Morse et al 2009), American civil juries' consideration of information withheld from them and the effects of such consideration on damages awarded (Greene et al 2008),

2. The grounded theory method

Grounded theory is an inductive method; this makes it different from standard sociological research methods, but perhaps more recognizable to lawyers familiar with case law research. After identifying a general area for study, researchers working with grounded theory go directly into collecting raw data. As data are collected, each item is compared against the other items that have already been analyzed and grouped into thematic categories. This process—'constant comparison' in grounded theory terminology—continues until no new categories emerge, which is called the point of data saturation. Once the data are saturated, the researcher should be able to identify a core theme or category that unifies the various categories and gives shape to the emergent theory. There are, then, effectively three stages of research in grounded theory: identification of the general area for study, concurrent data gathering and analysis to identify categories in the data (which comprises the overwhelming bulk of research activity), and identification of the core theme or category. These stages will be described in turn.

Identification of the area for study

In grounded theory, researchers are admonished not to begin with a specific research question, but only a broad area for investigation.[95] This prevents data gathering from being constrained by preconceptions and helps the researcher to avoid subconsciously 'forcing' the data to fit a preconceived theory.[96] Similarly, legal practitioners and academics working with case law are often admonished not to begin with too narrow a topic area or too specific a set of search terms, because this may exclude large numbers—even whole categories—of relevant cases.

Research for this book began with a general topic area (arbitral decision-making on substantive law matters) and two related research questions: do arbitrators decide matters of substantive law in ways different from national courts and, if so, what factors other than the governing law affect arbitral decision-making? These research questions were identified before data gathering and analysis began, but no explanatory theoretical framework was conceived or considered in advance.

Data gathering and analysis

In classical sociological research (and in empirical research generally) data are gathered according to principles of statistical sampling. Before data gathering begins, an attempt is made to identify the characteristics of the population being studied and a statistically representative sample of that population is drawn for study. If the sample is not representative of the whole, the results will not be generalizable to the entire population.[97]

variations in the rules governing access to records among the fifty US states (Chamberlin et al 2007, adopting multiple research methodologies, including grounded theory), the effects of a statute regulating the performance of government agencies on the practices of five US federal health care agencies (Frederickson and Frederickson 2006), the efficacy of defence lawyer advocacy on criminal sentences handed down by US federal judges after the enactment of mandatory sentencing guidelines (Etienne 2004), and corporate in-house counsel's understandings of their professional ethics (Gunz and Gunz 2002).

95 Corbin and Strauss 2008, 162.

96 Kelle 2005, 3.

97 L Cohen et al 2007, 108.

In grounded theory research, by contrast, data are sampled to help develop theory, rather than to be statistically generalizable ('theoretical sampling' instead of 'statistical sampling'). Grounded theory also differs from standard sociological research in that data gathering continues concurrently with data analysis, rather than being completed before analysis begins.[98] The basic premise of theoretical sampling is that the researcher chooses sources of data (interviews, survey responses, texts or any other possible source of information) based on whether the data will help to identify and describe social norms, and not on the basis of statistical representativeness or generalizability.[99] Theoretical sampling maximizes the researcher's opportunities to develop concepts about the data, uncover similarities and differences, and identify relationships between concepts. Theories developed from theoretical sampling are more likely to be robust—to accurately describe the social context of the community being studied.[100]

As data are gathered, they are categorized (coded) according to the 'constant comparison' method:

> As the researcher moves along with analysis, each incident in the data is compared with other incidents for similarities and differences. Incidents found to be conceptually similar are grouped together under a higher-level descriptive concept.... This type of comparison ... allows the researcher to differentiate one category/theme [from another] and to identify properties and dimensions specific to that category/theme.[101]

To be valid, categories must be 'analytic'; that is, they must not merely rephrase the raw data but rather conceptualize their characteristics.[102] Thus, for example, if arbitrators were frequently to describe 'cost-effectiveness' as a virtue of ICA, the category would not merely be 'cost-effectiveness' or 'price', but might instead be 'client service', since the motivation for arbitrators' concern for cost-effectiveness is that consumers of arbitration services want dispute resolution to be quick and cheap. Other aspects of ICA rules and practices, such as the freedom of the parties to choose their procedures (within limits), might also fall under the category of 'client service'.

In practice, the constant comparison method requires the researcher to consider new items of data one-by-one and compare them with previously analyzed items.[103] Data are coded for assignment into one of the categories that have already been identified or, if they do not fit into one of the existing categories, a new one is created. In addition, items of data that have been given the same code are continually compared with each other. This within-code comparison is intended to 'uncover the different properties and dimensions of the code'.[104]

Data relating to international arbitral decision-making were sampled from three main areas: original interviews with international commercial arbitrators, the published writings of arbitrators, counsel and commentators, and published arbitral awards. These were supplemented with research on the various rules of procedure and laws that are employed in international arbitrations, as well as the available quantitative information on international arbitration. These sources of data will be discussed in turn.

The primary original source of data is the interviews with international commercial arbitrators. These were conducted in person wherever possible, and otherwise by telephone. All of the interviews were recorded and transcribed for analysis. They were

98 Dey 1999, 5. 99 Skeat and Perry 2008, 102–3.

100 Corbin and Strauss 2008, 76. 101 Ibid, 73. 102 Dey 1999, 7.

103 Sociological studies often seek to make their findings more reliable by having two or more researchers separately code the data. However, given the scale of this study and the necessity of a background in arbitration law, the data for this book were coded by the author alone.

104 Corbin and Strauss 2008, 74.

'semi-structured'. There was not a single set of scripted questions that was posed to every interviewee; instead, a series of general topic areas, outlined in advance, was proposed for discussion, and interviewees were encouraged to speak freely on those topics or on related topics that came to mind. The semi-structured approach strikes a balance between informal and closed interview techniques. It increases the comprehensiveness of the data gathered and makes data collection more systematic, without closing off interesting areas of discussion or requiring interviewees to fit their responses into predetermined categories.[105] Semi-structured interviewing generates the most data suitable for constant comparison and therefore maximizes the opportunities for theoretically useful data to emerge from the interviews.[106]

In line with principles of theoretical sampling, interviewees were selected to present as wide a range of backgrounds as possible among the group of international arbitrators. The interviewees are not representative of all international arbitrators in a statistical sense; however, interviewing arbitrators with varying characteristics presented the best opportunities to uncover similarities and differences between their adjudicative philosophies and to identify relationships between the personal characteristics of arbitrators and their decision-making.

The bulk of the data were gathered from a wide range of written sources that might contribute to the development of a theory of arbitral decision-making, including all writings that express or describe standard practices in ICA or international arbitrators' values, interests, goals, or decision-making processes.[107] Grounded theory is most associated with the traditional sociological data-gathering strategies—interviews, surveys and field observations—but it is equally appropriate for a study of written texts. Glaser and Strauss emphasize that such 'library research' is useful to grounded theory researchers not only to sensitize them to theoretical categories that may emerge in later field research, but also as a source of data, which can include just about anything related to the group under study, including secondary sources found in the library.[108]

In traditional legal research, secondary sources—scholarly commentaries, for the most part—are considered inferior data when compared to the primary sources of legal research: treaty, statute, and case law. Here, however, interviews, commentaries, and arbitral awards are equally useful—and equally primary—sources of information about norms in ICA.

The academic writings, conference presentations, and interviews given by the various scholar-practitioners of arbitration are particularly useful because many arbitrators are successively adjudicators, counsel, expert witnesses, and commentators. As Ginsburg notes: 'In arbitration, perhaps more than any other field of law, the line between scholar and practitioner is blurred so that many leading scholars are involved in arbitrations, and many leading arbitrators take the time to write academic articles and books.'[109] This phenomenon is due largely to two facts: first, the primary generators of law in domestic systems—legislatures and judges—play a secondary role in arbitration; second, most arbitral awards are not published. The resulting legal void is filled by scholarly and institutional production of arbitration law and rules.[110]

[105] Cohen et al 2007.

[106] The template used for the interviews can be found in Appendix I.

[107] The sources of data considered are discussed in more detail in the following pages.

[108] Glaser and Strauss 1967, 176–80; Strauss and Corbin 1998, 58.

[109] Ginsburg 2003, 1340, citing, in particular, the writings of Gabrielle Kaufmann-Kohler and William W Park.

[110] Ibid, 1340–1.

Admittedly, such written data are not susceptible to rigorous statistical analysis. However, with theoretical sampling, the researcher 'need not be ... concerned with random sampling or similar procedures designed to provide a firm basis for generalization'.[111] Theoretical sampling is well suited for a field of study like ICA, where the available data are incomplete and potentially non-representative. Theoretical sampling permits the researcher to generate a robust theory based on whatever data are available.

Thus, for example, most of the institutional awards considered here come from International Chamber of Commerce (ICC) arbitrations, notwithstanding that the ICC accounts for a small percentage of the total international arbitral awards issued around the world. If data were sampled statistically—as opposed to theoretically—a smaller number of ICC awards would have to be considered so that the proportions of institutional awards discussed reflected the actual share of arbitrations conducted by the various institutions. However, the ICC publishes a larger proportion of its awards than other commercial arbitration institutions,[112] so that the total sample of published awards is skewed toward the ICC. Many arbitral institutions make no provision to publish any of their awards, so an attempt to ensure proportionality between the different institutions would leave the researcher without sufficient data to generate a theory.

The third major source of data is published arbitral awards, an obvious source of information about the decisions of international commercial arbitrators and, more broadly, about the norms that prevail in international arbitration. Much of the existing empirical research on arbitral decision-making focuses on published awards. However, awards are of limited usefulness; one must be careful not to generalize too freely from the published arbitral awards to make conclusions about arbitral decision-making generally or to compare arbitration with litigation.

For three reasons, the published awards cannot be treated as statistically reliable data regarding the outcomes in the entire body of international commercial dispute resolution: disputes resolved by ICA may not be representative of all cross-border commercial disputes, the published awards may not be representative of all awards, and the awards themselves present incomplete information about the arbitrations in which they were issued.

First, the disputes resolved by ICA are not necessarily representative of all cross-border commercial disputes. Disputes in ICA generally involve large multinational corporations or government entities on both sides of the contract. Moreover, at least with respect to arbitrations that arise out of submission agreements (where the parties agree to arbitration only after a dispute arises), parties may choose arbitration because they want the dispute to be resolved under rules that are not strictly legal (such as decision under amiable composition or according to industry usages).[113] As Drahozal notes, the differences in the types of cases that are brought to courts and to arbitral tribunals 'interfere with attempts to compare litigation with arbitration'.[114]

Second, it is impossible to determine whether the awards that are published are representative of the whole body of awards. There are no available data on a matter so

[111] Dey 1999, 38.

[112] By contrast, most investment treaty arbitral awards are publicly available. Current practices with respect to publication of commercial and investment awards are summarized in Karton 2012, 456–8.

[113] Carlston 1967, 47.

[114] Drahozal 2006a, 298 (citation omitted). Drahozal observes that for this reason, claims that arbitration is faster and cheaper than litigation may not be accurate.

simple as the total number of awards rendered, let alone on the results reached, because 'there are no agreed-upon criteria for what should be counted'.[115] There is no reliable way of determining how many ad hoc awards are published, and not every arbitral institution releases caseload statistics.[116] When institutions do report their caseloads, they do so inconsistently. Some report the number of open cases in their systems (which creates overlaps from year-to-year), others report only the number of cases filed since the institution's foundation, while still others include ad hoc arbitrations that rent the facilities of the institution.[117] Most report only the number of arbitrations filed, not the number of awards rendered; some do not distinguish domestic and international arbitrations; some count requests for the appointment of arbitrators together with requests for arbitration.[118]

All that can be said with certainty is that the published awards represent a small percentage of the total. The ICC publishes more arbitral awards than any other institution, and yet even the percentage of ICC awards published remains minute. By the end of 2004, approximately 13,000 arbitrations had been initiated at the ICC since its establishment as an arbitral institution. Of these, only 390 (3 per cent of the total) have an award published in the five-volume *Collection of ICC Arbitral Awards*.[119]

It is not only impossible to determine whether the sample of published awards is representative of the whole, but it is in fact likely that this sample is biased. The arbitral institutions, which are responsible for publishing the vast majority of the awards, do not publish a random sample. Institutions seek the permission of the parties to publish an award when they believe the award will be of particular interest to the arbitration community (as opposed to the legal community generally) or when publication advances the interests of the institution or of arbitration as a whole. Thus, for example, awards that address the jurisdiction of arbitral tribunals are more likely to be published, as are awards involving *lex mercatoria* or amiable composition. A former Secretary-General of the ICC Court of International Arbitration observed of the ICC's collection of awards: 'Only those awards in which arbitrators have felt least constrained to apply national law have been published.'[120]

Given such selective publication policies, it is difficult to tell whether a given award is an outlier or represents a mainstream perspective. However, awards that are published receive disproportionate attention and may therefore have a disproportionate effect on subsequent awards. The *Hilmarton* case, in which French courts enforced both a vacated arbitration award in favour of the respondent and a subsequent award in favour

[115] Dezalay and Garth 1996, 6 fn 4.

[116] However, institutional arbitration appears to be preferred to ad hoc arbitration in the majority of cases. One survey indicated that only 14 per cent of arbitrations from 1998 to 2008 involving corporate parties were ad hoc. Even among arbitrations involving a state or state entity as a party, only 33 per cent were ad hoc. Corporations surveyed cited the reputations of the institutions and administrative convenience as their reasons for preferring institutional arbitration. PwC/QMUL 2008, 15.

[117] Naimark 2003, 105; Drahozal 2003, 25. As Dezalay and Garth note, successful arbitral institutions are likely to release at least this information, since 'the statistics ... serve the promotional purpose of attracting new clients by seeking to persuade them of past successes'. Dezalay and Garth 1996, 25.

[118] Drahozal 2003, 25.

[119] This figure was obtained by counting the number of distinct awards listed in the Table of Cross-Referenced Cases included in the most recent volume of the *Collection of ICC Arbitral Awards* (ICC Publishing, Paris 2009), which lists every ICC award originally published between 1974 and 2007. This statistic must be qualified by noting that not every arbitration that is initiated results in an award, so the 3 per cent figure refers to the percentage of arbitrations that were initiated, not the percentage of arbitrations in which an award was issued.

[120] Quoted in Craig, Park, and Paulsson 2001, 639 fn 39.

of the claimant,[121] generated much scholarly hand-wringing.[122] However, as Paulsson colourfully notes, the case is probably 'like a two-headed white rhinoceros which might give us a thrill in the cinema but does not really endanger our daily walk to work'.[123]

The third reason published awards should be treated with caution as a source of data is that interim and final awards present an incomplete picture even of the individual arbitrations from which they arise. While only a few arbitral awards are publicly available, procedural orders, terms of reference, and other such documents may actually be more important sources of information about the perspectives of arbitrators and their relationships with the parties and arbitral institutions. These are entirely unavailable to the scrutiny of researchers.

For all of these reasons, and because of the lack of a formal doctrine of *stare decisis* in ICA, one must be careful not to treat published awards like the judgments of national courts. They do not constitute statements of what 'the law' of international arbitration is on any given point. Nevertheless, they are an important source of information on norms in ICA and are referred to where they are helpful to the generation of a theory of arbitral decision-making.

The data considered also include the various rules of procedure applicable in international commercial arbitrations. More than other areas of human activity, law codifies its procedures, rendering them discernible without extensive interviewing or field observation.[124] The various arbitral institutions tend to update their rules of procedure frequently, so these rules are likely to reflect the current consensus (or at least broadly held beliefs) as to how arbitrations ought to be conducted. Accordingly, rules of procedure are good sources of evidence of the social norms of ICA.

The final category of data is statistics compiled by arbitral institutions and surveys of parties and arbitration practitioners.[125] All such quantitative studies suffer from methodological limitations, but they nevertheless provide useful information about the current state of ICA practice and of the priorities of ICA practitioners. Quantitative information is available on such matters as:

- the choice of arbitration versus litigation (whether and why parties choose arbitration);[126]
- the matters specified in arbitration agreements (such as the place of arbitration, the applicable law, the number of arbitrators, the arbitral institution selected, and the language in which the arbitration is to be conducted);[127]

[121] The mess was eventually cleaned up by the *Cour de Cassation*. See *Hilmarton Ltd v Omnium de traitement et de valorisation (OTV)* (1994) XIX Ybk Comm Arb 655 (Cour d'appel Paris, 19 December 1991) (enforcing an anulled award in favour of OTV), *aff'd*, *Hilmarton Ltd v Omnium de traitement et de valorisation (OTV)* (1995) XX Ybk Comm Arb 663 (Cour de cassation, 23 March 1994); *Omnium de traitement et de valorisation (OTV) v Hilmarton Ltd* (1996) XXI Ybk Comm Arb 524 (Cour d'appel Versailles, 29 June 1995) (enforcing subsequent award in favour of Hilmarton), *rev'd*, *Omnium de traitement et de valorisation (OTV) v Hilmarton Ltd* (1997) XXII Ybk Comm Arb 696 (Cour de cassation, 10 June 1997).

[122] See, eg, Davis 2002, 63–6; Gaillard 1999, 509–11.

[123] Paulsson 1998, 21.

[124] Corbin and Strauss 2008, 93–4.

[125] Since most investment arbitration awards are publicly available, some quantitative studies have been performed on the reasoning and outcomes in those awards. See, eg, Faulchald 2008 and three studies by Susan Franck: Franck 2011; Franck 2009; Franck 2007.

[126] Bühring-Uhle 1996, 129–34, surveying sixty-eight attorneys and arbitrators as to the advantages of arbitration relative to litigation; Naimark and Keer 2002, surveying parties and attorneys involved in arbitrations administered by the American Arbitration Association (AAA) from January to November 2000 as to their reasons for choosing arbitration.

[127] W&C/QMUL 2010, surveying commercial parties' preferences on a variety of issues, including choice of the seat of arbitration, the arbitral institution, and the number of parties;

- the frequency with which cases are settled (both pre- and post-award);[128]
- the frequency with which (unspecified) interim relief is applied for and granted;[129]
- the factors that influence parties' choice of arbitrator;[130]
- the parties' attitudes toward confidentiality;[131]
- the causes of delay;[132]
- the cost of arbitrations;[133]
- the substantive laws that parties tend to prefer;[134]
- the frequency with which general principles[135] and trade usages[136] are applied;
- the frequency with which arbitral tribunals render compromise awards;[137]
- the rate of voluntary compliance with awards; and [138]
- the success rate of court applications to enforce arbitral awards.[139]

These surveys reveal the preferences and interests of various participants in ICA and therefore can contribute to the development of a cultural theory of arbitral decision-making. However, there are no published quantitative studies related to ICA culture itself. The closest are the interviews with arbitration practitioners found in Dezalay and Garth's *Dealing in Virtue*.[140] These interviews provide data that is empirical but qualitative in character, and therefore cannot be expressed in terms of degrees of statistical confidence.

Identification of the core category

Once data saturation is achieved, the researcher may be able to integrate the various categories by discovering a single category or theme that dominates or unites the

PwC/QMUL 2008, surveying commercial parties on preferences among arbitral institutions and between institutional and ad hoc arbitration; Drahozal 2002, surveying new or revised national arbitration statues enacted in 1994–1999 and the place of arbitration in ICC proceedings to estimate the effect of enactment of new arbitration statutes on parties' choice of the seat of arbitration; Bond 1990, examining the provisions of arbitration clauses in proceedings filed with the ICC from 1987 to 1989.

128 PwC/QMUL 2008.

129 Naimark and Keer 2001, surveying arbitrators on the AAA international panel as to their participation in cases where interim relief was sought.

130 W&C/QMUL 2010, 25–8.

131 Ibid, 29–32.

132 Ibid, 32.

133 CIArb 2011.

134 W&C/QMUL 2010, 11–6.

135 Ibid, 15; Berger et al 2001, 91–3, surveying 2,733 attorneys, arbitrators, and academics, of whom 639 replied, as to their experience with arbitrations involving the use of general principles or *lex mercatoria*.

136 Drahozal 2000, examining arbitration statutes and rules and published awards.

137 Keer and Naimark 2001, examining a sample of fifty-four AAA international arbitration proceedings from 1995 to 2000 to study the frequently asserted claim that arbitrators 'split the baby'.

138 PwC/QMUL 2008, surveying commercial parties on their experiences with opposing parties' rates of compliance with awards.

139 Ibid, surveying commercial parties on their experiences in national court enforcement proceedings; van den Berg 1999, finding that enforcement was refused in 10 per cent of reported cases worldwide; Peerenboom 2001, 263–5, comparing enforcement rates and percentage of awarded damages recovered in Chinese courts as between awards rendered by the Chinese International Economic and Trade Arbitration Commission and foreign arbitral institutions.

140 Dezalay and Garth 1996.

other categories of data identified during the coding process. Identification of the core category is the final stage of grounded theory research:

> The core category ... is the concept [to which] all the other concepts will be related.... A central category may evolve out of the list of existing categories. Or, a researcher may study the categories and determine that though each category tells part of a story, none captures it completely. Therefore, another more abstract term or phrase is needed, a conceptual idea under which all the other categories can be subsumed.[141]

As data gathering and analysis proceeded, it became clear that the various categories emerging from the data could all be described as social norms. These had an obvious affinity with the kinds of norms that have previously been identified in studies of national or local legal cultures. In particular, they appeared to belong to two broader categories: those norms that arise from the institutional structure of the ICA system, and those that arise from international arbitrators' shared values. However, all of the individual norms are united in their shared characteristic of being aspects of the culture of ICA. Accordingly, 'culture' emerged as the core category and unifying theme.

3. Some disclaimers with respect to methodology and data

As in any kind of empirical research, the data relied upon in this book suffer from some weaknesses. These are not fatal to the conclusions drawn from the data, but should be kept in mind.

First, the descriptions of arbitral practices that exist in the literature should not be taken entirely at face value. The writings of arbitrators may depict only their personal experiences and beliefs. Accordingly, they remain merely anecdotal evidence of actual arbitration practices. As Ginsburg notes, even the much-touted harmonization of arbitral procedure may actually be an illusion formed from anecdotal evidence and a biased sample.[142] For the same reason, interview data must be used with caution because they are necessarily anecdotal and may present a skewed picture of the actual norms espoused by the bulk of arbitrators. Drahozal, one of the few empiricists studying ICA, bemoans this state of affairs:

> Much of our understanding of what happens in arbitration proceedings is based on anecdotal sources of information, such as reported court cases, published arbitral awards, and attorney 'war stories'. The problem with anecdotes, of course, is that it is difficult to evaluate whether the event described is typical or atypical, frequent or infrequent, ordinary or extreme.[143]

The fact that such sources of information may not accurately depict widespread arbitral practice does not mean that they are useless. Writings by arbitrators and interview data are important to the extent that they indicate the values with which ICA markets itself and the characteristics that international arbitrators consider to be important. Such data may not be statistically valid, but they are theoretically useful. In this way, the grounded theory method allows the researcher to draw robust conclusions from data that are statistically incomplete or biased.

The same cautious approach should be applied to the published arbitral awards cited here. As discussed above, the published awards cannot be treated as representative of the entire set of international commercial arbitrations, still less of the entire set

[141] Ibid, 104–5. [142] Ginsburg 2003, 1340.
[143] Drahozal 2003, 23. See also Drahozal 2006.

of international commercial disputes.[144] Accordingly, the published awards are useful not for their *rationes decidendi* (ie, what they say about the applicable law) but rather for what they reveal about ICA norms.

An additional methodological difficulty relates to the magnitude of cultural effects. The available data indicate that social norms do have some effect on arbitral decision-making, but it is difficult to measure the magnitude of this effect. Tamanaha has pointed out that many studies of cultural factors in judicial decision-making suffer from a 'distorting slant'—they set out to prove that judges' political ideologies affect their decisions.[145] These studies typically take the form of quantitative analyses of whether cultural factors such as political ideology correlate to a statistically significant degree with the outcomes of judicial decisions. Such a focus on *whether* culture has an effect obscures an arguably more important question: *how important* is that effect?[146]

Although this book considers qualitative, not quantitative, data, it nevertheless may suffer from the same weakness as the studies cited by Tamanaha: the extent of social norms 'impact on arbitrators' decision-making cannot be quantified. There is no definitive reply to this concern, except to say that the social norms described below are consistent with the published awards and help to explain the divergence in outcomes between ICA and national court litigation.

V. Conclusion

Although it is still a young field, ICA has reached a point in its development where its basic concepts are largely settled. Nevertheless, the justice provided by the ICA system remains opaque to outsiders. Even as the procedural aspects of ICA have become increasingly certain and transparent, arbitrators' decisions on the merits of international commercial disputes continue to take place in the proverbial black box. The resulting uncertainties have the potential to undermine ICA's legitimacy and popularity as a system of international dispute resolution.

Some model of arbitral decision-making on matters of substantive law is therefore needed, a model that will make sense of existing outcomes and predict future ones. Yet academic research on ICA continues to focus largely on jurisdictional and procedural matters, largely because confidentiality rules make ICA decision-making unsusceptible to both traditional doctrinal research and quantitative methods. Interdisciplinarity provides a way out of this quandary. Using sociological methods, the researcher can make use of the available (statistically inadequate) data to develop a robust theory of arbitral decision-making.

This book attempts to provide such a theory, using the techniques of grounded theory, an inductive sociological methodology in which theories of community behaviour emerge from analysis of the conduct and values of group members. Grounded theory is particularly apt for research on discrete areas of human interaction—like ICA—for which no generally accepted models exist.

The questions considered here are empirical; they concern whether arbitrators decide matters of substantive law in ways different from national courts and, if so, what factors other than the governing law affect arbitral decision-making. To answer these

144 See Section IV.2 of this chapter.
145 Tamanaha 2009, 686.
146 Ibid, 754.

questions, data were gathered from interviews with arbitrators, the writings of arbitrators and other commentators on ICA, published awards, relevant statutes and rules of procedure, and statistical studies. These data were compared against each other in order to discern themes or categories within them and, eventually, a core category that unites the various patterns in the data. That core category is the imprecise but powerful notion of culture.

Culture is defined here as a complex of norms that condition behaviour both by shaping the thinking of members of a community and by creating a community consensus or peer pressure that discourages deviation from those norms. Any model in which 'culture' is held up as a key to understanding some observed behaviour will necessarily be indeterminate and impressionistic. And yet, culture is a powerful, inescapable force shaping all aspects of human conduct, including adjudication. In the ICA system, as in any definable community, repeated interactions between members of the community inexorably lead to the development of a culture specific to that community. The ICA culture that is emerging from this process shapes the conduct of members of the ICA community, including the decision-making of arbitrators.

From the data gathered for this book, the following theory of international arbitral decision-making emerged: the decisions of international commercial arbitrators are driven in part by a culture specific to the ICA community, a culture that is defined by a set of norms shared by international commercial arbitrators. The next two chapters explicate this cultural theory in detail, describing each of the social norms that emerged from the data and explaining the ways that international arbitral decision-making is shaped by those norms.

3

Norms Arising from the Institutional Structure of International Commercial Arbitration

> What I like about the international arbitration community is that … it's not some sort of self-protection society, where the infirm or those … who are not good are shaded from criticism. If someone is poor at their job, it will get out there.… It's enormously competitive. And that's a good thing. Choice is key. There are choices of venues; there are choices of arbitrators; there are choices of law firms. And that is … what gives the user trust in the process.[1]

I. Introduction

Judges are state officials, while arbitrators are private citizens. Judges are paid by the government, and may be part of the broader civil service, while arbitrators are paid by the parties. Judges are randomly assigned to cases, while the parties individually select their arbitrators. Judges adjudicate full time, while arbitrators are freelancers, openly competing with each other for work. Judges enjoy strong job security, regardless of the quality of their decisions, while arbitrators are reliant on maintaining a reputation for high quality decision-making. Judges can order enforcement of their own judgments, while arbitrators must rely on the goodwill of courts to enforce their awards. Judges make a fixed salary, while arbitrators earn more the more they work.[2] Judges' decisions may be appealed on points of law, while there is in general no appeal on issues of fact or law from the decision of an arbitral tribunal (although the decision may be set aside[3] or refused enforcement). Courts are tied to a particular country's legal system, while arbitral tribunals apply and are regulated by many different laws—they have no *lex fori*. Courts are permanent, while arbitral tribunals are ad hoc. Courts are physically rooted, while successful arbitrators regularly work with a variety of arbitral institutions and in a variety of locations all over the world.

Institutional structures are an important component of communities and their cultures.[4] This chapter deals with three categories of institutional differences that correspond to distinct aspects of ICA culture: the sources of international arbitral authority

[1] A London-based independent arbitrator, interviewed for this book.

[2] A 2000 survey by Gotanda revealed that when given the choice (ie, when the administering institution does not impose a particular fee system), most arbitrators charge fees based on the amount of work done (by an hourly or daily rate) rather than under a fixed fee or *ad valorem* (percentage of the amount in dispute) calculation. In addition, a significant percentage of arbitrators (although still a minority) charge cancellation fees if a case is settled prior to the hearing. Gotanda 2000.

[3] The term 'set aside' is used here interchangeably with 'annul' and 'vacate'.

[4] See, eg, Bell's comparative study of the judiciaries in five European countries, which focuses on the effects of institutional factors, such as recruitment and selection methods, avenues of promotion and means of management and governance. Bell 2006, 13–34. Bell justifies his adoption of an institutional perspective on three bases: that law is an 'institutional fact', that legal actors operate primarily through institutions, and that judiciaries relate to and are accountable to the wider society as institutions. Ibid, 6–10.

and the constraints on that authority, the professional context within which arbitrators work, and the competitive market forces operating in the ICA system.

II. Sources of and Constraints on Arbitral Authority

The most fundamental difference between arbitrators and judges is that judges are officers of state—they derive their authority ultimately from the coercive power of their respective governments—while arbitrators are private contractors—they derive their authority from the will of parties that enter into arbitration agreements. So far, this is not controversial. However, the extent to which arbitral authority is a function of party autonomy continues to be disputed.[5] The following section canvasses the major schools of thought as to the sources of and constraints on international arbitral authority.

1. Sources of international arbitral authority

Some arbitrators maintain that ICA derives its force *entirely* from the parties' choice. Robert was among the first to make this argument:

> Except for the eventual necessity of rendering an enforceable award, the law has no influence on the formulation, the promulgation, and the voluntary execution of an award. It is possible to consider that arbitration derives none of its institutional force from the law, and develops entirely from the will of the parties, via the contractual expression of that will.[6]

This position is often called the 'consensual theory' or the 'transnational approach'. Its most important implication is that arbitration can be entirely delocalized, or separated from national laws and court systems, in particular those of the seat of arbitration. In its extreme form, the consensual theory denies national courts any role except in the enforcement of arbitral awards and grants arbitrators the power to establish any procedure or apply any substantive rule that the parties permit.

The consensual theory is controversial because it assigns no jurisdictional importance to national laws and courts.[7] State courts (with the possible exception of those in France), have long resisted the consensual conception of arbitral authority. For example, in *Bank Mellat v Helliniki Techniki SA*, Kerr LJ, himself a leading figure in ICA, wrote 'despite suggestions to the contrary by some learned writers under other systems, our jurisprudence does not recognize the concept of arbitral procedures floating in the transnational firmament, unconnected with any municipal system of law'.[8]

The opposing theory is often called the 'jurisdictional theory' but Gaillard labels it the 'monolocal approach'. It emphasizes the fact that an international arbitration must take place somewhere, and therefore can only exist to the extent that a single national legal order—that of the jurisdiction that is the seat of the arbitration—permits it to exist.[9] The classic formulation of this theory is Mann's 1967 screed against the consensual theory, entitled *Lex Facit Arbitrum* ('the law makes the arbitration'). Mann decries the notion that 'the autonomy of the parties ... may produce a contract without

[5] For a relatively brief overview of the different theories of arbitral authority, see Yu 2004 and 2005. The philosophical underpinnings of the different theories are explored in depth in Gaillard 2010a.

[6] Robert 1967, 229. [7] Ibid, 15. [8] [1984] 1 QB 2901, 301.

[9] Gaillard 2010a, 35–9.

law . . . so that arbitrators are not called upon to apply any fixed rules of a specific system of law, but may have resort to a law of their own creation'.[10]

Of course, it is true that 'in the legal sense no international commercial arbitration exists', since arbitration cannot exist without national laws and national courts, at least as an enforcement system.[11] More recent commentators have advocated a third theory:

> Transnational private law is one among multiple regimes of cross-border governance, but one distinguished by its particular mode of governance: indirect intervention through private contestation and ordering. Through private law, the state offers a set of background norms and processes that can be used by private parties to make claims against each other. The state has a necessary role in this plural system, but it forgoes dominant 'command and control' regulation, and acts rather as a kind of indirect 'facilitative' actor.[12]

Gaillard describes this theory as 'multilocal' or 'westphalian'. It sees arbitration as deriving not from a single order—that of the seat of arbitration[13]—but rather from 'all the legal orders that are willing, under certain conditions, to recognize the effectiveness of the award'.[14] The multilocal theory recognizes the fact that jurisdictions other than the seat may legitimately insist on respect for their mandatory laws when recognizing and enforcing arbitral awards.[15] It is often characterized as occupying an intermediate position between the transnational and monolocal theories.[16] However, the multilocal theory is more properly understood as an update or refinement of the monolocal theory that takes into account the overlapping claims of multiple national legal orders. The monolocal and multilocal theories share a focus on the role of state power in constructing the international arbitral system. Both emphasize that neither arbitration agreements nor arbitral awards would be enforceable without the active cooperation of states.

Nevertheless, it is equally obvious that arbitrations can only exist with the will of the parties, so the consensual theory cannot be ignored. Arbitrators may ultimately be empowered by states, but they are proximately empowered by the parties. In particular, it is the parties that define the scope of the arbitrators' powers and that appoint and pay them.

Thus, on the macro level, arbitrators' and judges' obligations flow in different directions: 'Unlike the state official or politician, whose duty is to the national interest, the lawyer-diplomat can develop an intellectual capital which transcends particular national legal fields.'[17] More concretely, the difference in who 'employs' judges (the state) and arbitrators (the parties) affects how these adjudicators are selected and remunerated.[18]

Whether this difference in the source of judicial and arbitral authority makes it impossible for arbitrators to be independent of the parties is controversial.[19] Menkel-Meadow argues that conflicts of interests are 'systemic' and 'inherent' in ICA;[20]

[10] Mann 1967, 158 (citations omitted).

[11] Ibid, 159.

[12] Wai 2005, 475

[13] The *situs*, or seat, is the jurisdiction in which the arbitration legally takes place—the jurisdiction whose arbitration law governs the arbitration. The hearings and other proceedings may occur elsewhere.

[14] Gaillard 2010a, 24–5.

[15] For a brief but comprehensive description of the nature of mandatory laws and their relationship to public policy, see Bermann 2007.

[16] See, eg, Gaillard 2010a, 24–5.

[17] Picciotto 1997, 1021.

[18] Franck 2006, 509.

[19] The effect of the arbitrator-party relationship on arbitral decision-making on the individual level will be discussed in the following section.

[20] Menkel-Meadow 2002, 956.

others, such as Franck, argue that, in the abstract, the differences in arbitrators' and judges' sources of authority 'are minor and should not affect an adjudicator's capacity and willingness to render impartial decisions'.[21] However, it is reasonable to conclude that this institutional difference in the sources of their authority makes arbitrators more likely than judges to see matters from the point of view of the parties and to be more attuned to the interests of the parties than to the interests of the legal system and the society as a whole. (This is apart from the issue of party-appointed arbitrators' relationships with the parties that appoint them, a potential source of bias that will be discussed below.[22])

International arbitrators' own perspectives seem to bear out this observation. Although arbitrators recognize the importance of state law, they tend to see their power as deriving from the will of the parties. Arbitrators may debate the proper approach to determining the jurisdiction of ICA tribunals, but seem all to be consensualists at heart. For example, a Swiss practitioner who now acts almost exclusively as an arbitrator said: 'the arbitrator ... gets his mandate from the parties; he is appointed by the parties. The state court judge is an official of the state, and has a totally different authority than an arbitrator.' An interviewee with a common law background noted that, because arbitrators' authority comes from the parties, arbitrators must 'manage' that authority.

Indeed, every arbitrator interviewed for this book characterized arbitrations as 'belonging' to the parties in some sense. One interviewee said: 'I take a more deferential approach. Fundamentally, it's the parties' process.' Another interviewee, a French practitioner and academic, said: 'You are an arbitrator because you have been appointed as an arbitrator and it's the parties' arbitration; it's for them. So you are at their service.' An American attorney put it this way: 'When I sit as an arbitrator ... I think of providing a service that the parties have contracted with me to provide. I do think of myself as having a real obligation to be flexible and responsive to their needs and desires—the mode of dispute resolution that ... they expect when they do arbitration.'

The national laws of the seat and the mandatory laws of other jurisdictions come to the fore only when courts annul an award or refuse to enforce it. However, this concern, too, was characterized by several interviewees in terms of an obligation *to the parties* to render an enforceable award. The duty to render an enforceable award is expressly imposed by many of the various arbitral rules of procedure,[23] but interviewees took this duty seriously and imbued it with a kind of moral force. For example, one London-based barrister described his role in this way: 'You have a very specific task, particularly in jurisdictions where there is very limited right of recourse against your award. There's a legal obligation on you and also, I would say, a moral obligation to very carefully consider the decision you're going to make. That for me is a key point.'

If the arbitration belongs to the parties, so too does the award. Interviewees were clear that they write the award with the parties and their specific dispute in mind. Several even contrasted their party-oriented perspective with the broader systemic perspective that national court judges must take into account. One interviewee observed:

> Awards ... may touch on and decide a general point of interest. But they tend to do so in a very ... abbreviated manner, because they are not for external publication. They are for the

[21] Franck 2006, 508–9 (citations omitted). [22] See Section III.1 of this chapter.

[23] A typical provision is art 32(2) of the Arbitration Rules of the London Court of International Arbitration ('LCIA Rules'), which requires tribunals to 'make every reasonable effort to ensure that an award is legally enforceable'.

benefit of the parties and possibly the institutions. They provide reasons sufficient only for those purposes. Whereas a judgment in a court is written for the public; the judge is in a sense accountable not only to the parties but ultimately to the court of appeal if it goes that way.

Another interviewee, a Swiss arbitrator and academic with a reputation for taking an intellectually and legally rigorous approach to drafting awards, described the difference in this way: 'the judge will also write for other judges—maybe it sets precedent, maybe not *stare decisis* but still persuasive, etc. A court judgment has a function in developing the law. That is not at all what I have to do. I'm not developing the law. I'm trying to decide this case and nobody will ever read it, hardly, and it will not change the law.'

Beyond developing the law, arbitrators draft awards with the parties—in particular the losing party—in mind. Most rules oblige tribunals to provide reasoned awards, but arbitrators see it as their job to explain their decisions in a way that the parties will accept and will understand. As one put it: 'Because you get the mandate from the parties you try to find the solution or to solve the case in a way that takes account of what really happened, because in the end you also want to have the parties accept your decision even if they don't like it, at least they say "That's how it was, we have to bear the legal consequences."'[24] Another interviewee expressed a similar sentiment, and took the opportunity to criticize some arbitrators (especially certain members of the older generation) for failing to explain their decisions in a legally and commercially rigorous manner:

> I think the most important thing is that when you read the award, as a party, you should say 'Yes, that makes sense. If I had known—in fact I should have known and I could have known—that these were the rules and that is how they should have been applied.' ... If you achieve that, you reconcile the parties with the function of the legal system, which is to be predictable....
>
> That is very general, but I feel that it is an important thing. You get too many people who talk to you about discretion. They're like wise men under the tree.... To me, that's almost shocking ... I don't think we're supposed to be wise men under the tree; we are supposed to adjudicate the contractual dispute. People work hard; they make predictions. They expect something. They have computed for their own budget how much this contract was going to be worth to them. And when you are an arbitrator you have to respect that; you can't just say 'my wisdom, fairness ... '.

The self-imposed obligation to explain the outcome in a way that the parties will accept takes on an additional dimension due to the internationality of ICA. One Swiss interviewee noted that he always takes into account the necessity of drafting the award in such a way that it will be comprehensible to counsel and parties from a variety of legal systems:

> What we have normally is parties from all over the world, with totally different backgrounds, represented by totally different kinds of lawyers, not lawyers that were all trained at the local university and then took the bar here and know how we do things here. So you have to write in a very different way if you want to explain things to, say, a party from Argentina.

2. Constraints on international arbitral authority

Grants of authority are invariably accompanied by corresponding constraints on the exercise of that authority. The decision-making of arbitrators, like that of all adjudicators, occurs within the boundaries delineated by those constraints. Accordingly, the

[24] See also Tschanz 2009.

decision-making of arbitrators can only be understood within the context of the constraints upon it. This issue will be examined first with respect to formal constraints that derive from the applicable laws and rules (legal norms), and second with respect to informal constraints (social norms).

Arbitrators act within three layers of formal, rule-based constraints. First, the agreement of the parties determines the scope of the tribunal's jurisdiction, whether through an arbitration clause in a contract, by a submission agreement, or (in the case of ICC arbitrations and sometimes in ad hoc arbitrations) by terms of reference. If the tribunal exceeds this authority, as when the parties did not freely and lawfully choose arbitration, or when the tribunal rules on issues not submitted to it, or when the tribunal is constituted in a manner contrary to the agreement of the parties, any eventual award may be set aside or refused recognition and enforcement, as per article V(1)(a), (c) and (d) of the New York Convention.[25]

The rules of procedure constitute second layer of constraints. These are the rules of the administering institution if it is an institutional arbitration, and frequently the UNCITRAL Rules of Arbitration ('UNCITRAL Rules') if it is an ad hoc arbitration.[26] Failure to abide by the rules of procedure can result in removal of an arbitrator or annulment of the award. However, when it comes to the conduct of the hearing, these rules are often very general or provide for flexibility. They place few constraints arbitrators' power to structure the proceedings in the manner they deem appropriate. Moreover, they seldom place any significant constraints on arbitrators' ability to choose, determine, and apply the governing substantive law.

Applicable national laws constitute the third layer of formal constraints on arbitral authority. The New York Convention provides that recognition and enforcement of an award may be refused if the party against whom the award is invoked was 'unable' to present its case.[27] As a result, many national arbitration laws permit the annulment of an award or the refusal of recognition or enforcement if the tribunal did not give both parties full and equal opportunities to state their cases and to respond to the other parties' cases. For example, the UNCITRAL Model Law on International Commercial Arbitration ('UNCITRAL Model Law') states: 'The parties shall be treated with equality and each party shall be given a full opportunity of presenting his case.'[28] Similarly, the English Arbitration Act 1996 requires the tribunal to: 'act fairly and impartially as between the parties, giving each party a reasonable opportunity of putting his case and dealing with that of his opponent'.[29]

In addition, under article V(2)(b) of the New York Convention and every national arbitration law, courts may set aside awards or refuse them recognition or enforcement if they contravene the fundamental public policy of the state in which the application is made. Generally, the tribunal is bound by any mandatory provisions of law of the seat of arbitration; however, tribunals must also consider the mandatory laws of other states where enforcement of the award is likely to be sought.

[25] Convention on the Recognition and Enforcement of Foreign Arbitral Awards (adopted 10 June 1958, entered into force on 7 June 1959) 330 UNTS 3 (New York Convention).

[26] The UNCITRAL Rules were designed to be used in ad hoc international arbitrations and, when promulgated in 1976, were the only rules available for that specific purpose. Born 2009, 151. See also Lew et al 2003, 25. Unless otherwise noted, all references to the 'UNCITRAL Rules' are to the 2010 version of those rules.

[27] Article V(1)(b). [28] Article 18.

[29] Section 33(1)(a). Violation of s 33 can result in annulment of the award under s 68(2)(a) if the violation caused 'substantial injustice' to one party.

A key characteristic of the relationship between national law and ICA is that, in annulment or recognition and enforcement proceedings, the focus is on procedural matters. Not only is there in general no appeal process within international commercial arbitration, but also, generally speaking, judges may not set aside an award or refuse enforcement on grounds that the arbitrators made an error of law or otherwise made a wrong decision. There are, in essence, no formal constraints on the arbitrators' ability to err in choosing the governing substantive law (unless they ignore the express choice of the parties), determining the content of that law, or applying the law to the facts.[30] Carbonneau wryly puts the matter thus: 'The content of the governing *lex*, however chosen, is quite malleable ... with the degree of malleability being determined by the arbitrator's ingenuity.'[31] As Rogers points out, this state of affairs vests arbitrators with broad, virtually unreviewable decision-making power: 'Even clear mistakes of law in arbitral awards are virtually immune from appellate review.'[32]

By contrast, judges must apply the law—substantive and procedural—as written in domestic statutes and as interpreted by superior courts. If they make an error of law, it may be overturned on appeal. In some jurisdictions, arbitrators are subject to liability for negligent performance of their duties, while judges everywhere enjoy blanket immunity.[33]

Broadening the disparity between judges and arbitrators is the fact that arbitrators in ICA may recognize and apply general principles of international commercial law, also called '*lex mercatoria*', the 'new law merchant', 'a-national law', or 'transnational law'. The very existence of such principles, let alone their applicability to the resolution of actual disputes or their importance in practice, is controversial. However, they are in many ways central to ICA's self-image. It is therefore worth making a brief digression to discuss the place of general principles of law in ICA.

The importance of general principles of law is often overstated. Only a small percentage of contracts provide for the application of general principles.[34] As the ICC reported: 'In 79.8% of the contracts giving rise to disputes referred to ICC arbitration in 2007, the parties had specified the law applicable to the merits. They opted for state laws in all but three contracts.'[35] The three exceptions called for the application of the UNIDROIT Principles, the CISG, and the rules of the Organisation for the Harmonisation of Business Law in Africa (OHADA).[36] Thus, in no dispute filed with the ICC in 2007 did the parties call for the direct application of 'general principles' or '*lex mercatoria*'.[37] Similarly, in a study of arbitration clauses in disputes filed with the ICC over roughly the second half of the 20th century, Dasser found that only 0.3 per cent referred to *lex mercatoria* or general principles.[38]

[30] The rules regarding substantive law determinations in ICA will be discussed in greater detail in Chapter 5.

[31] Carbonneau 2004, 1204.

[32] Rogers 2002, 414–5 (citations omitted).

[33] Arbitrator immunity is a controversial subject and the rules vary greatly from jurisdiction to jurisdiction. See Rutledge 2004; Franck 2000.

[34] The available empirical evidence is discussed in Drahozal 2005, 536–44. One interviewee, a specialist in construction and engineering disputes, said that in his field, 'the reason there's arbitration at all is because the standard form has specified it. There are only a dozen standard forms that matter and none of them calls for general principles or amiable composition. In one or two, they actually say, "There will be no *compositeur*-ish behaviour by the tribunal." There's no question of it—parties want a court-like approach'.

[35] ICC Statistical Report 2007, 12.

[36] Ibid.

[37] Ibid.

[38] Dasser 2008, 140.

Contracts calling for the application of general principles tend to come from a few specific areas, such as contracts involving Middle Eastern government entities or investment guarantee contracts involving the World Bank's Multilateral Investment Guarantee Agency.[39] In other cases where parties choose to be governed by general principles, it is often because 'there was no published and publicly available national law on point. In other words, the new law merchant applied only in the absence of national law, not in lieu of national law'.[40] Finally, there is some evidence that both parties and tribunals are calling for the application of general principles less frequently than in the past; from 2003 to 2007, the percentage of arbitration clauses in ICC disputes that called for the application of such principles declined from 1.2 per cent to 0.5 per cent.[41]

Nevertheless, general principles constitute a potentially important body of law to which many arbitrators are dedicated, and which is almost entirely absent from national courts. The dedication of arbitrators and arbitral institutions to promoting general principles is evident in the publication policies of the major institutions. For example, as was noted above, the ICC has prioritized the publication of arbitral awards where the tribunal does not apply national laws.[42] Such a policy exists only to promote the legitimacy of general principles as a basis for the resolution of international commercial disputes.

In addition, as a reflection of the doctrine's roots in public international law, clauses providing for some manner of general principles remain common in contracts involving governments or government enterprises: 'The government does not wish to submit to the laws of a foreign state. A private party will not wish to have the contract governed by the laws of the foreign government since they may be changed to his disadvantage after the contract is made.'[43] Of course, private parties need not resort to general principles to protect themselves from their sovereign contractual partners; other means exist, such as expropriation insurance, stabilization or renegotiation clauses in the contract, and choice of the law of a 'third state'.

Finally, general principles are notoriously indistinct. The flexibility of general principles means that decisions applying them provide some of the most direct evidence of the actual preferences of arbitrators. The 'standard explanation' for why parties would not contract for the application of general principles is that they are 'too vague and uncertain to serve as a useful substitute for national law'.[44] Indeed, the primary criticism of general principles is that they are so vague as to constitute a mere façade for the preferences of the arbitrator: 'While not completely standardless, [general principles] and *lex mercatoria* tend to be very elastic concepts whose content changes as much with the arbitrator as with the industry.'[45] Thus, the way arbitrators select and apply general principles of international private law tells us a great deal about what arbitrators think the law ought to be.

Interviewees were highly aware of the absence of constraints imposed upon them by the applicable laws and rules, especially with respect to their decisions on the merits. They expressed the obvious point that this gave them greater freedom than national court judges: '[there is] practically no court control over the application of the law, of the substantive law. I'm sure that is an important factor that makes arbitrators more free

[39] As one interviewee observed, contracts involving general principles or amiable composition tend to be 'intensively located in a few particular kinds of trade practice'.

[40] Drahozal 2005, 526.

[41] Drahozal 2009a, 1039; see also Dezalay and Garth 1996, 63.

[42] See Chapter 2, Section IV.3.

[43] Lando 1989, 143–4.

[44] Drahozal 2005, 546.

[45] McConnaughay 1999, 471.

to apply the law than a judge, who knows he has a court of appeal above him.' However, interviewees also described themselves as feeling a countervailing duty to the parties to restrain the urge to make arbitrary decisions. One said: 'As an arbitrator, because there are so limited possibilities of appeal against your decision, that makes you cautious.'

More generally, the gap between the constraints on judicial and arbitral authority does not seem so wide when one includes informal constraints imposed by social norms. Arbitrators, like judges, do not want their awards annulled or denied enforcement. Indeed, despite the high degree of freedom afforded them by the limited means of recourse against an award, the arbitrators interviewed for this book were keenly aware of the risk that their awards may be annulled or refused enforcement by the courts. This concern permeates their thoughts in every stage of their involvement in an arbitration, from accepting an appointment to issuing a final award. Throughout the interviews, whenever an issue arose that touched on a ground for non-enforcement of awards, interviewees used phrases like 'you have to be careful' or 'I would be very cautious'.

This concern most obviously applies to procedural matters, such as ensuring that the tribunal stays within the scope of submission to arbitration and ensures that both parties have a reasonable opportunity to present their cases. But it also carries through to the drafting of the award. One interviewee, who frequently presides over arbitrations seated in Switzerland, spoke of the need to keep courts in mind when drafting an award, especially since judges in many jurisdictions are unfamiliar with ICA law and practice. After discussing the ways that awards can be drafted to increase their acceptability to the parties, he added:

> Of course I will write for the Swiss Federal Supreme Court, the one that is breathing down our necks.... But that's by no means the only court I am writing for. I am also writing for the courts in the place of enforcement, if I can predict it.... I had a case that had to be enforced in eastern Siberia.... I had to explain things, especially in the early days—this was a case that I had to do in the early days when they just came out of the Soviet system and started doing things in a modern way. You have to explain things to these judges.

Rendering an award that is the subject of a successful challenge implies (in arbitrators' perception, if not always in fact) a failure on the part of the tribunal. It is a black mark on an arbitrator's résumé and may even affect his or her ability to garner future appointments. Even if an award is not published or challenged in a public court proceeding, the parties will see it and will be able to evaluate the arbitrator's skill and conscientiousness. Given how small and tightly-knit the arbitration community remains, both exemplary and incompetent work will affect an arbitrator's prospects. Franck is therefore correct to conclude that: 'While arbitrators and judges are subject to different review processes, both processes provide an opportunity to evaluate their conduct.'[46]

In addition, increasing publication of awards, greater sophistication of the parties, and more frequent use of ready-made rules like those promulgated by the International Bar Association (IBA) mean that arbitrators now have less control over procedures than they did in the past.[47] Modern arbitral rules have also removed earlier constraints on the parties' freedom to choose the applicable substantive and procedural rules.[48] The parties' power in these areas balances the almost unconstrained power that arbitrators have over the decision on the merits.

[46] Franck 2006, 511. [47] Rogers 2002, 416 (citation omitted).
[48] See Chapter 4, Section II.1–2.

III. The Professional Context of Arbitration

International arbitrators work in a professional milieu entirely different from that of judges. Two important factors specific to ICA must be addressed: the multiple roles played by arbitrators and the fact that arbitrators are appointed by the parties.

1. Arbitrators' multiple roles

An important difference between judges and arbitrators is that the individuals who are appointed as arbitrators also participate in arbitrations in other capacities: as advocates, consultants, expert witnesses (hired by the parties or by the tribunal itself), and (in the case of the ICC's Court of International Arbitration) reviewers of awards.[49] Indeed, it is practically impossible to be appointed as an arbitrator in a major international dispute without prior experience in one or more of these roles.[50]

Three consequences arise from this state of affairs. The first is the greater likelihood in arbitration than in litigation that an adjudicator will have a prior professional relationship with a party or counsel that could create an inference of bias or an outright conflict of interest and duty. However, such relationships are, with adequate disclosure by arbitrators, relatively easy to police. Moreover, they do not substantially differ from potential conflicts experienced by judges, many of whom (at least in common law countries) were previously practising lawyers.

The second consequence is that arbitrators, counsel, and expert witnesses often maintain ongoing personal and professional relationships. Arbitrators are not only likely to have worked together with counsel or expert witnesses in the past, they may work together in the future on an unrelated dispute, as co-counsel, as consultant and client, or as counsel and arbitrator with the positions reversed. In addition, while members of the same law firm may not appear in front of each other, arbitrators who are barristers may generally hear arguments by barristers from the same chambers.[51] Arbitrators are often in a position to appoint other arbitrators, either when co-arbitrators choose a tribunal chair or when arbitrators serve on the boards of arbitral institutions that act as appointing authorities.

Repeated interactions between arbitration practitioners are often not coincidental, but rather the result of mutual referrals. As Dezalay and Garth note, the 'exchange of favours is essential to success in arbitration, a career dependent on personal relations'.[52] For this reason, international arbitration is often described as a 'club'.[53] Judges, on the

49 The ICC Court's review is nominally limited to the form of the award but often goes beyond this. One interviewee, a former UK representative on the ICC's Commission in International Arbitration, reflected on the character and effects of the ICC Court's review: 'The ICC Court scrutinizes awards not only on the grounds of form to see whether they will be capable of being enforced, but also looks at the reasons because a complete deficiency of reasons might be regarded as a defect in form. And it will provide advice on how to restructure the reasons or suggest different reasons. But it's only advice; it can't actually make you do it. And if you don't want to do it there's not much that it can do in the sense that, although the reasons may not be good, they are the reasons.'

50 Retired judges, who are popular as arbitrators, are an exception to this trend. However, high-level judicial experience can substitute for experience as an arbitrator; in addition, the retired judges who find success as arbitrators may have had experience as arbitration counsel prior to being elevated to the bench.

51 *Hrvatska Elektroprivreda, dd (Croatia) v Slovenia*, ICSID ARB/05/24, award of 6 May 2008 (Tribunal's Ruling regarding the participation of David Mildon QC in further stages of the proceedings).

52 Dezalay and Garth 1996, 124.

53 See, eg, Menkel-Meadow 2002, 958–9; Ridgway 1999, 51; Dezalay and Garth 1996, 10 (quoting a 'well-informed New York partner').

other hand, must not fraternize with advocates or potential witnesses, especially in states where judges are drawn from the ranks of prominent advocates, and may not act as advocates or expert witnesses while they are on the bench. For example, the House of Lords held in 2003 that lawyers who serve as part-time judges may not appear as counsel before a panel of the Employment Appeal Tribunal consisting of one or two lay members with whom they had previously sat, because such arrangements give rise to a real possibility of subconscious bias, and thereby undermine public confidence in the administration of justice.[54] These characteristics of the ICA community give rise to legitimate concerns regarding the independence of arbitrators.

Even more importantly, arbitrators are likely to have in the past and will in the future encounter the advocates appearing before them, with the positions reversed. Dezalay and Garth see such fluidity of roles as a benefit:

> The principal players ... acquire a great deal of familiarity with each other, and they develop also, we suspect, a certain connivance with respect to the role held by the adversary of the moment. The extraordinary flexibility of this rotation of roles contributes greatly to the smooth running of these mechanisms of arbitration.[55]

Such a statement may well be shocking to those who take conflicts of interest seriously. Indeed, there is cause for concern, given that an arbitrator's future livelihood may depend on the goodwill of the other participants in a current arbitration. As Garth notes, 'the world of ICA operates to a great extent as a "favour bank": Those who can provide a favour for the individuals at the core tend to get rewarded with referrals and recognition.'[56] There is thus a strong incentive to cooperate with the other participants in an arbitration and to conform to accepted practices and standards.

Nevertheless, several interviewees praised the close relationships between arbitrators and counsel and the fluidity with which individuals move between the two roles. One interviewee, who described his practice as 'about 50–50 acting as counsel and arbitrator', described the fluidity of roles as creating greater incentives for professionalism:

> It's an advantageous way of practising. If you are a counsel, it's good to be an arbitrator also, so that you can remember when you are arguing a case what it's like to be receiving the argument.... It is a small world; you often see the same people before you and then you argue a case before them. That, I think, is not bad because it's a way of ensuring a higher standard of practice, honesty, being genuine. You won't get away with being less than honest, if you are going to face the same people two years later in a different case.[57]

[54] *Lawal v Northern Spirit Ltd* [2003] UKHL 35 [21]–[23].

[55] Dezalay and Garth 1996, 49.

[56] Garth 1997, 11; Dezalay and Garth also note: 'It is good arbitration politics to thank business lawyers or other acquaintances who bring nice arbitration matters by letting them have limited access to the arbitration market. This system of exchange of favours is essential to success in arbitration, a career dependent on personal relations.' Dezalay and Garth 1996, 124.

[57] Other interviewees also emphasized the benefits they derive personally from acting as both arbitrator and advocate. For example, one French interviewee who regularly acts in both capacities commented: 'I think sitting as an arbitrator helps me a lot be effective as a lawyer addressing an arbitration tribunal or even a state court.... Because it helps me realize that only clear, important, convincing arguments are of any use and that all of the little legal discussions you advance in argument and there's a counter-argument but then in the reply, you criticized the counter-argument and you will cite another case and then they will again reply—all of that will not convince anybody.... But I like oral arguments, which I think carry much more weight to convince a tribunal. There, you have to completely forget about all these tiny things. Be very strong and straightforward. That I derived from my experience as an arbitrator.'

The only major arbitral rules of procedure that limit role switching are those of the Court of Arbitration for Sport. The Code of Sports-Related Arbitration ('CAS Rules') provides that only arbitrators on a list maintained by the CAS may be appointed.[58] In the 2009 revision to the CAS Rules, the 'most significant change' was a 'prohibition of the double-hat arbitrator/counsel role'.[59] Article S18 of the CAS Rules provides that arbitrators on the CAS list may not act as counsel for parties before a CAS tribunal. The CAS's stated goals in prohibiting such role-switching were 'to limit the risk of conflicts of interest and to reduce the number of petitions for challenge [to arbitrators] during arbitrations'.[60]

One arbitrator, who is familiar with CAS and investor-state arbitrations, noted that such a provision may make sense in fields that involve a relatively small number of legal issues that present themselves with frequency. This arbitrator has no qualms about role-switching in commercial arbitrations, but disapproves of it in investment arbitrations:

> I don't think you can be an arbitrator and counsel at the same time in different cases in investment arbitration, just because of the issue conflicts, because you always find the same notions and the same standards in investment treaties. When you have to define what fair and equitable treatment is as an arbitrator and then you have to argue something different or the reverse as counsel ... that is not credible. You don't have this problem in commercial arbitration because you have a negotiated contract between two private parties. The decision affects these two parties and it's specific to this contract.

Another interviewee made a similar point, that the CAS prohibition on role-switching should not be applied more widely:

> The rule ... is helpful in the close environment of the CAS. But in the international field I'm not sure such a general rule would make much sense.... There is a tendency of some 'guru arbitrators' to ... lose sight of the perspective of party counsel. It's important as arbitrator to always imagine 'How would I react as party counsel to the decision I make now?' A small example is time limits. Some arbitrators have no connection anymore to acting as a party representative; they set unrealistically short time periods or don't take into consideration attorneys' problems in setting dates for hearings.

The close relationships between arbitrators and counsel are also manifested in a high degree of collegiality and informality in their interactions. Several interviewees emphasized the lengths that they go to in order to establish a friendly and cooperative working relationship with other arbitrators and with the parties.

Some spoke of the importance of socializing with other members of a tribunal, such as one London-based arbitrator who makes it a habit, when sitting in London, to invite the other members of the tribunal to his house for dinner. Another arbitrator found that such socializing reduces disagreements within the tribunal and contributes to unanimous awards: 'In my experience, it's generally a very good relationship. We get along well. We'll have lunches, sometimes dinners. And generally we come to an agreement.'

[58] CAS Rules, S3, S6.3 R33, R40.2, R54 available at <http://www.tas-cas.org/d2wfiles/document/4962/5048/0/Code20201220_En_2001.01.pdf> accessed 27 August 2012.

[59] Court of Arbitration for Sport, 'Press Release: The Court of Arbitration for Sport (CAS) Amends Its Rules' (1 October 2009).

[60] Ibid. For an in-depth discussion of the CAS's rule change, see Brubaker and Kulikowsky 2010.

Interviewees often described themselves as 'equal to' the parties. This, they said, is in contrast to judges, who 'need a sort of aloofness'.[61] For example, one interviewee described the importance of maintaining an informal tone in hearings. Arbitrators, he said, are 'equal' to the parties, while a judge is 'superior'. Arbitrators are invariably selected because the parties consider them to be appropriate for the case in question. The interviewee noted that, upon entering a hearing room, he/she might offer to pour coffee for the parties, as a way of showing them respect and encouraging a cooperative atmosphere. He concluded: 'You have to keep your independence but also earn the parties' respect, and you can earn that respect by not being "above" or overly distant from them.'

Other interviewees spoke of the need to work with the parties to create a cooperative atmosphere. One called the relationship with counsel 'a give-and-take ... you need to keep the trust of the parties and have a sort of civilized relationship with counsel, which is based on agreements and not on orders'. Another interviewee spoke of the importance of having a good 'bedside manner'.[62] A third expressed the satisfaction she feels from achieving a collaborative relationship with the parties and their counsel:

> I would hope ... that you create a good working relationship, a good cooperation, with counsel so that they know they can contribute to the resolution of the case.... My biggest reward is when I close a hearing and I have a feeling everybody is happy ... One party will lose, or half lose; but at least it will have had the impression that it was heard, that it was treated fairly. And that's really the goal.

The collegiality prized by arbitrators is also illustrated by ICC Case No 8694 of 1996. There, the tribunal thanked 'the parties' counsels for their competence, professionalism, courtesy, and good humour manifested during the course of the arbitration. Without such a cooperative and constructive approach, our work would have been much more difficult'.[63] Former ICC Secretary-General Yves Derains characterized the tribunal's statement, which was not unusual, as 'refreshing', 'encouraging', and characteristic of the 'comradely spirit' of ICA.[64] Dezalay and Garth go even further:

> In the community of the initiated, the proximity and interchangability of roles makes the advocates comport themselves in a very subtle manner as auxiliaries of the arbitral tribunal. Defending the interests of their clients in a case does not push them to actions that jeopardize their own credibility or, worse still, the social legitimacy of arbitration. Such an attitude would have been equivalent to professional suicide in building the practice of international commercial arbitration.[65]

[61] Indeed, several interviewees noted that judges sometimes have difficulty making the transition to arbitrating because they are used to being separate from the parties, above them. One interviewee put it sharply: 'Some old-fashioned judges would have a problem [arbitrating] because they think that they're high and mighty.'

[62] 'Arbitrators are there because the parties want them to be there. And arbitrators, generally speaking, have very good bedside manner. They know how to deal with people and so on. Often judges have no bedside manner, they're so used to being the god-like figure that everybody defers to.'

[63] Award in ICC Case No 8694 of 1996 [1997] JDI 1056 (author's translation) ('*Le Tribunal exprime sa reconnaissance aux conseils des parties pour leur compétence, professionnalisme, courtoisie, et bonne humeur manifestés pendant le déroulement de l'arbitrage. Sans une telle coopération et approche constructive, notre travail aurait été beaucoup plus difficile.*').

[64] Ibid.

[65] Dezalay and Garth 1996, 56–7. This is explicable in part by mere professional courtesy and something similar could be said of judges. However, due to the interests and constraints described here, the effect is likely to be stronger among arbitrators than among judges.

Of course, collegiality has it limits; in the end, arbitrators must maintain their authority. But there is a balance to be struck. Observed one interviewee: 'You have to be respected and make people accept what you tell them and not because you force them, but because they believe you are right. But also listen to them and be modest. People who are both modest and have authority—you have to look for them.' Similarly, arbitrators would not allow socializing to create grounds for a challenge to them or to the award. For example, one arbitrator mentioned that he might occasionally have social contact with both counsel during a hearing, if they are all travelling to the same city, but that he would never see one party's counsel separately: 'if you are travelling in a cab you make sure are both parties have people in the cab with you. You absolutely don't do anything with one party alone'.

A third consequence of the fluid roles played by arbitrators is so-called 'issue conflicts', situations where actual bias, or an appearance of bias, arises from the adjudicator's relationship with the subject matter of the dispute, as opposed to a relationship with a party.[66] Because they tend to speak and publish frequently in academic and professional contexts, arbitrators may have committed themselves to particular points of view on issues that arise in a dispute in which they have been appointed; they may also have taken a position on the same legal issue in an unrelated dispute.

Parties are free to choose arbitrators who are generally predisposed to the legal or factual theory of their case.[67] Indeed, party-appointed arbitrators are often selected because the party and its counsel expect the arbitrator to be sympathetic to the arguments that the party intends to make. As Mosk notes: 'Doctrinal sympathies or antipathies are not disqualifying. A small distributor bringing an action for wrongful termination might be attracted to an arbitrator who is known to believe that the law should be zealously applied to curtail abuse of a dominant position.'[68] Carter even asserts that '[s]uch potential receptivity is one of the advantages of arbitration, whether international or domestic, in which parties can quite legitimately "shop" for arbitrators with specific backgrounds and experience'.[69]

In general, interviewees noted that it is often a mistake to try to choose an arbitrator based on their predispositions, partly because other qualities are more important and partly because one can never be certain how an arbitration will develop. There are no available statistics, but it seems likely that only a small number of arbitrators are chosen on this basis.[70] However, these kinds of predispositions can cross into outright bias. The problem of issue conflicts (although not necessarily under that name) has been noted by commentators[71] and, on occasion, has arisen in proceedings challenging arbitrators.[72] Still, existing codes of conduct and impartiality standards may be insufficient to address issue conflicts.[73]

66 See Brubaker 2008. 67 Craig, Park, and Paulsson 2001, 196.

68 Paulsson 1997, 15. 69 Carter 2000, 295–6.

70 At least in commercial arbitrations; the problem is arguably more acute in investment arbitration, where the recurrence of a relatively small number of issues makes it possible for arbitrators to establish themselves as state-friendly or investor-friendly.

71 See, eg, Grigera Naón 1999, 119 ('Neutrality should be understood not only as premised upon the independence and impartiality of arbitrators but also upon their mental openness and disposition.'); Singhal 2008, 125; Brubaker 2008.

72 See, eg, a pair of Dutch cases arising from an investment treaty dispute: *Republic of Ghana v Telekom Malaysia Berhad* (District Court of the Hague, 18 October 2004), HA/RK 2004, 667; *Republic of Ghana v Telekom Malaysia Berhad* (District Court of the Hague, 5 October 2005), HA/RK 2004, 788, reprinted in (2005) 23(1) ASA Bull 186.

73 For analysis of the relevant provisions of the major institutional rules, see Brubaker 2008, 126–34.

2. Appointment of arbitrators by the parties

Perhaps the most obvious concern regarding the independence of arbitrators arises from the fact that the parties appoint the arbitrators, or most of them, in the majority of international disputes.[74] The perception that party-appointed arbitrators are by definition biased has serious implications for the legitimacy of ICA.[75] All arbitrators are required by the rules of procedure to act neutrally, that is, both to judge the dispute with an open mind and to refrain from advocating for the parties that appointed them.[76] However: 'A certain perception of reality and a distaste for hypocrisy cause some practitioners to conclude that one should simply expect that a party-appointed arbitrator will not behave as impartially as one appointed jointly or by a neutral authority.'[77]

The bare fact that arbitrators depend for their livelihood on the continuing favour of the parties—or more properly their counsel[78]—affects their independence and impartiality. As a 'leading member of the pioneering generation' put it when interviewed by Dezalay and Garth, to be 'really independent', an arbitrator must be older than seventy-five and so not dependent on further arbitration business.[79] A 'senior English arbitrator' interviewed by Dezalay and Garth mused that: 'You're often appointed a party arbitrator by someone with whom you have worked before.... You know you're going to work with him again. Does that unconsciously bias one? I think it's a difficult one.'[80]

Yet, there is no objective evidence that party-appointed arbitrators systematically favour the parties that appoint them, and there is anecdotal evidence that most awards are unanimous.[81] Lowenfeld writes: 'The suspicion ... that the chairperson decides and the other two arbitrators are simply other kinds of advocates is not borne out in the practice I have seen in the international commercial arena.'[82] Interviewees echoed this observation; several said that they had never encountered a truly partial co-arbitrator, or that they had encountered one only once or twice in a hundred arbitrations.

Arbitrators from some cultures are reputed to see their role as a party-appointed arbitrator as a kind of advocate. One interviewee recounted a case where he was a party-appointed arbitrator. The lawyer who represented the other party, a personal friend, told the arbitrator (after the award was issued) that the lawyers who had appointed the

[74] Institutional rules generally permit the parties to agree that they will appoint (separately or jointly) one or more of the arbitrators. Moreover, under most of the major arbitral rules of procedure, selection by the parties is the default position. See, eg, ICC Rules art 12(3)–(4); ICDR Rules, art 6; UNCITRAL Rules, arts 7–10. An exception is the LCIA Rule, art 5, which makes the default position selection by the LCIA Court. However, under art 7, the parties can agree that they will nominate the arbitrators, and such agreement will derogate from the default rule in art 5. In practice, there is little difference from the other sets of rules.

[75] It has also been blamed for other negative perceptions of arbitration, such as 'the persistent myth that arbitrators "split the baby"'. Keer and Naimark 2001, 576.

[76] Redfern and Hunter 2004, 236. Some domestic arbitration rules allow for the appointment of explicitly non-neutral arbitrators. For example, the Commercial Arbitration Rules of the AAA, which apply to US domestic arbitrations, provide that party-appointed arbitrators need not meet standards of impartiality and independence if the parties 'have specifically agreed ... that the party-appointed arbitrators are to be non-neutral'. S R-12(b).

[77] Paulsson 1997, 13–4.

[78] As one interviewee observed: 'Whenever I say "parties," I'm really meaning "counsel." Most clients don't have enough knowledge to take an informed view.'

[79] Dezalay and Garth 1996, 35 fn 3. [80] Ibid, 50.

[81] One interviewee said of majority awards: 'I have encountered it, but it really is quite rare. I think if you were to be quite brutal and frank, if you have three people of equivalent and experience in background, the chances of that arising are extremely slim.'

[82] Lowenfeld 1987, 53.

arbitrator were disappointed that he did not share with them discussions within the tribunal.

A more common concern is identification with a party that comes from a career representing similar parties. As one interviewee put it: 'it isn't necessarily that you're deliberately doing it; it's part of your background actually. Here, you get an insurance claim, Bermuda Form or something, and appoint a QC who's spent his life representing insurance companies and drawing up these bloody forms. And he'll be very pro-insurer, instinctively. It's not quite fair to call it partisanship; it's just part of their makeup'.

Probably the main reason biased arbitrators are rare is that a reputation for overt partisanship will harm arbitrators' career prospects in the long run, as they will lose influence over their fellow arbitrators.[83] One English interviewee said:

> You never derogate from being entirely independent and neutral as a co-arbitrator. That is your stock in trade as a good arbitrator. The reason why you would get appointed in the future is because you are totally neutral and independent and you are not an advocate for the party that appoints you. That is the kiss of death for your reputation if you ever start doing that.

Partiality is a 'kiss of death' because partial arbitrators lose credibility with the tribunal. After all, as one interviewee pointed out, 'in a three-person tribunal, you need at least two votes to win.... If someone is partial, then the chair tends not to listen to that person, and the ability of a partial arbitrator to influence an independent and capable chairman is much diminished'. The other members of the tribunal cannot help but notice even subtle attempts to sway the proceedings on behalf of a party, such as asking helpfully leading questions of the counsel who appointed the arbitrator, or sharply questioning the other party's witnesses. As one interviewee noted: 'As a tribunal, the minute you see that one of you is partisan, [that arbitrator is] completely side-lined ... so it's not at all helpful for them, or for their client.'[84]

The most significant danger therefore lies with those who arbitrate infrequently, and who therefore 'may not appreciate or be cognizant of these informal market mechanisms'.[85] As Park notes: 'A considerable disjunction exists between the arbitration aficionado and the newcomer. For the latter, there exists no arbiter of proper procedure.'[86] Arbitrators who seek repeated appointments by the same party present a particular problem. 'In the case of an arbitrator who considers that his only chance lies with the party which has already named him once, this might result in more or less dissimulated, but nevertheless systematic, favouritism.'[87] Not surprisingly, arbitrators take seriously the risk that they will be perceived to be biased. One interviewee, who comes from an Asian country that has produced only a few prominent arbitrators, related that he tends to turn down appointments from parties of his nationality simply to avoid the perception that he will want to support their positions.

Many arbitrators see the role of party-appointed arbitrator as distinct from that of chair. The chair takes on additional procedural responsibilities, manages the hearings,

[83] Cf Webster 2003, 129–30. This is particularly so because the two party-appointed arbitrators usually select the presiding arbitrator, either directly or by deciding who is placed on the lists maintained by the various arbitral institutions. 47 per cent of survey respondents cited 'likelihood arbitrator will be able to influence Chair of tribunal' as a factor in their choice of a party-appointed arbitrator. W&C/QMUL 2010, 26.

[84] Franck makes a similar point: 'In multi-million and multi-billion dollar disputes, parties are likely to be unwilling to appoint an arbitrator who is likely to be challenged, who cannot fully consider ... the facts and laws at issue and who may be incapable of delivering an enforceable award.' Franck 2006, 517.

[85] Ibid. [86] Park 2002, 292. [87] Paulsson 1997, 14.

and typically drafts the award. More important for present purposes is the notion that, as Lowenfeld puts it, 'one of the principal functions of a party-appointed arbitrator is to give confidence in the process to the parties and their counsel'. [88] Several interviewees acknowledged that when they act as a party-appointed arbitrator, they take on the additional obligation of ensuring that all of the party's arguments have been understood by the tribunal and are at least addressed in the award. One interviewee put it this way: 'If I am party-appointed, I interpret my remit as ensuring that my co-arbitrators dealt with and considered all of the arguments that have been put forward by the party that appointed me.' Another said:

> [Party-appointed arbitrators] see their job as ensuring that the party that appointed them is not ... going to have an injustice, the decision is going to be justifiable vis-à-vis this party.... To be frank, I think there's nothing wrong with that. I want to make sure that when the party that appointed me reads the award, that they will understand why they win or why they lose. Especially if they lose, because ... there's no review and usually there are large stakes and therefore a party that loses would want to have all their defences not just decided, but decided in a convincing way. That, I think, is my job. It doesn't change the outcome but it is important that supporting reasons are convincing.

In any event, despite the risk of bias presented by party-appointed arbitrators and the cost of employing three arbitrators rather than one, tripartite tribunals 'are not withering away'.[89] Of parties that reported a preference as to the number of arbitrators, 87 per cent preferred three-member tribunals.[90] Carter concludes that the sense of control that accompanies the act of choosing one's own adjudicator outweighs cost and bias concerns.[91] The presence of a party-appointed arbitrator also reassures parties that at least one arbitrator is a known quantity, reducing the risk of a 'runaway tribunal'.[92] Finally, the presence of party-appointed arbitrators is said to improve the legitimacy of the ICA system by making awards more acceptable to the losing party.[93]

IV. International Commercial Arbitration as a Competitive Marketplace

Arbitrators, arbitral institutions, and even states compete with each other for a larger share of the dispute resolution market. The pervasive impact of market competition constitutes an important institutional distinction between arbitration and litigation.

The field of ICA was once 'the delightful discipline of a handful of academic aficionados on the fringe of international law' but has now become 'a matter of serious concern for a great number of professionals'.[94] Starting with a series of high-profile oil arbitrations in the 1970s, large US- and UK-based multinational law firms began to enter the field. These firms, with clients and offices around the world, expanded the ICA market. ICA became a multinational market because its primary consumers were

[88] Lowenfeld 1995, 62. [89] Carter 2000, 295.

[90] W&C/QMUL 2010, 25. 'Respondents said that three arbitrators lead to greater neutrality, less risk of a poor decision and a more "balanced" award. The desirability of being able to appoint one of the three arbitrators was another factor cited by respondents. A panel of three arbitrators also offers the opportunity to have a diversity of background and experience that may be useful in particular disputes, such as those with a great deal of technical evidence.'

[91] Carter 2000, 295. [92] Paulsson 1997, 14.

[93] Mosk 1988, 254; Paulsson 1997, 14. [94] Paulsson 1985, 2. See also Garth 2002.

themselves multinational: multinational fora for multinational firms.[95] This phenomenon, combined with an explosion in cross-border transactions generally, has led to an increase in the use of ICA services.[96] The potential profits have increased accordingly, leading to the entry into the field of many new practitioners.[97] As one interviewee observed:

> It has become a business, but it didn't used to be a business; it used to be a vocation. If you talk about certain people, of a certain generation in France, for example.... There are still people who see this as a sort of privilege ... and it is a privilege, but it has become a business and I think rightly so. Obviously the service that you are rendering, if it's done well it's very valuable.

The modern ICA system encompasses a variety of arbitrators, arbitral institutions, and fora, all anxious to distinguish themselves from their competitors. As Dezalay and Garth describe it:

> Arbitration is often presented quite overtly as a kind of market where the clients are able to choose from a palette of potential arbitrators according to the nature of their problems, their affinities, and above all their strategies. The parties—and their advisors—thus choose their terrain, their arms, and the rules of the game that will govern their confrontation.[98]

As this observation highlights, the key factor in competition within arbitration is that the parties call the shots. Carbonneau and Janson conclude: 'At the end of the day, transborder adjudication will be guided by the dictates of the marketplace and the international commercial community.'[99]

Despite the existence of increasing numbers of international arbitrators and arbitral institutions, there is 'a growing convergence in procedures and mutual goals'.[100] Since a rising tide of arbitral business lifts all boats, cooperative efforts to improve the standing of ICA as a whole have accompanied the increase in competition among arbitrators and institutions.[101] The process of competition reveals the rules and practices that are more effective and more attractive to disputing parties; these are quickly copied, so that the field progresses en masse. Thus, even without any *stare decisis* doctrine (and even without most decisions being reported), ideas and trends become disseminated when arbitrators work together and when they meet in conferences and social settings.

A good example of the role of competitive forces is provided by Rogers. She charts the increase of transparency within ICA in recent years and ascribes this change to the effects of market competition among arbitrators and arbitral institutions:

> ... rather than external pressure, [transparency gains] are the product of a range of collective, institutional and individual initiatives, leavened by a healthy dose of competition and drawing upon collaterally disclosed information.[102]

Understanding the operation of market forces in ICA is key to understanding the type of justice that ICA provides.[103] Competition is now so intrinsic to the operation

95 Dezalay and Garth 1996, 7 (citation omitted). See also Flood 2007.

96 Since different institutions use different systems to count arbitrations filed with them, it is difficult to come up with global numbers. However, the rate of change within a single institution can be measured. The ICC registered 32 new arbitrations in 1956, 210 arbitrations in 1976, 337 arbitrations in 1992, 452 arbitrations in 1997, 529 arbitrations in 1999, and 599 arbitrations in 2007—an increase of about twenty times over fifty years. Similarly, the AAA-ICDR administered approximately 100 international arbitrations in 1980, 207 in 1993, 510 in 2000, and 621 in 2007—an increase of more than six times in just twenty-seven years. Born 2009, 68.

97 Helmer 2003, 41.

98 Dezalay and Garth 1996, 209.

99 Carbonneau and Janson 1994, 221–2.

100 Thirgood 2004, 342.

101 Rogers 2006, 1313–4 (citations omitted).

102 Ibid, 1322.

103 Dezalay and Garth 1996, 8–9.

of the international arbitral system that it constitutes a social norm. Competition in ICA takes place on three levels: arbitrators and would-be arbitrators compete with each other for appointments, arbitral fora (institutions and states) compete with each other to host arbitrations, and practitioners of arbitration collectively compete for market share against other forms of dispute resolution.

1. Competition between arbitrators

Judges have security of tenure and income and a full-time workload assigned to them, while arbitrators are free agents, without tenure, and must attract the cases that they decide.[104] Arbitrators normally will not be aware of a dispute until and unless they are approached to adjudicate it.[105] Moreover, arbitrators' work product is, for the most part, only seen by the parties, their counsel, and in-house lawyers at the arbitral institution.[106] (When awards are published, the arbitrators' names are sometimes listed, even when the parties' identities are redacted.[107]) The result is a market for arbitration services that is far from transparent.

Consequently, competition between arbitrators must occur in alternative venues that allow them to demonstrate their expertise and build a reputation within the ICA community. Junior counsel and academics who hope to 'graduate' to being arbitrators may seek in-house positions at arbitral institutions,[108] work toward partnerships in major law firms,[109] serve as officers of arbitral institutions, take academic positions at universities (even if they work primarily within law firms or as barristers),[110] give presentations at academic conferences, publish academic papers, write for blogs or online fora, and teach at training events for practitioners.

The elite arbitrators maintain their dominance in part by 'defining themselves through writings, conferences, and meetings of the community of experts in international commercial arbitration'.[111] There are now hundreds of treatises and guidebooks on such topics as the drafting of arbitration agreements, the selection of arbitrators, and effective advocacy in arbitration. Such resources 'are principally the work of the

[104] Historically, English judges received no fixed salary but instead kept the court fees as their compensation. At least one judge believed this to be the cause of English courts' so-called hostility to arbitration: 'there was a great competition to get as much as possible of litigation into Westminster Hall for the division of spoil. [Judges] had a great jealousy of arbitrations whereby Westminster Hall was robbed of those cases ... Therefore, they said that the courts ought not to be ousted of their jurisdiction'. *Scott v Avery* (1856), 5 HL Cas 811.

[105] It is, of course, possible for arbitrators to hear about a dispute through the ICA 'grapevine' or from their professional activities. In such cases, they are able to (and sometimes do) lobby the parties' counsel to be appointed; however, such blatant marketing is likely to be frowned upon.

[106] That said, some arbitrators try to write their awards in a manner that will catch the attention of the lawyers who read them. Said one interviewee: 'I try to write awards that are also fun to read. I have a principle: the first sentence of the award should be such that the reader will want to read the second sentence. And the second should be written so he wants to read the third. I admit, once you have the reader down one page you are already pretty good; afterwards it probably gets boring.'

[107] Rogers 2006, 1323 fn 64.

[108] Dezalay and Garth 1995, 38, calling working for an institution 'the quick route' to arbitration expertise.

[109] See Alford 2003, 88: 'the Anglo-American juggernaut we know as the modern international law firm is the defining feature affecting the industry today'.

[110] Professorships are especially prized. Toby Landau, an English barrister and Visiting Professor at King's College, University of London, noted that '[i]n my particular field, the title of professor may be of greater value than that of QC'. Swallow 2004.

[111] Dezalay and Garth 1995, 31 fn 9.

top international arbitration specialists, who use these publications as a form of elite advertising'.[112]

One interviewee described publishing as integral to his career: 'Having a certain stature even if you're not a professor is still important. If people like to read what you write, this is a good beginning to get appointed.' Another interviewee, who was initially sceptical, came to see the professional value of publishing in garnering appointments:

> I did not know this before I arrived. I really thought the way you became an arbitrator was to basically get your friends to appoint you then show how good you are and get appointed again. I did not think you could get much mileage from writing or making your views known; they're my views, why would they be better than somebody else's views? I didn't really think it was a waste of time, but almost. And I was wrong. They are very important and are taken seriously.[113]

Maintaining a presence at conferences is considered de rigeur, particularly for arbitrators who are trying to make a name for themselves.[114] The topic was raised by several interviewees. One said: 'The conferences are good for the younger ones to be known; to get their profiles raised so that we're conscious that they exist. We're aware that they can speak in public, they are articulate. We're not going to be ashamed when our client is in the room. It is necessary for the younger ones to start, definitely.' Another interviewee, who said that he continues to attend a large number of conferences despite now being more senior, pointed out the peculiarity but also the benefits of advocates and adjudicators marketing themselves to each other at conferences:

> It's a little bit of an odd field ... when you're at a conference, the arbitrators ... are selling to their employers, who are ... lawyers.... There's a sense that often lawyers are seeing their future career as arbitrators and all of those dynamics are very, very awkward.... For that reason, there's a utility to arbitration conferences that, I think, is not present in certain other kinds of professional gatherings of employers; there's judges and advocates really mixing together.

There are now so many conferences that some arbitrators fret about overexposure. One interviewee, who left a private advocacy practice to become a full-time arbitrator, said:

> Early on when I started I did a lot of that because people had to understand my change [from full-time advocacy to full-time arbitrating].... And now I go less for very many reasons ... I find over-exposure in this field is a real threat, a real danger. You have to be careful.... People think you are at the conferences because you have no work.... Conferences are a double-edged sword and you have to choose your public.

Of course, many arbitrators and would-be arbitrators publish and speak at conferences for less mercenary reasons. ICA is known to be a field for academically minded lawyers, and many arbitrators have an intrinsic intellectual interest in research. One interviewee, who has maintained parallel careers as a practitioner and academic for many years, said that his practice would be sufficient for most people but that he enjoys giving lectures and seeing his words in print. Whether he has something useful to contribute is for others to judge.[115]

112 Rogers 2006, 1321.

113 Several interviewees noted that, when considering appointments, they look closely at a candidate's publications, given that publications are sometimes the best available indication of a potential arbitrator's views. As one interviewee put it: 'What they've written, we always read. Although they can change their mind, what they've written is something at least. They cannot claim they didn't know what they had written.'

114 This phenomenon is discussed in Garth 1997.

115 Even as this interviewee explained his intrinsic interests in publishing, he acknowledged the role of the market in determining the value of his commentary.

In addition to serving as venues for advertising, academic and professional journals and symposia are effective means for disseminating both standard practices and innovations. Jones cites the annual symposia organized by the LCIA at Tylney Hall for providing an effective forum in which participants and observers can 'pick up, in a relatively short space of time, a range of current ideas and trends which would otherwise be quite unavailable'.[116] This phenomenon highlights an essential feature of competition: it acts as a harmonizing (or at least homogenizing) force. Those seeking to break into the ranks of arbitrators are constrained to emulate the résumés, practices, and perspectives of the elite, thus reinforcing existing values and standards.

Indeed, it is arguable that the primary beneficiaries of arbitral competition (and of the massive expansion of the field in the last few decades) have been the small cadre of elite arbitrators. Summarizing the interviews they conducted with numerous practitioners in the mid-1990s, Dezalay and Garth relate that: '[T]he same, relatively few, names of arbitrators were repeated over and over on both sides of the Atlantic.'[117] Indeed, a 'leading arbitrator of the new generation' told Dezalay and Garth that: 'There are, I suppose, forty to fifty people in Western Europe who could claim that they make their living doing this.'[118]

The field has expanded greatly since the 1990s, when Dezalay and Garth conducted their research, but a few elite arbitrators continue to dominate. Several interviewees find this state of affairs to be understandable and defensible. Said one interviewee: 'A relatively small number of people get a large number of cases. This has been criticized by many people, including arbitral institutions. But to me, it's just perfectly logical … if you're a good cardiac surgeon, a good house painter, you'll get a lot of repeat work. It's inevitable.' Another interviewee explained the dominance of a small number of arbitrators as a function of the risk involved whenever a party chooses an arbitrator: 'They want certainty; they want people they can trust. They don't want mavericks; they want a safe pair of hands; they want dependable consistency. That's why it's a small field, because people go towards people they have total confidence in, and there's not that many people around.'[119]

The demand for these few leading arbitrators has created problems. Writing in 2004, Fellas noted that: 'Some arbitrators are in such demand that they are booked well over 18 months ahead.'[120] The packed schedules of these arbitrators are enough of an issue that 'availability' now counts as one of the most important factors in parties' choice of an arbitrator.[121]

Webster expresses a common perception: 'A chairman who cannot meet the parties' reasonable expectations as to dates for hearings is probably also going to have problems taking the time to read submissions prior to the hearings and to review the documents and submissions in preparation for deliberations.'[122] More than one interviewee complained that some of the most prominent arbitrators are overextended: 'when somebody

[116] Jones 2006, 282. Other ICA conference organizers now routinely describe their own events as featuring 'Tylney Hall-style discussions'.

[117] Dezalay and Garth 1996, 8.

[118] Ibid, 50.

[119] Another interviewee put the matter even more bluntly: 'Basically, you don't appoint someone you don't know. It's too risky.'

[120] Fellas 2004, 80–1.

[121] W&C/QMUL 2010, 25. Availability 'was emphasized by a number of interviewees as an extremely important factor and an issue of increasing concern'. Ibid.

[122] Webster 2003, 133. Note that arbitral rules have begun to be adapted in response to this problem. In 2011, the ICC began requiring appointed arbitrators to disclose not just their potential conflicts but also their availability. Fry 2011.

is so well known, so famous, that person may not be in a position to pay proper attention to the case. They have too many cases. Or somebody who pays more attention to the bigger cases than the smaller cases. Somebody who relies on assistants rather than himself or herself. That causes a problem.'

All of the interviewees communicated the sense that they work in a competitive marketplace, where they must differentiate themselves from their competitors. Most often, they emphasized their case management skills. Some characterized technical backgrounds as an asset, especially for certain specialist fields (in particular engineering/construction disputes).[123] Others highlighted their expertise in certain types of transactions, such as joint ventures, or in certain industries, such as oil and gas. A few pointed out the importance of multilingualism, and of training (or at least experience) in both common law and civil law. Many spoke of the importance simply of being personable, of getting along well with other arbitrators and with counsel.

One aspect of the community of successful arbitrators is the number and extent of direct personal links between prominent arbitrators of different generations. Notes Garth:

> ... clubs are built on the basis of personal relations, not just abstract resumes.... This personal dimension gives considerable importance to meetings, such as conferences, where individuals can both assess the market value of resumes and build relationships of trust and respect. It is also not surprising that many who are brought into international commercial arbitration are in fact disciples of those already in the field.[124]

Many leaders of the current generation of arbitrators were the protégés of well-known members of the previous generation: Albert Jan van den Berg worked under Pieter Sanders, numerous Swiss arbitrators under Pierre Lalive, Yves Derains, and Julian Lew under René David, James Carter under Jack Stevenson, David Rivkin under Robert von Mehren. Dezalay and Garth conclude: 'The systems of patronage may no longer be as extreme as the European legal dynasties of the past, but they are artificial recreations of the same phenomenon.'[125]

The dominance of the small number of successful arbitrators and the dynastic connections between arbitrators of different generations have led some to describe ICA as a 'cartel'[126] or 'mafia'.[127] Taking issue with such characterizations, Paulsson argues:

> ... whereas an operating mafia would bar entry to outsiders, the milieu of international arbitration has shown repeatedly its eagerness to welcome new outstanding arbitrators. In fact there is a short supply of people who command the kind of transnational respect which is essential in this context.[128]

Entry into the international arbitration services market is not barred to newcomers, as would be the case with a cartel. Still, Paulsson's own emphasis on 'transnational

[123] However, as one interviewee (a generalist) noted, many disputes involving highly technical transactions turn on more ordinary questions of commercial law: 'Even if you have some highly esoteric industry, a lot of space related work on satellites and what have you. Sometimes it can be quite useful to have people who understand something about either that business or the relevant technologies, sometimes the disputes turn out to be very commercial in nature and happen to be about, you know, satellites. How useful is it then to have somebody who knows a lot about satellites? Maybe not as much as you think ... people are hard working lawyers or arbitrators. It is our business to learn industries.... In many cases, having broad experience, judgement, and commercial understanding, rather than intensive industry background, is the key factor in my selection of arbitrators.'

[124] Garth 1997, 11.

[125] Dezalay and Garth 1996, 40.

[126] Rogers 2005, 960.

[127] Dezalay and Garth 1996, 83.

[128] Paulsson 1997, 19.

respect' highlights the importance for would-be arbitrators of esteem from the ICA community.

ICA is no longer dominated by quite so small a cadre of 'grand old men'—almost entirely white, male, and European—as it was prior to the 1980s.[129] However, it cannot be denied that, as Hacking put it in a response to Paulsson: 'Any grouping of professionals which becomes exclusive will tend to operate (intentionally and unintentionally) against the arrival of new persons into their ranks.'[130] Indeed, as a general rule, access to the ranks of international arbitrators continues to be controlled by the dominant arbitrators. They hold positions of authority at arbitral institutions (thereby exerting influence upon who gets appointed as an arbitrator) and, informally, are in a position to recommend particular up-and-comers. This effect is compounded by the fact that past experience as an arbitrator is considered among the most important qualifications for appointment as an arbitrator.[131] Indeed, commercial parties report that the 'ability to select experienced arbitrators' is one of the main reasons they choose arbitration over litigation.[132] They cite prior experience as an arbitrator as second only to 'open-mindedness and fairness' in influencing their choice of both sole/presiding arbitrators and party-appointed arbitrators. As a result, 'the market for international arbitrators operates as a relatively closed system that is difficult for newcomers to penetrate'.[133]

Despite its privileged position, the current generation of leading arbitrators should not be—and clearly is not—complacent. One arbitrator, among the most in-demand in the world, remarked that: 'In the end, the market selects you on the basis of your performance, really.' As Ogus notes: 'The fact that a particular set of [standards] has become ... dominant ... does not necessarily mean that it is, and will remain, the most efficient (in the sense of meeting consumer preferences at lowest cost) of the alternatives available.'[134] Indeed, arbitrators' writings indicate a concern that arbitration must continue to evolve or the field as a whole will wither. Crowter and Tobin's hand-wringing is typical: 'if the conduct of arbitrations is not efficient, even expeditious, arbitration may fall into disfavour as the preferred forum for the resolution of international commercial disputes'.[135]

If there were a perfect market for arbitration services, competitive forces would inevitably lead to improved arbitration services. However, a variety of factors make the current market highly imperfect. Severe 'information asymmetries prevent the market ... from being fully competitive'.[136] The confidential nature of arbitral work means that 'professional credibility and word-of-mouth recommendations ... play a significant role'.[137] 68 per cent of corporate counsel surveyed in 2010 said that they lacked sufficient information to make an informed choice about arbitrators independently of input from external counsel (who are more likely to be familiar with the ICA community).

[129] Dezalay and Garth 1996, 10. Despite some increase in diversity, the leading arbitrators continue to be overwhelmingly white and male. The Chambers and Partners 2012 list of the thirty-two 'most in demand arbitrators' includes only two women (Gabrielle Kaufmann-Kohler and Brigitte Stern) and one non-white (Michael Hwang). <http://www.chambersandpartners.com/Global/Editorial/36194> accessed 23 August 2012. Who's Who Legal's 2012 list of twenty 'most highly regarded individuals' in the field includes three women (Judith Gill, Gabrielle Kaufmann-Kohler, and Lucy Reed) and no non-white practitioners. <http://www.whoswholegal.com/news/analysis/article/29384/most-highly-regarded-firms-commercial-arbitration-2012/> accessed 23 August 2012.

[130] Hacking 1998, 75.

[131] Webster 2003, 129; Redfern and Hunter 2004, 233.

[132] PwC/QMUL 2008, 5.

[133] Rogers 2005, 967–8.

[134] Ogus 2002, 424.

[135] Crowter and Tobin 2002, 301.

[136] Rogers 2005, 968 (citing Rutledge 2004, 195).

[137] Franck 2006, 516.

With such input, 67 per cent felt that they could make an informed choice.[138] The survey authors note that, even with the input of counsel, 33 per cent of respondents were not confident that they could make an informed choice of arbitrator, which 'seems rather low considering the importance of making a good appointment'.[139]

Several interviewees commented on the important role played by personal knowledge of the candidates in their decisions on whom to appoint. Said one: 'If you're counsel and you're asked to suggest arbitrators, you're obviously going to flick through, in your memory, the kind of people who are the right kind of people for the job.' Another interviewee discussed relying on the kinds of factors that no outsider could know, even referring to it as proprietary information:

> Sometimes I have some confidential information how this arbitrator has behaved ... because when I saw the same arbitrator previously he or she was very good [but] recently became tired and doesn't pay attention to the case. Or recently that person lost a really good assistant.... Those things are all proprietary information that is not easy to figure out.

2. Competition between arbitral fora

Competition between arbitral fora—both institutions and states—is no less fierce or significant than that between individual arbitrators. As one might expect, competition between arbitral institutions, as with competition between individual arbitrators, has engendered a high degree of convergence in arbitral rules of procedure. However, differences remain. In addition, there is now almost complete freedom on the part of the parties to designate any state as the seat of the arbitration.[140] Arbitration lawyers will choose the institution and the state which provide the best likelihood of reaching the desired outcomes at the lowest cost.[141]

Like individual arbitrators, these competing fora are sensitive to any innovations introduced by their competitors. Beneficial innovations quickly spread, leading to a general harmonization in institutional rules of procedure and national arbitration laws: 'If there are efficiency advantages to particular rules, we might expect a trend toward harmonization under conditions of market competition. Indeed, long-time observers of the arbitral process have observed greater efficiencies over time.'[142] This process is exemplified by the widespread and continuing adoption of national arbitration laws based on the UNCITRAL Model Law,[143] which was intended to further 'the development of harmonious international economic relations' by establishing an arbitration law 'acceptable to States with different legal, social and economic systems'.[144]

138 W&C/QMUL 2010, 27. 139 Ibid.

140 This aspect of party autonomy is guaranteed in all of the major arbitration rules, usually by a provision that if the parties have not chosen the seat of arbitration, then a specified procedure will apply for choosing the seat: UNCITRAL Rules, art 18(1) (the tribunal may decide); ICDR Rules, art 13(1) (the tribunal may decide); ICC Rules, art 18(1) (the ICC Court may decide); LCIA Rules, art 16.1 (London, unless the LCIA Court decides otherwise).

141 Ogus 2002, 421. In this model, lawyers act as 'transaction cost engineers'.

142 Ginsburg 2003, 1344.

143 Legislation based on the UNCITRAL Model Law has now been enacted in ninety-two jurisdictions (including seven US states and all ten Canadian provinces). It was originally promulgated in 1985. In its first decade, thirty-three countries adopted it; in its second decade, there were thirty-four adoptees; and in the past six years, there have already been twenty-five adoptees. <http://www.uncitral.org/uncitral/en/uncitral_texts/arbitration/1985Model_arbitration_status.html> accessed 20 July 2012.

144 These statements are taken from the preamble to the UN General Assembly resolution that adopted the original UNCITRAL Model Law. UNGA Res 40/72 (11 December 1985).

Competition between arbitral institutions

One might wonder why international arbitral institutions, which are after all not-for-profit entities, might be so concerned about competing for a greater share of the arbitration market. One interviewee described competition among the institutions as arising from the desire of those who run them to enhance or at least maintain the institution's position in the international arbitration world. The senior officials of arbitral institutions do not receive banker-style bonuses, but they are anxious to ensure that the case loads of their institutions continue to grow year-on-year. The interviewee concluded: 'They are running a service and there is nothing wrong with trying to persuade people that the institution runs an effective service.'

The growing arbitration market and increased competition have redounded largely to the benefit of the handful of dominant institutions: the ICC, LCIA, American Arbitration Association (AAA) and its international disputes division, the International Centre for Dispute Resolution (ICDR), and (for investment treaty arbitrations) ICSID.[145] Newer entrants, particularly in Asia, have begun to earn a greater market share,[146] but most remain essentially regional institutions and do not yet seriously challenge the market leaders for the highest-stakes disputes. For example, in a 2008 survey, only 3 per cent of corporations involved in ICA reported ever having participated in SIAC arbitrations, and that was the highest rate for any Asian arbitral institution.[147] This number has undoubtedly risen in the years since 2008, and SIAC is arguably the model up-and-coming institution. This is the result of a conscious programme of raising SIAC's profile. As one interviewee, who is involved with SIAC's governance, proudly related:

> We have had an enormous leap in a number of cases in Singapore. SIAC has developed now into one of the leading arbitral institutions in the world in terms of its caseload and recognition, It's very, very strong.... These things don't happen without planning and execution....
>
> We have to make sure that our case administration is the world standard or equal to the best in the world. That involved a lot of training, recruiting the right personnel. We reviewed our practice notes.... We hosted the ICCA Congress, which was the biggest ICCA Congress held.... We now have a fully international board. The majority is non-Singaporeans on it. It's been re-developed as a very international institution. One can see that from the fact that parties come from so many different countries.

Historically, the ICC held a 'position of quasi-monopoly' on the highest-stakes cases; it is no longer pre-eminent, but remains the 'central institution'.[148] The AAA/

[145] See Dezalay and Garth 1996, 9. Similarly, London, Geneva, and Paris remain the most popular arbitral seats, although Tokyo and Singapore now eclipse New York. W&C/QMUL 2010, 19.

[146] In 2008, survey respondents reported 'an increased preference for regional arbitration institutions', in particular (in Asia), the Hong Kong International Arbitration Centre (HKIAC), Singapore International Arbitration Centre (SIAC), and the Chinese International Economic and Trade Arbitration Commission (CIETAC). To take one example, arbitrations filed at the HKIAC nearly doubled from 2003 to 2007, while those filed at the ICC increased by only 3 per cent over the same time period. PwC/QMUL 2008, 15. A 2010 survey indicated that the market share of regional institutions, especially Asian ones, has continued to increase, although corporations continue to be concerned that institutions have 'proven themselves' or possess a solid 'track record'. W&C/QMUL 2010, 22.

[147] PwC/QMUL 2008, 15. In 2010, in response to a similar but differently worded question, 2 per cent of survey respondents reported that, in the previous five years, they had been involved in more arbitrations administered by SIAC than by any other institution, and this rate was higher than for any other institution not located in Europe or the United States. W&C/QMUL 2010, 22.

[148] Dezalay and Garth 1996, 45. 56 per cent of survey respondents reported having been involved in an ICC arbitration from 2005 to 2010, more than any other institution. 50 per cent cited the ICC

ICDR now attracts a larger number of disputes, but they come from a smaller number of repeat parties. A 2008 survey indicated that 45 per cent of corporations active in ICA had been involved in ICC arbitrations, while only 16 per cent had been involved in AAA/ICDR arbitrations.[149] Although the presence in the United States of many large multinational corporations would suggest that the AAA would be popular with parties of any nationality, the AAA's share of cases where neither party is American remains modest.[150] Helmer suggests that 'The really big cases get to the AAA only when the American party's economic power is overwhelming'.[151]

There are three domains of competition between arbitral institutions. First, institutions seek to attract prominent arbitrators to serve on their boards of directors (which go by a variety of names) and to appear on their lists of arbitrators.[152] However, since arbitrators may appear on the lists more than one institution, and the most in-demand arbitrators appear on many institutional lists, competition in this area is not intense.

Attracting notable arbitrators matters most for new or regional arbitral institutions seeking to build a global clientele. For example, the Dubai International Arbitration Centre (DIAC) states in its website that it 'regularly updates its lists of highly-skilled national and international arbitrators experienced in different fields of trade and business'.[153] Other younger institutions, like SIAC, CIETAC, and the Australian Centre for International Commercial Arbitration (ACICA), also have such panels, but two of the best-established institutions, the ICC and LCIA, just provide access to databases of available arbitrators.[154]

The second potential arena of competition is fees. Arbitral institutions charge a fee for administering arbitrations, generally set at a percentage of the amount in controversy, and may also mandate a fee schedule for arbitrators. Institutions can compete on both, although arbitrators' fees make up a much larger proportion of the overall costs than the institution's administrative fees.[155] The overall costs of institutional administration, along with such matters as whether fees are due up-front or at the end of arbitrations, are cited by consumers of arbitration services as important factors in their choice of institution.[156]

Several arbitral institutions, especially the less-well-established, advertise their 'very competitive rates'.[157] For example, for a dispute with US$1,000,000 in controversy

as their preferred institution. W&C/QMUL 2010, 23. The ICC's continued prominence is explicable in part by its long history. As Dezalay and Garth note, 'history is a key legitimator in the legal field'. Dezalay and Garth 1996, 45 (citing Weber 1954).

149 PwC/QMUL 2008, 15.

150 Craig, Park, and Paulsson 2001, 3.

151 Helmer 2003, 42.

152 These panels and lists vary in their characteristics. Some institutions maintain exclusive panels, in the sense of fixed lists of arbitrators from which appointments must be made. Others have panels from which the institution will draw when called upon to make an appointment, while some institutions maintain just 'sources of information' on available arbitrators and their relevant experience. Jones 2006, 285.

153 <http://www.diac.ae/idias/services/diac/advantages/> accessed 20 July 2012.

154 Jones 2006, 285.

155 Administrative fees charged by an institution typically amount to about 2 per cent of the total costs of an arbitration. See ICC Commission 2007, stating that the sources of costs in ICC arbitrations were 82 per cent for counsels' fees and expenses, 16 per cent for the arbitrators' fees, and 2 per cent for the institutions' fees. A survey of other institutions produced general agreement that the split in costs of arbitration is similar to that found in the ICC survey. Scherer 2011b. See also CIArb 2011, 11–12.

156 W&C/QMUL 2010, 22.

157 The DIAC <http://www.diac.ae/idias/services/diac/advantages/> accessed 23 August 2012.

and three arbitrators, the ICC charges US$21,715 as its administrative fee (not counting a registration fee) and allows its arbitrators to charge between US$14,627 and US$64,130 for their fees.[158] Meanwhile, the DIAC charges only around US$5,450 and sets arbitrators' fees at around US$5,000–US$21,000,[159] and the ACICA charges around US$7,800 in administrative fees.[160] Institutions sometimes lower their fees in absolute numbers, as the ICC has done repeatedly.[161]

Institutions can also compete for arbitrators' favour by reducing or removing restrictions on the fees arbitrators may charge. For example, the ACICA Arbitration Rules state only that arbitrators should be compensated according to an hourly rate agreed to by the parties or, failing such agreement, determined by ACICA, and that this rate should be commensurate with the nature of the dispute, the amount in dispute, and the standing and experience of the arbitrator.[162] Some arbitral institutions impose fee arrangements that many arbitrators will not accept, effectively limiting the range of arbitrators available to the parties.[163] On the other hand, higher fee schedules may drive away disputing parties.[164]

Some recently amended rules of arbitration provide for flexible or high fee arrangements, but provide means to discipline arbitrators who may abuse their power to set their own fees. For example, the 2010 revision of the UNCITRAL Rules provides that, promptly after its constitution, the tribunal must notify the parties how it proposes to determine its fees and expenses. The parties may raise objections with the tribunal and with the appointing authority (if one was used), which has the power to adjust the tribunal's fees if they are not 'reasonable in amount, taking into account the amount in dispute, the complexity of the subject matter, the time spent by the arbitrators and any other relevant circumstances of the case'.[165] The 2012 ICC Rules go a step further; they direct the ICC Court to take into account, inter alia, 'the timeliness of the submission of the draft award' when it sets arbitrators' fees.[166] This provision was intended specifically to permit the ICC Court to adjust the fees of arbitrators if they unduly delay in rendering a decision.[167]

Third, and most importantly, arbitral institutions compete based on the efficiency and effectiveness of the services they provide and the procedural rules they impose on parties that contract for arbitration under their auspices. Arbitral rules were cited as the third-most important reason for choosing a particular institution, while such factors as the efficiency which institutions' secretariats manage disputes, their expertise in managing particular types of disputes, and their ability to administer arbitrations worldwide were also cited as influential.[168]

158 <http://www.iccwbo.org/Products-and-Services/Arbitration-and-ADR/Arbitration/Cost-and-payment/Cost-calculator/> accessed 19 August 2012.

159 <http://www.diac.ae/idias/resource/doc/en/DIACTableOfFees_1July2011.Eng.pdf> accessed 23 August 2012.

160 <http://acica.org.au/assets/media/Rules-inc-emergency-provisions.pdf> accessed 19 August 2012.

161 Dezalay and Garth 1996, 44. The SIAC advertised in 2003 that it was reducing the fee it charged for appointing arbitrators. <http://www.siac.org.sg/cms/index.php?option=com_content&view=article&id=87:siac-cuts-appointment-fee&catid=43:archive-2003&Itemid=96> accessed 20 August 2012.

162 ACICA Arbitration Rules, art 40.

163 Webster 2003, 123.

164 Methods of remunerating arbitrators and restrictions on the fees arbitrators may charge were cited as factors in parties' choice of an institution. W&C/QMUL 2010, 22.

165 Art 39.

166 ICC Rules Appendix III, art 2(2). Unless otherwise noted, all reference to the 'ICC Rules' are to the 2012 version of those rules.

167 Fry 2011.

168 Ibid.

While differences continue to exist between the rules of various arbitral institutions, they tend to take the same approach on the important issues. These rules are periodically amended to reflect business preferences,[169] and in particular with an eye to improving efficiency. Successful innovations tend to be copied, so 'competition among arbitration institutions ... has moved their respective technical details closer to conformity'.[170] A recent example of this phenomenon is the spread of provisions for the appointment of an emergency arbitrator to rule on urgent applications for interim relief prior to the constitution of the tribunal. The Arbitration Institute of the Stockholm Chamber of Commerce and the Singapore International Arbitration Centre both amended their rules in 2010 to provide for appointment of emergency arbitrators.[171] The ICC followed in 2012.[172]

There are some notable exceptions. For example, the ICC maintains a 'Court of International Arbitration' composed of notable arbitrators nominated by each country whose national chamber of commerce is affiliated with the ICC. The members of the Court review each award drafted by tribunals organized by ICC. This practice is unique; other institutions do not formally supervise their tribunals' awards. This measure of 'quality control' provided by the ICC Court is credited as one of the reasons for the ICC's continued success.[173] One commentator even asserted that the scrutiny of the award performed by the ICC Court 'may explain the infrequency with which national courts have set aside ICC awards'.[174]

Other institutions have adopted unusual rules designed to attract a particular type of party. For example, some regional institutions seek out a niche by giving the domestic party a linguistic advantage. The Rules of the Hungarian Chamber of Commerce provide in article 8(5) that international arbitrations (ie, those where the two parties come from different countries) must be conducted in Hungarian, while the rules of the Polish Chamber of Commerce and the DIAC include a presumption that international arbitrations will be conducted and the awards rendered in Polish and Arabic, respectively.[175]

Many in the ICA system see the variety among different institutions' rules of procedure as a virtue in itself. It gives parties a range of options, allowing them to select the institution and the rules that best suit the particular characteristics of their contract or their dispute. This attitude is illustrated by an anecdote told by a senior English arbitrator interviewed for this book. In the early 1980s, when the LCIA was revamping its rules, the interviewee disagreed with a colleague about some matter. The colleague replied that the interviewee's point was well taken, but that the LCIA's rules should reflect its own character and style. The rules might not be attractive to everyone but they will work; parties who like the rules will use them, and those who do not will not.

169 Wood 2004, 402, noting that the ICC Rules are periodically updated to reflect the current 'business climate'.

170 Malloy 2002, 45.

171 For the Arbitration Rules of the Arbitration Institute of the Stockholm Chamber of Commerce, Appendix II; for the Arbitration Rules of the Singapore International Arbitration Centre, art 26.2 and Schedule 1.

172 ICC Rules, art 29.

173 See, eg, Weisman 2007, 75; Bishop 2003, 34.

174 Coe 1997, 209. This assertion may well be correct, but it should be noted there is no statistical evidence that ICC awards are set aside less often than the awards of the other major arbitral institutions.

175 See Webster 2003, 123–4.

Competition between states

Like arbitral institutions, states also compete to attract international arbitrations to their jurisdictions. For example, the Law Society of England and Wales published a brochure to promote England and Wales as 'the jurisdiction of choice' for both litigation and arbitration.[176] Nor are these efforts limited to public relations campaigns. In 2010, some German courts began permitting English language proceedings. In support of the plan, one German lawyer argued: 'The focus on the German language has been perceived as a disadvantage for German courts in regards to being a centre for commercial litigation.... [T]his is a way for German courts to be more competitive and attractive.'[177]

States have also established or amended their national arbitration laws in order to make them more 'friendly' to international arbitration, in particular by removing restrictions on arbitration procedures or by narrowing the grounds on which awards may be challenged.[178] As Kerr puts it, countries have engaged in 'open rivalry' to provide attractive venues for ICA.[179] This process is exemplified by the 1979 and 1996 revisions to the English Arbitration Act, the 'main object' of which was 'to attract arbitration to London'.[180] After the 1979 Act was passed, there ensued a 'scramble among western European nations' to compete for that business.[181]

The 'common feature' of the new and newly amended arbitration laws of the last twenty years is that they expand the scope of party autonomy (in matters such as choosing the governing substantive and procedural rules of law) and the scope of arbitral powers (in matters such as competence-competence[182] and the issuance of interim orders), while restricting the role of national courts.[183] The primary systemic effect of this regulatory competition has been to detach ICA 'from the scrutiny and regulation of the national court systems'.[184] For example, in its marketing materials, the HKIAC trumpets the fact that: 'Hong Kong's courts are considered pro-arbitration and take a "hands off" approach with respect to arbitration.'[185] Similarly, the SIAC advertises that

[176] <http://www.lawsociety.org.uk/documents/downloads/jurisdiction_of_choice_brochure.pdf> accessed 20 July 2012.

[177] A Collins 2010, 15. This kind of competition also takes place within countries. In 2012, New York State established a task force to study how to make New York more attractive to litigants. The Chief Judge of New York, Jonathan Lippman, said in his annual address that he was tired of 'losing' commercial cases to other states. Palazzolo 2012.

[178] This phenomenon has been recognized by the courts. For example, in *West Tankers Inc v RAS Riunione Adriatica di Sicurta SpA (The Front Comor)* [2007] 1 All ER (Comm) 794 [18] (HL), Lord Hoffman noted that 'arbitration cannot be self-sustaining. It needs the support of the courts; but ... it is important for the commercial interests of the European Community that it should give such support ... an important aspect of the autonomy of the parties is the right to choose the governing law and seat of the arbitration according to what they consider will best serve their interests'.

[179] Kerr 1985, 7.

[180] Park 1983, 38 (referring to the 1979 Act). See also Lord and Salzedo 1996, ix ('One of the aims of the 1996 Act is to enhance England's competitive position as an international arbitration center.'); Mustill 1989, 53 ('One must take note of the efforts made by individual nations to make their arbitration laws ... more attractive.') This effort appears to have been successful. From 2005 to 2010, London was the world's most popular arbitral seat. W&C/QMUL 2010, 17.

[181] Park 1989, 680.

[182] Competence-competence refers to the power of tribunals to determine whether they possess jurisdiction. Courts retain the right to take a 'second look' at the tribunal's jurisdiction after an award has been issued and either to set aside that award or refuse it recognition or enforcement on the ground that the tribunal did not possess jurisdiction.

[183] Bernardini 2004b, 115.

[184] Dezalay and Garth 1996, 7 (citation omitted).

[185] <http://www.hkiac.org/index.php/en/why-hong-kong> accessed 20 August 2012.

the Singaporean courts 'offer maximum judicial support of arbitration and minimum intervention'.[186]

The French arbitration law that came into force in 2011 exemplifies the new generation of arbitration statutes.[187] It has the stated goal of sustaining Paris's leading role as a seat of arbitration, and seeks to accomplish this goal in large part by reducing opportunities for parties to involve the courts.[188] For example, it permits parties to waive their right to seek annulment of an award in front of the national courts at the seat of the arbitration,[189] and provides that a challenge to an award does not automatically result in suspension of enforcement proceedings before a French court. Rather, under article 1526, a suspension must be specifically requested and will be granted only if enforcement of the award would be 'highly detrimental to the rights of the party requesting the suspension'.[190]

Courts have unsurprisingly been reluctant to surrender substantive and procedural control of arbitrations taking place within their jurisdictions. However, such reluctance has been overcome due largely to market forces. As Leahy and Bianchi point out, the use of arbitration in international commercial disputes is self-reinforcing:

> As the use of international arbitrations grows in commercial contexts, many governments and business entities in non-Western and developing states are realizing that they must 'opt in' to the Western system of arbitration in order to maintain and grow business relationships with Western partners.[191]

As Ginsburg notes, in many countries, the number of international arbitrations held hardly justifies the legislative effort to draft and approve a new arbitration law designed to make the jurisdiction a more attractive *situs*.[192] However, the benefits of adopting an arbitration law that conforms to the international state-of-the-art go beyond attracting arbitrations. It symbolizes a state's friendliness to international commerce. More directly, if a country adopts an arbitration law based on the UNCITRAL Model Law, lawyers trained in that country will be better able to compete for business overseas and to negotiate arbitration clauses with foreign investors.[193]

States sometimes use blunter tools to attract arbitrations. In 2008, Singapore enacted a five-year tax break on income of Singaporean practitioners related to international arbitrations when the hearings are held in Singapore. This effectively reduced the cost of holding hearings in Singapore. Singapore also removed a requirement that foreign professionals obtain a temporary work visa to participate in arbitrations and mediations

[186] <http://www.siac.org.sg/index.php?option=com_content&view=article&id=47&Itemid=65> accessed 20 August 2012. An interviewee elaborated: 'Singapore's got a lot of natural advantages as a venue for arbitration, because of its geographic location. It has an excellent court system and judges who understand arbitration. It ticks all of the boxes for what one requires in an arbitral venue. That helps enormously.'

[187] For a comprehensive description and assessment of the changes brought by this statute, see Carducci 2012.

[188] Scherer 2011a.

[189] *Code de procédure civile*, art 1522; amendments enacted by the Decree No 2011-48 of 13 January 2011. Unofficial English translation available at <http://www.iaiparis.com/pdf/FRENCH_LAW_ON_ARBITRATION.pdf> accessed 20 July 2012.

[190] Ibid, art 1526.

[191] Leahy and Bianchi 2000, 58. They speculate that the next step in this regulatory competition may be for countries to modify their rules setting security requirements. Ibid, 47; see also Rogers 2002, 349–50: 'Any nation interested in participating in the global economy must adjust its laws to accommodate the demands of international arbitration.'

[192] Ginsburg 2003, 1343.

[193] Ibid.

there.[194] As a Singapore-based interviewee observed, Singapore's rise to prominence as an arbitral venue would not have been possible without significant governmental support: 'The support given is very important … the encouragement of the government officials, making available their time, making available support systems, and facilitating legislative changes such as allowing foreign lawyers and foreign arbitrators to be involved…. More and more liberties were granted by them.'

States can also compete to attract arbitrations through their substantive laws and their court systems. Parties that choose a particular state's substantive law to govern their dispute are likely to choose that state as the seat of the arbitration.[195] After all, the arbitration law of the arbitral seat will govern the arbitration, and the courts of that jurisdiction will have the power to set aside an eventual award. Attracting arbitrations to its jurisdiction will bring revenue to the state and will make it more likely that parties will hire advocates and arbitrators from that state (who are the most likely to be expert in that state's law).

A country with a competent and impartial judiciary and a well-developed body of domestic commercial law will be preferred as an arbitral venue over one with rudimentary laws and incompetent or corrupt judges. The 'formal legal infrastructure' of a state (including such factors as the 'arbitration-friendliness' of the state's arbitration laws, its courts' track record of enforcing arbitration agreements and awards, and the neutrality and professionalism of its judiciary) was cited by corporate counsel as the most important influence on parties' choice of a seat of arbitration.[196]

For example, parties in the shipping and insurance industries continue to choose English law, even where there is no English party and despite the fact that England is no longer economically dominant in either industry. The primary explanations are that, especially in areas where England was historically dominant, English law is more finely developed (and therefore more predictable) and the English bar and courts more expert than those of other countries. Several interviewees commented that, in their experience, English law is in fact becoming more popular among non-English parties, even beyond the sectors where it has traditionally been chosen. One non-English arbitrator based in London related that, in his practice, he is seeing more and more contracts with no connection to England that contain a choice of English law: 'English law as the governing law is really starting to take a prominent place, probably beyond all others.'

A well-developed set of laws and a high-quality judiciary may not be enough to attract arbitral business, as a number of factors that are not strictly legal can also play a role. Said a senior London-based independent arbitrator:

> I've had Paris law firms that have told me they're moving people over here because of the infrastructure … all the services you can get here, the court reporters and interpreters and all that kind of stuff. It's the infrastructure. You can get a brilliant Turkish interpreter tomorrow if you want it in London, which you can't always do elsewhere.

America provides an interesting case in point. US commercial and arbitration laws are well developed,[197] the judiciary (in the federal courts at least, which are the ones

194 See the SIAC press release: <http://www.siac.org.sg/pdf/20080411-WP.pdf?phpMyAdmin=OP8vu698 vunuzJZYZoW2%2CoDB3yb> accessed 20 August 2012.

195 Corporate counsel reported that the law governing the substance of the dispute was the second most important influence (after the quality of the state's legal infrastructure) on their choice of the seat of arbitration. W&C/QMUL 2010, 18.

196 Ibid.

197 However, the arbitration laws are quite dated, as the US Federal Arbitration Act (FAA) has not been updated since it was enacted 1925, before the drafting of the New York Convention. On the shortcomings of the FAA, especially those related to its age, see Bermann 2011a.

foreign parties are likely to encounter) highly professional. However, many non-US lawyers are put off by the complexity of US federal and state laws (and the corresponding mass of precedents), 'which seem extremely tricky, and even bizarre, to foreign parties and lawyers trained in different legal traditions'.[198] For this reason, Helmer asserts that American courts and the laws of American states are not chosen as frequently as English courts and law in situations where neither party is American or English.[199]

Finally, some countries present advantages or disadvantages unrelated to their legal systems. Switzerland and Sweden are preferred for their political neutrality. Thus, the Stockholm Chamber of Commerce built up a reputation in the 1970s and 1980s as a neutral site for arbitrations between western and Soviet bloc corporations.[200] Despite the reservations that many foreign parties have about the US courts and US legal system, some parties choose to arbitrate in the US because the respondent has significant assets there.[201]

3. Competition with other forms of dispute resolution

The pervasiveness of competition in the international arbitral system does not mean that competition is all-encompassing; there are many areas in which the interests of different arbitrators and different arbitral institutions converge. First, arbitrators and arbitral institutions tend to support globalization and free trade.[202] Self-interest partly accounts for this phenomenon—more cross-border transactions will mean more international arbitrations—but arbitrators tend to be committed free-traders.[203]

Second, arbitrators recognize that they are dependent upon cooperation from national courts; without courts willing to enforce arbitration agreements and arbitral awards, 'the effectiveness of the entire arbitral process (and its attractiveness to international business) will be undermined'.[204] Until recently, courts limited the scope of arbitral authority and reserved the right to supervise arbitral decision-making.[205] Arbitrators and arbitral institutions have successfully lobbied national legislatures, executives, and courts to enact laws supporting international arbitration.[206]

Third, arbitrators and arbitral institutions actively cooperate to promote arbitration (over other forms of ADR and litigation) as the preferred method for resolving international commercial disputes.

As a result, extolling the virtues of ICA (especially its superiority over litigation) is part of the business of an arbitrator. Many arbitrators seldom miss an opportunity to proclaim arbitration's superiority. For such arbitration apologists, arbitration is 'a valuable commodity as yet too little known but capable of being proved superior to its competitors',[207] while courts are 'unaccustomed to international commercial transactions

198 Helmer 2003, 42.

199 Ibid. Helmer provides no statistical support for this assertion, but several interviewees agreed.

200 Born 2009, 165–6. Similarly, one interviewee ascribed Singapore's increasing popularity as an arbitral seat to the fact that Singapore is 'a truly neutral venue in Asia'.

201 Alford, 86.

202 Trakman 2006, 29; Thirgood 2004, 344.

203 Such an ideological position is itself attributable in part to arbitrators' identification with business interests and their internationalist values. See Chapter 4, Sections III and V.

204 Thirgood 2004, 346.

205 See Section II.2 of this chapter.

206 Thirgood 2004, 344.

207 Minoli et al 1967, vii. This statement was made more than forty years ago, but the sentiment persists.

and ... [their] laws and practices are not adequate to deal with them'.[208] Effective promoters of ICA are lauded by their fellow arbitrators. For example, in their introduction to a *liber amicorum* for Martin Domke, Minoli, Pearson, and Sanders praise Domke for having been a 'shrewd ... salesman' for arbitration during his extensive travels: 'Always the gospel of Arbitration has been preached *con brio* and tirelessly.'[209]

Arbitration treatises and student textbooks typically include, in their first chapters, lists of the advantages of arbitration.[210] Moreover, arbitration scholars continue to publish arguments for arbitration's importance and prescriptions for how to ensure that arbitration remains, as in the title of one such article, the 'preferred option for international dispute resolution'.[211]

Too often, academic commentary on ICA takes the form of cheerleading; as Rogers notes, most commentators in domestic contexts are 'sceptics who focus on the ... power differentials that characterize most disputes', but 'international commercial arbitration scholars have traditionally been insiders.... When they criticize the system and call for improvement, their tone is most often that of loyal opposition from within, not that of external detractor.'[212] (Investment treaty arbitration, on the other hand, has attracted some persistent lines of criticism, in particular that both arbitral tribunals and the system of bilateral investment treaties itself systematically favour corporations over developing states[213] and that inconsistent awards regarding inadequately defined substantive rights threaten the legitimacy of the system.[214])

Not surprisingly, arbitrators tend to take wide views of arbitral jurisdiction and the arbitrability of disputes. Doctrines such as interpretation *in favorem validatis*, widely applied by arbitrators, tilt jurisdictional disputes toward a finding that jurisdiction exists.[215] The tribunal's decision in consolidated ICC Cases Nos 6515 and 6516 is typical. The arbitration agreement read as follows:

> Any eventual dispute between the Parties arising herefrom should be ironed out by the Parties undertaking to make all necessary efforts for settling them amicably. However, if a dispute finally had to be litigated, it would be by Arbitration in Athens, in accordance with the provisions of the International Chamber of Commerce.[216]

The tribunal found this clause to be 'defective under a number of respects'—the indefiniteness of the statement that the parties 'should' attempt to 'iron out' the dispute, the reference to 'provisions' of the ICC as opposed to its rules of procedure, the reference to 'litigation' of the dispute. However, it held that 'none of these defects ... is of such gravity as to vitiate the clauses'.[217]

208 Redfern and Hunter 2004, 31. 209 Minoli et al 1967, vii.

210 For this kind of list, see, eg, Born 2009, 70–89; Redfern and Hunter 2004, 26–54; Lew et al 2003, 4–8.

211 Crowter and Tobin 2002. For another example of this type of article, see Carbonneau 2009b.

212 Rogers 2006, 1324 (citations omitted), noting that arbitration has only 'recently ... attracted some skeptics, who are calling for ... reforms'. However, even these critics remain few in number and 'their proposals have demonstrated an appreciable sense of reserve'. Ibid, 1325. Dezalay makes a similar point: 'In the world of arbitration, academics and practitioners frequently work together as arbitrators and advocates and there is no activist community to speak of' (Dezalay 2007, 163).

213 See, eg, Sornarajah 2006; Chimni 2004.

214 See, eg, Franck 2005; Afilalo 2005.

215 There is no single doctrine of interpretation in favour of validity, but rather an attitude that is exhibited in a variety of circumstances where the arbitral tribunal's jurisdiction is contested. For example, where it is alleged that a valid arbitration agreement exists but the dispute is outside the scope of that agreement, there is 'a strong tendency to favour a broad interpretation of arbitration clauses'. Lew et al 2003, 151–2. See also Hanotiau 2011.

216 (1999) XXIVa Ybk Comm Arb 80 [1]. 217 Ibid, [54].

In a similar vein, an empirical study of ICC awards by then ICC Secretary-General Schwartz revealed what he called a 'liberal' view of arbitrability. Schwartz reviewed over 500 ICC awards rendered over five years and found not a single award in which the tribunal held that the dispute referred to it was unarbitrable.[218] As Thirgood wryly comments on these findings: 'It is clearly in the ICC's interests to create as many new opportunities for arbitration as possible (provided that in doing so it does not jeopardize the enforceability of its awards or its good reputation).'[219]

Arbitral institutions actively encourage this trend. When the ICC revised its rules in 1998, ICC tribunals' jurisdiction was expanded to include 'disputes not of an international character' if the parties so provide in their arbitration agreement.[220] Derains and Schwartz—both former Secretaries-General of the ICC Court of International Arbitration—write that the purpose of this revision was to allow an ICC tribunal to extend its jurisdiction to cases 'where the international character of the dispute may be in doubt'.[221] The equivalent provision in the 2012 Rules goes a step further. It refers simply to 'the resolution of disputes'. In other words, the ICC arbitrations under pre-1998 Rules were limited to disputes of an international character. Next, they were presumptively limited to such disputes under the 2010 Rules but the parties could provide otherwise. Today, under the 2012 Rules, they are no longer limited at all in that way.

Competition between arbitrators and courts is largely one-sided. Judges and national legislators derive no personal benefits from attracting more lawsuits to their courts; they even encourage parties to go to arbitration. Courts tend to see arbitration as, at minimum, a means of easing their crowded dockets.[222] As Ridgway notes, increasing international trade will generate an increasing number of cases, which may overwhelm already-overworked national judicial systems.[223] Perhaps in response to this development, states 'have overcome their historical mistrust of arbitration ... to consider that it represents an important factor of stability and development in transnational economic relations'.[224] The role of national courts has therefore 'evolved from the supervision and control of the arbitrator's activity to the more fruitful one of co-operation with a view to more efficient conduct of the proceedings'.[225]

Despite the cooperative attitude of most national courts, arbitrators must overcome the fact that courts have an inherent legitimacy. Not surprisingly, '[t]he international arbitration community is deeply concerned with its real and perceived legitimacy.'[226] Indeed, ICA as a field must continually justify its legitimacy: 'Large portions of international arbitration procedure can be explained as attempts to maximize the legitimacy of a process detached from the normal sources of authority.'[227]

218 Schwartz 1994, 19. Courts may or may not have agreed that these 500 disputes were arbitrable; however, without access to the awards on which Schwartz based his study, it is impossible to reach any conclusion regarding abitrators' and judges' differing conceptions of arbitrability.

219 Thirgood 2004, 351. The limitation on the enforceability of ensuing awards remains important. As Mistelis notes, one could argue an arbitral tribunal has no duty to respect national standards of arbitrability. Nevertheless, a tribunal 'should on its own initiative deny jurisdiction if the dispute is inarbitrable on the basis of the facts submitted by the parties'. Mistelis 2009 [1]–[18].

220 Art 1. 221 Derains and Schwartz 1998, 22.

222 For example, Bales and Eviston note, in the context of civil litigation in the US, 'without pre-dispute arbitration, court dockets would be overloaded with claims'. Bales and Eviston 2010, 11.

223 Ridgway 1999, 52. For budgetary reasons, states are generally reluctant to increase the number of judges, even as the population and the number of claims filed increase.

224 Bernardini 2004b, 118–9 (citations omitted). 225 Ibid, 115. But see Wallace 1990.

226 Rogers 2006, 1335. 227 Park 2003, 1257–8.

Today, one of the major concerns expressed by interviewees is ensuring the legitimacy of ICA in developing countries. This is a greater issue in investment arbitration,[228] but ICA also suffers from a perception that it is largely a creation of the global North, foisted upon the global South. One interviewee described the current state of affairs:

> I personally see one of the bigger challenges for arbitration is to make certain we have a diversity of players from the developing world. Now, diversity is a word that can very easily be [limited to] gender diversity ... one could put together a series of tribunals that would be all women, but ... because all the women would be either from New York or London or Washington—big firm solicitors or very senior barristers.... [If] the parties are from the developing world then all they see are three Western faces.... We need to look at the buy-in from the rest of the world. This does not detract from the importance of gender diversity but we need to pursue in parallel diversity in all its forms.

Primarily, this means promoting arbitration as sophisticated enough to serve the multifarious needs and interests of international commerce and reliable enough to trust with the resolution of major disputes. The sophistication is provided largely by ICA's academic sheen. As Dezalay and Garth describe it: 'The academic theorization of arbitration ... gave the field ... a sophisticated legal expertise suitable for high-level practitioners. This academic pedigree has helped promote the acceptance and recognition of arbitration throughout much of the world.'[229]

Reliability concerns are somewhat more intractable; indeed, they may well be endemic to arbitration. In 1938, before the modern era of international arbitration, Judge Learned Hand memorably wrote that 'arbitration sometimes involves perils that surpass those of the sea'.[230] In 1965, when ICA was just beginning to coalesce as a distinct field of law, Martin Domke called 'predictability of result' the 'principal challenge' facing arbitration.[231] As discussed above, the internecine nature of the arbitration community continues to raise concerns about conflicts of interest.[232] Moreover, informal procedures can lead to denials of due process, cross-cultural misunderstandings can lead to serious miscommunications, and unsupervised and unaccountable arbitrators can render superficial or clearly erroneous awards.

The last concern is the most serious. Given arbitrators' lack of any inherent authority over the parties, 'the success ... of arbitration as a means of resolving disputes depend[s] upon the quality of ... the skills, training and experience of those involved'.[233] Consequently, faulty or inadequate awards not only 'destroy any trust parties can have in a particular panel, but ... also destroy the parties' trust in arbitration'.[234] As Ridgway notes, trust is critical in ICA, which depends for its effectiveness on a high rate of voluntary compliance.[235]

[228] Some commentators have criticized the investment arbitration system for being biased in favour of (mostly Western) investors and against developing states. The debate has now produced a voluminous literature. See generally Waibel et al 2010.

[229] Dezalay and Garth 1996, 42.

[230] *Canadian Gulf Line v Continental Grain Co*, 98 F2d 711, 714 (2d Cir 1938).

[231] Domke 1965, 14. See also Redfern 2003.

[232] See Section III.1 of this chapter.

[233] Jones 2006, 276.

[234] Giovannini 2003, 351.

[235] Ridgway 1999, 50. The ICC has estimated that over 90 per cent of its awards are complied with voluntarily. Lalive 1984, 319. However, Drahozal notes that an empirical basis for that estimate is not provided, and it appears to be based entirely on anecdotal reports of members of the ICC Court. Drahozal 2009a, 1040 fn 41. Survey data indicate that the rate of voluntary compliance is indeed high, although not as high as the ICC asserts. 84 per cent of corporations regularly involved in international arbitration reported that the opposing party had honoured an award in more than three quarters of the disputes in which the respondent was involved. PwC/QMUL 2008, 8. However, these figures are difficult to verify, as only about half of the arbitral institutions have any system in place for

As a result of these concerns, arbitrators and arbitral institutions have promoted more detailed rules on conflicts of interest and arbitral ethics,[236] drafted clearer and more harmonized rules of procedure,[237] increased transparency in such matters as the selection and challenge of arbitrators,[238] required reasoned awards,[239] advocated for the publication of more awards,[240] and established training and certification programs for would-be arbitrators.[241]

V. Conclusion

The institutional structures of the ICA system are important components of ICA culture. Based on those structures, it is possible to predict a variety of effects on international arbitral decision-making.

Whatever jurisdictional theory one subscribes to, it is clear that arbitrators derive their authority from both state legal orders and the agreement of the parties. Similarly, both state laws and the parties' agreement place constraints on the exercise of that authority. However, within the culture of ICA, the parties are the primary focus, since they are the direct cause of the tribunal's existence and since they select and pay the arbitrators.

These are purely logistical realities, but their predictable consequence is that international arbitrators will identify with the perspectives and interests of the parties. Arbitrators interviewed for this book did not characterize the parties as limiting their authority, although parties do often agree to limit the power of the tribunal (for example, by restricting the scope of submission to arbitration to a narrow set of issues, or by agreeing to limited document production or short hearings). The mirror image of this tendency is that international arbitrators perceive the risk of non-enforcement of an award—and the corresponding risk to their reputations and their livelihoods—as the primary checks on their authority. Accordingly, interviewees referred to state laws

monitoring arbitrations after the award is rendered. Ibid, 16. Similar findings from other surveys are summarized in Drahozal 2009a, 1040.

236 See generally Rogers 2006.

237 Jolivet 2006, 270. In particular, attention has been paid to streamlining rules of procedure to increase the speed and lower the cost of arbitration. Crowter and Tobin 2002, 301.

238 For example, the LCIA now publishes its decisions on challenges to arbitrators, despite the fact that its rules do not require publication. See 11(2) LCIA News 1 (June 2006). In its 2012 revision to its Rules, the ICC decided not to begin publishing decisions of the ICC Court on challenges to arbitrators. Fry 2011. The two approaches may be explained by differences in the institutional structure of the LCIA and the ICC. An interviewee pointed out: 'It would be difficult for the ICC to publish its decisions on challenges, because those decisions are formally taken by the ICC Court of Arbitration at plenary sessions at which thirty or more members of the ICC Court may be present. The LCIA procedure is more formalistic. A tribunal of one or three members of the LCIA Court are appointed to adjudicate upon the challenge and make a reasoned decision. At the ICC, there is a report from the Secretariat, a report from the Rapporteur, and then it is very much the essence of the meeting at the plenary session of the Court. And it may not be unanimous.'

239 Rogers 2006, 1316–7. The increase in detailed reasoning in arbitral awards is illustrated by the fact that, on average, published arbitral awards have increased dramatically in length over time. Rogers canvassed the ICC awards published in the Yearbook of Commercial Arbitration and noted that the average length of ICC awards in the volumes for 1986 and 1987 were 5.7 pages and 8.4 pages, respectively, while those for 2003 and 2004 were 16.5 and 20 pages. Ibid, 1317 fn 64. See also Park 2002, 823: 'The marketplace has pushed international arbitration toward reasoned awards.'

240 Rogers 2006, 1323 fn 64.

241 Grizel 2006, 167.

mainly in terms of the limits that they place on arbitral decision-making.[242] Of course, state laws also empower arbitrators in the first place by enforcing both arbitration agreements and arbitral awards.

Identification with the parties does not translate into identification with *one* party. Despite the obvious risk of bias presented by the direct appointment of arbitrators by parties, party-appointed arbitrators are not systematically partial. Incidents of party-appointed arbitrators who act as advocates for 'their' parties are rare, and such conduct is stigmatized in the ICA community. Market competition obliges arbitrators to maintain neutrality (or at least the appearance of neutrality); biased arbitrators lose credibility with their fellow tribunal members, so parties are unlikely to appoint arbitrators with a reputation for partiality.[243]

By contrast, market forces may not discipline the tendency of arbitrators to cooperate with each other and with the counsel who appear before them. It is unclear how much the fluidity of arbitral roles and the personal and financial ties between arbitrators and counsel affect the decision-making of arbitrators. However, it seems reasonable to conclude that market and social forces act together to disincentivize arbitrators from making decisions that might harm the interests of the ICA community (which overlap with but are distinct from the interests of the parties who employ that system). Market forces affect ICA culture in other ways. They create an incentive to redesign arbitral procedures to better serve the needs of the parties—the primary consumers of arbitration services. Similarly, market forces may lead arbitrators away from substantive rules of law, such as *lex mercatoria*, that are disfavoured by parties.

Competition also acts as a harmonizing force, as beneficial innovations are quickly copied, and as would-be arbitrators market themselves in terms of the career paths of the currently dominant generation. Conferences and publications serve as a means for arbitrators to advertise their expertise (especially since almost all commercial arbitration awards are confidential) and also provide avenues for the dissemination of new ideas among arbitrators and counsel.

Despite the trend toward 'professionalization' or 'judicialization' of ICA, arbitral decision-making is relatively unconstrained when it comes to determinations of substantive law. Beyond a choice of the governing law (which appears in most cross-border contracts), parties' agreements typically do not address the way in which the tribunal should apply the governing law. Similarly, national laws do not normally intrude upon the arbitrators' decision on the merits; the grounds for non-enforcement of awards are almost entirely jurisdictional and procedural.

Combined with the confidentiality of awards and the lack of a *stare decisis* doctrine in ICA, these institutional facts mean that arbitrators largely need not concern themselves with developing the law in a systemic sense when they render awards. Interviewees repeatedly emphasized that the award is 'for' the parties, and not for any larger constituency. As one interviewee put it, he is a 'problem-solver' not a 'policy-maker'.

This not to say that international arbitrators ignore notions of legal coherence when they render awards. For example, they routinely refer to national court judgments on

[242] The limits that interviewees most frequently referred to are the requirement to obey state mandatory laws and the requirement that both parties have an adequate opportunity to present their cases.

[243] These phenomena are also reinforced by the neutrality norm, which will be discussed in Chapter 4.

matters of national substantive law. However, international arbitrators are not directly supervised by courts of appeal and must make their decisions acceptable primarily to the parties (and in some cases, to a lesser extent, to arbitral institutions). One would therefore expect both the substance of their decisions and the style in which those decisions are written to display less concern for legal formalism and more concern for commercial reasonableness.

4

Norms Arising from the Values Shared by International Commercial Arbitrators

Consulting the entrails of a disembowelled chicken might perhaps be off limits. Negative attitudes about augury aside, however, very few constraints limit the manner in which arbitrators go about their jobs.[1]

I. Introduction

In a system with few constraints on arbitrators' power to adjudicate the merits of disputes, social norms are particularly important in guiding and legitimizing international arbitral justice.[2] Shared norms promote harmonization of decision-making in a system that otherwise has little to encourage internal consistency. Thus, to protect the legitimacy of the ICA system as a whole, arbitrators have an interest in displaying (or at least declaring) their adherence to the prevailing norms.

Most studies of norms in arbitration focus on their impact on rules of procedure[3] or on the role of the arbitrator in managing arbitral proceedings.[4] Little work has been done on the impact of ICA norms on substantive rules or decisions on the merits.[5] It is not surprising that studies of norms in arbitration have focused on procedure. After all, correspondences between procedures and norms are easy to draw: if arbitral tribunals value neutrality, they will adopt procedural rules such as those ensuring the independence of arbitrators and requiring that both parties have the opportunity to plead their cases. However, similar correspondences can also be drawn between arbitral decision-making on substantive law matters and arbitrators' shared normative goals.

This chapter considers four social norms that constitute elements of an incipient ICA culture: party autonomy, the service of business, neutrality, and internationalism.

II. Party Autonomy

Party autonomy is the factual, legal, and ideological core of international arbitration. In their academic writings and awards, arbitrators frequently praise the soundness of this principle and affirm its importance. Party autonomy is 'fundamental'[6] and

[1] Park 2002, 281. [2] Ibid, 288.

[3] See, eg, Berger 2006, considering evidentiary privileges; Kaufmann-Kohler 2003; Karamanian 2003, and Elsing and Townsend 2002, considering common law and civil law influences on the conduct of hearings; Rogers 2006, arguing that three 'normative goals' undergird all arbitral procedures, namely 'neutrality, effectiveness, and party autonomy'; Jolivet 2006, considering the proper scope of confidentiality in arbitration); Fellas 2004 and Rau and Sherman 1995, considering fairness and efficiency in arbitral procedures.

[4] See, eg, Webster 2003 and Böckstiegel 1997, considering the balance between party and arbitrator control of the proceedings; Rogers 2002, Carter 2000, and Lowenfeld 1995, all considering conflicts of interest for arbitrators; De Vara 2004 and Bühring-Uhle et al 2003, both considering the role of the arbitrator in mediating disputes or encouraging settlements.

[5] But see Carbonneau 2004. [6] Böckstiegel 1997, 25.

'archetypical'.[7] In cases of doubt, it is the 'guiding principle'[8] and 'general rule' in arbitration.[9] It 'prevails almost universally'[10] and reigns 'supreme' among the principles of private law to which ICA is subject.[11] Pamboukis even describes ICA as 'the jurisdictional expression of increasing individual freedom'.[12]

At the most basic level, party autonomy is simply a fact of international arbitration, a characteristic of the system. Unlike national courts, which exist as permanent organs of the state, arbitral tribunals exist only when and to the extent that parties cause them to exist. For an arbitration to occur and for a tribunal to have any authority, the parties must have freely and mutually chosen both the arbitral forum and the arbitrators. As one tribunal put it:

> It is a fundamental principle that any arbitration must be founded on the consent of all the parties thereto and the consent must be recognized as such by law. Especially in an international arbitration ... the consent of each party must be unambiguously demonstrable if any resulting Award is to be safely enforceable.[13]

Accordingly, Redfern and Hunter refer to party autonomy as the 'foundation stone' of arbitration generally, and of international arbitration in particular.[14]

Legal rules expressing the party autonomy principle extend beyond the jurisdiction of the tribunal. It pervades every stage of an arbitration, from the power of the tribunal itself, to the choice of applicable procedural and substantive rules, to the composition of the tribunal, to the conduct of the proceedings, and finally to the form of the award. In other words, in nearly every aspect of the arbitration, the parties can decide for themselves and the tribunal will follow almost any agreement made by the parties.

Finally, party autonomy has become a norm. It is now so well and widely entrenched that it is difficult to remember that current notions of party autonomy emerged only recently.[15] The relevance of party autonomy to all stages of arbitration law and practice is neither necessary nor accidental. Rather, it has come about because of a concerted and prolonged effort by proponents of arbitration to enshrine party autonomy within the treaties, national arbitration laws, rules of procedure, national court judgments, and international arbitral awards that collectively constitute the body of international arbitration law. Party autonomy has become so pervasive because arbitrators have dedicated themselves to expanding its scope.

The evolution of arbitration law toward virtually complete party autonomy is well documented—especially by the same arbitrators who have promoted this trend—and need not be recapitulated in detail here.[16] The importance of party autonomy as a norm is evidenced by the fact that states and arbitral tribunals have progressively given way in favour of the parties' choice.[17] In other words, they have voluntarily diminished their own powers over the arbitral process so that party autonomy could be expanded. Two examples will illustrate this phenomenon: the increasing ability of the parties to avoid

[7] Blanke 2006, 335–6. [8] Redfern and Hunter 2004, 315.

[9] Kaushal 2006, 183.

[10] ICC Case No 7920 of 1993 (1998) XXIII Ybk Comm Arb 80 [1].

[11] Van Harten and Loughlin 2006, 140. [12] Pamboukis 2009, [7–9].

[13] ICC Case No 7453 of 1994 (1997) XXII Ybk Comm Arb 107 [10].

[14] Redfern and Hunter 2004, 135.

[15] As recently as 1968, English courts took the position that a choice of England as the seat of arbitration constituted a choice of English law as the substantive law governing the contract. *Tzortzis & Sykias v Monarch Lines* [1968] 1 Lloyd's Rep 337 (CA).

[16] See, eg, Lew et al 2003, 16–29; Chatterjee 2003; Böckstiegel 1997.

[17] Grizel 2006, 167.

national courts and the increasing ability of the parties to determine the conduct of arbitral proceedings.

1. The parties' freedom to avoid national courts on matters of substance

When parties choose arbitration, their 'ultimate desired legal consequence' is to avoid national court systems (except for the enforcement of an eventual award).[18] If the parties had not wanted to avoid court resolution of their dispute, they would not have chosen arbitration in the first place.[19] On the other hand, states have significant interests in supervising arbitrations: when a state is the site of an arbitration or when enforcement of an award is sought against a national of the state or against assets located within it. However, the parties' autonomy to choose final resolution of their disputes by arbitration has progressively displaced states' authority to see that their own laws are enforced.

Nearly every country now explicitly provides for a right to choose arbitration and for enforcement of that choice. The New York Convention, to which 148 states, including nearly every major trading nation, are parties,[20] requires national courts to enforce valid arbitration agreements (ie, to dismiss court actions concerning contracts containing arbitration clauses) and requires courts to enforce procedurally valid arbitral awards, even if those awards misapply the governing substantive law.

Court control of substantive aspects of arbitral awards

The exclusion of substantive review of awards by national courts is a primary purpose of the New York Convention,[21] and substantive review by the courts is considered 'contrary to the spirit' of ICA.[22] After all, if arbitral awards can be reviewed on their merits by national courts, then the parties' goal of avoiding court resolution of their disputes is frustrated.[23] As Craig points out, what a court might describe as an 'error of law' is, at heart, 'a claim that the arbitrators did not reach the result a court would have'.[24]

Countries have long differed on the propriety of judicial control over the decisions of arbitrators on the merits, with the common law states generally being more willing than the civil law states to impose such supervision.[25] However, previously robust regimes of

[18] Kerr 1985, 1–2.

[19] Arbitrators' advocacy for wide party autonomy to avoid national courts is related to the service of business norm, discussed below in Section III of this chapter. Writes Shilston: 'The widespread desire of arbitration producers is to disengage arbitration to the maximum from state litigation systems in the best interests of servicing international commerce' (Shilston 1987, 51).

[20] <http//www.uncitral.org/uncitral/en/uncitral_texts/arbitration/NYConvention_status.html> accessed 20 July 2012. The only economically important jurisdiction not a party to the New York Convention is Taiwan, which withdrew from the Convention when it lost control of the 'China seat' in the United Nations.

[21] McConnaughay 1999, 468–9.

[22] Grizel 2006, 166. See also Rigaux 1982, 274, asserting that international arbitration would be 'denatured' and would 'lose its essential value' if awards were subject to court review as a matter of course (author's translation).

[23] This rationale was a motivating factor in the drafting of the Model Law, the provisions of which preclude courts from reconsidering the merits of disputes decided by arbitration. Model Law Explanatory Note [14].

[24] Craig 1988, 213.

[25] See, eg, the comparative analysis of different national approaches to competence-competence in Born 2009, 877–965. This phenomenon is nicely illustrated by the historical disparities between the approaches taken by Canada's common law and civil law jurisdictions. Bachand 2009.

substantive judicial review have retreated over the last few decades. Courts 'have made fidelity to the parties' arbitral preferences a cardinal principle of arbitration law'.[26] The modern 'light-handed attitude'[27] is exemplified by the UNCITRAL Model Law, which contains 'no provision ... for any form of appeal [to the courts] from an arbitral award, on the law or on the facts, or for any judicial review of the award'.[28]

Some states continue to make provision for substantive review of arbitral awards. In the United States, courts have vacated awards where the tribunal 'manifestly disregards' the law.[29] However, this doctrine—always a narrow exception—appears now to have been entirely abrogated. In *Hall St Associates v Mattel Inc*,[30] the US Supreme Court, resolving a split between different the federal circuit courts,[31] held that judicial review of an arbitral award under the US Federal Arbitration Act is limited to the grounds specifically enumerated in the statute.[32] Therefore, all 'non-statutory' grounds of judicial review are inoperative, including manifest disregard of the law.[33] Smit concludes that 'manifest disregard ... is probably dead'.[34]

English law has long been inimical to the notion that arbitral awards are unappealable to the courts. The earlier (1889–1950) versions of the Arbitration Act freely permitted parties to petition the courts to review the determinations of arbitral tribunals on points of law.[35] Indeed, in the Court of Appeal, Lord Denning reasoned that agreements made to arbitrate disputes in England were made under the assumption that points of law could be referred to its courts.[36] Many English lawyers and judges passionately defended this position and, more generally, assailed the notion of arbitration entirely detached from the courts. Sir Michael Kerr, for example, noted that: 'In England, we often speak in laudatory terms about a partnership between the courts and arbitrations under our system.'[37]

However, in 1979 and then more thoroughly in 1996,[38] England largely reversed its previous position. Under the Arbitration Act 1996, arbitral awards containing errors of law are, in the normal course, 'unassailable'.[39] Section 69 of the Act does preserve a

[26] Bermann 2009, 1014. See also De Ly 1994. [27] Newman 2009, 1230.

[28] Redfern and Hunter 2004, 500.

[29] *Wilko v Swann*, 346 US 427, 436–7 (1953), articulating the 'manifest disregard' test in dictum followed by subsequent courts, overruled on other grounds, *Rodriguez de Quijas v Shearson/American Express, Inc*, 490 US 477 (1989). See generally Rubins 2001.

[30] 128 S Ct 1396 (2008). [31] Reuben 2009, 1105.

[32] *Hall St*, 128 S Ct 1396, 1400: 'The question here is whether statutory grounds for prompt vacatur and modification may be supplemented by contract. We hold that the statutory grounds are exclusive.'

[33] Reuben 2009, 1106.

[34] Smit 2009, 999. Note, however, that a similar common law doctrine in India, 'patent illegality', appears to be alive and well. See, eg, the decision of the Supreme Court of India in *Oil & Natural Gas Corporation Ltd v SAW Pipes Ltd* (2003) 5 SCC 705, 727 ('Patently illegal award is required to be set at naught; otherwise it would promote injustice.'), as well as two recent decisions of the Delhi High Court considering whether a delay in the issuance of an award can amount to patent illegality: *Union of India v Niko Resources Ltd* and *Oil India Ltd v Essar Oil Ltd*, both unreported as of the time of writing and available at <http//practicalacademic.blogspot.in/2012/08/whether-undue-delay-can-constitute_28.html> accessed 29 August 2012.

[35] Park described pre-1979 English law on judicial supervision of arbitrations as 'the apogee of intervention'. Park 1980, 91.

[36] *Halfdan Greig & Co v Sterling Coal & Nav Corp (The Lysland)* [1973] 1 QB 843 (CA).

[37] Kerr 1985, 2.

[38] 'Exclusion agreements' contracting out of some aspects of judicial review of arbitral awards were first permitted by the 1979 Act. See generally Park 1980.

[39] Sheppard 2005, 66, commenting on the House of Lords' decision in the *Lesotho Highlands* case.

right to petition a court to review the substantive determinations of an arbitral tribunal. However, parties may contract out of section 69,[40] and the provision contained in all standard form arbitration agreements to the effect that an eventual award will be final and binding has been held to constitute a valid waiver of the right of review.[41] Moreover, most institutional rules of procedure provide that arbitrations organized by that institution are final, so whenever parties contract for institutional arbitration, they thereby contract out of section 69.[42]

In the unlikely event that the parties have not expressly or impliedly contracted out of section 69, English courts must give leave to apply for judicial review,[43] which they will do only when two requirements are met: first, the issue must involve interpretation of English law,[44] and second, either the tribunal's decision must be 'obviously wrong' or the issue must be one of 'general public importance and the decision of the tribunal is at least open to serious doubt'.[45]

This shift in English law came in response to widespread criticism from arbitration practitioners that the English system of judicial supervision was inappropriate.[46] Lord Hacking, one of the early parliamentary sponsors of the Arbitration Act 1979, related that 'a distinguished partner of a distinguished Wall Street law firm ... [considered it] to be a matter of professional negligence to allow an English arbitration clause in any contracts'.[47]

Court control of arbitrable subject matter

The only remaining significant limitation on the parties' freedom to choose arbitration (and thereby to exclude national courts) is that the subject matter of the dispute must be arbitrable under national law (effectively, under the national law of the seat of arbitration and of any countries where enforcement of the award is sought). Under article II(1) of the New York Convention, courts may decline to enforce an arbitration agreement if, according to the court's national law, it does not concern 'a subject matter capable of settlement by arbitration'. Typically, an unarbitrable subject matter is one that the state considers to be inappropriate for private adjudication because it affects the rights or interests of the general public.[48] Examples include the validity of patents and trademarks.[49]

The arbitrability doctrine limits both the power of arbitrators and the autonomy of parties.[50] Here, too, however, party autonomy is greater than in the past; several subjects once considered unarbitrable are now arbitrable. As Lew relates, the decreasing relevance of the arbitrability doctrine is a significant development: 'Most jurisdictions now accept that where parties have agreed that their disputes should be resolved by arbitration there is no good legal or policy reason to reserve any of these issues for the courts.'[51]

[40] s 69(1).
[41] *Sanghi Polyesters Ltd v The International Investor (KCFC)* [2001] 1 Lloyd's Rep 480.
[42] *Lesotho Highlands Development Authority v Impregilo SpA* [2006] 1 AC 221 (HL), referring to the ICC Rules.
[43] s 69(2)(b). [44] ss 69(1) and 82(1).
[45] s 69(3)(c). [46] see Schmitthoff 1977. [47] Hacking 1979, 1.
[48] Mistelis 2009 [1–6]. This kind of arbitrability is sometimes referred to as 'objective' arbitrability, as opposed to 'subjective arbitrability', which is concerned with the legal capacity of parties to submit disputes to arbitration. Ibid [1-13].
[49] See generally Mantakou 2009. [50] Pamboukis 2009 [7-4].
[51] Lew 2006, 193.

The most prominent example of this trend is antitrust/competition claims,[52] but disputes over securities transactions also fit the trend. In the US, disputes arising under the federal Securities Act had been unarbitrable. However, the US Supreme Court overturned this doctrine in its 1974 decision in *Scherk v Alberto-Culver*, and did so in near-hyperbolic language that indicates the extent to which courts have relinquished their traditional power to regulate arbitration agreements. The court wrote that a 'parochial refusal by the courts of one country to enforce an international arbitration agreement' would not just 'frustrate' the purposes of such an agreement,[53] but would also 'imperil the willingness and ability of businessmen to enter into international commercial agreements'.[54]

The trend toward recognizing more subject matters of disputes as arbitrable has continued. In 2009, the US Supreme Court upheld the arbitrability of employment discrimination claims where the relevant collective bargaining agreement contains an arbitration clause.[55]

Arbitrability also plays a role at the enforcement stage. Under article V(2)(a) of the New York Convention, an arbitral award may be set aside or refused recognition and enforcement if it concerns an unarbitrable subject. In the *Mitsubishi* case, which is mostly remembered for the US Supreme Court's permitting arbitration of antitrust claims, the court noted that US national courts would have another opportunity at the enforcement stage to ensure that America's 'legitimate interest in the enforcement of antitrust laws has been addressed'.[56] A similar evolution has occurred in the EU, culminating in the ECJ's decision in the *Eco-Swiss* case, which held definitively that competition claims are arbitrable.[57]

Continuing areas of court control of substantive matters

None of the above is to say that parties may avoid entirely the application of national laws. As long as arbitral tribunals must rely on national courts to enforce their awards, those courts will insist on enforcing certain mandatory laws—laws that relate to the fundamental public policy of the state. Arbitrators accept the right of courts to set aside awards on the narrow ground of violation of fundamental public policy as the price of court enforcement of the vast majority of awards.[58] Under the New York Convention, article V(2)(b), national courts may set aside an award or refuse to enforce it if enforcing the award would be contrary to national public policy. This principle is in turn expressed in the various national arbitration laws. For example, the UNCITRAL Model Law provides in article 34(2)(b)(ii) that courts may set aside an award on the ground that it is contrary to the public policy of the *situs*, and in article 36(1)(b)(ii) that courts may refuse an award recognition or enforcement for the same reason. More specifically, the English Arbitration Act 1996, section 1(b), provides that the procedure of an arbitration, regardless of the parties' agreement, is subject to such safeguards as are necessary in the public interest.

[52] For a list of court decisions in a variety of countries reversing previous doctrines to permit arbitration of contracts implicating antitrust issues, see Redfern and Hunter 2004, 165–8.

[53] 417 US 506, 516 (1974).

[54] Ibid, 517.

[55] *Penn Plaza v Pyett,* 129 S Ct 1456 (2009).

[56] *Mitsubishi Motors Corp v Soler Chrysler-Plymouth Inc*, 473 US 614, 628 (1985).

[57] Case C-126/97 *Eco Swiss China Time Ltd v Benetton International NV* [1999] ECR I-3055. Lew describes as 'remarkable' the ECJ's conclusion that competition issues are arbitrable, especially since competition law is something of a 'holy cow' for the EU. Lew 2006, 193.

[58] McConnaughay 1999, 454.

Analogously, many national arbitration laws specify that tribunals are bound by mandatory laws. For example, the English Arbitration Act 1996 provides in section 4(1) that a set of mandatory provisions, listed in Schedule 1 to the Act, have effect notwithstanding any contrary agreement of the parties. However, when an arbitration takes place in a country whose arbitration law does not contain such a list (including jurisdictions which have adopted the UNCITRAL Model Law), arbitrators must still respect mandatory laws of the seat of arbitration. A core duty of the arbitral tribunal, expressed or implied in all arbitral rules of procedure, is to deliver an enforceable award.

2. The parties' freedom to choose the procedures of their arbitration

One of the reasons parties choose arbitration over litigation is a desire to avoid 'strict adherence to the procedural rules applicable in the national courts of the country in which they take place, or indeed any particular set rules other than those expressly agreed to'.[59] Today, party autonomy is the 'guiding principle in determining the procedure to be followed in an international commercial arbitration'.[60] As one interviewee put it: 'I think a lot of what really is important to parties in commercial arbitration is to be able to have the proceeding that they want to have, you know? That degree of autonomy and control is really very important.'

Current national arbitration laws and arbitral rules of procedure permit the parties to agree on 'all aspects of an international arbitration procedure, subject only to certain limitations of mandatory law'.[61] Parties may even choose a procedure that appears to the arbitrators to be unfair or inappropriate, except that parties may not agree to waive basic due process protections.[62]

Parties usually agree on the arbitral procedure, either by selecting an institution to administer the arbitration (in which case the institution's rules of procedure apply) or, if the parties choose ad hoc arbitration, by selecting an existing set of rules to govern the proceedings (often the UNCITRAL Rules). All modern institutional rules follow the general model that, for every aspect of procedure that is not prescribed by the rules, the parties may agree and, if they do not, the arbitrators will decide. To a greater or lesser degree, they also permit the parties to derogate from the rules. The LCIA Rules exemplify such permissiveness: article 14.1 provides that: 'The parties may agree on the arbitral procedures and they are encouraged to do so.'[63]

As with substantive review of arbitral awards by national courts, the current state of affairs regarding procedure is a recent development. Compared with arbitration laws and rules of procedure enacted prior to the 1980s, modern rules generally contain few non-derogable procedural rules and provide that the arbitrators may decide on the procedure only if and in such areas as the parties do not agree.[64] This last point is the most important, as the rise of party autonomy over procedural matters has come directly at the expense of the power of the arbitrators to control the proceedings, especially

[59] Borris 1999, 2–3.

[60] Redfern and Hunter 2004, 315.

[61] Böckstiegel 1997, 25.

[62] Born 2009, 1749; Fouchard, Gaillard, and Goldman 1999, [1701]–[1702].

[63] The right of parties to choose their procedures is not, of course, unlimited. Article 14 of the LCIA Rules provides that procedures chosen by the parties must be consistent with various 'general duties' of the tribunal, including the duty to act fairly and impartially as between the parties, adopt procedures suitable to the circumstances of the arbitration, and avoid unnecessary delay and expense.

[64] Borris 1999, 3.

with respect to the conduct of the hearing. While arbitral rules of procedure 'once left vast discretion to the arbitrator' on such matters as the manner of the presentation of evidence, form of submissions and time limits, 'modern rules have … shifted more control to the parties'.[65]

Since institutional rules of procedure are drafted by committees of leading arbitrators and counsel, it is reasonable to conclude that arbitrators have deliberately ceded power to the parties. Some arbitrators are explicit about this policy preference. For example Wang and Cao, two of the architects of the 2005 version of the CIETAC Arbitration rules, entitled their article on the new rules: 'Toward a higher degree of party autonomy and transparency'.[66]

3. Party autonomy as a social norm

Party autonomy acts primarily as a constraint on the power of arbitrators. Arbitrators do sometimes impose their procedural preferences on the parties; however, such occurrences are rare and, when they do occur, they are criticized. One interviewee even said: 'You are much more constrained by party autonomy than by the rules of procedure.' Ridgway describes a case in which the arbitrators imposed a hearing schedule on the parties as an example of the tribunal 'riding roughshod',[67] and Böckstiegel characterizes such situations as 'horror stories'.[68]

As a result of rules that prioritize party autonomy, such horror stories have become rare: 'Limitations on party autonomy have declined during recent decades.'[69] Indeed, arbitrators' efforts to enshrine party autonomy, in particular with respect to the parties' choice of the substantive law, have been so successful that Böckstiegel could conclude in 1997 that: 'The wide acceptance of party autonomy in national laws throughout the world might arguably be considered as leading to party autonomy being today a general principle of law.'[70] The *Institut de droit international* has also characterized party autonomy as one of 'the fundamental principles of private international law'.[71]

Practical reasons exist for preferring broad party autonomy. For example, party autonomy over the arbitral process counterbalances the 'vast' power arbitrators possess in the form of an unappealable final award,[72] and party agreement on choice of law and the conduct of the proceedings improves buy-in to the arbitral process and therefore acceptance of an adverse outcome.[73] However, if practical concerns were paramount, we would see debates on the optimum level of party autonomy for one rule or another. Instead, arbitrators tend to agree universally that party autonomy should be as expansive as possible. This consensus is best explained by the proposition that party autonomy is a norm of arbitration.

Arbitrators tend to perceive party autonomy to be a—perhaps *the*—core desire of commercial parties in international arbitration. Böckstiegel writes:

65 Rogers 2002, 353.

66 Wang and Cao 2005, stating that the changes made to the rules were 'designed to respect party autonomy at a higher level in the arbitral process' 117.

67 Ridgway 1999, 50–1. 68 Böckstiegel 1997, 25.

69 Ibid. 70 Ibid.

71 *Institut de droit international*, 'The Autonomy of the Parties in International Contracts Between Private Persons or Entities' (Basel Session 1991). <http//www.idi-iil.org/idiE/resolutionsE/1991_bal_02_en.PDF> accessed 20 July 2012. The resolution expressly reserves the question of whether parties are free to choose transnational rules of law.

72 Rogers 2002, 411. 73 Borris 1999, 4.

... party autonomy is fundamental to the functioning and development of private economy systems at the national level, as well as of international trade and investment. The business community has a strong interest in shaping its relationships to its need and advantage and in selecting its own systems of dispute settlement.[74]

Arbitrators often characterize the gradual expansion of party autonomy as a function of the 'recognition' by legislatures and judges that the interests of the international commercial community are served by a robust doctrine of party autonomy.[75] Writings by arbitrators tend to contrast their own 'enlightened' respect for party autonomy with the 'parochialism' of national courts.[76] For example, Georges Delaume characterizes the expansion of legal support for party autonomy as an unambiguous victory of arbitration over national courts and a cornerstone of arbitration's ability to adapt to the needs of international commerce:

In recent years [party autonomy] ... has conquered new grounds heretofore denied to it ... Modern statutes and treaty provisions, together with enlightened judicial decisions, increasingly and relentlessly have given new dimensions to party autonomy in an effort to cope with the needs of transnational commerce and eradicate from national systems a former parochialism out of context with the necessities of contemporary economic and commercial relations.[77]

Donahey even proclaims: 'party autonomy gives the parties the flexibility necessary to structure the procedure in a way best suited to their needs. It is this flexibility that has led to the success of commercial arbitration and made it the preferred means of resolving international commercial disputes.'[78]

When the parties do not agree on a procedure, the tribunal may decide. Even then, however, most arbitrators try to reach an agreement with the parties on the way the arbitration should proceed. One interviewee observed that 'You can't start dictating to parties how they should approach their cases'. Another said, 'if an agreement is possible, I would want them to agree. Provided of course that it is within certain parameters, because I would not want to be bound to a party agreement that is not practicable or the like. But usually then they would not agree.' A third interviewee, who prides himself on active management of his arbitrations, pointed out that most disagreements on procedure between the tribunal and the parties should be resolved in the parties' favour:

After all ... in case management, you are guiding the parties in a direction in which they are not unhappy to go. In arbitration essentially, you start off with what the parties agreed to as the procedure and you build on that. You don't normally tear up what they've written.... If the practitioners are experienced, they will tell you why it was agreed in this way, and you will pipe down, settle down and say, 'That's fine. If that's what you want, that's what you'll get.'

Interviewees also justified their evidentiary practices in terms of party autonomy. For example, one interviewee said that he hesitates to engage tribunal experts because the parties do not like the loss of control a tribunal-appointed expert entails:

... a lot of opposition by the parties, on the whole.... They've got their own experts, you see, and they're in control. They know what the expert is going to say because he talks to them before

74 Böckstiegel 1997, 25. 75 Ibid.

76 See, eg, Newman 2009, 1239: 'International arbitration is but one example of a larger movement to promote reforms facilitating international commerce and cooperation, and the avoidance of parochial discrimination by the State'; McConnaughay 1999, 454, referring to national courts' 'parochial notions of procedure or justice'.

77 Delaume 1988, 282. 78 Donahey 1992, 42.

he gives evidence. With a tribunal expert, you don't know what he or she is going to say. And you have to pay for it!

Another interviewee, a London-based independent arbitrator, noted that national evidentiary norms are generally inapplicable in ICA. The interviewee gave the example of hearsay evidence, which would be inadmissible under common law rules. If the parties want to introduce such evidence, they may; the tribunal will simply assign it less weight.[79]

Arbitrators' acceptance of near-total party autonomy over procedure trumps both their personal interests and their view of the interests of the parties. For example, the longer the proceedings take, the more expensive they are for the parties and (when arbitrators are paid by according to an *ad valorem* calculation) the less profitable they are for the arbitrator. However, arbitrators are frequently admonished to allow the parties to direct the proceedings even if this leads to what the arbitrator perceives to be a waste of time.[80] Implicit in such admonitions is the notion that the interests of the arbitral system are congruent with the wishes of the parties. One arbitrator gave the example of adjournments that violate the agreed hearing schedule:

> You are much more constrained by party autonomy. What do the parties want to do? They'll often change their timetables by agreement. For example, let's say they wanted to go off and mediate, and they say 'May we have an adjournment of the timetable for the next four weeks?' without specifying why. You know why. A court would be much more reluctant to suddenly allow the established timetable to be ignored. But as an arbitrator, that is never a problem.

Party autonomy also affects the way that tribunals decide the merits of disputes. In general, arbitration agreements specify the issues that the parties are submitting to the tribunal, and the tribunal may not assert its jurisdiction over additional issues, except that arbitrators must ensure that any applicable mandatory rules are observed. Once the tribunal's jurisdiction over a dispute is established, questions continue to arise over the particular legal issues to be resolved. One interviewee expressed caution about even referring to issues that the parties have not raised:

> It's not up to the tribunal to put a case for a party. It is a matter of great importance. The tribunal may ask a question but you need to be very careful. If neither party wants to raise a particular issue, then unless the issue is a core issue, such as whether or not the tribunal has jurisdiction ... the tribunal does need to be cautious.

Another way in which party autonomy affects merits determinations has to do with the ascertainment of the content of the governing law. Unlike national courts, international arbitrators are regularly called upon to decide under laws with which they are not familiar.[81] They must learn the content of that law somehow, the main sources

[79] But see a recent decision of the Swiss Federal Supreme Court, *Y and Z v U, V, W and X* (Federal Supreme Court, 23 January 2012) Cases 4A 526/2011 and 4A 528/2011. The sole arbitrator refused to hear a witness because the party proffering the witness failed to demonstrate why the witness's testimony would be relevant. The losing party sought to have the award set aside on the ground that its right to be heard had been violated. Federal Supreme Court denied the application, holding that an arbitrator's refusal to hear evidence does not, in itself, violate a party's right to make its case.

[80] See, eg, Fellas 2004, 80; Park 1988, 629.

[81] See, eg, Kaufmann-Kohler's reflection: 'Reflecting back on the cases in which I have been involved as an arbitrator ... I realized that I have resolved disputes under German, French, English, Polish, Hungarian, Portuguese, Greek, Turkish, Lebanese, Egyptian, Tunisian, Moroccan, Sudanese, Liberian, Korean, Thai, Argentinean, Colombian, Venezuelan, Illinois, New York ... and Swiss law. Do I know these laws? Except for New York law, which I learned many years ago and would not pretend to know now, and Swiss law, which I practise ... the answer is clearly no. So how did I apply a law

being the submissions of the parties, expert witness testimony and the arbitrators' own research.[82]

This issue is connected to an ongoing debate concerning the nature of international arbitrators' duty to apply the law. There is general agreement that international arbitrators have a duty to apply the governing substantive law. The debate has to do with the implications of that duty in specific instances[83] and on the range of powers that arbitrators possess to help them in discharging their duty. For example, one central question that appears to be unresolved is whether the *iura novit curia* principle applies in arbitration (so that arbitrators would be under an *ex officio* duty to determine the content of the applicable law), or whether it is up to the parties to prove the content of the law.[84]

Very few national laws or rules of procedure address the means by which arbitrators should determine the content of the governing law; those that do address the matter do so in ways that leave tribunals a great deal of discretion.[85] Accordingly, it would appear that each arbitral tribunal is free to determine this matter for itself. However, it seems that an international arbitral practice prioritizing party autonomy is now crystallizing.

This issue seems to have come to the fore only during the last decade, so there is little commentary available. The most notable publication is a report with recommendations by the International Commercial Arbitration Committee of the International Law Association (ILA). Similar documents are regularly applied in ICA as codifications of international arbitral practice in other areas, most prominently the International Bar Association's Guidelines on Conflicts of Interest in International Arbitration and its Rules on the Taking of Evidence in International Commercial Arbitration. It is too soon to know whether the ILA Report will gain similar prominence, but if one is searching for international rules on the ascertainment of the applicable law, it is a good place to start.

The ILA Report gives a series of recommendations. Taken together, they assign the tribunal primary responsibility for ascertaining the relevant legal issues and the contents of the legal rules necessary to resolve those issues, but encourage tribunals to be guided by the parties. In other words, they chart a middle course between a continental-style *iura novit curia* rule and an English-style foreign-law-as-fact rule.

The ILA Report recommends that tribunals raise promptly the topic of the ascertainment of the applicable law. Tribunals should seek to secure the parties' agreement on the relevant procedures, such as whether the parties will make submissions with

unknown to me? By ignoring it? By focusing on the facts and the equities? How did I become educated in the law? How did counsel teach me?' Kaufmann-Kohler 2005, 631.

[82] The permutations are numerous. Should the parties' submissions include argumentation only? Or should they present primary source materials, in particular statutes and regulations? Should they present case law? What about cases from civil law jurisdictions? Is evidence of the drafting history of statutes appropriate? Should expert witness reports cite these kinds of sources? In the oral hearing, what kinds of information should be presented by live testimony? Should expert witnesses be subject to cross-examination? Should the parties provide the experts, or should the tribunal hire its own expert? To what extent should arbitrators bring their own research or knowledge to bear, and if so, what obligations do they have to present their research to the parties for comment?

[83] For example, Paulsson and Mayer have debated the circumstances in which an arbitral tribunal may refuse to apply a national law on the ground that it conflicts with a hierarchically superior national or international law. Paulsson 2008; Mayer 2011.

[84] See, eg, Landolt 2012; Waincymer 2011; Isele 2010; Kaufmann-Kohler 2006; Kaufmann-Kohler 2004b; Lew 2000.

[85] See Chapter 5.

materials attached or will prove the law through expert witnesses. Except for matters that might jeopardize the enforceability of an eventual award (such as public policy and the scope of the submission to arbitration), arbitrators should not introduce legal issues or propositions of law that the parties have not raised. Arbitrators are not confined to the parties' submissions and may conduct their own research, but should receive information about the applicable law primarily from the parties. If an arbitrator discovers a relevant legal issue or binding authority that has not been raised, the parties should be given an opportunity to comment.[86]

Commentators who have addressed the issue reached similar conclusions. For example, Kaufmann-Kohler suggests this transnational rule:

> The parties shall establish the contents of the law applicable to the merits. The arbitral tribunal shall have the power, but not the obligation, to conduct its own research to establish such contents. If it makes use of such power, the tribunal shall give the parties an opportunity to comment on the result of the tribunal's research.[87]

Interviewees tended to share this perspective. With respect to allocation of the responsibility for proving the law, even arbitrators from civil law systems seem to agree that *iura novit curia* is inapplicable in ICA. Instead, the common law position that it is up to the parties to prove the law was generally endorsed. One interviewee observed: 'Most arbitrators from different legal systems I've sat with, or appeared before, do require some detail as to "Well, explain to me why we should do this? We need this explained. We can't make the case out for you." And I think ... this slightly adversarial [as opposed to inquisitorial] approach has started to emerge more and more.'

On determining the means by which the parties ought to prove the content of the governing law, interviewees concurred that this is something on which the parties should agree. One said simply: it's up to the parties. If the parties want to introduce expert witnesses, arbitrators will hear them. If the parties want to submit bundles of statutory and case law, the arbitrators will read them. In general, interviewees said that they do not hire tribunal-appointed experts on legal matters, even if they would appoint experts to explain technical matters. One said: 'I never hire an independent expert on the governing law issues. I usually hear the parties' arguments and if they introduce legal experts on both sides I hear the expert opinions.'

On the whole, however, interviewees said that they often found it unnecessary for the parties to introduce expert witnesses on the content of the applicable law. One interviewee said that expert witnesses 'are usually not very helpful. The examination is not very fruitful ... because they are under the instruction of the party that appointed them and they very often simply argue the case of the party'. Another interviewee observed that where you have a professor as an expert witness, they can sometimes try to take over the decision-making from the tribunal. Where there are two professors as experts, the tribunal may decide on the basis of which professor was more impressive or persuasive. He added: 'Professors sometimes preach; that's not what arbitrators need. Then the tribunal asks itself, "Who gave the better presentation—Professor X or Professor Y?".' (On the other hand, one interviewee who acts regularly as counsel prefers to hire expert witnesses on the applicable law because 'The credibility of our argument is stronger if we have an expert and it's sort of an opportunity to repeat the argument'.)

[86] ILA Report on the Applicable Law 2008, 213–20.

[87] Kaufmann-Kohler 2006, 181. Similar proposals can be found in Landolt 2012, Waincymer 2011, and Lew 2000.

Instead, most interviewees preferred what some referred to as the more common modern approach, which is for the parties simply to argue the content of the applicable law in their written and oral submissions. One interviewee with a common law background observed:

What tends to happen more frequently now is the parties have lawyers from the relevant legal system before you. They don't bother with experts and you get them to submit on it and they will give you their opinion through their submissions, supported by the text of laws or court decisions or anything else that they regard as relevant and then they can be questioned by the tribunal. I don't find it particularly difficult. There are some difficult cases but it's not nearly as difficult as some might make out.

Interviewees were unanimous that tribunals should be able to do their own research, but should never apply a legal doctrine or refer to a source of authority without giving the parties an opportunity to comment upon it. One said, 'there is an invariable law that if you come up with any clever ideas that the parties haven't raised you have to immediately tell them'. Another interviewee concurred: 'I would not be shy in saying "I want assistance on the following points." One can't make it up as one goes along, regardless of how clever one thinks one might be.... But then the parties would have to have a clear opportunity to brief the point and understand the case of the other.' An interviewee who acts primarily as counsel noted that: 'It drives me crazy when I receive awards that are based upon some rationale ... where they've come up with an approach that was never raised with the parties, not given an opportunity to respond to.'

4. Party interests and systemic interests

In deciding individual disputes, judges must pay attention to systemic interests, such as the development of legal doctrine, the concerns of users of the dispute resolution system generally, and the overall functioning of the legal system. On the other hand, arbitrators' deference to party autonomy leads them to identify with the parties' interests, rather than with the system's. One consequence of arbitrators' identification with the parties' interests is a diminished sense of obligation to follow the law.

Judges have an institutional duty to the legal system: to apply the law and to ensure that the rules they lay down are of general applicability. This duty is usually implicit but is sometimes spelled out explicitly. For example, under the Rome I Regulation on the law applicable to contractual obligations, judges in EU national courts must consider 'the proper functioning of the internal market' when they apply the Regulation's conflict of laws rules.[88]

By contrast, arbitrators are not required to consider the proper functioning of a market or of the legal system generally. They are obliged to obey the law, but if arbitrators take into account other circumstances, such as commercial interests or equitable concerns, there is nothing (within limits) that can stop them. For this reason, commentators have suggested that the arbitrators' duty is to obey not only the law, but also the interests of the parties and the requirements of justice.[89]

Of course, equitable rules exist in national legal systems as well, and judges often tailor their stated interpretations of the law to the equities of a particular dispute. Yet a

[88] Rome I Regulation, Recital 6.

[89] Jones 2006, 281; Carlston 1967, 48. Cf Tschanz 2007, arguing that, in light of the 'goals of arbitration', an international arbitral award need only (1) put an end to the dispute, (2) with *res judicata effect*, (3) do that by applying the law, (4) after a fair trial.

difference in mentality is discernible.[90] As Mayer puts it: 'A judge's mission and obligations ... consist in ... defining the respective rights of the parties as they result from the applicable law. [The parties] do not expect him to upset the established order so as to impose, in breach of the law, what he subjectively considers as fair.'[91] By contrast, writes Mayer, the international arbitrator owes no strict 'duty of obedience' to the law.[92] Then-Associate Justice Rehnquist of the US Supreme Court argued that this is all to the good: a 'less frequently realized advantage of arbitration ... is that its process usually need not produce a body of decisional law which will guide lawyers and clients as to what their future conduct ought to be'.[93]

The party autonomy norm and arbitral 'lawlessness'

The phenomenon of arbitrators paying more attention to the equities of a dispute or the particularities of a contract than to the applicable law gives rise to what has been called the 'lawlessness' of ICA. Opinion is divided on the extent to which arbitral lawlessness actually exists and whether it ought to exist.[94] Many arbitrators consider lawlessness to be one of arbitration's most important positive characteristics: 'A principal virtue of international commercial arbitration is its lawlessness, its ability because of its unrestrained flexibility to accommodate the enormous procedural, presentational, and decisional ... differences that typically exist among parties to multinational transactions.'[95] Similarly, Reuben argues that:

> The notion of substantive 'correctness' or 'accuracy' historically has had little place in arbitration precisely because arbitration calls for the exercise of worldly judgment that is informed by a variety of considerations that may not lend themselves to an objective notion of correctness or accuracy, such as knowledge of economic considerations in the securities industry or professional standards and practices in the construction industry.[96]

Some interviewees appeared to endorse this perspective. One told the following anecdote:

> I recently had a case about the outfitting of a business jet. It was a contract between a businessman who ordered a so-called 'green aircraft' and one of the outfitters that did the job. There were a lot of problems in the outfitting process and problems with an important outfitting feature that took too long to install. One of the questions was: gross negligence or simple negligence? We looked at the overall situation and formed an opinion. Many aspects come in when you consider the circumstances: When was the contract entered into? Did the principal know that the outfitter had little experience with the specific type of aircraft versus other types of aircraft? Did he accept the risk? ... These are all aspects which may or may not be relevant from a strictly legal point of view. But you look at them all and form your opinion, your overall opinion. Then you write the award ... with a view to the end result that the arbitrators find fair.

90 Cotterrell 1997, 162. 91 Mayer 2001, 240.

92 Ibid, 235–6, referring to the 'ancient conception' of arbitration as entailing 'equity being mixed with law', even in cases not involving amiable composition. Hermann makes a similar point: 'the settlement of international commercial disputes is always more of a problem of equity than of law'. Hermann 1983, 200.

93 Rehnquist 1977, 5.

94 For example, in one case, the tribunal wrote that it 'cannot accept the suggestion made by the claimant to evaluate the lawfulness of the claims in the present case without reference to any national system of law'. ICC Case No 7263 of 1994 (1997) XXII Ybk Comm Arb 92 [8].

95 McConnaughay 1999, 522. 96 Reuben 2009, 1129. See also Ulmer 2011.

A version of this attitude, common among international arbitrators, is the notion that the applicable law is in some way subordinate or secondary to the contract. Many international commercial disputes, it is argued, are resolvable based on the facts and the terms of the contract alone. As one interviewee put it: 'Very often you don't need the applicable law that has been chosen by the parties. It is not that relevant. What is relevant is what is written in the contract.' Another interviewee, a former judge from a common law jurisdiction, criticized 'weak' arbitrators who go too quickly to the legal issues:

> They will aim to see whether they can decide the case on the contract or a point of law, rather than first getting a full factual background. That can be, in a sense, a sign of weakness. That is to say, they don't have enough experience and knowledge to make an assessment of the facts, so they don't want to go into the facts. They want to go down the road ... as we all do, that they are most happy with. They take comfort in the law, because that's all they know.[97]

Such a position may be shaped by the detailed drafting style of most modern contracts. This is especially true when the contract was concluded on the basis of a sophisticated form, like the FIDIC form for construction contracts or the Bermuda form for insurance contracts. These forms are highly detailed and are frequently updated to take account of judicial interpretations. Moreover, detailed contracts in what has traditionally been thought of as a common law style are becoming more common. One Swiss interviewee reflected that: 'You used to see short contracts written on a napkin, things like that. Classical type. But nowadays even in the civil law jurisdictions they are more sophisticated.'

Not all arbitrators support such an open-ended characterization of the arbitral mandate. Nearly all international arbitrators are lawyers, after all, and are accustomed to thinking in terms of legal rules. In some cases, they will apply national laws even if they are not required to do so. Said one interviewee: 'Applying *ex aequo et bono* frees you from applying any national standard, but if ... there are strong ties to a particular law, you might find in your role as *amiable compositeur* that the application of that law was the most predictable or the fairest thing you could do.'

Even if no reference is made to national laws, *ex aequo et bono* awards often end up looking quite similar to legally based awards:

> One of the things that is really quite strong in ... my *ex aequo et bono* approach, and I know this from quite a few other people who sit in the same sort of cases, is that *ex aequo et bono* is not simply 'Tear up the contract and decide whatever it is you think is right.' ... *Pacta sunt servanda* is a fundamental tenet of justice, that if people are going to agree to something, they are going to be kept to it ... *Ex aequo et bono* probably requires arbitrators to have a fundamental sense of 'This result isn't right, and I'm going to do what is right and just.' But the parties will see where it's coming from—it's not simply a tossed coin or something like that.

Arbitrators might naturally prefer to adjudicate under general principles or *lex mercatoria* because it grants them almost unfettered discretion to implement the rules that they favour. But parties are wary of such loss of control, and party autonomy governs. Dezalay and Garth note that the Anglo-American practitioners they interviewed were 'nearly unanimous in their denunciation of a doctrinal construction that, according to them, allows academics to avoid the rigorous analysis of the facts, the formal law, and even the terms of the contract'.[98] In general, arbitrators, counsel, and commentators

[97] A different interviewee with a common law background made a similar point, and observed that fact-finding is an important but often overlooked skill for international arbitrators.

[98] Dezalay and Garth 1996, 41.

with common law backgrounds have been sceptical of the *lex mercatoria*, amiable composition,[99] and other doctrines that increase the scope of arbitrators' discretion in deciding the merits of disputes.[100] Commercial parties seem to share the same scepticism; they rarely choose *lex mercatoria*.[101]

Nevertheless, some arbitrators assert that lack of rigour in arbitral decision-making is a response to the parties' preferences. For example, McConnaughay argues that 'elastic rules of decision' and 'the absence of reasoned opinions' are of great value to commercial parties from non-Western legal traditions, particularly from East Asia.[102] Ridgway summarizes the argument that commercial parties as a whole prefer decisions that are not overly 'legal':

> Some commentators contend that parties opt for arbitration—whether domestic or international—specifically because they want 'rough justice', a decision in equity. Indeed, some commentators argue that one inherent advantage of international arbitration ... is the freedom it gives an arbitrator to do justice even where strict application of the law might require another result.[103]

In ICC Case No 7181 of 1992, the parties agreed on a procedure to determine the amount of damages but the tribunal nevertheless decided to calculate the damages 'equitably'. In that case, the parties disagreed on the amount of damages recoverable but jointly submitted that the tribunal should appoint an expert to determine the damages. The tribunal declined. It reasoned that, since the damages depended on an assessment of the parties' behaviour and on certain factual determinations, 'an expert appraisal could not give the Arbitral Tribunal precise elements of valuation of these factors. In the absence of such precise elements, the Arbitral Tribunal prefers ... to determine, without further delay, the amount of damages *ex aequo et bono*'.[104] This approach appears to be common; one interviewee observed that: 'In case of calculation of damages I would say that it's not that unusual for a tribunal not specifically under an equity power to apply that principle in the calculation of damages.'[105]

In ICC Case No 11849 of 2003, the parties disagreed as to the applicable rate of interest on any damages awarded. The contract was governed by the CISG, which contains no provisions relating to the rate of interest. The parties each argued for the application of their own states' laws to set the interest rate. However, the tribunal rejected both arguments, on the basis that: 'In international arbitration, arbitrators have the broadest powers to determine interest on the basis of the most appropriate rate, without resorting to any rule of conflict.'[106]

The arbitrators interviewed for this book seemed to recognize that commercial parties generally prefer the substantive law rules applicable to their dispute to be as certain

[99] See Chapter 5, Section II.2.

[100] See, eg, Mustill 1988, 86, describing the *lex mercatoria* as something that the common lawyer is 'tempted to regard as a non-subject, having no contact with reality save through the medium of a handful of awards which could well have been rationalized more convincingly in terms of established legal principles'; Rubino-Sammartano 1992, 5 asserting that: 'The difficulty which some common law jurisdictions meet when they face a request to decide *ex bono et aequo* ... is well known.'

[101] See Chapter 3, Section II.2.

[102] McConnaughay 1999, 502. McConnaughay, an American-trained lawyer and academic, practised in Tokyo and Hong Kong.

[103] Ridgway 1999, 52.

[104] ICC Case No 7181 of 1992 (1996) XXI Ybk Comm Arb 99 [60].

[105] The interviewee noted that in some legal systems, it is perfectly acceptable for the adjudicator to simply determine an amount of damages in consideration of all the circumstances, without explaining how the quantum was calculated.

[106] ICC Case No 11849 of 2003 (2006) XXXI Ybk Comm Arb 148 [81].

as possible, and therefore disfavour discretionary doctrines like general principles and amiable composition. One said: 'in contract negotiations they shy away from *ex aequo et bono*. Nobody wants to take responsibility for an *ex aequo et bono* decision because that can really go both ways'. Another characterized the entire debate over the *lex mercatoria* as 'more a discussion amongst lawyers as opposed to discussion amongst the people who count, mainly the clients who write contracts'.

In deference to what they see as the parties' preferences, interviewees generally expressed a cautious attitude toward amiable composition and the application of general principles or *lex mercatoria*. One said simply: 'If they don't choose it, I don't feel at liberty to apply it.' Another said that when an award is decided under general principles, this is often with the agreement of the parties, even if that agreement is not mentioned in the award:

> You'll find that most of the time it will be agreed in the Terms of Reference. Given the paucity or lack of certainty about what the law might be, they actually agree that the arbitrators may if they think it fit apply the *lex mercatoria* ... They've done it by agreement ... by their own volition. But they don't tell you that; it might come out in a question and answer section but they don't tell you.

One interviewee, a former judge, even questioned whether general principles are really any more flexible than national laws:

> The law gives you the freedom and flexibility to arrive at a just result which is in accordance to the law. You don't actually have to say 'I'm applying equity or *lex mercatoria*.' The only thing it does is that you don't have to justify your conclusion by reference to a body of law that doesn't quite give you the answer you are looking for. In other words, you don't have to interpret the law first and say this is what the law means, therefore this is the conclusion we want to arrive at.'[107]

Another aspect of arbitral lawlessness is arbitrators' reliance on 'good faith' as a purported general principle of international commercial law, even when applying the substantive law of a country that contains no general requirement of good faith.[108] For example, in an ad hoc award from 1982, the tribunal held that a party's argument:

> ... contradicts both the general principle of good faith and the fundamental principle *pacta sunt servanda*, both principles forming the basis of all contractual relations, particularly in international affairs, and which are specifically enshrined in international commercial usages and international law.[109]

Arbitrators with common law backgrounds have made similar assertions. For example, DiMatteo writes that: 'The meta-principles of good faith, fairness in the exchange, and the duty to inform are implied into contract by most arbitral regimes.'[110]

ICA is not, of course, an entirely lawless forum, nor are arbitral awards devoid of reference to legal authority. An award that runs contrary to the parties' agreement, for example by deciding under amiable composition without authorization, is subject to

[107] This perspective was echoed by another interviewee, who noted that amiable composition provisions in a contract only lead the tribunal to be 'more bold' stating outright that they are deciding based on equitable considerations.

[108] See, eg, ICC Case No 6197 of 1995 (1998) XXIII Ybk Comm Arb 13 [42]; ICC Case No 3267 of 1979 (1982) VII Ybk Comm Arb 96, 100; Hamburg Friendly Arbitration Award of 15 January 1976 (1978) III Ybk Comm Arb 212, 213; ICC Case No 1784 of 1975 (1977) II Ybk Comm Arb 150.

[109] Ad hoc award of April, 1982 (1983) VIII Ybk Comm Arb 94, 116, citing ICC Case No 1939 of 1971 [1973] Rev Arb 145; ICC Case No 1526 of 1968 [1974] JDI 919.

[110] DiMatteo 1997, 83.

annulment or refusal of enforcement.[111] But even if a 'lawless' award is enforceable, it is still likely to be contrary to the wishes of the parties. If parties want to have their dispute arbitrated by non-lawyers exercising 'commercial judgment' instead of 'legal analysis', it is within their power to convene an appropriate tribunal. Yet the vast majority of parties appoint qualified lawyers as their arbitrators.[112]

The 'judicialization' of ICA

It is often stated that the leading arbitrators of this era are better-versed in arbitration law than their forbears, and that their awards are more likely to be grounded in legal principles.[113] Indeed, many regard lawlessness as a hallmark of an earlier era, when arbitrators were known more for their personal wisdom and gravitas than for their legal expertise. Today, the argument goes, parties do not want 'the open-textured discretion of international arbitration's past';[114] instead, 'businesses use international arbitration to provide a neutral, adjudicative dispute resolution process where arbitrators independently apply the law to facts, and this in turn promotes the legitimacy of international arbitration'.[115] Where once 'grand old men' dominated the field, today it is the multinational law firms, 'with their tight organizational structure, integrated services, global network of offices, and team mentality'.[116] As Dezalay and Garth relate, members of the new generation 'assert, even citing Max Weber in one instance, that the time has come for the "routinization of charisma" essential to the transition from the stage of artisans to that of mass production'.[117]

A growing literature exists which documents the 'judicialization' or 'professionalization' of ICA, a trend associated with this generational turnover.[118] Some contend that the process has gone too far, so that arbitration is no longer cheaper, faster, and fairer than litigation.[119] Many of these critics associate greater legalism and procedural complexity with an Americanization of ICA.[120]

The generational shift should not be taken for more than it is. While modern arbitrators are technocratic compared with the previous generation, the relationship between arbitrator and disputing party is such that arbitral decision-making remains more open to the influence of subjective and contextual factors than judicial decision-making. Dezalay and Garth themselves conclude that 'that this project of routinization—even

[111] Berger 2010, 55. [112] Franck 2006, 503 (citations omitted).

[113] Dezalay and Garth 1996, 36, calling today's leading arbitrators 'technically better equipped in procedure and substance'. See also Faulconbridge and Muzio 2009, 1349–52, crediting the involvement of global law firms with the increase in professionalism among arbitrators and counsel.

[114] Franck 2006, 504. [115] Ibid.

[116] Alford 2003, 88. Of course, not all arbitrators or arbitration practitioners are associated with multinational firms. However, of 105 leading international arbitration practitioners recognized by Chambers and Partners in 2012, 79 are or were partners in major law firms (75 per cent). Around half of the remainder are English barristers. <http//www.chambersandpartners.com/Global/Search/PracticeArea/57> accessed 23 August 2012.

[117] Dezalay and Garth 1996, 37, quoting an interviewee.

[118] See, eg, Schneider 2006, describing increased judicialization in international dispute resolution generally; Hansen 2003, referring to judicialization of investment treaty arbitration under the North American Free Trade Agreement; the various contributions to Lillich and Brower 1994, describing two trends in ICA that fall under the rubric of 'judicialization': increased judicial intervention in the arbitration process and greater procedural intricacy and formality in arbitration procedures.

[119] See, eg, Stipanowich 2010; Seidenberg 2010.

[120] See, eg, Martinez-Fraga 2009; Helmer 2003; Alford 2003; Reed and Sutcliffe 2001; Ulmer 2001.

judicialization—of arbitration … cannot be completely accomplished. Despite the changes, there remains a vital element of personal relations in this field'.[121]

The generation of the grand old men developed a lawless system of arbitration in response to a perceived desire by commercial actors for informal and equitable decision-making.[122] The legal specialists of the current generation of arbitrators have reacted to parties' concerns about the arbitrariness of arbitral decision-making by writing awards arrived at by tight legal reasoning. Both the prior charismatic arbitrations and the current technocratic arbitrations have been shaped by arbitrators' desire to serve what they believe to be the wishes of the parties.

Confidentiality

Arbitrators also defer to party interests by preserving near-total confidentiality in the face of increasing criticism. Few national arbitration laws mention confidentiality, but it is indisputably a core principle of arbitration: 'Most scholars and practitioners agree that a presumption of confidentiality—whether implied or explicit—exists between the parties to an international commercial arbitration.'[123] More specifically, the confidentiality of arbitral hearings is guaranteed by all the major institutional arbitration rules.[124] The final award, similarly, is private. The ICDR Rules are typical: an award may be made public 'only with the consent of all parties or as required by law'.[125] Even when there is no specific confidentiality provision in the arbitration agreement or the applicable rules, 50 per cent of parties surveyed consider international arbitrations to be confidential.[126]

If enforcement of an award is sought in a national court, the existence of the dispute, the award, and possibly documents that were generated or disclosed during the arbitration may become public.[127] If an arbitration gives rise to an action in court, 'parties' expectations about the privacy and confidentiality of their arbitral proceedings are often disappointed, or even negated'.[128] English courts have expressly held that arbitration agreements contain an implied condition of confidentiality extending to all documents produced in an arbitration proceeding.[129] However, the Australian High Court (among others) has held that the confidentiality principle does not necessarily extend to prevent the disclosure of documents or other evidence presented in an arbitration.[130]

[121] Dezalay and Garth 1996, 46.

[122] See, eg, ICC Case No 10329 of 2000 (2004) XXIX Ybk Comm Arb 108 [29] (citing 'the need to secure transactions for the safe functioning of the trade against too stringent formalities').

[123] Brown 2001, 970–1. See also Smit 2000, 573–4: 'There is a general assumption that arbitration is a private process that is presumptively confidential.'

[124] See, eg, ICC Rules, art 21(3); UNCITRAL Rules, art 28(3).

[125] Art 27. Some recently enacted institutional rules explicitly state that, unless a party objects, the institution may publish the award in redacted form if it is of academic interest. See, eg, the Rules of Arbitration of the Chamber of Arbitration of Milan ('CAM Rules'), art 8(2), official English translation available online: <http//www.camera-arbitrale.it/Documenti/cam_arbitration-rules_2010.pdf> accessed 20 July 2012.

[126] W&C/QMUL 2010, 29.

[127] However, studies indicate that a majority of awards are voluntarily complied with. See Chapter 3, Section IV.3.

[128] Brown 2001, 975.

[129] See, eg, *Hassneh Insurance Co of Israel and Others v Steuart J Mew* [1993] 2 Lloyd's Rep 243 (QB).

[130] *Esso Australia Resources Ltd and Others v Plowman (Minister for Energy and Materials) and Others*, 128 ALR 391 (1995). For an American case reaching a similar conclusion on this point, see *United States v Panhandle Eastern Corp*, 118 FRD 346, 349–50 (D Del 1988).

In the *Bulbank* case, the Swedish Appeals Court took the position, characteristic of the modern trend, that confidentiality, including of arbitration documents, is an implied characteristic of all arbitrations, but that it is not absolute.[131]

That confidentiality continues to be the general rule in ICA is surprising. Arbitrators are concerned with the legitimacy of ICA and transparency is a core characteristic of any legitimate system of adjudication. National legal systems that issue secret court decisions are rightly criticized for such a practice. Indeed, arbitrators generally agree that increased (even default) publication of awards would be beneficial to arbitration.

Numerous potential benefits of publication have been described in the academic literature.[132] Publication of arbitral awards would contribute to the development of international commercial law generally by establishing a body of persuasive precedents.[133] This could in turn improve the efficiency of the arbitration system as a whole, since confidentiality precludes the accretive 'case-by-case lawmaking such as has been claimed to lead to the efficiency of the common law'.[134] Publication of awards could also increase the predictability of arbitral proceedings,[135] aid in the training of current and future arbitrators,[136] and enhance the quality of arbitral awards, both by exerting pressure on arbitrators to articulate their reasoning clearly[137] and by providing objective information on which to judge the qualifications of potential arbitrators.[138]

Arbitrators also have a personal interest in increased publication of awards. They would be able to advertise the quality of their work product. They would be more able to influence subsequent tribunals. And they might also gain more confidence in their own decisions if they were subject to public scrutiny.

Finally, complex international transactions often produce multiple disputes involving several parties that are connected by separate contracts. Consequently, multiple arbitrations might arise out of the same circumstances and, if each is kept confidential, may be resolved in inconsistent ways.[139] To be sure, inconsistent judgments do not occur often, but 'when they do occur they raise doubts about arbitration's reliability and the authority of arbitral awards'.[140] There is at least one major example of inconsistent awards, the *CME/Lauder* arbitrations.[141]

To deal with this problem, courts have advocated the consolidation of arbitration proceedings in cases where the disputes arise out of the same facts, where the same disputed issues of law are implicated, or where there is a danger of inconsistent findings.[142] Some modern arbitral rules of procedure provide for the joinder of additional parties or

[131] See Swedish Appeals Court Report 1999.

[132] The argument that more international arbitral awards should be made publicly available is by now well known, even trite. See, eg, Karton 2012; Rogers 2006; Ong 2005; Raymond 2005; Gu 2004; Gruner 2003; Buys 2003; Brown 2001; Tashiro 1992.

[133] Daly 2007, 125 fn 221. It would also help to legitimize the *lex mercatoria* by making it more certain and accessible, an avowed goal of some arbitrators. Park 1989, 673–4.

[134] Ginsburg, 1344.

[135] Brown 2001, 1014.

[136] Ibid, 1019.

[137] Kaczmarek 2000, 314.

[138] Smit 1986, 31–2.

[139] Brown 2001, 1017. Strict confidentiality also permits parties to adduce different—even inconsistent—evidence in different proceedings without fear of consequence.

[140] Brekoulakis 2009, 1176–7 (citations omitted).

[141] *CME Czech Republic v Czech Republic* (Svea Ct of Appeals 2003) (2003) 15(5) World Trade and Arb Materials 171; *R S Lauder v Czech Republic*, Final Award of 2002 (2002) 14(3) World Trade and Arb Materials 35; *CME Czech Republic BV v Czech Republic*, Partial Award of 2001, (2002) 14(3) World Trade and Arb Materials 109.

[142] See, eg, *Cable Belt Conveyors, Inc v Alumina Partners of Jamaica*, 669 F Supp 577 (SDNY 1987), aff'd 857 F2d 1461 (2d Cir 1987).

the consolidation of related claims.[143] However, joinder and consolidation are generally possible only where multiple disputes arise out of the same complex of contracts, so that the same disputing parties are involved and known to each other. Even if the rules permitted consolidation in broader circumstances, it could only come about when a party to one of the arbitrations knows about the other arbitration(s)—something made difficult by confidentiality rules.

Similar systemic benefits cannot be claimed in defence of confidentiality of awards.[144] As Lo argues, the only principled, normative reason to enforce confidentiality is the protection of trade secrets and other undisclosed information of economic value.[145] Such information could easily be kept private even if the bulk of the arbitral proceedings and the award were made public. Despite the clear theoretical and practical case for curtailing confidentiality, it remains well entrenched in arbitral rules of procedure.

Confidentiality is justified primarily on grounds of party autonomy: commercial arbitrations are the products of private agreements between contracting parties. Even if publication of awards would improve the quality of arbitral justice, ICA is in the end a private system; parties should be able to choose confidentiality over effectiveness if they so desire.[146] (This is in contrast to investment arbitrations, which implicate 'clear and strong public interests';[147] the case for limiting confidentiality is therefore stronger in investment than in commercial arbitrations.[148])

However, no arbitration is truly the concern of the parties alone. The types of complex cross-border transactions resolved in ICA frequently impact third parties, such as shareholders, creditors, or debtors of a party; they may also implicate public interests.[149] Even if a given dispute is truly of concern to no one other than the parties, their interests would not outweigh the systemic benefits of publication of awards outlined above.

Increased transparency would benefit the arbitrators, the arbitral institutions, and even the consumers of international arbitration services as a group. The only explanation for the perpetuation of confidentiality is that parties to arbitrations continue to demand it and that individual arbitrators and arbitral institutions continue to accede to the parties' desires.[150] According to a former ICC Secretary-General:

> ... users of international commercial arbitration ... place the highest value upon confidentiality as a fundamental characteristic of international commercial arbitration. When enquiring as to the features of international commercial arbitration ... confidentiality of the proceedings

[143] See, eg, ICC Rules, arts 7 (joinder) and 10 (consolidation); SIAC Rules, art 24(1)(b) (joinder); SCC Rules, art 11 (consolidation).

[144] The party and systemic interests served by publication and confidentiality of awards are not mutually exclusive. See Karton 2012.

[145] Lo 2008, 245–6. Many justifications of the confidentiality presumption mention the protection of trade secrets and similar information. See, eg, Menkel-Meadow 2002, 962.

[146] Brown 2001, 1019. After all, Brown notes, in ICA, the parties rather than the taxpayers pay for the use of the adjudication system.

[147] Bjorklund 2009, 1287.

[148] Delaney and Magraw 2008, 756. 'In some cases, it is the mere presence of the State or a State entity that gives rise to the need for transparency. In other cases, it is the subject-matter, the issues at stake, the political situation in the host State, or the amount of potential financial liability that gives rise to questions of public interest or public concern and, thus, the need for transparency.'

[149] As the Australian High Court found in the *Esso/BHP v Plowman* case.

[150] Rogers notes that increases in transparency in ICA that have occurred are 'under-appreciated' because the parties 'are regarded as the principal obstacle against transparency for the benefit of the general public'. Rogers 2006, 1309.

and the fact that these proceedings and the resulting award would not enter into the public domain was almost invariably mentioned.[151]

Although parties do not seem to consider confidentiality to be the essential reason for recourse to arbitration, 62 per cent of respondents to one survey described confidentiality as 'very important' to them, and a further 24 per cent described it as 'quite important'.[152] The parties' desire to preserve confidentiality is understandable. If the existence of a dispute is secret, or even just the resulting award, then customers of the losing party will not have the opportunity to worry about a producer's reliability, nor will stock analysts have the opportunity to raise concerns over a company's litigation liabilities. Professional reputations can be maintained and money need not be spent on public relations damage control. More broadly, commercial entities as a matter of principle prefer to control the disclosure of any information about their businesses.[153]

If either of the parties does want to publicize an award, it can be leaked, usually without consequence.[154] On the other hand, arbitrators who breach confidentiality may be subject to termination of their contracts or even personal liability.[155] There is, moreover, at least one case in which a court fined an arbitral institution for breaching confidentiality.[156] Thus, it is clear that confidentiality acts primarily to bind *arbitrators and arbitral institutions*, at the behest and for the benefit of the *parties*. Arbitrators and arbitral institutions often see it as their duty to maintain confidentiality even when an arbitral decision has given rise to state court proceedings.[157] As such, the principle of confidentiality in ICA provides further evidence that arbitrators view service to the parties as their primary duty—another norm of ICA.

III. The Service of Business

Judges are state officials, officers of the court. In most civil law countries, they spend their careers as members of the broader civil service. In common law countries, practising lawyers appointed to the bench are expected to set aside their previous affiliations and serve the public interest. Their duty is to the law itself—court justice is public justice.

151 Bond 1995. It should be noted that, while there is general agreement that confidentiality is a factor motivating parties' choice of arbitration, there is conflicting empirical evidence as to the weight parties place on it. See W&C/QMUL 2010, 29; Pryles 2004, 415; Naimark and Keer 2002, 203–8.

152 W&C/QMUL 2010, 29. However, only 35 per cent of survey respondents stated that they would cease to use arbitration if it ceased to offer the potential for confidentiality. A similar number (38 per cent) stated that they would continue to use arbitration. Ibid, 30.

153 Menkel-Meadow 2002, 962.

154 The only remedies now generally available when a party breaches confidentiality are injunctions against further disclosures and (more controversially) money damages. Smureanu 2011, 166–7. Obtaining even these unsatisfying remedies can be difficult in practice. Brown 2001, 1016. A good recent example of essentially consequence-free disclosure of an award by a party occurred following an arbitration between Kingsbridge Capital Advisors, a private equity investor, and AlixPartners, a consultancy. See Balthasar 2012.

155 Fouchard, Gaillard, and Goldman 1999, 617.

156 A Spanish court imposed a fine on the Associatión Europea de Arbitraje de Derecho y Equidad under the Personal Data Protection Act for wrongfully releasing information about the parties to a third party. Reported in Hamilton and Maestre 2009.

157 Jolivet 2006, 269, asserting that arbitrators and arbitral institutions should 'ensure that all possible efforts are made to maintain the confidentiality of the arbitral proceedings'.

Arbitrators are private individuals. They provide a service (resolution of disputes) and are compensated for that service by their clients (the disputing parties). As Gélinas puts it: 'international arbitration exists to serve the needs of international business'.[158] Lord Mustill takes the argument a step further: 'Commercial arbitration exists for one purpose only: to serve the commercial man. If it fails in this, it is unworthy of serious study.'[159] The same principle applies to individual arbitrators: 'The idea that … the arbitrator is bound to respect the parties' will in exercising his or her role and, more generally, in discharging his or her duties, has prevailed for a long time. That the arbitrator is the servant of the parties is … a widespread view.'[160]

Arbitration is characterized by two social norms that relate to the service of business: an ideal of client service and an orientation toward the interests of the international commercial system.

1. Arbitration as a service industry

At its heart, arbitration is a service industry. As one interviewee put it: 'I do think of myself as somebody who is providing paid service to the parties. When I'm sitting as an arbitrator, the parties are entitled to the service they are paying you for.' The relationship between arbitrators and disputing parties (and their counsel) is one characterized by collegiality, informality, and an identification by the arbitrators with the mutual interests of the parties before them. Arbitrators work to ensure that the parties see the arbitration process as serving their needs: 'Unlike judges, arbitrators must inevitably treat the parties and their lawyers as having something of the aura of a clientele, whose goodwill, understanding and respect for the tribunal's authority must be cultivated and preserved.'[161] This attitude can be seen in the active manner with which arbitrators manage the proceedings, the attention arbitrators pay to reducing costs and delays, and arbitrators' efforts to encourage settlements.

Active case management

Arbitrators frequently take an active role in managing the proceedings. Cremades describes the ideal method as 'interactive' adjudication: 'rather than invoking prerogatives which may be challenged or provoke negative reactions, the arbitrator should from the very beginning of the proceeding make an effort to establish a fruitful line of communication with the disputing parties and their counsel.'[162] Cremades describes such a method as being distinct from both the inquisitorial and the adversarial method.[163] Parties appear to prefer this kind of proactive role,[164] and arbitral rules of procedure

[158] Gélinas 2000, 117.

[159] Mustill 1988, 86. See also Fortier 2001, 121, characterizing Mustill's statement as 'the essential creed of the commercial arbitrator'.

[160] Bernardini 2004b, 114.

[161] Kerr 1997, 124.

[162] Bernardini 2004b, 116–7, citing Cremades 1999, 157. Jones makes a similar point, stressing that the 'consensual, if not cooperative, nature of arbitration requires a distinct and unique approach to traditional litigious skills and practices, despite having much in common with them.' Jones 2006, 275–6.

[163] Ibid.

[164] W&C/QMUL 2010, 25. 'Excessive flexibility or failure to control the process' was cited by survey respondents as the second-most-significant reason (after 'bad decision or outcome') why parties were disappointed by an arbitrator. Ibid, 26.

have evolved to support it. For example, the 2010 version of the UNCITRAL Rules require the tribunal to establish a provisional timetable for the arbitration, and to revisit that timetable where appropriate.[165]

Such an emphasis on case management appears to be a preoccupation of the current generation of arbitrators and ICA counsel. One interviewee predicted: 'I think over time arbitrators who adopt a more proactive approach ... will be favoured by the parties because of the time and cost of international arbitration.'

A recent study by Schultz and Kovacs seems to support this proposition.[166] Taking as their starting point the notion of symbolic capital, they surveyed ICA practitioners on the qualities they look for when they select arbitrators. One finding, which the authors call 'probably the most striking attribute revealed in the results', is that 'arbitrators today must possess strong management abilities'.[167] From this, Schultz and Kovacs posit that a third generation of arbitrators, whom they call 'managers', has succeeded the two generations identified by Dezalay and Garth ('grand old men' and 'technocrats').

Interviewees for this book were unanimous in their belief that arbitrators should actively manage the proceedings so as to serve the collective interests of the parties. They rejected the notion that an arbitrator should act purely as an umpire in the manner of a common law judge. One interviewee observed:

> I'm a great believer in getting my hands right in the mud, right up to here [gestures at her elbow], and I think the parties appreciate the fact that you care about their dispute and that you show that you care by getting down to the nitty gritty with them, rather than just sitting there.

In particular, interviewees emphasized the importance of holding a procedural conference as early in the proceedings as possible, not only to determine how the arbitration will go forward, but also to establish a good working relationship. Interviewees noted that it is helpful to have not just counsel but also party representatives at this meeting:

> For instance, it is useful to have a very good first session where you discuss procedure. You have counsel there, and you also have party representatives. You have the general counsel of the company, or a representative from the justice or trade ministry of a state. They may not be used to this process—some are, but many are not. It's important that they get a good impression ... of the way the tribunal handles matters. That is what I mean by management skills: practically and technically, how do you draft a calendar; what comes first, what comes next; what do you do if there is an issue that disrupts the calendar; these kinds of things.[168]

More generally, the importance of case management skills was raised in nearly every interview. As one interviewee related: 'You need a decent office, you need an organization. Robert Briner used to say that "arbitration is mostly logistics", and he's absolutely right. It's getting organized, having a system.'[169] Such abilities are particularly important for sole arbitrators and chairs. For one interviewee, an independent English

165 Art 17(2). On this phenomenon generally, see Bernardini 2004b, 115.

166 Schultz and Kovacs 2012. 167 Ibid, 170.

168 Another interviewee gave an example of the benefit of bringing party representatives to the procedural conference. When counsel ask for an extension due to a schedule conflict, 'the arbitrators peer over at the party on the other side, the in-house lawyer, and say, "Is that the schedule you want or do you want this over sooner?" Often, you get a different response.'

169 This interviewee proudly pointed out the wheeled cabinets that cluttered his office and the colour-coded filing system he had developed for his own use: 'I have a nifty system for these kinds of things. A lot of others have probably similar systems.'

arbitrator and former law firm partner, this presents an advantage for arbitrators who have a law firm background:

As a sole arbitrator or chairman one of your main duties is to manage the process effectively. Case management skills are therefore important. That's where having been a partner at a law firm is helpful, because you're used to schedules and deadlines. And you know if you have got to get something done by the end of May, you'd better start now. Because ... people sometimes get overtaken, don't they: 'Oh my god, is it the end of May already?' I think organization is so important.

Minimizing costs and delays

One of the purposes of effective case management is to minimize costs and delays. Like any other service, ICA can be promoted both on the quality of the service delivered and on the low price charged for it. Arbitrators and arbitral institutions tend to emphasize vigilance in reducing the time it takes to complete an arbitration and the costs associated with the process. As Lloyd declared in his introduction to a survey on costs conducted by the Chartered Institute of Arbitrators: 'There is no room for complacency.'[170]

ICA is often claimed to be faster and cheaper than litigation. Whether this is in fact true is debated,[171] but many criticisms of the cost of ICA inappropriately compare it with the cost of domestic litigation. In the context of international disputes, if the parties go to litigation, at least one of them will be forced to proceed in a foreign court, employ additional foreign lawyers unfamiliar with its business (who will require more time to prepare), and translate all of the relevant documents into the language of the court (a time-consuming and expensive process).[172] In any event, commercial parties generally perceive arbitration to be a cost-effective option.[173]

Interviewees tended to downplay the importance of costs, even as they acknowledged that arbitration is not as fast and cheap as in the past, and that national court processes in some countries are faster and cheaper than in arbitration.[174] For the most part, they argued that accuracy and thoroughness are more important to the parties than economy.[175] One arbitrator complained that case management skills are frequently overrated relative to skill in writing awards:

One quality that is particularly appreciated is the skill at managing the hearings, which I think is overrated, because it is less important than drafting a good award, which doesn't count so

[170] CIArb 2011, i. One survey respondent commented: 'The topic of costs is hardly glamorous.... Although it is the last thing to be dealt with in any arbitration, it is usually the first thing on the client's mind.' Ibid, iii.

[171] Pearson 1967, 210–1; Fellas 2004, 79; Sussman 2009.

[172] Redfern and Hunter 2004, 26.

[173] See Naimark and Keer 2002. However, survey data indicate that the commercial parties that describe themselves as 'dissatisfied' with their experiences with international arbitrations do so in part because of 'increased costs of arbitration and delays to proceedings'. PwC/QMUL 2008, 5. Delays in the process or in the issuance of the award were described as sources of disappointment in particular arbitrators. W&C/QMUL 2010, 26.

[174] On the other hand, they pointed to the finality of arbitral awards as a reason why arbitration remains more efficient than court litigation in many jurisdictions. One senior English arbitrator said: 'I think costs and saving time has gone out the door. But I suppose you have an advantage that, on the whole, it's one stop. You can perhaps go on some sort of appeal but normally it's just one stop. And that's helpful because across the road they go to the High Court, Court of Appeal, Supreme Court, and now the European Court of Justice. It just never stops [whistles and gestures spiraling upward with his finger].'

[175] Park makes an extended version of this argument in Park 2010.

much in your reputation. People see you for two weeks and either they are impressed or not and that counts.

Even so, arbitrators are much more likely than judges to weigh the costs and benefits of additional procedures and, potentially, to sacrifice meticulous exploration of a dispute for the sake of efficiency.[176] Borris writes:

> While fairness is the most important aspect, the second test to which procedural rules should be subject is 'efficiency'. In international commercial arbitration, more than in other types of litigation, the parties are commercial companies and business people for whom one of the reasons for choosing arbitration is the desire for a quick decision.[177]

Interviewees supported Borris's assessment. They stressed that the procedure adopted for a case should be adapted to the specific circumstances of the case. For example, they indicated that they often convene a separate hearing on one or two threshold legal arguments, in the hope that resolving these points would lead parties to settle their dispute.

On the other hand, in cases where such a procedure would not be efficient, arbitrators will proceed differently. One interviewee, a specialist in construction and engineering disputes, indicated that in construction disputes, there are rarely legal issues the resolution of which would lead the parties to settle:

> Is it really cost effective to make an inquiry into the legal aspects and to resolve them first to see whether that settles the case? In construction, the answer is generally no ... The best thing to do is to find out what the case is about and by using the procedural techniques available, to try to do so in a way that will bring the parties closer together in the sense that they get a better understanding of the strengths and weaknesses of their case.

As a general matter, Griffin describes the goal of international arbitral tribunals as: 'to seek a workable compromise ... in order to achieve efficient administration of justice without rendering the process over-burdensome.'[178] Redfern and Hunter describe a trend toward shorter live hearings and greater reliance on documentary evidence, characterizing this 'as a necessary step in the interests of economy of time and costs in cases that often involve arbitrators, lawyers, experts, [and] company executives ... operating away from their home bases'.[179] The ICC convened a task force to identify the techniques that most effectively reduce time and costs in arbitration.[180]

The German arbitrator Karl-Heinz Böckstiegel has been praised for his efficient management of arbitrations.[181] The so-called Böckstiegel Method involves assigning a total amount of hearing time to each party, then strictly enforcing the total while allowing the parties to decide how to allocate that time among opening and closing statements and examination of witnesses.[182] Such a method may work against the interests of a given party in a given dispute, but the Böckstiegel Method is praised because it reduces costs and is therefore in the interests of commercial parties generally. However, it may be moving out of favour—none of the arbitrators interviewed for this book said that they typically or frequently use it.

176 See Kaufmann-Kohler 2004a.

177 Borris 1999, 5.

178 Griffin 2000, 19. For a similar statement, emphasizing that efficiency must be balanced with fairness, see Bernardini 2004b, 121.

179 Redfern and Hunter 2004, 380.

180 The task force's report was published as ICC Commission 2007.

181 Especially in Paulsson 2001.

182 Ibid, 608. See generally Bockstiegel 2005.

Most institutional rules do not require arbitrators to adopt efficient procedures in areas where they have discretion. For example, the AAA/ICDR Rules state only that: 'Subject to these rules, the tribunal may conduct the arbitration in whatever manner it considers appropriate.'[183] However, the LCIA Rules impose a general duty on the part of arbitrators to adopt suitable procedures, 'avoiding unnecessary delay or expense, so as to provide a fair and efficient means for the final resolution of the parties' dispute'.[184]

The importance of customizing procedures to the particulars of each dispute was a common point made by interviewees. They emphasized that each arbitration is different and that the role of the arbitrator is to consult with the parties to determine how the procedure can be adapted to their specific needs. Rivkin calls his preferred procedure the 'town elder' model; he advocates that tribunals start with a blank slate in each arbitration and add only those procedures (eg, oral hearings, witness statements, document production) that are necessary to resolve the dispute.[185] Similarly, Rivkin suggests that tribunals identify threshold legal issues and resolve them first so as to avoid unnecessary legal and factual submissions. For example, if a contract excludes the recovery of consequential losses, an early determination to this effect can save the parties the expensive process of calculating and preparing submissions on the quantum of consequential losses.[186]

Interviewees (including those who act primarily as counsel) tended to blame the parties and their advocates for rising costs in ICA. Interviewees cited in particular the tendency of advocates to make too many arguments and raise too many objections ('Some counsel take a scattergun approach and raise every conceivable matter.'[187]), the size of legal teams ('You get the most appalling overmanning of cases by the law firms.'), the 'prevalence of defensive practice', and an arms race to hire the best advocates in a global market ('You want to hire … the best lawyers in the world. That becomes expensive.').

As one interviewee noted, parties do not always want the more expensive process requested by their counsel:

> I know there are some arbitrators who say that if the parties have agreed to certain procedures there is nothing they can do, and I disagree with that strongly.… I don't equate the parties and their counsel. Sometimes counsel have a different interest. Sometimes counsel don't know that cases can be run in a different way or they don't explain it to their clients. I think part of the job of arbitrators is to speak directly to the parties and make sure that they are comfortable with the proceedings and show them the way the case can best be handled.

On the other hand, some interviewees indicated that counsel are more likely to be sympathetic to streamlined procedures than their clients. As one interviewee pointed out:

> If you've got responsible counsel and responsible parties who are there to fight, then you've got to get on with it. You can't wave a magic wand and say 'This dispute is going to be settled through high-minded clap-trap in blogs or in articles or in guidelines or in whatever.' People are there to fight. And, in the serious case, where there is a lot of money at stake, there is not a client I have ever met who will say, 'Oh but you know I read this article about saving costs in arbitration, so

[183] Art 16(1).

[184] Art 14.1(ii). See Crowter and Tobin 2002, 304, praising the LCIA Rules for placing upon tribunals an affirmative duty to adopt efficient procedures.

[185] Rivkin 2008. [186] Ibid, 381.

[187] Another interviewee concurred: 'People tend to argue everything, some might actually say they argue too much. There's actually lack of discrimination about what's a good case and what's a bad case. Chuck absolutely everything at it. Even the best law firms in the world, the most prestigious law firms, you see in their pleadings they chase everything.'

let's just be cautious about the documents we look for on discovery.' Not at all. The instructions are: 'Leave no stone unturned.'

Encouraging settlements

Many arbitrators consider it their duty to move the parties toward settlement.[188] In one survey, 'a large majority of respondents (86%) thought that facilitating a consensual solution is one of the functions of the arbitral process'.[189] In another, several respondents indicated they were more likely to settle disputes in arbitration than those before a national court.[190] By contrast, while judges do encourage settlements and issue orders intended to expedite cases in front of them, their concern is as much with waste of the court's time as it is with waste of the parties' money.[191] Thus, for example, the Civil Procedure Rules (CPR) of England and Wales require judges actively to manage cases, including helping the parties to settle[192] or encouraging them to use an alternative dispute resolution procedure.[193] However, in considering what courses of action to take, judges are to keep in mind an overriding objective of the CPR, that cases should be allotted 'an appropriate share of the court's resources, while taking into account the need to allot resources to other cases'.[194]

The topic of settlements seemed to cause some angst among the interviewees; it was one of the few areas of significant disagreement between them. The responses fell roughly into four groups, which are distinguishable on the basis that each of the four groups prioritized a different ICA social norm.

The first group of interviewees emphasized the nature of the arbitrators' relationship to the parties—that they have been hired to provide the specific service of ruling on the dispute. If the parties want a halt to proceedings in order to settle, the arbitrator should grant it, but should not otherwise get involved. As one interviewee put it:

> I don't think that's a core function of an arbitrator. Plainly there can be instances where the arbitration process helps the parties to focus on the issues involved and contributes to a settlement. Plainly the arbitration process can be flexible in allowing the parties that want to achieve a settlement to do it, in terms of schedules and postponements and other kinds of flexibility.... But I don't think encouraging settlement *per se* is part of what arbitrators should really appropriately be doing.

Another interviewee explained his practice of giving space for settlement without actually encouraging it: 'I might decide liability and then say, "Hope you can agree on quantum on the basis of the findings on liability. But if you can't, come back." And I often say that on costs. "Here's the award, if you can deal with costs by yourself do so, but if you can't, come back."'

The second group of interviewees, which was the largest, acknowledged that settlements are often in the parties' economic interests[195] but expressed the concern that

---

188 See generally M Collins 2003.

189 Bühring-Uhle et al 2003, 82.

190 PwC/QMUL 2008, 6. However, this effect cannot be entirely put down to encouragement by the arbitrators; 43% of settlements occurred before the first hearing. Ibid, 7.

191 Of course, judges encourage settlements for reasons other than merely to clear their dockets. Here, too, culture may play a role; for example, Japanese judges, like Japanese arbitrators, are known to take an active role in encouraging settlements. Cole 2007, 32.

192 s 1.4(f).

193 s 1.4(e).

194 s1.1(e).

195 One interviewee noted that, in his experience, more cases are settling than in the past. He ascribes this to the current poor economy: 'The last two years, I've had a much higher rate of settlement ... than I have ever had before. I think that's a ramification of the economic times we are

proactive efforts to secure a settlement would impact their neutrality and leave an eventual award open to challenge. As one put it, if the arbitrators were to share their preliminary opinions on any point of fact or law: 'In my view you could overturn the award. You can't indicate that you've made up your mind until the end of the arbitration.' Another interviewee, a former judge, said: 'You have to be careful because you don't know enough about the case, you have to do it very cautiously. I came closest to it as a judge, and people then say "He made up his mind against us."' One interviewee, an engineering/construction specialist, expressed his concerns thus:

> Once you start to get involved in the terms of settlement you're losing your neutrality. If you've got a lot of experience in the engineering-construction field … and someone comes to you with some draft terms, you look at them and you can see, this one could be tightened up to the advantage of party A and that one could be tightened up to the advantage of party B. So whatever you say you're actually not being neutral. You're assisting one or the other party. So you simply can't get involved in drafting terms.

The third group of interviewees appealed to party autonomy, arguing that arbitrators may get involved with settlement discussions, but only if the parties specifically request it and expressly agree to every step. An Australian interviewee pointed out the broader context within which disputes come to arbitration:

> International arbitration is expensive and time consuming. Invariably, the parties try to negotiate. It would be outstanding if they didn't try to negotiate. Arbitrations are a last resort. It's pretty naïve to say to the parties, 'Have you considered trying to resolve this amicably?' You know they got big law firms involved. Of course they know the ropes. It is very, very occasionally appropriate to say something.[196]

These interviewees tended to emphasize the limits of arbitrators' understanding of the dispute. One pointed out that settlement negotiations may well be ongoing during the arbitration without the tribunal's knowledge:

> When I sit as an arbitrator it sometimes seems to me that my colleagues believe themselves to see things—particularly my older colleagues—that the parties don't see. I'm not so sure. When I am engaged as counsel, often there is an awful lot going on, with respect to consensual resolution and possible settlements and what have you, I don't think the arbitrators are aware of.

Another interviewee observed that the tribunal is often not privy to the commercial context within which the dispute arose, and therefore cannot know whether a settlement is possible or even appropriate:

> You will probably know little about the true commercial interests of the parties because sometimes the case is mysterious. Why are they fighting? The answer is they're not fighting so much about this, they're fighting about something else. The two managers on either side never saw eye-to-eye; that's why they are here today, because it's a personal dispute. It may be driven by natural reasons, it may be driven by the bank … You may take a course which actually undermines the position of the parties to achieve a settlement because you've taken away a bit of leverage, unintentionally, which one party needed to have.

living through. Companies may not have the resources—or might not wish to expend enormous resources—on a big case. They might find that the respondents don't have much money and there is not much point in continuing the arbitration.'

[196] Another interviewee, a London-based barrister, made a similar observation: 'A point comes where you have to be sensitive to the fact that, if they have come this far in the process, then they are here for a reason and they may simply say "We are here to have this decided upon".'

The last group of arbitrators felt that their duty to help the parties resolve their dispute in an economical fashion outweighed other considerations. Most but not all of these arbitrators were trained primarily in Germany or Switzerland, which have a long tradition of judges encouraging settlements and a reputation for arbitrators who are active in settling disputes. These arbitrators tended to emphasize the limits of the parties' understanding of the 'big picture'. One arbitrator, a Swiss law firm partner, described his motivations for encouraging settlements:

Very often parties can lose themselves in wrong arguments ... and so the case evolves and develops and gets lost in a lot of details and a lot of bad places that are not important, not relevant. That costs a lot of money and takes a lot of time. I think that it is helpful after the first or second exchange of briefs, that you sit together with the parties and that the arbitrators—but generally only if the parties agree to it—present their preliminary opinions on the basis of the evidence that has so far been produced ... I call them preliminary views conferences. Hopefully, you also encourage the parties to not only be present with their attorneys, but also with people from management who are responsible for the case so they get a first hand impression of what may come, in terms of the decision.

Another interviewee expressed this point of view more plainly. When asked if it his policy to encourage settlements, he replied: 'Only if you thought you needed to say it because somebody needed to hear it.'

Other manifestations of the service mindset

The drive for efficiency also affects other aspects of arbitration. The tendency of tribunals to admit extrinsic evidence of the parties' intentions when interpreting contracts[197] can also be explained by tribunals' desire to serve the interests of the parties before them and of business generally. Although considering a wide range of extrinsic evidence may lengthen proceedings, there are compensations. Eschewing the complex common law procedural rules decreases the number and complexity of motions and submissions to be prepared by counsel and thus shortens the proceedings and reduces the cost. Moreover, objective interpretation and the exclusionary rules, whatever their merits, often confuse litigants and lead to results that appear unfair:

The by-product of almost every parol evidence dispute is a client who is angry either because he has not been given his day in court or because the opposing party has been permitted to prove [the existence of] an oral agreement that the client claims was not made and which his attorney assured him could not be proven.[198]

Arbitrators also serve the interests of the parties in the way they exercise their power to choose directly the substantive law applicable to the dispute (absent a choice by the parties). In practice, choosing the applicable law via a direct choice (*voie directe*) most often 'consists in finding a significant connecting factor between the contract and the law which the arbitrator decides to apply'.[199] Accordingly, choice of law under *voie directe* frequently yields the same law that application of a country's choice of law rules would provide. However, *voie directe* has also been employed in a manner designed to give voice to party autonomy in cases where the parties have not agreed on an applicable law. A 1984 ICC award provides an example. There, the contract did not specify the

197 See Chapter 7.

198 Sweet 1968, 1046.

199 Derains 1996, 521.

governing law, and the law of Switzerland and of another country were the only laws connected to the contract. The tribunal directly applied Swiss law, on the ground that:

> ... the law of country X might partially or totally affect the validity of the agreement.
> It is then reasonable to assume that from two possible laws, the parties would choose the law which would uphold the validity of the agreement....[200]

The reasoning employed by the tribunal is analogous to the *in favorem validatis* doctrine, common to both civil law and common law jurisdictions, according which contracts should be construed to make them valid because the parties could not have intended to enter into an invalid contract. The arbitrators must have felt that, although they were making the choice of law, the best way to proceed was to determine the presumed intention of the parties with respect to the applicable law. Thus, arbitrators strive to apply the parties' intentions, even where the parties have not expressed their intentions.

Arbitrators' use of their *voie directe* power to give voice to the parties' unexpressed but presumed intentions also helps to improve the efficiency of the choice of law process. It is often observed that, traditionally, the choice of law process has been marred by complexity and uncertainty,[201] although the increasing resort to presumptions about the parties' intent makes choice of law in some national courts more predictable than it has been in the past.[202] Such uncertainty imposes systemic costs:

> Uncertainty at the time of contracting means that the parties cannot easily determine the standard of conduct to which they should conform or how to price contract rights and duties.... Uncertainty about choice of law at the time of litigation can increase both the costs and frequency of litigation.[203]

In general, managing risk associated with the application of an unforeseen substantive law is of interest to parties in international commerce. More specifically, Ribstein has identified a number of reasons why parties might want to specify a particular governing law in their contract: to avoid mandatory rules in the national law that would otherwise be held to be the proper law of the contract, to avoid the uncertainty of the choice of law process and to protect against post-contractual opportunism by a party seeking to change the law (as in a contract with a foreign sovereign).[204] Arbitrators, by the way they use their power to make a *voie directe*, help to reduce the costs associated with the application of a law unforeseen by the parties at the time they concluded their contract.

2. The 'specific needs' of international commerce

In a much-quoted passage, Justice White of the US Supreme Court wrote that arbitrators should not be held to standards of 'judicial decorum' because arbitrators' effectiveness depends on them being 'men of affairs, not apart from the marketplace'.[205] It is

[200] ICC Case No 4145 of 1984 (1987) XII Ybk Comm Arb 97. See also ICC Case No 7154 of 1993 [1994] JDI 1059, where the tribunal reached a similar result for the same reason.

[201] Berger 2010, 10, citing various German-language sources characterizing choice of law in courts as 'a jump in the dark'.

[202] Especially in those jurisdictions covered by the Rome I Regulation.

[203] Ribstein 1993, 254.

[204] Ibid, 247–55.

[205] *Commonwealth Coatings Corp v Cont'l Casualty Corp*, 393 US 145, 150 (1968), reh'g denied, 393 US 1112 (1969).

no accident that many of the world's international arbitral institutions (and most of those located in civil law jurisdictions) are attached to chambers of commerce. Such institutions benefit from 'a double sponsorship—that of the world of business, since the parent organization remains a major business group, and that of the world of learned jurists'.[206] Arbitrators have come to see themselves as actors not just in an international legal system, but in international commerce as well. One interviewee contrasted the arbitral and judicial roles on the basis that arbitrators play a constructive role in improving commercial relationships:

> What you want when you are an arbitrator is somehow to be constructive, as opposed to a judge, which I think can be quite a destructive way of acting, in the sense that you keep breaking relationships. As an arbitrator you are, of course, asked to break relationships, but sometimes in certain cases there is scope for a role to allow business to carry on, just generally, to be part of the wheels of business. And to basically, perhaps, be on hand ... to allow skirmishes to be smoothed over. It's a more constructive way of adjudicating than a judge. I have never been a judge but that's my impression.

Many arbitrators maintain that developing a robust system of private international dispute resolution was a precondition to the emergence of the modern era of globalized commerce. Briner, a former President of the Iran–United States Claims Tribunal, writes:

> [A]rbitration accompanied the growth of international commerce. It saw its role as offering the tools best suited to international business to resolve disputes whenever they arose. The major institutions especially see their role in facilitating the growth of international business by offering the necessary tools to resolve the disputes arising in international business.[207]

As Lew puts it, arbitration has 'survived the test of time ... because it has served the users well. It has met the needs of those business entities which have considered national courts to be unsuited to their needs.'[208] Dezalay and Garth argue that, since a commercial system cannot function without an effective, predictable, and legitimate dispute resolution system, arbitration is itself a commercial institution:

> The workings of international commercial arbitration have a considerable impact on the security of business investments and on the transaction costs of resolving transnational disputes. International commercial arbitration, therefore, should be seen as a key institution in the structuring of international markets.[209]

Trakman comes to a similar conclusion: 'Despite the fragmentation of global trade along bilateral and regional lines, international commercial arbitration has remained a vital, yet adaptable, constant in the world trade equation.'[210]

Many arbitrators appear to have taken the small step from seeing themselves as an integral part of a system to seeing themselves as indispensable to the system's functioning. For example, international arbitrators tend to overestimate the share of international commercial disputes that are resolved by arbitration. Berger asserts that: 'About ninety percent of international economic contracts contain an arbitration clause.'[211]

[206] Dezalay and Garth 1996, 45, referring specifically to the ICC.

[207] Briner 2000, 444. [208] Lew 2006, 180.

[209] Dezalay and Garth 1996, 7. See also Drahozal 2000, 107, calling international lawyers 'transaction cost engineers', citing RJ Gilson, 'Value Creation by Business Lawyers: Legal Skills and Asset Pricing' (1984) 94(2) Yale LJ 239, 253–6.

[210] Trakman 2006, 29.

[211] Berger 1993, 8 fn 62. A similar claim is made in A van den Berg, *Arbitragerecht* (WEJ Tjeenk Willink, Zwolle 1988) 134.

However, as Born notes, the 90 per cent figure 'lacks empirical support and is almost certainly substantially inflated: in reality, significant numbers of international commercial transactions—certainly much more than 10% of all contracts—contain either forum selection clauses or no dispute resolution provision at all'.[212] In a 2010 survey, 50 per cent of multinational companies that had a dispute resolution policy in place reported that their policies either required arbitration or preferred it to state court litigation.[213] In addition, as discussed above in Chapter 3, proponents of ICA are apt to engage in a kind of arbitral apologetics, proclaiming arbitration's virtues in every possible forum.[214] Such writings are, to an extent, mere marketing; if fewer parties choose arbitration, then arbitrators as a group will lose business. Judges, on the other hand, have no personal stake in the number of cases brought to court.[215]

Dismissing arbitral apologetics as no more than self-promotion is unfair. Many arbitrators believe passionately in the essential role of arbitration within international business and, in particular, in arbitration's superiority over litigation for the resolution of international commercial disputes. Arguments for arbitration's indispensability often take the form of a list of the general deficiencies of litigation, such as its purported slowness and expense in comparison with arbitration. However, arbitrators are most likely to cite the 'inability' of litigation to respond to the 'specific needs' of international commercial dispute resolution.[216]

Such factors as informality of procedure and cost-effectiveness are the most visible ways in which ICA responds to the needs of business, but arguably more important is the commercial mentality that arbitrators bring to their decision-making. As business norms and practices evolve, arbitrators endeavour to keep up. Dezalay and Garth write that 'the increasing importance of particularism in law, especially in commercial law, comes from pressure exercised by merchants to have their legal affairs treated by specialized experts'.[217] By contrast, arbitral commentators assert, the legal principles applied by courts have always lagged behind evolving commercial usages:

> In the Middle Ages, the regular courts were interested primarily in property disputes and breaches of the King's peace. The 'gap' between accepted trade practices and the Common Law, which was devoid of mercantile custom, made those courts inappropriate. Judges who were ignorant of commercial norms compounded the problem.[218]

Arbitrators continue to point out various ways in which national laws are inadequate to the task of regulating modern international commerce. For example, in ICC Case No 9427 of 1998, the dispute concerned an on-demand guarantee. The governing law, that of a Baltic state, had no provisions dealing specifically with on-demand guarantees.

212 Born 2009, 70. Born allows that in cross-border commercial (as opposed to financial) transactions, the parties are 'more likely than not' to include an arbitration clause in their contracts. This figure 'permits one to fairly say that international arbitration is the preferred means for contractual dispute resolution, but more ambitious statistical claims are unsustainable.'

213 W&C/QMUL 2010, 6.

214 See Chapter 3, Section IV.3.

215 That said, judges have raised concerns regarding the migration of commercial cases out of the courts and into arbitration. In particular, some have worried that the diminishing number of commercial disputes that go to trial (either because the parties settle or because they resort to alternative dispute resolution) means that commercial law is not developing properly or evolving to reflect changing commercial circumstances. See, eg, Haarhuis and Niemeijer 2006 (concerning the Netherlands); Galanter 2004 (concerning the US). However, the expression of such concerns supports the underlying contention that judges' primary concerns are systemic, while arbitrators' primary concerns are with the parties.

216 Petsche 2005, 10; and Cuniberti 2009.

217 Dezalay and Garth 1996, 117 (citation omitted).

218 For example, bills of exchange, which came into common use by the mid-16th century, were not recognized in law until the late 17th century. Yarn 2004, 970 (citation omitted).

The tribunal 'decided to apply such legal principles relating to on-demand guarantees which are generally applied in international banking practice'.[219] Thus, faced with a gap in the applicable national law, the tribunal applied general principles, notwithstanding that neither party had asked the tribunal to do so.

Arbitrators also distinguish themselves from national court judges by touting their own commercial expertise. Although there exist courts with special expertise in commercial disputes (most notably the Commercial Court in London and Delaware's Chancery Court),[220] most national courts are of general jurisdiction. Judges therefore hear all types of cases and are unlikely to have special expertise in commercial matters. International arbitrators, on the other hand, tend to adjudicate only commercial and investment disputes, and may develop specialties in particular commercial sectors, such as construction or oil and gas. By choosing arbitration, parties can choose adjudicators who are expert not only in the applicable law but also in relevant commercial norms and practices.[221]

Interviewees were unanimous in expressing their view that commercial experience and a commercial perspective are essential for effective arbitration. To be effective, arbitrators must understand the commercial context of disputes. One interviewee, a partner at a Swiss law firm, expressed this idea:

> You have to have good analytical skills, so that in a short time you get to know what the case is about, you're able to discern the interests of the parties that lie behind their positions and that means you have to have a certain commercial experience, and I think that the best arbitrators are those that have a long career behind them as advisors to parties to commercial transactions.[222]

A London-based barrister, with extensive experience in both arbitration and litigation, put the point in these terms:

> Parties want you to understand that they've got a big commercial dispute which is a real burden for them and they're trying to cope with it as best they can. It's costing them a lot of money, it's taking up huge amounts of management time and you need to be sympathetic to the commercial background that both parties will be experiencing in fighting a major case. Judges in my experience are often quite oblivious to all this commercial background.

Another way in which arbitrators distinguish themselves from judges on the basis of specialized expertise is in their use of transnational contract law. Since transnational contract law—in codified or uncodified form—is generally unavailable (or simply not raised) in national court proceedings,[223] judges are unlikely to gain much expertise with it. Transnational contract law therefore functions as a *droit savant*—a specialized field of knowledge understood only by specialists.[224] It is telling that arbitrators are most likely to refer to general principles when the applicable national law provides no rules or no commercially sensible rules to resolve a legal issue.[225] As one interviewee put it:

> The UNIDROIT Principles are statements of the obvious, and only really useful in countries which have no developed system of law. For example, if you go to Central Asia then you have to

[219] ICC Case No 9427 of 1998 (2002) XXVII Ybk Comm Arb 153 [7].

[220] On such specialist courts and their relationship with ICA, see Drahozal 2009b.

[221] Smit 1986, 15; see also Kitagawa 1967, 133, arguing that there are very few judges 'competent to manage foreign transactions'.

[222] A similar point was made by a Canadian interviewee, who observed that facility with numbers is an important but underrated skill.

[223] See Chapter 5, Section II.2.

[224] Dezalay and Garth 1996, 91.

[225] See Section V of this chapter.

use *lex mercatoria*. No one really knows what the answer is. If you applied the law ... you won't find the answer there, or the answer wouldn't be acceptable, so you have to reach for something else.'

More generally, attention to the 'specific needs' of international business gives rise to a commercial mentality that exists alongside a legal mentality in the minds of arbitrators. One interviewee said simply: 'I like to think my approach would be fact-based and commercial in nature. In other words, if at all possible to focus on the basic business aspects of the case.' Hermann declares more broadly that: 'It is fundamental to arbitration that it should solve disputes according to commercial practice and common sense, arriving at a result considered fair in a particular business community.'[226] Collins contrasts what he sees as the 'commercial reasoning' employed by arbitrators with the 'private law reasoning' employed by courts:

Private law reasoning is relatively closed to the competing normative considerations governing contractual behaviour outside the discrete communications system provided by the formal contract itself. As a result, it cannot translate expectations grounded in business relations ... into its default standards for regulation. Commercial arbitration appears to be favoured precisely because it can provide ... reasoning which marries adjudicated outcomes with business expectations more closely.[227]

This mindset is exemplified by one interviewee who said that there are really only two rules of contractual interpretation: 'Common sense is one. Commercial sense is the other.'

The primary practical manifestation of this commercial mentality is the primacy given in arbitral awards to arguments based on trade usages and commercial reasonableness. As Schmitthoff notes: 'The interaction between international commercial usage and international arbitration is very close.'[228] Cremades makes a similar observation: 'International arbitrators have always been closer, and thus more familiar with, the usages and practices of international commercial trade than local judges.'[229] Arbitrators thus oblige what they see as the preference of businesses to be judged according to the standards of their industries, and not according to a priori rules of general contract law imposed upon them by the legal system.

Trade usages can be successfully pleaded in court if the party relying on the usage proves both that the usage is regularly observed in the industry in question and that the opposing party was aware of the usage.[230] In an apparent exception to their usual deference to party autonomy, arbitral tribunals sometimes apply trade usages when the parties have not raised them, and may find that a trade usage governs even absent evidence that the parties were aware of it.[231] For example, in ICC Case No 7661 of 1995, the

226 Hermann 1983, 221.
227 H Collins 1999, 187.
228 Schmitthoff 1985, 23.
229 Cremades 1999, 167.
230 For a usage to be incorporated into a contract under English law, there must be evidence that the parties implicitly intended to be bound by the usage; this requires evidence that both parties were actually aware of the usage and that the usage is consistent with the express terms of the contract. Cheshire, Fifoot, and Furmston 2001, 146–7.
231 Under the major international contract law instruments, parties are deemed to be aware of relevant trade usages and must take active steps to inform themselves. With respect to the CISG, see Schmidt-Kessel 'Art 9' 2010, 191. (Under CISG art 9(2), if it can be shown that a relevant usage is 'objectively known', then a 'lack of due care' is imputed to a party that claims ignorance of the usage.) With respect to general principles, the online CENTRAL compilation of *lex mercatoria* rules, Principle I.2.2, adopts a similar position: <http://www.trans-lex.org/output.php?docid=903000> accessed 20 July 2012. This reversal of the standard posture in domestic legal systems indicates the greater deference to trade usages in international than in national commercial laws.

tribunal argued that it was 'unlikely that a seller would accept a lower price to account for an event, known or unknown, that may never happen'. Consequently, the tribunal found that the contract did not include a guarantee against certain unforeseen financial contingencies.[232] In ICC Case No 9443 of 1998, the tribunal considered a contractual obligation that, on its plain language, was perpetually renewable unless both parties expressly repudiated it. The tribunal interpreted the term differently, on the ground that 'such an obligation is irreconcilable with general principles of international commerce. It is unimaginable that two corporations will be obliged to cooperate eternally without one or the other being able to put a stop to the cooperation.'[233]

Parties' attempts to exclude the application of trade usages may not deter tribunals. For example, in ICC Case No 8873 of 1997, the contract contained an express term that it was governed entirely by Spanish law, to the exclusion of all other laws.[234] Nevertheless, the tribunal found that it had also to consider 'international commercial usages', which for the tribunal meant a consideration of the *lex mercatoria*.[235] In the tribunal's conception, the *lex mercatoria* is not a 'law', but rather must always apply to international disputes because it embodies international trade usages.

There are even cases where arbitral tribunals disregarded express contractual or statutory terms in light of trade usages. Such cases are explicable on the basis that the norm in favour of trade usages is consistent with party autonomy; tribunals appear to assume that, regardless of their express agreement, parties also intend to be bound by applicable trade usages. For example, ICC Case No 3820 of 1981 involved a sale of food products in instalments. Payment was to be by documentary credit, which provided that the seller could draw down the credit, 'provided goods have been received by opener'. The buyer refused the goods and argued that this meant that it had not received the goods, so the preconditions for payment had not been met. The Dutch sole arbitrator wrote that documentary credits must be interpreted 'not ... in accordance with specific national laws ... but in accordance with the practices that apply on this subject in international trade'. He held that, contrary to its express terms, the letter of credit must be read to include situations where 'the opener could have received the goods if he had wanted to'.[236]

Institutional rules of arbitration and national arbitration laws reflect arbitrators' desire to ensure that applicable trade usages be enforced. Article 21(2) of the ICC Rules

[232] ICC Case No 7661 of 1995 (1997) XXII Ybk Comm Arb 149 [17]. While this can be seen as simply an application of common sense, and not a specific trade usage, it remains that such arguments are made from the point of view of practice rather than law. Another example of interpretation of a party's intent based on commercial reasonableness is consolidated ICC Cases Nos 6515 and 6516 of 1994 (1999) XXIVa Ybk Comm Arb 80 [15].

[233] ICC Case No 9443 of 1998 [2002] JDI 1106 (author's translation): '*Un tel engagement serait également inconciliable avec les principes généraux du commerce international. Il est par exemple inimaginable que deux sociétés puissent s'obliger à coopérer éternellement sans que l'une ou l'ature puisse mettre fin à la coopération.*'

[234] ICC Case No 8873 of 1997 [1998] JDI 1017: '*Ce Contrat sera entièrement régi par le droit espagnol, à l'exclusion de tout autre droit.*'

[235] Ibid: '*on devra prendre en considération également, dans le contexte de la loi nationale choisie par les parties, les usages de commerce international*'.

[236] ICC Case No 3820 of 1981 (1982) VII Ybk Comm Arb 134, 136. See also ICC Case No 7063 of 1993 (1997) XXII Ybk Comm Arb 87, awarding interest at the prevailing rate of inflation despite acknowledging that an applicable provision of Saudi law prohibited an award of interest; ICC Case No 3316 of 1979 (1982) VII Ybk Comm Arb 106, holding that, in a documentary credit, 'unconditional' should not be interpreted literally, since in banking practice it is often used as a synonym for 'irrevocable'.

requires that: 'The arbitral tribunal shall take account of the provisions of the contract, if any, between the parties and of any relevant trade usages.' This is so regardless of the applicable law.[237] A survey of ICC awards indicates that ICC tribunals have regularly cited the previous versions of rule 21(2).[238]

The ICC rule is not an isolated example. In a 2000 survey of arbitral institutions, Drahozal found that thirty-two of the forty-four largest commercial arbitration institutions require arbitrators to take trade usages into account.[239] As for national arbitration laws, prior to 1985, references to trade usages were rare.[240] Since 1985, the situation has changed dramatically; most statutes enacted or amended after that date contain provisions requiring arbitrators to take trade usages into account.[241] This trend is likely to continue because businesses are well served by processes that judge their behaviour according to the standards specific to their industries.

The *lex mercatoria* can also be seen as a manifestation of arbitrators' preference for trade usages, and of their belief that the parties also prefer to be governed by trade usages. One conception of the *lex mercatoria* is as the set of trade usages specifically 'adapted to the conditions of international commerce'.[242] In ICC Case No 8365 of 1996, the respondent contested the applicability of *lex mercatoria* on the ground that it is not a complete system of law, that it can only serve to fill gaps in and help interpret the applicable national law, and that the enforceability of an award founded on *lex mercatoria* was therefore doubtful.[243] Nevertheless, in the absence of a choice of law by the parties, the tribunal decided to apply 'the terms of the contract and trade usages'. It also referred to 'international arbitral precedent', which it characterized as: 'largely applying … general principles of law, trade usages and international customary law, or *lex mercatoria*'.[244] Indeed, proponents of *lex mercatoria* argue that the universalized, formalized language of *lex mercatoria* gives a patina of law to what are essentially trade usages, enhancing their legitimacy as a basis for arbitral decision making.[245]

IV. Neutrality

The neutrality of the adjudicator is an essential aspect of any legitimate system of adjudication, but a neutral judge is not the same thing as a neutral forum. In the context of international commerce, national court systems are institutionally incapable of being entirely neutral as between the parties. ICA, on the other hand, is institutionally

[237] Craig, Park, and Paulsson 2001, 331.

[238] See, eg, ICC Case No 6527 of 1991 (1993) XVIII Ybk Comm Arb 44; ICC Case No 5713 of 1989 (1990) XV Ybk Comm Arb 70; ICC Case No 5314 of 1988 (1995) XX Ybk Comm Arb 35; ICC Case No 5485 of 18 Aug 1987 (1989) XIV Ybk Comm Arb 156; ICC Case No 4237 of 1984 (1985) X Ybk Comm Arb 52; ICC Case No 3540 of 1980 (1982) VII Ybk Comm Arb 124; ICC Case No 3493 of 1983 (1984) IX Ybk Comm Arb 111; ICC Case No 3380 of 1980 (1982) VII Ybk Comm Arb 116; ICC Case No 2930 of 1982 (1984) IX Ybk Comm Arb 105.

[239] Drahozal 2000, 112.

[240] Ibid, 118.

[241] English translations of these statutes are collected in International Handbook 2010. This trend is traceable in part to the enactment since 1985 of approximately seventy statutes based on the UNCITRAL Model Law, which includes a provision to this effect, art 28(4).

[242] ICC Case No 8385 of 1995 [1997] JDI 1061 (author's translation). Petsche 2005, 15; see also Flood 1996, 170; Rogers 2002, 351–2. For a similar characterization of the medieval *lex mercatoria*, see Berman and Kaufman 1978, 225.

[243] ICC Case No 8365 of 1996 [1997] JDI 1078.

[244] Ibid, 1079 (author's translation).

[245] Cf Flood 1996, 170.

neutral. Arbitrations do not take place in the home court of either party.[246] Neither party is more familiar with the procedures than the other; neither is put at a linguistic disadvantage; neither takes the risk that the judge will be a xenophobe or that the laws will be biased against foreign parties.[247] Resolution of international commercial disputes by arbitration means that neither party is a 'foreign' party.[248] Commentators assert that the neutrality of the arbitral forum is one of the most important reasons parties choose arbitration over litigation,[249] an assertion that is supported by surveys.[250]

Interviewees echoed these concerns. Several made the point that, for modern cross-border commercial disputes, arbitration is the only viable choice, since neither party will be willing to submit to the other's home courts. One interviewee said that avoiding each other's national courts is 'by far the most important consideration' for parties. Another said of ICA: 'internationally it's the only way of resolving disputes. It gives a neutral forum to both parties and gives them a real opportunity to present their own case, with their own lawyers, in the language of the contract'. A third called arbitration 'the only game in town' for companies engaged in cross-border commerce.

Park argues that without the existence of the neutral forum provided by arbitration, modern cross-border commerce would be much diminished:

> The special *raison d'être* of international arbitration means that the parties often place a premium on freedom from the type of judicial scrutiny that would impinge on procedural neutrality.... the prospect of foreign court intervention will chill cross-border economic cooperation....[251]

Even when outright xenophobia is not implicated, parties often face difficulties when litigating in foreign courts, a phenomenon that has been acknowledged by national court judges. In *Fiona Trust v Privalov*, Lord Hoffman noted that parties choose arbitration 'on the grounds of ... neutrality, expertise and privacy.... they ... do not want to take risks of delay and, in too many cases, partiality, in proceedings before a national jurisdiction'.[252] The fact that arbitrators are not officials of the states in which the proceedings take place is particularly important when state entities are parties to the disputes.

1. Neutrality as a social norm

Arbitration's reputation for neutrality is perhaps surprising. While the arbitral forum is neutral, the institutional structure of arbitration is such that individual arbitrators ought to be *less* neutral than national court judges. Neutrality requires independence and impartiality—that the adjudicator must be neither objectively beholden to a party nor subjectively biased.[253] Compared with national court judges, arbitrators are both more beholden to parties (because they depend on the parties for appointments) and more likely to have previously expressed opinions on factual or legal issues related to

[246] Franck 2006, 501.

[247] See Park 2003, 1256: 'Absent reliable arbitration, judicial proceedings might go forward in a foreign language and perhaps before a xenophobic judge in a country lacking a tradition of judicial independence.'

[248] Franck 2006, 501, referring to arbitration as a 'geographical half-way house'.

[249] Redfern and Hunter 2004, 26; see also Fellas 2004, 79–80.

[250] Drahozal and Ware 2010, 452.

[251] Park 2003, 1257.

[252] *Fiona Trust & Holding Corp v Privalov* [2008] 1 Lloyd's Rep 254, 256 (HL).

[253] On the distinction between independence and impartiality, see Redfern and Hunter 2004, 238–9.

a dispute they are adjudicating (because they tend to publish in academic and trade journals).

Since ICA lacks the institutional force of state power and its own internal enforcement system, it depends on the perception of its legitimacy.[254] Yet, given the close and fluid professional relationships between arbitrators and counsel, one might be justified in concluding that bias and personal conflicts of interest are endemic to arbitration.

As discussed in the previous chapter, market competitive forces constrain arbitrators from acting in an overtly partial manner and constrain counsel from appointing biased arbitrators. Neutral arbitrators are clearly what the parties want: for both sole/presiding arbitrators and party-appointed arbitrators, 'open-mindedness and fairness' was cited as the most important factor in parties' decisions on whom to appoint.[255] Interviewees emphasized that open-mindedness is particularly important, given that the parties come from different countries with different legal systems and traditions. One said:

> The ... feature that I think marks a good arbitrator is just an open mind. An open mind towards different cultures, and a curiosity also for these different cultures. Which then in turn gives the parties a confidence that you will look at this case in a fair way and also, in recognition of their own position and of the values which exist in their cultures and made them act as they did.

Most parties will not appoint arbitrators who lack credibility with other members of the tribunal. Moreover, arbitrators are cautious not to create grounds for challenge to themselves or to their awards. As one interviewee ruefully said: 'Challenging arbitrators for conflict is a new way of appealing. You don't like the way the case is going so you find a conflict and try to get rid of the arbitrator.'

However, the threat of lost appointments is not, in itself, sufficient. There will always be some arbitrators who are willing to compromise their reputations on behalf of a repeat client. Perhaps more importantly, there will always be those who conclude that the close relationships between arbitrators and counsel and the existence of party-appointed arbitrators mean that conflicts of interest are not just prevalent in ICA, but systemic. A strong social norm constraining arbitral behaviour is therefore necessary not only for ICA to maintain neutrality (and therefore its legitimacy), but also to continue to market its neutrality as a selling point.

In their writings and awards, and in the interviews conducted for this book, arbitrators reveal the power of the neutrality norm. As Dezalay and Garth relate, arbitrators promote a 'cult of disinterestedness'.[256] Indeed, the arbitral literature is filled with praise for the exemplary neutrality of arbitrators and admonishments for arbitrators to maintain that neutrality.[257] In particular, arbitrators are well-advised to maintain what Park calls 'cultural neutrality', meaning that, if the parties' nationalities were reversed, the result would not change.[258] For this reason, it has become standard for the presiding arbitrator to be a 'prestigious foreigner', not only devoid of 'the interest or affiliations

[254] Park 2009, ix: 'If an evil gremlin sought to bring international arbitration into disrepute ... One course would be to allow service by biased arbitrators, thus tarnishing the neutrality of the arbitral process.'

[255] W&C/QMUL 2010, 25–6. [256] Dezalay and Garth 1996, 58.

[257] See, eg, Franck 2006, 506–7: 'Although all humans are inevitably influenced by their experiences, in international arbitration, parties ask arbitrators to put aside biases in order to fairly and impartially exercise their independent judgment and apply their expertise to the facts on the record to render a decision based upon the law.'; Redfern and Hunter 2004, 233: 'most experienced international arbitrators are adept at maintaining awareness of their own inbuilt preconceptions and ... cultural prejudice'.

[258] Park 1995, 103.

that would disqualify him in domestic arbitration, but also selected from a region and culture different from that of the parties involved'.[259] This is so regardless of whether the presiding arbitrator is chosen by the two party-appointed arbitrators or by the convening arbitral institution.

Of course, the fact that a potential chair's nationality is considered an important factor contradicts the assertions of many arbitrators that they can transcend their national backgrounds: 'When examining both procedural matters and the merits of the case, a chairman will have a natural tendency to refer to his national origins, however much they may be diluted and even modified by his or her international practice.'[260] Nationality restrictions are therefore common. The UK Supreme Court recently upheld the right of the parties to restrict potential arbitrators to persons of a particular religion or belief.[261] The same reasoning applies to restrictions on the nationality of arbitrators.[262]

The practice of appointing presiding arbitrators from a 'third country' accounts for the large number of arbitrators who come from small countries with reputations for neutrality (in particular Switzerland and Sweden). In one case, when the tribunal considered whether a contractual clause referring to the non-existent 'International Chamber of Commerce of Geneva' constituted a valid arbitration agreement, it reasoned: 'The defendant affirms that the "neutral aspect" of Switzerland was a determining factor for its decision. Hence, only a Swiss institution can be seized.'[263] Another example was given by a Francophone Canadian arbitrator, who cited this background as a professional advantage. Especially in arbitrations between American and European parties, a Canadian who speaks French is perceived by the parties as both neutral and able to understand their individual perspectives.

Like all social norms, neutrality in ICA is enforced by social sanctions meted out by other members of the community. Two clear examples were related given by a very senior arbitrator, who related two occasions where he publicly reprimanded co-arbitrators for acting in a non-neutral manner. (He noted that such occurrences are rare, but are more common in investor-state than commercial arbitrations.)

> I was chairing an important investor-state panel. The party appointed by the state asked a question which was suggestive against the argument of ... the counsel for the investor. He was a very distinguished arbitrator, but I objected to the question before any lawyer spoke. I said 'I will not allow the witness to answer that question.' My colleague looked at me. There was a pregnant pause, and he said 'I guess you're right, Mr. Chairman. I won't insist on an answer.' There is another case I remember ... again the arbitrator appointed by the state showed ... displeasure, if you wish, to a statement which was being made during the oral argument by counsel for the investor and it was obvious. I turned—and I said it loud enough for the parties to hear—I said, 'So and so, please be careful with your reactions during the hearing.' And [the reply came] ... 'I guess you're right. I apologize, Chairman.'

2. Neutrality in procedure and substance

Arbitral neutrality plays out in both the procedural and substantive spheres. Arbitrators and arbitral institutions strive to make their procedural rules neutral as between the

[259] Wilkey 1999, 80. [260] Webster 2003, 133.

[261] *Jivraj v Hashwani* [2011] UKSC 40. [262] See, eg, Gearing 2011.

[263] ICC Case No 7920 of 1993 (1998) XXIII Ybk Comm Arb 80 [11]. The Swiss reputation for neutrality is not absolute. Lowenfeld recalled an arbitration in which he served as a party-appointed arbitrator and experienced great difficulty in agreeing with the other party-appointed arbitrator on the identity of the presiding arbitrator: 'Another [candidate] was Swiss, in my judgment a very fair and conscientious arbitrator with whom I had worked in several other cases; he, too, was vetoed because "the Swiss are too favourable to multinational corporations".' Lowenfeld 1995, 63.

parties. After all, the parties may have chosen arbitration specifically to avoid national court procedures that would otherwise apply, procedures that give one party an advantage. A commonly cited example is the hostility with which many parties regard American-style document discovery.[264] International arbitral rules of procedure are therefore designed to be neutral, in that they resemble an international consensus of how an arbitration ought to proceed.[265] Lew describes only two limitations on the parties' and the tribunal's power to choose the procedures: applicable mandatory laws and the requirement to treat the parties 'fairly and equally'.[266] Failure to observe such fairness and equality constitutes grounds for courts to annul an award or refuse it recognition or enforcement.[267]

Arbitral rules of procedure are written to be neutral, but in deference to party autonomy, they generally permit the parties to contract for non-neutral procedures—so long as both parties have the opportunity to present their own cases and to hear the cases against them. The parties may choose to be governed by rules of procedure that are more familiar to one party than another, or choose to conduct the arbitration in one party's native language.

When the rules do not specify the procedures, and the parties do not make an agreement, arbitrators will often set the procedural rules ad hoc, either at the outset of an arbitration or as issues arise. In such cases 'a review of existing practice shows that such rules are generally pragmatic and seek to accommodate different procedural cultures whenever the actors come from different backgrounds'.[268] As one interviewee, a partner at a Swiss law firm, put it: 'the arbitrators … have to give both parties, coming from different cultures, the confidence that they can be taken seriously and that their needs and values are recognized'. Thus, when they have the opportunity to shape procedure, arbitrators act with an eye to protecting neutrality.

Similarly, several interviewees mentioned that the only occasion in which they would depart from acting neutrally between the parties is when one party seems to be at a severe disadvantage, typically due to counsel who are inexperienced in international arbitrations. Interviewees expressed a need for caution, but observed that their instinct toward providing a neutral dispute resolution procedure at times outweighs their caution. An experienced Australian arbitrator, who deals regularly with parties from developing states whose counsel may at times be 'outlawyered', characterized his practice:

> If one side has inexperienced counsel, and that does happen from time to time, there's sometimes the temptation to intervene. You have to be very careful, because each side has chosen its own counsel.… Tribunals have to be very careful not to be partial, not to help one side. If you take the attitude that you have to help one side, you are being partial. That's improper. But inevitably, there might be a little raising points here and there very discreetly. But you have to be extraordinarily cautious. It's a party's decision as to who they engage.

Arbitrators had little patience for more expert counsel who attempted to take advantage of the other side's inexperience. There were two situations that several interviewees

[264] See, eg, Stürner 2001, 15, characterizing US litigation as a 'procedural monster'.

[265] See generally Kaufmann-Kohler 2003, referring to the 'globalization' of arbitral procedure. For this reason, many arbitral institutions enact separate rules of procedure for domestic and international arbitrations.

[266] Lew 2006, 196.

[267] New York Convention, art V(1)(d); UNCITRAL Model Law, arts 18, 34(2)(a)(iv). See also Park 2003, 1264.

[268] Kaufmann-Kohler 2003, 1325 (citations omitted).

indicated would lead them to step in. The first was if counsel were badgering a witness who was unfamiliar with arbitration or who did not speak the language of the arbitration fluently. One interviewee, when asked whether he would step in if such a situation arose, said: 'If [the question] hasn't been understood, certainly, particularly with a foreign witness. Or if it's unfair actually.' The second situation that tended to irk arbitrators was when more experienced counsel raised multiple objections during the presentations or witness examinations of less experienced counsel. An interviewee observed:

> When you're in the tribunal, you have to ask yourself: do you trust counsel? You form your opinion as the case goes on. And you see whether you think counsel have been fair. Particularly in a case perhaps where a corporation is an East European company that has decided to represent itself with its own in-house lawyers and they're struggling. And then you're quite impressed if counsel on the other side recognize and give them a bit of slack, and aren't clever jumping up all the time.

When it comes to matters of substance, judges must apply the law neutrally as between the parties, but the laws that they apply may not themselves be neutral. A party is just as disadvantaged by having to work with unfamiliar foreign substantive law as it is by having to work with unfamiliar foreign procedures.[269] For this reason, parties often choose state substantive law based on their familiarity with the law and the fact that it is neither party's domestic law.[270]

In ICA, the neutrality norm also affects the substantive laws that arbitrators choose to apply. They not only apply the law neutrally as between the parties, but also choose laws that are neutral as between the parties. In other words, in ICA, the choice of substantive law is itself a tool to achieve neutrality. In ICC Case No 9771 of 2001, the tribunal reasoned that the mere fact that the parties had chosen to resolve their dispute by international arbitration meant that the parties could not have intended to apply either party's national law:

> It seems likely that the parties in this case—had they contemplated the matter—would not have been inclined to accept the case being treated with the application of the substantive law (or in the courts) of the other party's country. This may also be the reason why the parties agreed to have their dispute resolved in arbitration governed by the rules of an international arbitral institution.[271]

Similarly, in ICC Case No 7710 of 1995, the parties had not made a choice of law and had not conferred upon the tribunal amiable composition or *ex aequo et bono* powers. In such a context, reasoned the tribunal, 'one can only conclude that no national law can be judged adequate or suitable to regulate such transactions, without breaking the equilibrium of neutrality between the parties'.[272] Moreover, the mere fact that the

[269] 44 per cent of surveyed parties reported choosing their own national law if they were free to do so. If not, some sought choice of law agreements selecting a law similar to their own, including laws on which their national law was modeled (eg, Swiss law for Turkish parties) or laws that come from the same broad legal tradition (eg, American law for Canadian parties). W&C/QMUL 2010, 11–2.

[270] Indeed, this appears to be the most important factor in parties' choice of law. Ibid, 11. When parties choose a law other than their own national law, they most often choose English, Swiss, or New York law—all jurisdictions that are noted, among other things, for laws that are neutral with respect to the parties' nationalities and for judiciaries that are independent and highly professional. Ibid, 12.

[271] ICC Case No 9771 of 2001 (2004) XXIX Ybk Comm Arb 46 [18].

[272] ICC Case No 7710 of 1995 [2001] JDI 1148 (author's translation): '*on ne peut que conclure qu'aucune loi nationale a été jugée adéquate ou adaptée pour régir de telles transactions, sous peine de rompre l'équilibre de neutralité entres les parties*'.

parties submitted their dispute to ICC arbitration was 'clear proof ... that the parties preferred to delocalize the dispute resolution system with respect to all of their contracts in conformity with their strong preoccupation with regard to the neutrality of the substantive and procedural law'.[273]

In the ICA context, substantive neutrality means that the applicable rules must be derived from neither party's domestic law. The law of a third country could be selected, and sometimes the parties agree among themselves that a third country's law will apply. (For example, English law is popular for charterparties, regardless of the nationality of the parties.) In at least one case, a sole arbitrator considered applying (although he did not ultimately apply) the law of his own domicile as a neutral substantive law.[274]

However, choice of a third national law by the tribunal is considered by arbitrators to be an 'undesirable compromise', since instead of unequal familiarity, it usually engenders equal ignorance.[275] Instead, arbitrators tend to prefer to apply international contract law instruments or *lex mercatoria*. Often, application of general principles of international instruments is justified on the basis of neutrality. For example, in ICC Case No 10422 of 2001, the tribunal held: 'in the absence of an express choice of a third national law, the most appropriate solution in a case where it appears that the parties desire a neutral solution is to apply general principles of international contracts or *lex mercatoria*'.[276]

More generally, Petsche argues that arbitrators' participation in efforts to harmonize or unify the law of sales—either through the promulgation of international contract law instruments or the elaboration of general principles of international private law—is motivated by a desire to achieve neutrality:

> If ... the domestic laws of [different states] were identical, it would be irrelevant whether the laws of State A or those of State B apply. The achievement of substantive neutrality therefore requires uniformity of the law. This explains why international law-making efforts in the field of international commerce traditionally focus on the unification of the law.[277]

When making a *voie directe*, tribunals may choose to apply rules of law common to the legal systems of the parties' home states. This is called the '*tronc commun*' doctrine or 'cumulative application' of multiple laws.[278] In ICC Case No 7319 of 1992, the

[273] Ibid (author's translation): '*une preuve claire et la confirmation que les parties ont préféré la délocalisation du système de résolution des litiges eu égard à tous les Contrats en conformité avec leurs fortes préoccupations quant à la neutralité du cadre légal matériel et procédural dans leurs relations à long terme concrétisées par les Contrats*'.

[274] ICC Case No 8128 of 1995 [1996] JDI 1024. The parties were Austrian and Swiss and the arbitrator was German; the contract contained no choice of law.

[275] Petsche 2005, 14. Traditionally, many countries' courts refused to apply the law chosen by the parties if that law bore no relationship to the parties or to the transaction. Today, however, parties' right to choose the law of a country with no connection to the contract is generally acknowledged, except that mandatory laws of states connected to the dispute may have to be observed. See, eg, Rome I Regulation, art 3.3: 'Where all other elements relevant to the situation at the time of the choice are located in a country other than the country whose law has been chosen, the choice of the parties shall not prejudice the application of provisions of the law of that other country which cannot be derogated from by agreement.'

[276] ICC Case No 10422 of 2001 [2003] JDI 1142: '*à défaut d'indication expresse d'un tiers droit national, la solution la plus appropriée dans le cas où il apparaît que les parties désirent une solution neutre est d'appliquer les règles et principes généraux en matière de contrats internationaux ou lex mercatoria*'. See also ICC Case No 8128 of 1995 [1996] JDI 1024, applying the CISG on the basis that a 'neutral law' is desirable.

[277] Petsche 2005, 14. See, eg, ICC Case No 2886 of 1977 [1978] JDI 996.

[278] See generally Ancel 1990.

French and Irish parties failed to agree on the governing law. The sole arbitrator refused to apply either French or Irish law on the ground that this would be non-neutral; he also refused to apply general principles on the ground that the parties had not expressly or impliedly chosen them. Instead, he applied both French and Irish law cumulatively.[279]

Cumulative application of multiple national laws can also be employed in the choice of law process. In ICC Case No 12193 of 2004, the contract did not contain a choice of law clause. The parties were Lebanese and German and the seat of arbitration was Switzerland. The tribunal found that 'the cumulative application of the relevant conflicts rules ... on the one hand, of the parties' domiciles, and on the other hand, of the seat of arbitration, makes it possible to verify that these concur on the application of Lebanese law'.[280] Thus, the tribunal avoided the appearance of unfairness by demonstrating that various potential choice of law rules would yield the same result. Such methodology is also said to accord with party autonomy since the home laws of one party would not necessarily be known to—let alone consented to—by the other party; however, both parties 'can be expected to be conversant with provisions of law common to both of them'.[281] An interviewee made a similar point:

> A method which I like ... the cumulative method. You realize that the conflict of law rules in the country of the claimant is the same or points to the same law as the conflict of law rules of the other party. So you apply the law which is designated by both systems. That is equally predictable to both parties, so I think it's a good method.

A slight variation on this circumstance occurs in cases where the home law of one party clearly governs. In such circumstances, tribunals will sometimes note that the result would not have differed if the *other* party's home law had applied.[282] Several interviewees reported including such passages in their awards where possible. As a Swiss arbitrator put it:

> On the substance, I would try to look at all the legal systems that have contact with the facts and see if we can have common rules. There are different rules that can ... have the same sort of right or the same claim to be applied because they have contacts with the cases. I look at the substance of the rules to see if they are in fact compatible. It's a lot of work because there are always differences.... But I like to have alternative reasons so that I can say either law would have reached the same conclusion.

Such statements are legally gratuitous but do demonstrate the tribunal's commitment to substantive neutrality, and therefore enhance the legitimacy of the system, especially in the eyes of the losing party. One interviewee characterized this practice as intended purely to 'increase the acceptability of the award'.

V. Internationalism

'Internationalism' is defined here as a point of view that reflects a dedication to subordinating national perspectives and distinctions in favour of transnational or global

[279] ICC Case No 7319 of 1992 (1999) XXIV Ybk Comm Arb 141 [14].

[280] ICC Case No 12193 of 2004 [2007] JDI 1277 (author's translation): '*L'application cumulative des règles de conflit en présence, à savoir, d'une part celles des États dont les parties sont ressortissantes (le Liban et l'Allemagne), et d'autre part, celles du siège de l'arbitrage (la Suisse), permet de vérifier qu'elles convergent vers l'application du droit libanais.*'

[281] Ancel 1990, 67.

[282] This phenomenon is discussed further below, in the context of arbitrators' use of the comparative method. See Section V.3 of this chapter.

ideals. In practical terms, arbitral internationalism manifests itself in a desire among arbitrators to establish for arbitration an international space autonomous from national legal systems and traditions. Arbitral internationalism is related to the desire to detach arbitration from interference by national courts, but internationalism is rooted less in autonomy than in economic, social, and intellectual globalization.

The phenomenon of globalization does not reside only in institutions.[283] It is increasingly a mental and cultural phenomenon, a 'zeitgeist'.[284] ICA is thus part of a broader trend in the professions. Declining legal nationalism and greater acceptance of supranational and transnational decision-making bodies are trends that have been identified by socio-legal scholars. As Arthurs argues, even if institutions like the WTO were to dissolve and transnational trade and immigrant flows were to disappear: 'We would still be deeply implicated in a global system driven not only by trade and economics, but also by transnational social, cultural, intellectual and ideological forces ... a globalization of the mind.'[285]

This phenomenon has been observed in the legal profession. An academic literature has recently developed that explores transnational legal practice and new forms of globalization-related legal work.[286] Among practitioners, '[t]here is a long tradition in comparative and international law of the cosmopolitan lawyer working at the interface between legal orders'.[287] When business and trade become globalized, 'then there must also be a globalized sector of law'.[288] In recent years, the transnational, globalized sector of law has become both more relevant and more self-sufficient.[289] With an increasing number of lawyers working for multinational firms, and an increased ability of lawyers to become licensed in multiple countries, the practice of law itself increasingly crosses borders.[290]

Transnational legal practice arguably reaches its apogee in ICA:

> ... international arbitration is presently undergoing a process of harmonization in its basic notions ... [It] is uniquely and inevitably undergoing this process because, historically, it is

[283] International arbitral institutions are often themselves exemplars of globalization. For example, Grigera Naón sees the ICC as exemplifying the multicultural character of international commercial arbitration. Noting the multinational makeup of the ICC Court of Arbitration and of its secretariat, he concludes: 'All of this emphasizes the multicultural traits of the ICC arbitration system and guarantees the evenhanded administration of ICC arbitrations, free from cultural or other bias.' Grigera Naón 1999, 139.

[284] Flood 1996, 200. [285] Arthurs 1997, 222.

[286] See generally Terry et al 2008 (surveying developments related to the growth of transnational legal practice). For specific examples, see, eg, Roesler 2010, examining professional ethical standards in transnational human rights practice; Loza 2009, describing evolving, transnational standards of professional competence and responsibility; Rogers 2009, describing attempts by the American Bar Association to regulate cross-border practice by American-qualified lawyers; Terry 2009, describing similar efforts within the EU; Burkhart 2008, assessing the particular challenges of transnational real estate practice; Needham 2007, considering the role of foreign legal consultants in US law firm offices; Silver 2005, predicting the 'winners' and 'losers' from the globalization of legal services; Stewart and Conley 2007, calling for a common international approach to email service of process on foreign parties; von Mehren 2001, arguing that comparative legal training has a role to play in educating lawyers for transnational practice; Glenn 2000, describing an increase in judicial cooperation across borders; Abel 1994, arguing that US legal education has failed to adapt to the demands of transnational legal practice.

[287] Picciotto 1997, 1021. See also Riles 1999.

[288] Friedman 2001, 353. See also Dammann and Hansmann 2008.

[289] Friedman 1996, 65. See also Silver 2005, 897, noting that 'evidence of internationalization is ubiquitous in the legal services market'.

[290] Glenn 2000, 52.

one of the earliest examples of the attempts to adapt independent national legal systems to the relentless progress of international commerce.[291]

International arbitrators aspire to globalization of the mind, and success as an international arbitrator requires mental globalization. Compared with national court judges, international arbitrators tend to share a perspective increasingly detached from the national legal system and traditions in which they were trained, a preference for transnational sources of law over national ones and a sensitivity to the cultural and practical issues that arise when dealing across multiple cultures and legal traditions. As one interviewee, a Swiss arbitrator who has practiced in three different countries, put it:

> There's an international dimension that ... is absolutely key, it seems to me. There are different nationalities. You have to understand both sides.... You just don't handle an Italian party, a Russian party, a Polish party, a Thai party the same way. There are things you have be aware of, otherwise they are shocked by your behaviour.

Arbitral internationalism is visible in various phenomena, of which three examples will be discussed here: the increasing autonomy of arbitration from national laws, the cosmopolitan backgrounds and attitudes of international arbitrators, and arbitrators' use of comparative legal methodologies.

1. Internationalism and delocalization

Arbitrators tend to share the goal of creating a coherent, unified global dispute resolution forum that is more than a hodgepodge of national laws, practices, and cultures.[292] International arbitrators and national courts and legislatures now agree that international commerce requires 'harmonized solutions ... acceptable for parties from around the world'.[293] The purpose of ICA is therefore to 'provide a universal procedure for the settlement of international disputes detached, to the extent possible, from the particularities of national law'.[294] For this reason, international arbitrators tend to conceive of their field as something autonomous, not just an extension of 'domestic knowledge and usages with respect to business justice'.[295] Lew argues that 'international arbitration is, and should be recognized to be, an autonomous process for the determination of all types of international business disputes.... It has its own space independent of all national jurisdictions'.[296]

If ICA is to be an autonomous forum existing on a separate, international plane, it must be supported by the national systems of enforcement that make arbitration possible. This is a reality of our Westphalian world order. Arbitration agreements, rules of procedure, and awards 'can be given effect only by reference to some body of law prescribing such effect'.[297] Indeed, the autonomy that ICA already enjoys 'would not have been possible, and remains largely dependent upon, the benevolent eye, and active support, of national courts and legal orders'.[298]

291 Cremades 1999, 147–8. But see Dibadj 2008; and see also Silberman 2006.

292 See generally Smit 1986 and Paulsson 1983. Cf Carbonneau 2004, 1186: 'Processing international commercial claims through national courts leads to a decentralized system that is Byzantine both in its structure and operation.'

293 Helmer 2003, 57; see also Grigera Naón 1999, 118.

294 Craig, Park, and Paulsson 2001, 295, referring to the motivation for some of the 1998 amendments to the ICC Rules.

295 Dezalay and Garth 1996, 198.

296 Lew 2006, 181.

297 Smit 1989, 631.

298 Grigera Naón 1999, 120.

A brief history of delocalization

The commitment of states to support ICA is embodied in the 1958 New York Convention, which binds its signatories to enforce both arbitration agreements and arbitral awards.[299] As Lew relates, the New York Convention was 'the beginning of internationalism in arbitration'.[300] The previous regulatory regime is exemplified by the 1923 Geneva Protocol on Arbitration Clauses[301] and the 1927 Geneva Convention on the Execution of Foreign Arbitral Awards.[302] The Geneva Protocol provided: '[t]he arbitral procedure, including the constitution of the arbitral tribunal, shall be governed by the will of the parties and by the law of the country in whose territory the arbitration takes place.'[303] By contrast, the New York Convention expressly enshrines the parties' intent with respect to procedure above the law of the *situs* (except for mandatory rules).

The primary objective of the New York Convention was 'to insulate foreign arbitral awards from national judicial review at the award enforcement stage'.[304] It differed from the 1923 Geneva Protocol and the 1927 Geneva Convention by requiring for the first time that the courts of contracting states enforce, with only narrow procedural exceptions, all valid arbitration agreements and foreign arbitral awards.[305] 148 states are now parties to the New York Convention, including all major trading nations.[306] Although the New York Convention has been neither amended nor superseded, the process of detaching ICA from the vagaries of divergent national laws has continued through the adoption of national arbitration laws and rules of procedure that reduce opportunities for court interference with arbitrations. This process is usually called 'delocalization'.[307]

The term delocalization was coined to refer to the notion that a dispute need not be governed by the substantive law of the seat of the arbitration.[308] Since at least the 1980s, 'delocalization' has referred more broadly to the detaching of any aspect of the arbitral proceedings from national laws and courts.[309]

At one time, delocalization 'gave rise to passionate arguments',[310] especially in developing countries, which suspected that ICA was simply another means by which multinational corporations based in developed countries could exploit natural resources without fear of legal sanction. Today, many aspects of delocalization are no longer controversial, such as the parties' freedom to choose a different substantive law than that of the seat or to hold hearings in a different place than the seat.[311]

Courts in some states have gone so far as to recognize in explicit terms the autonomy of the arbitral order from national regimes. In the 2007 *Putrabali* case, the French *Cour de cassation* declared that 'An international arbitral award, which is not anchored in any

299 Arts II and III, respectively. 300 Lew 2006, 189.

301 Protocol on Arbitration Clauses (signed 24 September 1923) 27 LNTS 157.

302 Convention on the Execution of Foreign Arbitral Awards (signed 26 September 1927) 92 LNTS 301.

303 Art 2. 304 McConnaughay 1999, 468–9.

305 See the discussion of this evolution in Gaillard 2010a, 94–8.

306 Up-to-date information on the Convention's status can be found at: <http//www.uncitral.org/uncitral/en/uncitral_texts/arbitration/NYConvention_status.html> accessed 20 July 2012.

307 Also referred to as denationalization or deterritorrialization.

308 Kaufmann-Kohler has described this as 'physical delocalization', which she points out 'has already been achieved'. Kaufmann-Kohler 2003, 1318.

309 Sandrock 2001, 302–3. 310 Kaufmann-Kohler 2003, 1320.

311 Born 2009, 1675.

national legal order, is a decision of international justice'.[312] Similarly, the Swiss Federal Court held in 1994 that Swiss courts, when reviewing arbitral awards in the context of an annulment or enforcement proceeding, should base their decisions not on principles of Swiss law, but rather on 'transnational or universal public policy', including general principles of international law that apply 'regardless of the connection between the dispute and a given country'.[313]

Despite such developments, arbitrators recognize that, given the necessity of national courts as ICA's enforcement mechanism, total delocalization is as impossible as it is undesirable. In *Coppée Lavalin NV v Ken-Ren Fertilisers and Chemicals*, the House of Lords considered an application for security for costs in an ICC arbitration. Lord Mustill recognized the conflict between the necessity of court involvement and arbitrators' internationalist desires:

> On the one hand the concept of arbitration as a consensual process reinforced by the ideas of transnationalism leans against the involvement of ... a municipal court. On the other side there is the plain fact, palatable or not, that it is only a Court possessing coercive powers which could rescue the arbitration if it is in danger of foundering.[314]

Referring to development of codified instruments like the INCOTERMS,[315] Friedman makes a similar point:

> All this is supposed to constitute ... autonomous norm creation within the international economy.... But in the end all such customs and practices have to be validated somehow by national courts applying what they consider to be national law or rules that national law recognizes.[316]

This theme—a recognition of the necessity of national court involvement but a yearning for truly delocalized arbitration—has run through the international arbitration

[312] *PT Putrabali Adyamulia v Rena Holding* (2007) XXXII Ybk Comm Arb 299, 301 (Cour de cassation, 1ère civ, 29 June 2007). This decision built on a previous judgment of the Paris Court of Appeal, where the court referred to the existence of a 'genuinely international and universally applicable public policy' that would allow a tribunal to enforce a remedy precluded by the procedural law chosen by the parties. *Fougerolle v Procofrance* [1990] Revue critique de droit international privé 753 (Cour d'appel Paris, 25 May 1990) (author's translation).

[313] *Westland Helicopters Ltd* (Swiss Federal Supreme Court, 19 April 1994) ATF 1290 II 155 (author's translation). Among national jurisdictions, France and England are often described as occupying the two extreme positions. One interviewee, an Australian with an extensive international practice, observed: 'I have noticed a huge difference between the English and the French. The French will say that they are a long, long way towards de-localization and more or less, you can do anything you want to as long as it's not contrary to transnational public policy. If you sit in London, which is one of the centres of international arbitration, you find a lot of people there are not internationalists at all. They said this is an English arbitration, this is an English arbitration. I've had that put to me many, many times. You've got to follow what we do. There's an enormous gulf between London and Paris.'

[314] *Coppée Lavalin NV v Ken-Ren Fertilisers and Chemicals* [1994] 2 Lloyd's Rep 109 (HL) (speech of Lord Mustill).

[315] The INCOTERMS are a set of rules on delivery of goods and passage of risk in sales contracts. They were promulgated by the International Chamber of Commerce and are frequently incorporated by reference into sales contracts that include delivery of the goods.

[316] Friedman 2001, 356–7 (citations omitted). The same sentiment is expressed in the International Council for Commercial Arbitration's handbook for national court judges on the application of the New York Convention. See ICCA Handbook 2011, xi–xiii: 'The ultimate growth of the rule of law, the expansion of international arbitration for resolving cross-border disputes and enforcement of awards depend on the sovereign national courts. It is thus hoped that this Guide will also play its small part in assisting judges around the world to participate in this continuing harmonization process and use the Convention in a way consistent with its letter and spirit.'

literature for decades.[317] Lew refers to a-national arbitration as 'the dream',[318] while Smit calls it 'the epitome'[319] of international arbitration. According to Kennedy, delocalization is 'the whole point' of constructing an international arbitral order: 'If an international commercial transaction can be legally constructed in a regime detached from local legal cultures, in a place without public policy, the risks from prejudiced national public policy, intercultural misunderstandings, national elite rent seeking, or biased judiciaries can be diminished.'[320] One interviewee expressed this perspective in the following terms:

> Arbitration is in an area of its own, and the reason is simple: the parties have expressly excluded the courts of each other's countries, or any third country, by their agreement to arbitrate. It may be difficult to tell a national court judge that the parties do not want him or his court involved in the matter, but that is the result of an arbitration agreement. The parties are saying, in effect, 'You, judge, mind your own business. Please respect what we're doing. If either of us needs your help to get evidence, help us. If either party needs interim relief, and the court thinks it's right, help that party. And when one party seeks enforcement, help that party. But don't interfere; don't second guess the arbitrators.' That's what the parties want.

One aspect of delocalization is the development of separate legal regimes to regulate domestic and international arbitrations. Proponents of ICA have convinced many states that international arbitration is a self-contained, supranational system, and therefore that separate statutes should govern domestic and international arbitrations.[321] In the ninety-one jurisdictions (including several sub-national units) that have adopted legislation based on the UNCITRAL Model Law, international arbitrations are now governed by separate laws.[322] In addition, several countries, including France, Belgium, and Switzerland, have enacted their own statutes with different provisions for domestic and international arbitrations.[323] As might be expected, the provisions that govern international arbitrations provide for greater party autonomy and less court supervision than those that govern domestic arbitrations.[324]

The notion that ICA is qualitatively different from domestic litigation and arbitration is not universally shared. Lord Mustill, for one, wrote that he 'never understood why international arbitration should be different in principle from any other kind of arbitration'.[325] This is, however, a minority position. Some countries that previously distinguished between domestic and international arbitrations have retreated from this position. These changes are not due to a belief that domestic and international arbitration are equivalent, but rather to concerns that statutes that effectively treat national and foreign parties differently may conflict with treaty commitments to observe equal treatment.[326]

[317] See, eg, Pietrowski 2006, 386; Park 2003, 1265; Sandrock 2001, 320; Mayer 1995, 37; Smit 1989, 631; Paulsson 1981; Lalive 1976, 155; Mann 1967, 159. Lew argues that the debate goes back at least to the 1950s, when Frédéric Eisemann, then Secretary-General of the ICC International Court of Arbitration, lobbied for the establishment of denationalized international arbitration awards that would not be subject to annulment in any jurisdiction. Lew 2006, 179.

[318] Lew 2006, 179. [319] Smit 1989, 629.

[320] Kennedy 1997, 624.

[321] Park makes this case in the context of proposing changes to the US Federal Arbitration Act. Park 2003.

[322] For a list of jurisdictions that have adopted legislation based on the UNCITRAL Model Law, see <http//www.uncitral.org/uncitral/en/uncitral_texts/arbitration/1985Model_arbitration_status.html> accessed 20 July 2012.

[323] Park 2003, 1258. [324] Ibid. [325] Mustill 1992, 165.

[326] Park 2003, 1255 (citation omitted). Park cites as an example the fact that, 'under the now-superseded 1979 English Arbitration Act, pre-dispute waiver of appeal on points of law was not allowed between or among residents and/or citizens of the United Kingdom … The 1996 Arbitration

Delocalization and choice of law

The process of delocalization has been most clearly apparent in the evolution of choice of law rules in ICA. Under the traditional theory, sometimes called the '*lex fori*,' '*siège*', or 'jurisdictional' doctrine, by selecting a particular country as the site of an arbitration, the parties also impliedly chose that country's law to govern the merits of the dispute—a choice of forum was also a choice of law. This doctrine is now all but abandoned; however, as recently as 1968, English courts took the position that a choice of England as the site of arbitration entailed a choice of English law.[327]

Even if the *lex fori* doctrine did not apply, tribunals were traditionally bound by the choice of law rules of the seat of the arbitration.[328] Today, parties to arbitrations 'enjoy virtually unfettered contractual discretion to designate the law of whatever nation they wish as the law that will govern their transaction' irrespective of the choice of law rules of the *situs* or of any other states with which the arbitration is connected.[329] Moreover, if the parties do not agree on the applicable law, arbitrators are generally able to choose whatever choice of law rules they consider appropriate or to even avoid the choice of law process entirely and make a direct choice (*voie directe*) of the substantive law.[330] Thus, not only do parties have the right to substantively delocalize their disputes, but delocalization of the substantive law may also occur at the behest of arbitrators.[331]

Some have argued that the traditional choice of law process itself runs contrary to delocalization. As de Boer notes: 'In the choice-of-law process, international cases are, in a sense, "domesticated". They are stripped from their unruly international features and moulded to fit into the concepts and categories of national law.'[332] The basic presumption of choice of law rules is that different national legal systems are in conflict with each other, which is contrary to the universalizing spirit of arbitration.[333] Thus, if domestic choice of law rules are applied to international conflicts, they lead to the 'nationalization' of those disputes, something that is anathema to arbitral internationalism.

As a practical matter, proponents of ICA often cite the complexity of modern international transactions to argue that national choice of law regimes are inadequate. Barnes gives the following hypothetical example:

> ... [a] web site is maintained on a server located in London, a mirror site and server is maintained in Sydney, Australia, and persons from the United States, France, and Germany all transact business on the site. Which nation's law governs in the absence of an agreement? Which nation's laws should regulate affairs conducted on the site? Our legal regimes are currently struggling for answers to these questions....[334]

Act contained similar provisions, which never entered into force due to a perceived conflict with obligations within the European Union' 1255 fn 58. See also Rodner 2002.

327 *Tzortzis & Sykias v Monarch Lines* [1968] 1 Lloyd's Rep 337 (CA). The *lex fori* doctrine found adherents among arbitral tribunals into the 1990s. See, eg, ICC Case No 6527 of 1991 (1993) XVIII Ybk Comm Arb 44.

328 Sandrock 2001, 323.

329 McConnaughay 1999, 470. The national arbitration laws of a small number of jurisdictions, such as England and Switzerland, contain choice of law rules that apply in the absence of a choice by the parties.

330 For example, ICC Rules, art 21(1) provides: 'The parties shall be free to agree upon the rules of law to be applied by the arbitral tribunal to the merits of the dispute. In the absence of any such agreement, the arbitral tribunal shall apply the rules of law which it determines to be appropriate.' This notion entered the ICC Rules in the 1975 revision, and was aimed at 'liberating the choice of substantive law from national rules of conflict of laws'. Craig, Park, and Paulsson 2001, 321.

331 Sandrock 2001, 305. 332 de Boer 1994, 18. 333 Glenn 2001, 997.

334 Barnes 2005, 732–3 (quotations omitted).

Even in more straightforward factual situations, avoiding the choice of law process and the possibility that differing national laws might apply reduces the uncertainty involved in international transacting.[335] The application of domestic choice of law rules also imposes costs on parties to cross-border transactions in the form of expense, delay, and uncertainty.[336] It is therefore not surprising that international arbitrators frequently use the *voie directe* power.[337] Permitting the parties to make a choice of law or, absent such a choice, permitting the tribunal to make a *voie directe*, serves a variety of ICA social norms: party autonomy, the service of business, and internationalism.

Parties and arbitrators have exercised their autonomy to choose transnational rules of law unavailable via traditional choice of law analyses. Delocalization was therefore a necessary precondition to the development of transnational contract law generally, and in particular the modern *lex mercatoria*.[338] Unlike judges working under many national choice of law systems, arbitrators are able to choose both 'laws' and 'rules of law' (general principles of international law and the international contract law instruments) to serve as the substantive law governing a dispute.[339] Modern arbitration laws permit the parties or arbitrators to choose transnational rules of law and give meaning to this freedom by enforcing awards applying transnational rules. Delocalization has 'gradually freed [international arbitrators] from their traditional obligation to refer to national laws'.[340]

Delocalization and substance—the role of transnational law

For many arbitrators, the establishment of arbitration as autonomous from both national courts and national laws calls for the establishment of a purely international substantive law. This notion encompasses international law instruments like the CISG, but the desire for a substantive law that is both transnational and global is most manifest in the *lex mercatoria*, which 'should be seen as an aspect ... of the autonomy and universality of the international legal field'.[341] As one tribunal noted, general principles 'apply uniformly and are independent of the peculiarities of different national laws'.[342]

The development of a transnational substantive law is an explicit project for some arbitrators. However, some interviewees observed that transnational legal rules are coalescing without active assistance, as a by-product of the internationality of the ICA process:

> I'm not sure it's a conscious thing.... It's due in part to the fact ... in international arbitration that you have actors from different backgrounds—legal, cultural. So you may have counsel from different backgrounds, you may have arbitrators on the panel who are trained in different laws, and somehow everybody wants to get to some common denominator. When you deliberate within a tribunal, you would like to get to consensus.

Many arbitrators argue that the application of transnational law is generally desired by parties engaged in international commerce. As one interviewee put it: 'we see in

[335] David 1967, 60 (author's translation): '*le contrat international appelle l'application d'un véritable droit international ... non celle d'un droit national, dont le choix sera toujours quelque peu arbitraire, et bien souvent incertain*'.

[336] Glenn 2001, 997, concluding that the ability of ICA to save parties the costs of the choice of law process is a significant factor in the growth of ICA.

[337] Craig, Park, and Paulsson 2001, 320; Symeonides 2006, 213.

[338] Petsche 2005, 15.

[339] See Chapter V, Section II.2.

[340] Gélinas 2000, 122 (citation omitted).

[341] Dezalay and Garth 1996, 65.

[342] ICC Case No 8385 of 1995 [1997] JDI 1061.

arbitration as it develops that parties are having more confidence in the internationally minded arbitrator than they do in the nationally minded judge'. To the extent that this is true, arbitral internationalism is a manifestation of respect for party autonomy. Yet the internationalism norm sometimes competes with party autonomy. Arbitrators frequently refer to transnational rules of law where the parties have expressed no intention to apply them, or even where the parties have expressly chosen to be governed by national laws.

Where parties in international disputes do not make a choice of law, some tribunals see this as an indication of the parties' preference for general principles. In ICC Case No 9466 of 1999, the claimant argued that:

> the silence of the parties as to the law that should be applied to their contractual relationship may be construed as a significant indication of their will that their relationship be simply governed by the terms of the contract and/or ... by the general principles of international commercial contracts.[343]

The tribunal concurred:

> This is very likely true, and quite understandable in a situation where we are facing a combination of elements attributable to various different nationalities.... the tribunal is of the opinion that making reference to a specific national law may not be necessary in the present case.[344]

Similarly, in ICC Case No 8501, the parties made no choice of law, although their contract did refer to the INCOTERMS and the UCP. The tribunal held that these references to codified international trade usages indicated the parties' intention ('*volonté*') that their dispute ought to be resolved solely according to 'customs and usages of international commerce'.[345] Since the INCOTERMS and UCP did not, in themselves, resolve the dispute, the tribunal applied the CISG. The CISG was not applicable, since the respondent's domicile had not ratified it, but the tribunal nevertheless applied it as an expression of international commercial usages.[346]

Businesses tend to be suspicious of general principles and rarely call for their application because businesses prize predictability, while general principles are notoriously malleable. The continued interest in transnational commercial law, and the many scholarly writings on the subject that prominent arbitrators continue to produce, are best explained by arbitrators' ideological attachment to transnational contract law.[347]

For some arbitrators, party autonomy trumps internationalism. Interviewees frequently noted that, while they see the value of general principles, they would not foist them on unwilling parties:

> The parties don't see that as something necessarily desirable because it is not predictable from their point of view. So even though ... I'm one of those lawyers who is comfortable with general principles, the parties may not be, so I would not go there and impose it on them ... without some prior warning and asking for their views on it.

343 (2002) XXVII Ybk Comm Arb 170 [3].

344 Ibid [4]–[5]. But see ICC Case No 7319 of 1992 (1999) XXIV Ybk Comm Arb 141 [13]. There, the parties made no express or implied choice of law, but the tribunal nevertheless declined to apply general principles, reasoning that 'the failure of the parties to agree on the law governing the agreement cannot, in the sole arbitrator's opinion, be interpreted as an implied reference to some vague international legal or trade principles'. Instead, the tribunal applied the laws of the parties' home states concurrently. On the concurrent or cumulative application of multiple laws, see Section V.3 of this chapter.

345 ICC Case No 8501 [year unknown] [2001] JDI 1164.

346 Ibid.

347 On the disconnect between arbitrators' image of the universality of the *lex mercatoria* and the small number of cases in which it is actually applied, see Bernardini 2004a, 63.

However, most interviewees who expressed scepticism about the entire notion of *lex mercatoria* still indicated their willingness to apply the UNIDROIT Principles, which suggests that their objection to *lex mercatoria* is its uncertainty, rather than its transnational character. One interviewee, a French practitioner and academic, had this to say about *lex mercatoria*: 'I think it does not exist,... and it's a good thing that it does not exist. The UNIDROIT Principles exist. They are written, they are predictable, so why not use them?' The UNIDROIT Principles have emerged in arbitral practice as the best means to rationalize arbitral internationalism with the need to serve commercial parties' interests.

Similarly, interviewees who acknowledged that the parties generally do not want the application of transnational law argued that it maintains an important role in two circumstances. The first is when national laws are outdated or parochial. In such circumstances, many interviewees will at least propose to the parties that the rule ought to be replaced with an international one. For example, one interviewee saw general principles as serving a supportive role, 'mostly complementing what you think is applicable.... I look at the applicable law and I try to find support in some international rules. Where there is a gap in the applicable law, you look at these international rules to find the right solution'. Two specific examples were given by a French interviewee regarding his practice:

> When it comes to interpretation of a contract, there are good rules on interpretation [in the UNIDROIT Principles]. Why ... apply domestic rules on interpretation of the applicable law, which are ... only a *guide âne*,[348] not really rules of law, but advice—be reasonable, sensible? So why not take them from the UNIDROIT Principles, which are modern and the result of a consensus? Or the rules on interest ... it is most often absurd to apply the 3.6 per cent rate in the applicable law which is in fact meant for domestic situations and in the currency of the country. I will not hesitate, even if a certain law had been chosen ... to try to convince the parties at least that it is not reasonable and that there is a better provision in the UNIDROIT Principles.[349]

The second circumstance in which there was wide agreement among interviewees that it is appropriate to apply general principles when the parties have not called for them has to do with cases involving the cumulative application of multiple laws. When parties call for the application of the rules common to two or more legal systems, there will often be too few common principles to address every legal issue that arises in the arbitration. As one interviewee observed wryly:

> In practical terms, when you try to look at the common ground between Venezuelan law and international law, what are you going to get? *Pacta sunt servanda*? What you are going to get is a bunch of gaps. In my experience you fill those gaps with contractual interpretation, general principles, common sense.

Another interviewee described a similar approach: 'I've had some cases where you had the principles common to Turkish or Swiss and Belgian law and when there are no

[348] A French phrase referring to a very elementary guide, literally, a 'guide for fools'.

[349] The adequacy of national laws as they relate to the calculation of interest was a recurrent theme in the interviews. A Swiss arbitrator gave the example of a case governed by Swiss law in which damages were calculated in a foreign currency: 'Does it make sense to apply Swiss statutory interest of five percent a year to a currency ... which is devaluing very, very quickly and the interest rate is, I don't know, 80 percent, or something like that per year because the currency devalues so quickly that the interest rate is practically a hedge against devaluation? It has nothing to do with Swiss statutory law ... so I went into the UNIDROIT Principles.'

such principles ... I would fall back on general principles of law of the ... Klaus Peter Berger type.'[350]

Drahozal argues that writing about transnational law in academic journals and speaking about it at trade conferences allows arbitrators to 'signal' their 'legal internationalism'. He writes: 'Even if parties do not want to have their dispute resolved according to principles of transnational law ... they may still prefer an arbitrator with a transnational outlook and expertise as to a number of legal systems.'[351] Some arbitrators' eagerness to associate themselves with transnational law may therefore be related to competition between arbitrators.

Arbitral internationalism has also led arbitrators to promote international contract law instruments over national laws. For example, tribunals have applied the CISG and the UNIDROIT Principles in situations where courts would have applied national law, including before they went into effect[352] and when neither party submitted that they apply.[353]

Even when a national law does apply, arbitrators will frequently refer to international contract law instruments as evidence of an international consensus on a point of law,[354] or as expressions of applicable trade usages,[355] or to 'arrive at an internationally acceptable and economically sensible interpretation of the domestic law'.[356] Witz explains that the greater use of international instruments in ICA occurs: 'because international arbitrators are more accustomed and more favourably inclined to the application of international standards than are national judges'.[357]

Delocalization and procedure—the importance of 'international arbitral practice'

Arbitral internationalism can be seen most clearly in the evolution and status of what is most often called 'international arbitral practice'—the standard practices of international arbitrators reconceived as a legal norm. The particularities of those standard practices are beyond the scope of this discussion; what is striking is the extent to which

350 Berger is the director of the Centre for Transnational Law at the University of Cologne. See Chapter 1, Section I.

351 Drahozal 2005, 551, noting that this is particularly the case with respect to sole or presiding arbitrators.

352 Berger 1998, 140, citing ICC Cases Nos 5713 of 1989 (1990) XV Ybk Comm Arb 70 and 2438 of 1975 [1976] JDI 969 (both applying the UNIDROIT Principles).

353 See, eg, ICC Case No 11849 of 2003 (2006) XXXI Ybk Comm Arb 148 [9]. This award is discussed at greater length in Chapter 6, Section IV.2. Even if the CISG is applicable in litigation, courts are unlikely to determine *sua sponte* that it applies; one of the parties must argue for the CISG's application. In arbitration, on the other hand, some tribunals determine on their own initiative whether the CISG or one of the other international contract law instruments applies. See, eg, ICC Case No 8128 of 1995 [1996] JDI 1024. Schlechtriem also describes a case in which the contract contained an express choice of Russian law. The parties argued for conflicting interpretations of Russian domestic law but the tribunal found that the CISG applied as the Russian law pertaining to international sales contracts. Schechtriem 2005, 794.

354 See, eg, the award extract reported in Bonell 1996, 157: 'general legal rules and principles enjoying wide international consensus ... are primarily reflected by the UNIDROIT Principles'.

355 See, eg, ICC Case No 5713 of 1989 (1990) XV Ybk Comm Arb 70, where the tribunal declared there to be 'no better source' than the CISG from which 'to determine the prevailing trade usages'. On the basis that the CISG expresses prevailing international trade usages, the tribunal applied it even though neither party came from a state party to the CISG.

356 Berger 1998, 138. See, eg, the extensive use made of the UNIDROIT Principles in ICC Case No 8486 of 1996 (1999) XXIVa Ybk Comm Arb 162.

357 Quoted in Curran 1995, 179 (citation omitted).

ICA practitioners have developed a set of procedures that are global in character and not derived from any one national approach. They are often described as a hybrid of common law and civil law approaches, but many practices are specific to arbitration, such as the use of 'Redfern Schedules' for document discovery.

Several interviewees indicated that a close familiarity with international arbitral practice was essential to receiving appointments, especially as a tribunal chair. One interviewee explained: 'I'm sitting more as a chair than a co-arbitrator because normally the institutions try to find a chairperson, or the two co-arbitrators try to find a mutual person, with a good understanding of civil law and common law and a good understanding of international arbitration practice.'

Moreover, interviewees were unanimous in their denunciation of parties that want to have their arbitration governed by national procedural rules. Several told anecdotes of cases where they tried, with more or less success, to convince the parties to adopt international procedural standards, which they equated with modernity and global acceptability. One interviewee from an Asian country made this broad declaration:

> I always try to apply international standards rather than any particular national standard. I understand sometimes the parties from different jurisdictions might have different positions.... But my practice, when I act as chairperson particularly, is to try to introduce the modern standards of international arbitration. I am quite flexible in applying any procedural rules, but usually ask the parties to agree to adopt international standards. Normally it's quite successful.

While a given dispute may be resolved in a manner consistent with the rules and methods of a specific national legal system, the approach taken by the majority of international arbitrators is increasingly internationalized.[358] This international approach is also being codified both within ICA and in national laws. Documents like the IBA's Rules on the Taking of Evidence in International Commercial Arbitration and Guidelines on Conflicts of Interest in International Arbitration, which are in common use in ICA, were designed as crystallizations of existing practice, much in the manner that the American Restatements are intended to crystallize existing common law. Similarly, industry groups[359] and private law firms[360] have published their own compendia of best practices in international arbitration procedure.

Arbitral institutions and national legislators frequently look to international arbitral practice for guidance when updating rules and statutes. For example, the recently proposed amendments to the Dutch Arbitration Act have been described as necessary modernizations reflecting changes in international arbitral practice,[361] as have several provisions of the 2011 revisions to the French Code of Civil Procedure relating to arbitration.[362] However, the most prominent example is the UNCITRAL Model Law itself, which is often praised for codifying international arbitral practice on such basic matters as competence-competence and party autonomy in the choice of the governing law. States that have adopted the UNCITRAL Model Law often do so on the basis that

358 Cf Grigera Naón 1999, 118–9.

359 See, eg, various practice guidelines and protocols issued by the Chartered Institute of Arbitrators, available at <http://www.ciarb.org/information-and-resources/practice-guidelines-and-protocols/list-of-guidelines-and-protocols> accessed 30 August 2012.

360 See, eg, Debevoise and Plimpton LLP's 'Protocol to Promote Efficiency in International Arbitration', available at <http://www.debevoise.com/arbitrationprotocol/> accessed 30 August 2012.

361 van Zelst 2012.

362 See, eg, Carducci 2012; Yu and Ahmed 2012.

the Model Law 'reflects worldwide consensus on key aspects of international arbitration practice'.[363]

Commentators reinforce these trends by assessing institutional rules of procedure and national laws according to the extent to which they conform to international arbitral practice. For example, Luttrel and Moens praise the most recent revisions to ACICA Rules for reflecting 'international best practice',[364] while O'Reilly criticizes the English Arbitration Act 1996 for failing to: 'design its provisions for wide international use … the time has come to review the legislation with a renewed and vigorous international outlook'.[365]

Finally, international arbitral practice is frequently cited as a source of legal rules in its own right. This phenomenon is most visible in commentary, but also appears in arbitral awards, especially in investor-state arbitrations. For example, Lew argues that international arbitral practice is a foundation stone of the legitimacy of the entire ICA system: 'international arbitration does not depend on national courts for legitimacy; this exists as of right, based on the agreement of the parties, the New York Convention, and international arbitration practice'.[366]

In their awards, tribunals occasionally describe international arbitral practice as a source of procedural law. This is most common in investor-state arbitrations,[367] but also arises in commercial disputes. For example, the tribunal in ICC Case No 12703 held that 'the international arbitrator sitting in Switzerland is not required to apply either Swiss civil procedure rules or conflict of law rules. Where appropriate, reference may be made … to other national procedural laws or to apposite international arbitration practice'.[368] A more specific example is provided by ICC Case No 13507, where the sole arbitrator ruled that he was empowered to rule on costs and fees because 'general international arbitration practice … unequivocally vests the arbitrators with broad powers and flexibility to decide on cost allocation issues'.[369]

The overall effect of these developments is that ICA standard practices are hardening into a comprehensive, predictable procedural law that is increasingly detached from any national approach—increasingly delocalized.[370] Arbitral internationalism is not, of course, unlimited. Most importantly, under article V(2)(b) of the New York Convention, national courts may set aside awards or refuse them recognition and enforcement when the award or the arbitral procedure violates mandatory provisions of national law.[371]

[363] See, eg, Haydn-Williams 2011, referring to the Barbados Arbitration Act.

[364] Luttrell and Moens 2009, 521.

[365] O'Reilly 2010, 718.

[366] Lew 2009, 535–6.

[367] See, eg, *Railroad Development Corp v Republic of Guatemala*, ICSID Case No ARB/07/23, award of 18 May 2010 [128]–[131]; *Archer Daniels Midland Co and Tate & Lyle Americas v Mexico*, ICSID Case No ARB(AF)/04/05, award of 21 November 2007 [296].

[368] ICC Case No 12703 of 2003 (2008) XXXIII Ybk Comm Arb 63 [24]. See also the partial award on jurisdiction and admissibility in ICC Case No 6474 of 1992 (2000) XXV Ybk Comm Arb 11.

[369] ICC Case No 13507 (2010) XXXV Ybk Comm Arb 158 [17].

[370] These trends are not limited to arbitration, but extend to international dispute resolution more generally. The increasing commonalities in procedure among international tribunals are explored in Brown 2007.

[371] A prominent recent example is *Dallah Real Estate and Tourism Holding Company v The Ministry of Religious Affairs, Government of Pakistan* [2010] UKSC 46, refusing recognition and enforcement of an ICC award rendered against the government of Pakistan on the ground that, under the national law of France, the seat, Pakistan was not a party to the arbitration agreement. One legal basis for such decisions is New York Convention, art V(1)(a), which provides that awards may be refused recognition and enforcement if the parties' arbitration agreement is invalid under the law applicable to it or under the law of the seat of arbitration.

Here, too, however, the ICA community has pushed for national courts to apply international standards. Commentators generally agree that, when applying article V(2)(b), international rather than national public policy should be applied.[372] In this context, 'international public policy' means the public policy of a state that underlies the state's private international law. In other words, it is still the public policy of a state—just a subset of that public policy which pertains to international matters.[373] This is in itself a significant step in the direction of delocalization. However, some commentators take the further step of arguing that states should apply transnational public policy (also called 'truly international public policy') that is, the public policy of the entire world, and not of any one state.[374]

For now, national legislatures have resisted the application of international public policy.[375] However, national courts have applied such a standard without explicit statutory authorization.[376] The notion of transnational public policy, which does not appear to be supported by the text or legislative history of article V(2)(b),[377] has not been adopted by any country. However, if courts around the world come to apply truly international public policy when they consider the enforceability of international arbitral awards, one of the last significant links between ICA and national laws will be removed, and ICA will be one step closer to the ideal of a-national arbitration.

2. Arbitrators' cosmopolitanism

ICA practitioners are increasingly multilingual, multicultural, and multinational. Just as both procedure and substance in ICA have become increasingly delocalized, so too have arbitrators themselves. As characteristics shared by the leading arbitrators, Rogers cites linguistic ability, 'multi-national educations' and 'multi-faceted, multi-cultural legal training'.[378] Such attributes reinforce arbitrators' image of neutrality and legitimize them to their international clientele. As Garth puts it, potential arbitrators 'must demonstrate ... an attitude that might be termed "cosmopolitan".... The "legal nationalist" has a very difficult time making it into the international arbitration world'.[379] Cremades, a prominent Spanish arbitrator, argues that professionalism in arbitration is largely defined by the arbitrator's ability to avoid legal nativism and think internationally: '... the truly international arbitrator is one whose ... professionalism leads his decision to be independent from the "bag and baggage" of the system or national systems from which he originates'.[380]

[372] See the authorities cited in ILA Report on Public Policy 2002, which itself recommends that the standard be one of international public policy.

[373] ILA Public Policy Resolution 2002.

[374] An important early text is Lalive 1987. See also, eg, Pryles 2007b and several contributions to van den Berg 2007.

[375] But see the French Code of Civil Procedure, art 1502(5). A few other states' national arbitration laws provide for the application of international public policy. See Born 2009, 2834.

[376] Some examples from different jurisdictions include *Parsons & Whittemore Overseas Co v Rakta*, 508 F2d 974 (2d Cir 1974) (US Court of Appeals for the Second Circuit); *Judgment of 18 January 1990* (1992) XVII Ybk Comm Arb 503 (German Federal Supreme Court); *Judgment of 9 October 2003* (2007) XXXII Ybk Comm Arb 474 (Portuguese Supreme Court); *Judgment of 4 December 1992*, (1997) XXII Ybk Comm Arb 725 (Milan Court of Appeal).

[377] Born 2009, 2837. [378] Rogers 2005, 958–9. [379] Garth 1997, 10–1.

[380] Cremades 1999, 165.

Two other characteristics shared by international arbitrators are that they tend to speak English plus at least one other language fluently[381] and that they have lived in two or more countries. Indeed, such a background is becoming an informal requirement for entering the field. For example, Baker & McKenzie, a large international law firm, boasts that every member of its 'Global Arbitration Team' has 'either studied or worked abroad.... This is essential for understanding the possibilities offered, the forces working, and the pitfalls hidden in international arbitration'.[382]

Such marketing language should not be taken too literally, but it does indicate the premium that consumers of ICA services place on linguistic abilities and international experience.[383] Along these lines, Grigera Naón praises the ICC secretariat for its multiculturalism, which 'guarantees the even-handed administration of ICC arbitrations',[384] and Kennedy observes that ICC lawyers are likely to be introduced to strangers by their linguistic expertise or disciplinary specialty, while UN staff are identified primarily by their nationalities.[385]

Just as parties are likely to seek out arbitrators with cosmopolitan backgrounds, lawyers with cosmopolitan backgrounds are more likely to be interested in practising international arbitration law. One interviewee, now based in a major world capital, left their home country in part to 'get away from its parochial mentality' and 'to find an international aspect to the practice of law'.

As Dezalay and Garth note, many of the key solicitors who developed international arbitration in England 'were ... drawn to ICC-style arbitration because of their own cosmopolitan, hybrid backgrounds—for example, they were born or educated abroad, including especially German immigrants; or they had foreign, typically French, spouses'.[386] Such self-selection is likely to increase, thus strengthening the effects of cultural norms.

These observations were supported by interviewees. As mentioned above, they are not intended to be a representative sample of all arbitrators, or even of highly active arbitrators, but their example is illustrative of trends in ICA. With respect to languages, all twenty interviewees speak English fluently and work regularly in English; ten speak at least three languages and eleven are sufficiently proficient in at least two languages to conduct arbitrations in them.[387] Of the eight interviewees who are native English speakers, five are sufficiently proficient in another language to read legal documents and converse in it.

With respect to training and experience, ten of the interviewees studied law in at least two countries and eight have formal training in both common law and civil law systems. Eight practised or taught at universities in at least two different countries.

The interviewees who speak more than one language or were trained in more than one legal system invariably pointed to their multinational backgrounds as a reason for their effectiveness as arbitrators and their success in garnering appointments.

381 One German practitioner affirmed that: 'it is already accepted that English is the language of international arbitration'. A Collins 2010, 16.

382 Wittinghofer 2007, 5.

383 It is arguably as important for counsel as for arbitrators to possess multicultural expertise, since they will need to persuade arbitrators who come from a variety of legal backgrounds. Jones 2006, 279.

384 Grigera Naón 1999, 139.

385 Kennedy 1997, 586–7.

386 Dezalay and Garth 1996, 136.

387 Counting Mandarin and Cantonese as different languages. They are often lumped together in arbitrators' CVs, but proficiency in one does not permit even basic understanding of the other, so they are counted separately for present purposes.

A London-based arbitrator who speaks English, French, and Russian, and was trained in both civil law and common law, said that these were significant assets:

It's absolutely essential in this field to have, if not languages, certainly the cultural awareness at the very, very least.... In the big firms nowadays I don't think they even consider you if you have only one language ... that certainly wasn't the case in my day. I think also that my civil law-common law background was invaluable [to the firm where the interviewee was first hired], although at the time I did not realize it.

An Australian arbitrator, who has significant experience with Asian legal systems and also studied in Germany, made a similar point about cultural awareness:

Firstly, it's desirable to have experience in more than one legal system. But beyond that, it's desirable to have a broader, cross-cultural sensitivity and experience. It's not simply the fact that laws differ from place to place. The significance of the contract, and the approach to the law and the role of law differs from place to place. One has to understand that they come from a different system and you have to make allowances and be fair. I think one needs to have a much broader perspective to be an international arbitrator than to be a judge in a national legal system.

The theme of cross-cultural sensitivity was raised by every interviewee. One arbitrator, who works only in English and neither studied nor practised abroad, said that even being married to a spouse of a different nationality was in itself a benefit: 'You get aware that when somebody says something, it may not come out straight right away.'[388] For example, interviewees said that they might alter the way they manage an arbitration depending on the nationality of the parties and their counsel. When asked whether it is appropriate to encourage the parties to settle, a Swiss arbitrator said that the appropriate course of action depends in part on the parties' backgrounds:

I'm not among those who say that's out of the question; an arbitrator shouldn't do it. But you do have to be careful; you really have to choose where it will be well received and where it will not and that may depend on the cultural background and the legal background of counsel and the parties. If I proposed it to Swiss and German parties, they will find it very natural, but if I have English and Australian counsel they will think it's totally outrageous.

Several interviewees articulated their role as including helping parties from different traditions and counsel from different legal systems to understand each other. Said one interviewee: 'It's part of my job to make, not necessarily make the parties converse, because obviously often they are no longer able to do that, but certainly to make sure that they have a conduit.' Several interviewees gave examples of circumstances in which they acted as 'cultural translators' (in the words one interviewee), either between the parties or between one party and other members of the tribunal. One arbitrator, from an East Asian country, gave the example of a case that turned in part on the meaning of some internal documents generated by a Japanese corporation:

We normally have these memos, these internal documents that will circulate among the members of the company, including comments. It's quite a unique form of internal document.... there are a lot of internal documents in the Japanese language. You can interpret them into English but it's almost impossible actually and straightforwardly to interpret from Japanese into English because from the beginning Asian languages are very vague....

But even when you find some way to overcome linguistic barriers in international arbitration, you have more importantly the cultural things like the ... working atmosphere in companies

[388] At least three of the interviewees are married to a spouse who was raised in a different country and has a different native language.

that is different from the working atmosphere in European countries. So you need to really properly explain the working relationship and how decisions are actually made. Those things are quite important, more than just explaining the documents and what the parties agreed.

Perhaps as a result of their own cosmopolitanism, some interviewees expressed impatience with counsel who are not equally cosmopolitan. When asked for examples of arbitrations where problems arose between the tribunal and the parties, interviewees often gave examples that involved counsel who were insufficiently attuned to legal and cultural variety. Several became frustrated with counsel who could not clearly explain a foreign legal concept or misunderstood opposing counsel's perspective. Interviewees were particularly irritated with counsel who were not sensitive to linguistic or cultural differences when cross-examining witnesses. One English arbitrator called out his compatriots as particular offenders: 'You get English counsel who say, "I put it to you that …" and the witness doesn't have the faintest idea. What is he talking about? So I say, "Do you think you could rephrase that?" But they often say, "I put it to you that you didn't say that." And you wonder, what's the question?'

3. Arbitrators' use of comparative methodology

The internationalism of arbitrators can also be seen in what Berger calls their 'natural comparative approach', that is, the tendency of arbitrators to consider the way different legal systems approach an issue before them, even when it is clear that only one substantive law governs the resolution of the dispute.[389] Indeed, the use of comparative law methodology is an often-cited attribute of arbitral decision-making.[390] One interviewee described his background as an academic comparativist as unimportant for marketing purposes, but fundamental to being an effective arbitrator: 'Did it help getting appointments by saying I've been a professor and so on? I don't think so. Is having a wide background in comparative law? … Absolutely. It's as Andy Lowenfeld quite rightly said, "arbitrations are comparative law in action".' Pierre Lalive gave advice to would-be arbitrators along the same lines:

> The arbitrator should have a good command of contract law, commercial law, procedure, private international law and preferably also public international law. On top of this, he should have a certain amount of training in and experience of *comparative law* and the comparative method, by having a good working knowledge and understanding in at least two of the great legal systems of the world, common law, civil law, Moslem law, etc.[391]

National courts may not have similar levels of in-house comparative law expertise. The US Supreme Court has written of the difficulty that courts experience in 'conducting complex exercises in comparative law' in order to determine whether 'the law applied by the alternative forum is as favourable … as that of the chosen forum'.[392] Admittedly, arbitrators do at times misapply national laws with which they are unfamiliar;[393] however, they are more likely than judges to be familiar with the contract law of multiple legal systems. Almost of necessity, successful international arbitrators must

389 Berger 1998, 130.
390 See, eg, Sourgens 2007; Stoffel 2001; Rogers 1998; Kennedy 1997; Siqueiros 1993.
391 Lalive 1986, 16 (emphasis in original).
392 *Piper Aircraft Co v Reyno*, 454 US 235, 251 (1981).
393 Perhaps most famously in the *Klöckner* arbitration. See Chapter 6, Section IV.2.

possess such knowledge, since most international arbitrations involve parties from at least two different legal systems.[394] Glenn even argues that ICA constitutes important evidence that 'comparative legal thought is possible at the level of individual dispute resolution in spite of multiplication of sources and major differences in styles and manner of legal thought'.[395] Arbitrators' cosmopolitan backgrounds enable them to think in terms of multiple legal systems, and their cosmopolitan attitudes encourage them think in such a manner.[396] Thus, arbitrators' use of the comparative method is a manifestation of internationalism.

ICA's philosophical development has been influenced by the comparativist tradition in international law, which stresses the commonalities between legal systems and posits that unification of law will best be achieved by focusing on the law that governs private relationships, rather than relationships between states.[397] The Hague Peace Conferences of 1899 and 1907, which led to the creation of the Permanent Court of Arbitration and—indirectly—to the Permanent Court of International Justice, were peopled by comparativists who believed in international law—public and private—as a universalist project.[398] Several prominent arbitrators first gained a reputation as academic comparativists[399] and a background in comparative law endows a potential arbitrator with the kind of legal cosmopolitanism that is an element of the emerging international arbitration culture.

International arbitrators regularly employ the comparative method in at least three situations that arise frequently. First, tribunals that refer to general principles of international law will demonstrate the generality of such principles by citing various legal systems in which those principles appear. Indeed, some argue that the *lex mercatoria* is not a corpus of legal principles at all, but rather a 'methodological approach centred on comparative legal analysis'.[400] According to Gaillard, the commentator most associated with this theory, transnational law consists of 'deriving the substantive solution to the legal issue at hand ... from a comparative law analysis which will enable the arbitrators to apply the rule which is the most widely accepted'.[401] Transnational rules themselves 'are understood as a methodology drawing from a number of sources pursuant to the comparative law approach'.[402]

Even if general principles exist independently of national laws, proving their content almost invariably requires a comparative law exercise.[403] Nolan and Sourgens describe the process necessary to prove the content of a previously unrecognized general principle as having five steps: (1) identify the factual issue requiring legal resolution, (2) identify the legal systems that may bear on the issue, (3) assemble a relevant sample of

[394] The same is true for counsel. Since arbitration allows the parties to 'dictate the laws and rules governing their disputes ... in order to utilize these choices, attorneys must have a basic understanding of foreign procedures'. Secunda 2006, 709–10 (citation omitted), arguing that courses in arbitration law should instruct students in a variety of *lex arbitri* models from different countries and in the practices of various major arbitral institutions.

[395] Glenn 2001, 984.

[396] Pietrowski 2006, 377; Wilkey 1999, 97.

[397] Kennedy 1997, 623.

[398] Pietrowski 2006, 373 fn 2.

[399] Such as Berthold Goldman, one of the fathers of the modern *lex mercatoria* and, more recently, Klaus Peter Berger and George Bermann.

[400] Petsche 2005, 59.

[401] Gaillard 2001, 61. But see Delaume 1989.

[402] Ibid, 68. See also Glenn 2001, 999, calling general principles of international law a 'form of comparative legal practice'.

[403] A comparative investigation is unnecessary only when a general principle has already been recognized. The content of such principles may be proven through the rulings of international tribunals and domestic courts, transnational legal codifications, and scholarly publications. See Nolan and Sourgens 2009, 524–32.

those systems and determine whether they contain common principles relating to the factual issue, (4) verify whether any differences between those systems have a practical effect, and finally (5) determine whether the principle can be appropriately characterized as a principle of international law.[404]

Tribunals do not necessarily follow these steps punctiliously, but they do describe in general the way they go about determining the content of general principles. ICC Case No 7263 of 1994 provides an example. The claimant was the Ministry of Defence of a state referred to as Country X. The respondent, a US military contractor, asserted that the claimant lacked authority to initiate the arbitration because the constitution of Country X required approval of the Ministerial Council and notification to parliament prior to the initiation of arbitrations regarding public or government property. The approval had not been sought, nor the notification made. The claimant maintained that the relevant provision of the constitution required approval only of arbitration agreements, not initiation and notification of arbitrations in individual cases. The tribunal agreed with this interpretation and found that it was 'more consistent with … the general principles governing international arbitration, and with the "trade usages" which the Tribunal is bound to apply pursuant to article 13(5) of the ICC Rules'.[405] The universality of this interpretation was 'confirmed' by the fact that 'Rules similar to the relevant article of the Constitution of Country X are not rare in the constitutional and administrative law of various countries'.[406]

Second, in cases where the parties disagree as to the applicable substantive law, tribunals will consider both laws. For example, ICC Case No 6850 of 1992 involved German and French parties. Although the tribunal held unanimously that French law governed the dispute, it also wrote that 'we may not ignore the provisions of German law, as the arbitral clause was concluded by officers of a German company'.[407] Such references to inapplicable national laws are partly a function of arbitrators' desire to remain neutral; comparative law 'provides the means to do justice to all legal systems involved'.[408] In this regard, party-appointed arbitrators often play the role of a 'translator' of national laws and legal cultures; they take it upon themselves to explain to the rest of the tribunal the perspective of the party that appointed them.[409]

Even in cases where it is clear that one party's law applies, tribunals sometimes take pains to demonstrate their sensitivity to the different perspectives that parties from different states might bring to a dispute. This phenomenon demonstrates the comparative law expertise of many international arbitrators. In ICC Case No 9302 of 1998, the dispute concerned a distributorship agreement between German and Colombian parties. The contract contained a choice of law clause selecting German law. Although the tribunal applied German law, and only German law, it also noted relevant aspects of Colombian law to demonstrate to the Colombian party that the tribunal understood its perspective:

It appears to the arbitral tribunal there was a genuine *bona fide* dissent between the parties. This may be due to a different understanding and practice of commercial contracts, the Colombian

[404] Ibid.

[405] Award in ICC Case No 7263 of 1994 (1997) XXII Ybk Comm Arb 92 [9]. The reference to trade usages is striking; for this tribunal, even national constitutions should be interpreted in accordance with international commercial practice.

[406] Ibid [21].

[407] ICC Case No 6850 of 1992 (1998) XXIII Ybk Comm Arb 37 [8].

[408] Berger 1998, 131.

[409] Lowenfeld 1995, 65. When arbitrators help each other to 'bridge any cultural gap to understand the conduct and arguments' of both parties, they 'contribute not only to a more acceptable award, but also to a higher quality award'. Paulsson 1997, 15.

party emphasizing the formalities and '*Aussenverhaltnis*' [external relationship], while the German party attached more importance to the definition of the contract terms in the '*Innenverhaltnis*' [internal relationship]. The lack of interest of the Colombian party for specific contract terms can be explained by the fact that Colombian law provides sufficiently detailed rules for agency/distribution relationships on which the agent/distributor relies.[410]

Third, comparativism is sometimes forced upon tribunals by the parties, as where the parties agree to the cumulative or concurrent application of multiple laws.[411] In such cases, the tribunal must determine what legal principles are common to the laws that are being applied concurrently.

Doing justice to the different legal systems relevant to a dispute has a practical as well as a principled foundation. As Berger notes, an arbitral award that considers the national laws of both parties, even if only one of those laws governs the dispute, will be more 'palatable' to the losing party, which will in turn encourage voluntary compliance.[412] Arbitral internationalism improves participants' buy-in to arbitration and promotes compliance, thus enhancing the legitimacy of a system that cannot on its own force the losing party to comply with awards.[413]

VI. Conclusion

International commercial arbitrators, like everyone else, are products of their social context. They are shaped by their diverse national cultures and legal training, but are also guided by a combination of social norms that is specific to ICA. Some of these norms can be expressed in terms of values, ie, the normative priorities shared by arbitrators. Among the most important of these are party autonomy, the service of business, neutrality, and internationalism. The impact of these social norms can be seen in arbitrators' decision-making at every stage.

Arbitral tribunals take a wide view of arbitral jurisdiction. For example, they tend to hold that defective arbitration clauses do confer jurisdiction upon the tribunal. This comports with arbitral reverence for party autonomy and a desire to serve the interests of disputing parties that want to avoid each other's national courts.

When it comes to determining the procedures of the arbitration, statutes and rules of procedure permit the parties to determine the procedures they will use. Arbitrators encourage the parties to exercise this autonomy, convening hearings to help the parties decide upon procedures that are appropriate to the particularities of their dispute. Arbitrators will resist the parties' chosen procedures only when the procedures are non-neutral (giving rise to a risk that any eventual award will be set aside) or when the procedures are ill-suited to ICA, for example because they are too closely tied to one party's national court litigation procedures.[414] When arbitrators disapprove of the procedures chosen by the parties, they are more likely to try to convince the parties to

[410] ICC Case No 9302 of 1998 (2003) XXVIII Ybk Comm Arb 54 [33].

[411] Some of the best-known examples are cases decided by the Iran–US Claims Tribunal and the *Eurotunnel* arbitration.

[412] Grigera Naón 1999, 120; Berger 1998, 132.

[413] Lowenfeld argues that one of the roles of party-appointed arbitrators is to 'translate' legal concepts from the home states of the parties that appointed them into terms that the rest of the tribunal can understand. Lowenfeld 1995, 65.

[414] One interviewee recalled that once, 'as a younger, less experienced arbitrator', he acquiesced to the parties' agreement to use the US Federal Rules of Civil Procedure and 'it was a disaster'.

use harmonized international standards and less likely simply to overrule the parties (unless enforceability of the award is at stake).

Throughout the proceedings, arbitrators will take pains to ensure that both parties feel that they are being treated fairly and that their concerns are being addressed. This requires a command of the logistics of arbitrations, an understanding of commercial realities and a broad cultural sensitivity. As international arbitrators see it, their cosmopolitan backgrounds and their experience with international commercial disputes equip them with the necessary tools.

Similarly, arbitral rules of procedure and international arbitral practice prioritize party autonomy on choice of law. International arbitrators are likely to respect parties' choice of law, derogating from it only to comply with relevant mandatory laws. When a tribunal is called upon to make a choice of law, it will likely choose according to its understanding of the parties' presumed intention. Thus, for example, tribunals are unlikely to choose the national law of one of the parties, unless the circumstances show that the contract is closely connected only to that jurisdiction.

Today, ICA tribunals (unlike in the past, to some extent) are unlikely to choose transnational principles as the governing law of a contract, although they will apply them in the unlikely case that they are chosen by the parties. However, tribunals are likely to resort to transnational rules of law in circumstances where internationalism is not trumped by countervailing party interests. In particular, arbitrators are likely to refer to transnational law to fill gaps in the applicable law, whether those gaps arise because the parties chose a national law that is not comprehensive or because the parties called for the application of rules that are common to more than one jurisdiction. In addition, arbitrators may refer to transnational principles when a governing national law compels a result that is commercially unreasonable, for example when it imposes a rate of interest that is unrelated to the actual time value of money for the successful party.

When transnational law is invoked, tribunals almost invariably point to a codified instrument, such as the UNIDROIT Principles, CISG, INCOTERMS, or UCP 600. Codified instruments appeal to international arbitrators because they represent an international consensus. More importantly, they are predictable, and therefore palatable to commercial parties, which crave certainty.

Once the jurisdiction of the tribunal is established, the procedures determined, and the applicable law chosen, tribunals must reach a decision on the merits. This involves determining the content of the relevant legal rules and also determining the facts. Here, too, the parties take the lead. Rules of procedure and standard practice allow the parties to determine how the content of the law will be demonstrated and how the facts will be proven. Tribunals are unlikely to impose any particular evidentiary restrictions; if the parties introduce evidence of facts or law that the tribunal thinks are irrelevant, the arbitrators will simply disregard the evidence rather than exclude it. That said, arbitrators frequently attempt to streamline the proceedings by indicating to the parties the issues that they think deserve attention.

When arbitrators come to decide the merits of the case, they are likely to rely on the facts and the terms of the contract. Although they think in terms of legal rules (for example, by disfavouring entirely untethered *ex aequo et bono* decision-making), they are concerned that the result be commercially reasonable. Thus, for example, arbitrators refer frequently to trade usages, particularly when those usages are specific to the parties' industry, the type of transaction, or the parties' nationalities. This is so regardless of whether the governing law is national or transnational, and regardless of that law's standards for proving usages.

As the ICA community evolves, the values that international arbitrators share are increasingly likely to supersede their diverse national outlooks. Today, many arbitration specialists under middle age have spent their entire careers working only in ICA. They were hired by the currently dominant generation, and therefore have the characteristics esteemed by that generation—technical skill in arbitration law, cosmopolitanism (legal, linguistic, and cultural), and commercial sense. The social norms discussed in this chapter are therefore likely to be reinforced by the next generation of international arbitrators, and the trends discussed in this chapter are likely to harden into standard practices and shared assumptions.

PART II

INTERNATIONAL ARBITRATION CULTURE AND CONTRACT LAW

5

Substantive Law Determinations in International Commercial Arbitration: The Legal Rules

I. Introduction

Part II shifts the argument from the theoretical to the practical plane—it examines international arbitral decision-making in practice. Specifically, Part II tests the explanatory power of the theory developed in Part I by applying it to published decisions of international commercial arbitrators on discrete and well-defined areas of contract law. If the cultural theory of arbitral decision-making can explain the published decisions better than a traditional doctrinal analysis, then it is likely to be useful in predicting arbitrators' decisions in future disputes.

It is frequently said that ICA is merely a procedural alternative to litigation, that arbitrators and judges apply national laws similarly. Part II challenges these commonly held beliefs. The chapters that follow provide evidence that like cases will not necessarily reach like outcomes in ICA and national court litigation. In other words, Part II will show that the applicable legal rules—the subject of traditional doctrinal analysis—are in themselves insufficient to explain the way that international arbitrators make decisions on matters of substantive law. The field of commercial law is too vast and the percentage of unpublished arbitral awards too great for a comprehensive doctrinal analysis to be conducted. Accordingly Part II proceeds by conducting two case studies. These case studies each provide evidence that the outcomes reached in ICA do in fact differ from those reached in national court litigation. This evidence supports the proposition that international arbitrators approach substantive law matters from a different perspective than that of national court judges. The difference in perspective is, in turn, explicable by the cultural theory of arbitral decision-making developed in Part I.

Part II is composed of four chapters. Chapter 5 lays out the rules of law that pertain to substantive law determinations in ICA and shows how these differ from the rules that apply within national legal systems. Chapters 6 and 7 each present a case study; Chapter 6 considers the circumstances in which an aggrieved party may suspend performance in the face of non-performance by the other party without terminating the contract, while Chapter 7 considers the interpretation of contracts. Finally, Chapter 8 discusses the broader implications of the cultural theory of arbitral decision-making for the evolution of contract law.

Since arbitration remains fundamentally an alternative to litigation in national courts, the way that arbitrators apply doctrines of suspension of performance or interpret contracts can only be understood in comparison with the way that courts decide in similar situations. Consequently, each of the case studies presented in Part II considers the comparative legal context of the issue under examination by considering the differing applicable rules and approaches in common law and civil law jurisdictions. These are represented by five exemplars: the United States and England representing common law jurisdictions, and France, Germany, and Switzerland representing the civil law.

These countries were chosen because they exemplify some of the variety that exists within the common law and civil law and also because a significant portion of active international commercial arbitrators were trained in them. One would expect arbitrators to be influenced by the legal systems in which they were trained. Therefore, if results reached in ICA differ from those that would occur in the courts of England, the United States, France, Germany, and Switzerland, even when the substantive laws of those states apply to the merits of the dispute, this would constitute evidence that arbitral decision-making is influenced by norms distinct not only from the provisions of the applicable substantive law, but also from the legal systems and cultures of the arbitrators' home countries.

After placing the relevant legal issues in comparative context, each of the case studies examines the publicly available arbitral awards in which each issue arose. As will be seen, with both suspension of performance and contractual interpretation, international arbitrators reach outcomes that are largely consistent with each other but distinctly different from the results reached under any one national legal system.

The case studies discuss the various national laws that apply to the awards included in the case study. However, it is also necessary to provide some background on the rules generally applicable in ICA that pertain to substantive law, since these might be the source of any divergence in outcomes between ICA and national courts.

This chapter describes the legal rules specific to ICA that pertain to substantive law. It might seem that there could be no substantive law rules common to all international arbitrations; after all, arbitral institutions do not draft codes of substantive rules, only procedural rules. Moreover, there is no unified substantive law of ICA; different tribunals apply different substantive laws to the individual disputes brought before them. Accordingly, there should not be any legal rule that would cause arbitrators and judges to reach different outcomes on substantive law matters.[1]

However, there do exist rules specific to ICA that pertain to substantive law. Some of these rules relate to what might be called arbitral private international law; they govern the choice of law process and the range of substantive rules available. These rules may lead international arbitrators to apply different rules of law to a given dispute than national court judges would. Moreover, rules specific to ICA may lead arbitrators to apply a given law in a different manner than a national court judge would. To the extent that these rules do in fact lead to the application of different laws or the differing application of the same laws, they would provide a doctrinal explanation for any divergence in outcomes between ICA and national court litigation.

This chapter will consider each of these two possibilities in turn. First, it will describe three ways in which different rules of law may come to be applied to the same dispute in ICA and in national court litigation: differing choice of law rules, the availability of transnational rules in ICA, and the availability of amiable composition in ICA. Second, it will describe the rules relating to the ascertainment of the content of the governing law in ICA, which may lead international arbitrators to interpret a given law differently from national courts.

[1] This discussion does not address the substantive law applicable to the arbitration agreement, which may or may not be the same as the law applicable to the remainder of the contract. See, eg, Redfern and Hunter 2004, 147–53.

II. Application of Different Rules of Law in International Arbitration and National Court Litigation

Choice of law is a complex topic, and no attempt is made here to survey the full range of choice of law rules applicable in different states. However, this section will describe the three ways in which different rules of law may be applied to a given dispute in ICA than would be applied by national courts: the choice of law rules applicable to ICA, which differ from those that apply in any national jurisdiction; the availability of transnational rules of law in ICA that are either unavailable or unlikely to be applied in national court proceedings; and the power of arbitral tribunals, when acting (expressly or even implicitly) under amiable composition, to apply no legal rules whatsoever.

1. Choice of law in international commercial arbitration

In ICA, party autonomy in choice of law is nearly absolute.[2] International arbitral tribunals have no *lex fori*, and therefore no nationally generated choice of law regime and no inbuilt predisposition in favour of any national law.[3] They begin the choice of law process not from the point of view of any national system of law, but from the expectations of the parties. This was alluded to by the tribunal in ICC Case No 12073 of 2003, where the respondent argued that its representative did not have legal capacity to enter into the contract, and the result would be different depending on which law applied. The tribunal found: 'While national civil procedure laws and conflict rules applied by national judges typically follow substantive law on capacity (if any), international arbitrators do not have a *lex fori* and must also consider the contractual dimension of arbitral jurisdiction.'[4]

Thus, if the contract contains a clear choice of law clause, tribunals are generally bound to respect that choice.[5] Deference to a choice of law by the parties is, as one tribunal put it, 'standing practice' in ICA.[6] Such deference extends to permitting parties to choose to be governed by specific provisions or specific rules of law, and to derogate from aspects of the otherwise-applicable law. As the tribunal in ICC Case No 7047 of 1994 observed, 'the principle of party autonomy is not only understood as one of localization of a contract within the sphere of a given law but also as one allowing the parties

[2] This basic proposition is supported by the major treatises. See, eg, Born 2009, 2154: 'The freedom of commercial parties to choose the substantive law governing their business relations is uniformly affirmed'; Redfern and Hunter 2009, 195: 'It is generally recognized that parties to an international commercial agreement are free to choose for themselves the law (or the legal rules) applicable to that agreement'; Lew et al 2003, 414: 'Due to the universal acceptance of party autonomy in most developed legal systems and its origin in the express or determinable intention of the parties, it is now recognized that party autonomy operates as a right in itself.' But see Craig, Park, and Paulsson 2001, 101–2, arguing that there remained, at least as of 2001, some limits to the parties' absolute freedom of choice of law. On the evolution of the modern rule of party autonomy, (up to the 1970s), see Lew 1978, 73–5.

[3] See, eg, Silberman and Ferrari 2011, 277–81. However, the arbitration statutes of some states do prescribe a particular choice of law rule for international arbitrations seated in those states.

[4] (2008) XXXIII Ybk Comm Arb 63 [19]. See also Craig, Park, and Paulsson 2001, 322.

[5] The rules of procedure of most arbitral institutions require the tribunal to apply any laws or rules of law chosen by the parties. See, eg, ICC Rules, art 21(1); LCIA Rules, art 22.3; ICDR Rules, art 28(1); UNCITRAL Rules, art 35(1).

[6] ICC Case No 7047 of 1994 (1996) XXI Ybk Comm Arb 70 [14]. The tribunal also stated that the parties' choice of law can be overridden only by principles of international public policy, such as 'provisions to fight corruption and bribery' [16].

to depart from the otherwise applicable law'.[7] However, the autonomy principle is not unlimited; mandatory rules relating to fundamental public policies cannot be overridden by the parties' agreement:

> Even in international arbitration, the parties' agreement should not be allowed to prevail over *all* mandatory rules of national laws ... some rules are so important to the economic or social welfare of the country whose legislature enacted them that international arbitrators must be prepared to enforce them irrespective of the contrary intent of private parties.[8]

Aside from limitations imposed by compliance with mandatory provisions of the law of the seat of arbitration, there are only two generally applicable exceptions to the rule that tribunals must respect parties' choice of law. First, choices *in fraudem legis*, that is, made only to circumvent an undesired law, will not necessarily be enforced; second, tribunals sometimes apply, in addition to the law chosen by the parties, the mandatory laws of states other than the seat of arbitration where enforcement of the award may be sought.[9]

Party autonomy in choice of law does not always enjoy such a wide scope in national court litigation. To be sure, most national laws respect party autonomy in the choice of the substantive law, and have done so for some time,[10] and national jurisdictions have increasingly come to presumptively enforce contractual choice of law.[11] However, unlike with arbitration, some limits remain in different national laws, especially in states that have not recently updated their choice of law regimes. For example, many states' courts will not necessarily enforce a choice of law agreement that selects a law with no connection to the state in which the court sits.[12]

If the contract does not designate the governing substantive law, most national *leges arbitri* and most arbitral rules of procedure empower the tribunal to select the choice of law rule it considers most appropriate, and then to apply that choice of law rule to determine the governing law.[13] There are some outliers, Switzerland being the most prominent example; the Swiss Private International Law Statute and the Swiss Rules both provide that, in the absence of a choice by the parties, the tribunal must apply the rules of law with which the dispute has the closest connection.[14] In most cases, however, the tribunal need not employ a choice of law rule taken from a nation's private international law regime, and need not even apply a choice of law rule at all. Instead, the rules of most arbitral institutions permit the tribunal to designate an applicable law directly (*voie directe*); for example, the ICC Rules simply permit the tribunal, in the absence of a choice by the parties, to 'apply the rules of law which it determines to be appropriate'.[15] In sum, arbitral tribunals are more likely to enforce a contractual choice of substantive law than national courts and, absent such a choice, often avoid choice of law rules by making a direct choice of the applicable law.

[7] ICC Case No 7528 of 1993 (1997) XXII Ybk Comm Arb 125 [10].

[8] Ibid [12] (emphasis in original).

[9] Blessing 1997, 39–40. The application of mandatory rules other than those of the seat is an issue of some debate. See generally Bermann and Mistelis 2011. See also Borchers 2008.

[10] See, eg, Lew et al 2003, 414 (citing E Rabel, *The Conflict of Laws. A Comparative Study*, Vol I (2nd edn, U Michigan P, Ann Arbor 1958) 90); see also Lew 1978 [441].

[11] This trend is exemplified by the Rome I Regulation. See Section II.2 of this chapter. See also Briggs 2008, 381 (concluding that: 'As far as the common law is concerned, the right of parties to choose the law to govern their contract is practically unrestricted.').

[12] Dicey and Morris 2000, 1196–8.

[13] See, eg, UNCITRAL Rules, art 35(1); English Arbitration Act 1996, s 46(3).

[14] Articles 187(1) and 33(1), respectively.

[15] Article 21. See also ICDR Rules, art 28(1); LCIA Rules, art 22.3.

2. Availability of transnational rules of substantive law

In addition to national laws, other bodies of substantive legal rules exist that are frequently applied in ICA but are either unavailable or unlikely to be applied in national courts. In the context of international private law, 'rules of law' must be distinguished from 'laws'. The latter means the laws applicable in a state, whatever their source. Rules of law, on the other hand, are any statements of principle which have the character of legal rules but which are not 'law' applicable in any state.[16] The two most prominent examples of rules of law are international contract law instruments and general principles of international private law.

International contract law instruments

The major international contract law instruments were all drafted by representatives of both common and civil law jurisdictions. These instruments take one of two forms: conventions that mimic domestic statutes, or compilations of principles in the manner of the American Restatements.

Parties may expressly adopt the conventions as the governing laws of their contracts. More commonly, however, conventions typically provide that they apply when the parties have made no choice of law, and are domiciled in different states and choice of law analysis leads to the application of the law of a state party to the convention.[17] Generally, the domestic choice of law rules of contracting states provide that the convention will apply to contracts between parties from that state and another contracting state. These types of international contract law instruments are equally applicable in state courts and in ICA.

The two most prominent examples of these conventions are the CISG and its predecessor, the Uniform Law for International Sales (ULIS). These two instruments apply only to contracts for the sale of goods for commercial use. The CISG applies to contracts that have both sales and non-sales aspects, so long as the sales aspects form the 'preponderant part' of the parties' obligations.[18] If parties conclude two or more separate contracts, not all of which are contracts of sale, then the CISG applies to the contracts of sale and the otherwise applicable domestic law applies to the other contracts.[19]

These instruments potentially apply to a huge number of contracts. In practice, however, most lawyers and judges in many jurisdictions are not aware of the applicability of these conventions, so they seldom appear in the decisions of national courts.[20] Arbitrators, on the other hand, tend to be aware of them, to be receptive when the parties submit that they are applicable, and even to determine that they are applicable when the parties make no such submission. This can be seen in the case studies that follow in the next two chapters.

The second type of international contract law instruments—the compilations of principles—are often drafted by representatives of states but are not conventions to be ratified. The two best known are the UNIDROIT Principles and the PECL. These instruments most commonly apply when tribunals invoke them as embodiments of

[16] See, eg, Silberman and Ferrari 2011, 268–72. [17] CISG, art 1(1).
[18] CISG, art 3(2). See generally CISG-AC Opinion No 4. [19] Ibid.
[20] See Ziegel 2005. In the United States, Canada, Australia, and New Zealand combined, there were only seventy-nine published decisions under the CISG in the seventeen years from the date the CISG entered into force until 2005. In the same period, seven Western European civil law countries surveyed by Ziegel published decisions under the CISG in 765 cases. Ibid, 68. The only states in which the CISG is frequently applied by the courts are Germany and China.

general principles of international private law.[21] The UNIDROIT Principles and PECL may also apply directly as rules of law governing a contract if the parties so designate or, absent such a choice, if the tribunal chooses them. However, this is rare in practice.[22] More commonly, they are applied to interpret or supplement the CISG or to fill gaps in applicable domestic laws.[23]

These instruments do not have the status of governing law in national court proceedings even if the contract contains a clause choosing them as the governing law. For example, under the 1980 EC Convention on the Law Applicable to Contractual Obligations ('Rome Convention')[24] and under the Rome I Regulation (applicable to contracts concluded after 17 December 2009),[25] courts of EU member states cannot apply rules of law like the UNDROIT Principles or PECL. Under the Rome Convention, a contract may be governed by 'the law chosen by the parties', or, in the absence of such choice, by 'the law of the country with which [the contract] is most closely connected'. Similar rules apply under the Rome I Regulation.[26] Because these international instruments are considered 'rules of law', not 'laws', state courts have interpreted these words to require application of a national law, even if the parties explicitly choose rules of law.[27] Thus, if a contract contains an express choice of 'rules of law' in a proceeding before an EU state court, the court will disregard that choice and apply the national law designated by the Rome I Regulation.[28] In ICA proceedings, on the other hand, contractual disputes may be determined under rules of law.

[21] Farnsworth 1997, 3. A good example is PECL, art 1:101(3), which states that the PECL may be applied when the parties 'have agreed that their contract is to be governed by "general principles of law", the "lex mercatoria" or the like; or have not chosen any system or rules of law to govern their contract'.

[22] Empirical studies indicate that parties rarely choose transnational rules of law to govern their contracts. See, eg, Dasser 2008, 140. For awards where the UNIDROIT Principles were applied directly as the law governing the contract, see, eg, ICC Case No 7710 of 1995 [2001] JDI 1148; ICC Case No 8501 [year unknown] [2001] JDI 1164. In both cases, the parties did not make a choice of law and the tribunal chose the UNIDROIT Principles via *voie directe*. No awards could be found where the PECL were applied as the governing law.

[23] Berger 1998, 133; see also Garro 1995 and Mayer 2002. Examples of awards where tribunals have employed the UNIDROIT Principles in this manner include: ICC Case No 8547 of 1999 (2003) XXVIII Ybk Comm Arb 27 (to supplement the ULIS); ICC Case No 9333 of 1998 [2002] JDI 1094 (along with the CISG, to supplement Swiss law); ICC Case No 8486 of 1996 (1999) XXIVa Ybk Comm Arb 162 (to supplement Dutch law); ICC Case No 8817 of 1997 (2000) XXV Ybk Comm Arb 355 (to supplement the CISG); ICC Case No 8128 of 1995 [1996] JDI 1024 (to supplement the CISG).

[24] Convention on the Law Applicable to Contractual Obligations, 19 June 1980 (80/934/EEC), art 4.

[25] Regulation (EC) No 593/2008 of the European Parliament and of the Council of 17 June 2008 on the law applicable to contractual obligations (Rome I) (OJ No L 177, pp 6 ff) ('Rome I Regulation').

[26] Ibid, art 4.

[27] See, eg, *Shamil Bank of Bahrain v Beximco Pharm Ltd* [2004] EWCA Civ 19: under art 3(1) of the Rome Convention, only choice of law clauses selecting national laws are valid, and therefore a choice of law clause selecting Shari'a law was invalid. See Bantekas 2010, 1 fn 4: 'In this case it was held that the choice of Islamic law as the proper law of the contract was inoperable, given that Islamic law is not a quantifiable legal system which the courts can ascertain for the purposes of choice of law. In the field of arbitration, on the other hand, this does not constitute a problem at all.' Presumably, international arbitral tribunals could apply Shari'a because they are permitted to apply 'rules of law'.

[28] But see recitals 13 and 14 to the Rome I Regulation, which state that the Regulation: 'does not preclude parties from incorporating … into their contract a non-State body of law', and that: 'Should the Community adopt, in an appropriate legal instrument, rules of substantive contract law, including standard terms and conditions, such instrument may provide that the parties may choose to apply those rules'.

General principles of international private law

Some jurisdictions have considered permitting their courts to apply international contract law instruments like the UNIDROIT Principles and PECL.[29] However, another category of rules of law remains the exclusive province of arbitration: general principles of international private law. These remain entirely unavailable in national court litigation,[30] and prior to the 1970s, arbitration awards based on general principles of law were considered unenforceable.[31] Now, however, both arbitral rules of procedure and recently adopted national arbitration laws permit the parties to choose to be governed by 'rules of law', not just 'laws'.[32] For example, article 1496 of the French National Code of Civil Procedure (a provision that was introduced in 1975) provides for the application of the 'rules of law' considered 'appropriate' by a tribunal.[33] As a result of the spread of such provisions, international arbitral awards applying general principles as the substantive law governing the contract will now be enforced by most national courts.[34] In effect, national courts now uphold the freedom of parties to arbitrations to choose to be governed by general principles, even though they continue to prevent parties to litigation from making the same choice.

3. Arbitration without law: amiable composition and related doctrines

If the parties expressly so empower them, arbitral tribunals may decide disputes not on a legal basis, but instead on their own sense of fairness, commercial reasonableness, or trade usages. This can happen in two ways. First, parties sometimes include statements in the dispute resolution provisions of their contracts to the effect that, in addition to the applicable law, the tribunal should consider equity or trade usages, or alternatively that the tribunal may depart from the applicable law to the extent that it conflicts with equity or trade usages. In these situations, there is still a law or rules of law applicable to the substance of the dispute; however, the tribunal may disregard or supersede the law in the circumstances directed by the parties.

Second, the parties may empower the tribunal to act without reference to any governing law whatsoever. This broad equitable power is usually called amiable composition. Tribunals so empowered are often referred to in French as '*amiables compositeurs*'

[29] The European Commission proposed that the Rome I Regulation permit the application of non-state bodies of law, ie, 'rules of law'. See European Commission 2005. However, this proposal was not accepted.

[30] Briggs 2002, 159, noting that under the Rome Convention: 'a choice of the *lex mercatoria*, or of the law of Mars, not being the law of a country, cannot be upheld, because the Convention sanctions only the choice of the law of a country'. The only real exception is France, where *lex mercatoria* concepts have generally received a friendly reception from both commentators and courts. Sandrock 2001, 303.

[31] Rivkin 1993, 72.

[32] All major arbitral rules of procedure permit the parties or the tribunal to choose to apply 'rules of law'. In the drafting of the first version of the UNCITRAL Rules, 'law' was specifically chosen, as opposed to 'rules of law,' in order to preclude the application of non-state rules. Van Hof 1991, 226–7. By contrast, the current (2010) version of the UNICTRAL Rules provide for the application of 'rules of law': art 35(1). Similarly, ICC Rules, art 17(1) was drafted utilizing the term 'rules of law' specifically to permit the parties to choose to be governed by non-state rules. Craig, Park, and Paulsson 2001, 320.

[33] When it was adopted, the *Code de procédure civile* was unusual—possibly unique—for permitting the application of 'rules of law' in arbitration. Official translation available online: <http://www.legifrance.gouv.fr/home.jsp> accessed 20 July 2012.

[34] Rivkin 1993, 73–4; see also Lew 1978, 123.

or are said to decide '*ex aequo et bono*'. (These terms are synonymous as generally construed.[35]) In such cases, the tribunal may decide according to its own sense of justice without reference to any particular law: 'Amiable composition and *ex aequo et bono* make no pretence of standards: [they] generally are considered as an authorization to act *contra legem*, to depart from the law, to change the law or to reject a claim based on the law.'[36] Amiable composition clauses give tribunals much latitude—even more than when deciding under equitable principles.[37]

Although these two situations in which tribunals may exercise equitable powers are distinct, they are considered together for present purposes. What they have in common is that the parties have agreed that the tribunal should decide according to its sense of the appropriate outcome, even if this sense is not based on a legal rule or is contrary to the law that would otherwise be determinative. The discussion that follows focuses on amiable composition, but it also largely applies to cases where the parties choose a governing law and also direct the tribunal to take into account extra-legal factors such as trade usages, or to disregard the law as necessary to serve the interests of fairness or commercial reasonableness.

For a tribunal to possess the power of amiable composition, the parties must confer this power in express terms.[38] Many tribunals take this restriction seriously. For example, in ICC Case No 13278 of 2003, Spanish law governed the contract and the respondent proffered an argument based on general principles of *force majeure*. The sole arbitrator rejected this argument as unsupported by Spanish law and intended to entice her into exercising powers of amiable composition, which had not been conferred upon her.[39]

However, some tribunals have taken on amiable-composition type powers without an express conferral of those powers. For example, in ICC Case No 7369 of 1994, neither the Qatari respondent nor the Italian claimant raised any arguments regarding amiable composition or equitable principles. The tribunal conceded that it was 'bound to decide all issues by relying on the proper law of the Contract between the parties, as a result of the clear wording of the Applicable law Clause of the Agreement, which is also expressly reflected in the Terms of Reference adopted by the parties'.[40] However, the tribunal nevertheless based its decision on general principles of equity: 'the Tribunal has decided to consider these principles as part of its Terms of Reference, in its genuine and serious desire to be fair to both parties, by among other things, considering the general principles of equity'.[41]

Amiable composition clauses do not appear ever to have been common in international commercial contracts,[42] and are even less popular than they used to be.[43] As

[35] ICC Case No 11663 of 2003 (2007) XXXII Ybk Comm Arb 60 [17].

[36] McConnaughay 1999, 471–2 (quoting Sohn 1967, 332–3).

[37] Scheuner 1967, 282: 'The judge who refers to equity stays within the borders of existing law.'

[38] See, eg, ICDR Rules, art 28(3); ICC Rules, art 21(3); LCIA Rules, art 22.4; UNCITRAL Rules, art 35(2).

[39] ICC Case No 13278 of 2003 (2008) XXXIII Ybk Comm Arb 118 [9]. See also ICC Case No 11663 of 2003 (2007) XXXII Ybk Comm Arb 60 [17]; ICC Case No 9771 of 2001 (2004) XXIX Ybk Comm Arb 46 [60].

[40] ICC Case No 7639 of 1994 (1998) XXIII Ybk Comm Arb 66 [31].

[41] Ibid. See also ICC Case No 7181 of 1992 (1996) XXI Ybk Comm Arb 99 [60].

[42] 81 per cent of corporations surveyed in 2010 reported that they never use *ex aequo et bono* or amiable composition adjudication. Only 2 per cent often concluded contracts that contain *ex aequo et bono* or amiable composition clauses. W&C/QMUL 2010, 15.

[43] The only area where amiable composition is common is in sport-related arbitrations, especially those administered by the Court of Arbitration for Sport (CAS). Rule 45 of the CAS Rules provides that the parties may authorize CAS tribunals to decide *ex aequo et bono*. Statutes of the Bodies

an example of this trend, of fifteen published ICC awards involving contracts that conferred amiable composition powers upon the tribunal, only two were issued in the 1990s and none since 2000.[44]

Despite its rarity, amiable composition is worthy of mention for three reasons. First, the awards that have been decided under amiable composition must be understood as such, and not measured by the same standards as awards decided under legal rules. Second, all the major arbitral rules continue to permit parties to choose amiable composition, so the possibility, though diminished, is not dead.[45] Third, amiable composition is both historically and theoretically tied to the *lex mercatoria* doctrine. When tribunals are empowered to act as *amiables compositeurs*, they frequently take this as evidence that the parties intended to apply general principles.[46] Goldman goes so far as to assert that the inclusion of an amiable composition term in a contract constitutes a designation of general principles as the applicable law.[47] Most arbitrators and commentators do not subscribe to Goldman's wholesale identification between amiable composition and general principles; however, tribunals acting as *amiable compositeurs* may refer to general principles to give their decisions analytical structure and consistency.

III. Ascertainment of the Content of the Governing Law

The previous sections refer to situations where the rules might permit or direct arbitrators to apply different substantive principles (laws, rules of law, principles of equity) than a national court would apply. In other words, these rules may explain divergences in outcomes based on different substantive principles being applied to the same dispute. However, divergences may also arise from arbitrators interpreting a given law in a *way* that differs from the approach of national court judges; these are not conflict of laws questions, but rather content of laws questions.[48]

The means by which adjudicators ascertain the content of the governing law and apply that law to the facts of a dispute may affect the outcome of the dispute. This section examines whether any rules specific to ICA permit or direct arbitrators to apply the chosen law (including determining the content of that law) in a different way than national courts would do.

Working for the Settlement of Sports-Related Disputes, available at <http://www.tas-cas.org/rules> accessed 6 August 2012.

44 ICC Case No 1677 of 1975 (1978) III Ybk Comm Arb 217; ICC Case No 2216 of 1974 [1975] JDI 917; ICC Case No 2694 of 1977 [1978] JDI 985; ICC Case No 2879 of 1978 [1979] JDI 989; ICC Case No 3267 of 1979 (1982) VII Ybk Comm Arb 96; ICC Case No 3380 of 1980 (1982) VII Ybk Comm Arb 116; ICC Case No 3540 of 1980 (1982) VII Ybk Comm Arb 124; ICC Case No 3938 of 1982 [1984] JDI 926; ICC Case No 4265 of 1984 [1984] JDI 922; ICC Case No 4467 of 1984 [1984] JDI 924; ICC Case No 4972 of 1989 [1989] JDI 1101; ICC Case No 5103 of 1988 [1988] JDI 1207; ICC Case No 5118 of 1986 [1987] JDI 1027; ICC Case No 6503 of 1990 [1995] JDI 1022; ICC Case No 7986 of 1999 [2002] JDI 1071. This apparent decline in the number of amiable composition cases actually occurred earlier than the dates of these awards would indicate; a tribunal can act under amiable composition only if the contract empowers it to do so, and most of the contracts at issue in these cases were concluded years before the arbitrations were initiated. See also Rogers 2002, 353.

45 Redfern and Hunter 2004, 54.

46 See, eg, ICC Case No 3540 of 1980 [1981] JDI 914; ICC Case No 3292 of 1980 [1981] JDI 924; ICC Case No 3267 of 1979 (1982) VII Ybk Comm Arb 96.

47 Goldman 1979, 927.

48 ILA Report on the Applicable Law 2008, 195.

National legal systems differ profoundly in the ways that they direct judges to ascertain the content of the law and to apply that law to the facts of the case. There are three main categories:

> (i) those in which the court has considerable powers to apply foreign law and to ascertain its contents on its own motion (this is typically the approach followed in civil law systems); (ii) those in which the court is required essentially to rely on the initiative of the parties to plead and prove foreign law as if it were a factual matter (this is typically the approach of English-based common law systems); and (iii) those intermediate systems … where pleading foreign law primarily rests with the parties and where responsibility with regard to ascertaining its contents is divided between the court and the parties.[49]

There is thus no global standard in national courts against which ICA approaches may be compared. Moreover, it is generally agreed that domestic rules on the ascertainment of the governing law should not be applied by analogy to ICA.[50] Accordingly, this section will simply outline the rules that do exist in ICA that might direct arbitrators to ascertain and apply the law in a particular way. The first place to look for such rules is the parties' arbitration agreement. If the arbitration agreement guides or constrains the arbitrators' discretion in applying the governing law, it will be binding upon them. However, arbitration agreements differ from case to case, so no generally applicable rules may be derived from them. There are three possible sources of rules regarding the application of governing laws that apply to ICA generally or to a broad class of international arbitrations: national arbitration laws, arbitral rules of procedure, and international arbitral practice.

National arbitration laws invariably provide, in accordance with New York Convention, article V(1)(b), that both parties must have sufficient opportunities to present their cases. This due process notion implies that the parties must have a reasonable opportunity to address the legal issues in their dispute. Thus, for example, if the tribunal applies a rule or principle that was not invoked by the parties and does not give the parties an opportunity to express their positions, the award could be set aside or refused enforcement.[51]

Beyond this basic point, however, nearly all national arbitration laws are silent on the matter of how arbitrators ought to ascertain and apply the content of the applicable substantive law. There are three notable exceptions:

First, section 34 of the English Arbitration Act 1996 provides:

> (1) It shall be for the tribunal to decide all procedural and evidential matters, subject to the right of the parties to agree to any matter.
> (2) Procedural and evidential matters include …
> (g) whether and to what extent the tribunal should itself take the initiative in ascertaining the facts and the law.

This provision makes clear that it is up to the tribunal to decide the means by which it should ascertain the content of the applicable law, but provides no further guidance. This interpretation is supported by *Hussman (Europe) Ltd v Al Ameen Dev & Trade Co*,

[49] ILA Report on the Applicable Law 2008, 201–2 (citations omitted).

[50] There are a number of reasons for this. Some often-cited reasons are: national rules are founded on a distinction between 'national' and 'foreign' law, while ICA tribunals have no national law of their own; state courts, unlike ICA tribunals, exercise a public function and must consider the transparency and consistency of the rules on pleading and proof of foreign law.

[51] Cf ILA Report on the Applicable Law 2008, 215.

where the Commercial Court held that tribunals seated in London have no obligation to obtain evidence on the content of a foreign law, even if that law governs the dispute:

> If there is no suggestion by the parties that there is an issue under the applicable system of law which is different from the law of England and Wales, or the tribunal does not itself raise a specific issue, then the tribunal is free to decide the matter on the basis of the presumption that the applicable system of law is the same as the law of England and Wales.[52]

Second, article 1044(1) of the Dutch Code of Civil Procedure provides for arbitral tribunals to take advantage of mechanisms for the ascertainment of foreign law that were designed for cooperation between European national courts:

> The arbitral tribunal may, through the intervention of the President of the District Court at The Hague, ask for information as mentioned in article 3 of the European Convention on Information on Foreign Law.... The President shall, unless he considers the request to be without merit, send the request without delay ... and notify the arbitral tribunal thereof.[53]

Third, section 27(2) of the Danish Arbitration Act provides arbitral tribunals with a means of determining the content of European Union law, but does not apply more widely: 'If the arbitral tribunal considers that a decision on a question of European Union law is necessary to enable it to make an award, the arbitral tribunal may request the courts to request the Court of Justice of the European Communities to give a ruling thereon.'

Although there is no Swiss statutory provision relating to the ascertainment of the governing law by arbitral tribunals, the Swiss courts have held that the *iura novit curia* principle applies to international arbitrations with Switzerland as their seat.[54] A tribunal's failure to apply this principle is not in itself sufficient grounds for an award to be set aside; in *D doo v Bank C*, the Swiss Federal Supreme Court held that tribunals may rely entirely on the evidence of foreign law advanced by the parties and need not conduct their own research.[55] However, the Federal Supreme Court has set aside awards when the tribunal ruled on legal issues that were not raised during the arbitration and which came as a surprise to the parties.[56] The French *Cour de cassation* has taken a similar approach.[57]

In sum, the overwhelming majority of national laws do not direct arbitral tribunals to ascertain the content of the governing law in any particular way; the few that address this issue do so in a flexible, permissive manner. The only significant constraint on

52 [2000] EWHC 210 (Comm) [42].

53 Quoted in English translation in ILA Report on the Applicable Law 2008. The authors of the report note that, to their knowledge, this provision has never been invoked.

54 See, eg, *Westland Helicopters Ltd* (Swiss Federal Supreme Court, 19 April 1994) ATF 120 II 155. Similarly: 'In France the prevailing line of jurisprudence confirms the arbitrator's right (and even duty) to base the award on reasons deriving from the applicable law which have been included (even if implicitly) in the debate without an explicit invitation to the parties to comment upon it.' ILA Report on the Applicable Law 2008, 208 fn 42, citing *SGI v Ewbank*, (1993) Rev Arb 664, confirmed by the Court de cassation, (1995) Rev Arb 597.

55 *D doo v Bank C*, 27 April 2005, (2005) *ASA Bulletin* 719.

56 Compare Case No 4P.100/2003, 30 September 2003 (award set aside when the tribunal applied a contractual provision not invoked by a party and coming as a surprise to the parties) and *Bank Saint Petersburg plc v ATA Insaat Sanayi ve Ticaret Ltd* (Federal Supreme Court, 2 March 2001), (2001) *ASA Bulletin* 531 (award not set aside when the tribunal failed to inform the parties that its decision would be based on formal defects in a bank guarantee rather than on the guarantee's performance because this was not surprising to the parties).

57 *Conselho Nacional de Carregadores v Charasse* (Cour de cassation, 14 March 2006) (2006) Rev Arb 653.

arbitrators' powers to decide how to ascertain the content of the applicable law is that both parties must be given a reasonable opportunity to present their positions on the decisive legal issues.

Arbitral rules of procedure are similar. The sole exception is article 22.1 of the LCIA Rules, which provides:

> Unless the parties at any time agree otherwise in writing, the Arbitral Tribunal shall have the power, on the application of any party or of its own motion, but in either case only after giving the parties a reasonable opportunity to state their views …
>
> (c) to conduct such enquiries as may appear to the Arbitral Tribunal to be necessary or expedient, including whether and to what extent the Arbitral Tribunal should itself take the initiative in identifying the issues and ascertaining the relevant facts and the law(s) or rules of law applicable to the arbitration, the merits of the parties' dispute and the Arbitration Agreement.

This rule has two notable features. First, it states that arbitral tribunals have the power to act on their own motion to determine the content of the applicable law. Second, it requires them first to give the parties a reasonable opportunity to state their views.

Finally, if an international standard practice has emerged in ICA with respect to application of the governing law, international arbitrators will not be bound to follow it, but may feel obliged to do so or may feel that the exercise of their discretion ought to be guided by such a practice.

There does appear to be an international consensus on the following matters. First, international arbitrators tend to agree that the *iura novit curia* principle does not apply in ICA. Second, tribunals generally see the content of the applicable rules of law to be part of the parties' burden of proof, and leave the means of proving the law up to the parties' agreement. Third, if arbitrators do engage in their own research or raise any legal issues, they must give the parties an opportunity to present their positions.

In sum, therefore, the ICA rules on the way in which arbitrators ought to apply the law, just like the rules on which laws should be applied, impose few constraints on international commercial arbitrators.[58] Arbitrators may exercise their discretion in such a way that the outcome will differ from national court litigation, but there is no legal rule that would require or forbid arbitrators to interpret substantive laws differently from national courts.

IV. Conclusion

This chapter has described the rules of law applicable in ICA that might lead to divergence between courts and arbitral tribunals on matters of substantive law. Broadly

[58] This notion is borne out in the diversity of approaches visible in the very few published awards that consider the matter. For example, in ICC Case No 5418 (1988) XIII Ybk Comm Arb 102, the tribunal relied both on the submissions of the parties' expert witnesses and on its own research on the applicable law. In ICC Case No 7071 of 1994, the tribunal held that it was entitled to rely on its own research, to which it did not draw the parties' attention in advance, because the issues had been extensively argued by the parties in their written submissions and at the hearing. Unpublished; quoted in ILA Report on the Applicable Law 2008, 211. In *Iurii Bogdanov, Agurdino-Invest Ltd and Agurdino-Chimia JSC v Republic of Moldova*, an investment treaty arbitration administered by the Stockholm Chamber of Commerce, the sole arbitrator held that the parties should be given an opportunity to comment on any legal sources identified by the tribunal but that the tribunal was free 'to give the legal qualifications and determine the legal consequences that it deems appropriate, even if they were not pleaded by the parties'. SCC Award of 22 September 2005 [2.2.1], available at <http://italaw.com/documents/Bogdanov-Moldova-22September2005.pdf> accessed 21 August 2012.

speaking, they fall into two categories: rules that lead to application of different substantive laws and rules that lead to divergent applications of a given law.

Choice of law rules in ICA are such that the parties have almost total freedom to choose the governing law, even more than in modern national choice of law regimes (which themselves give wide scope to party autonomy). If the parties do not choose the governing law, the tribunal makes the choice. In most jurisdictions and under most arbitral rules of procedure, the tribunal has the power to choose the governing law or rules of law directly, without reference to any choice of law rule. Under some rules of procedure, tribunals cannot make a direct choice, but must instead apply a choice of law rule, then apply the law selected by that rule. In a small minority of jurisdictions and under some rules of procedure (most notably in Switzerland and under the Swiss Rules), tribunals may be required to follow a particular choice of law rule.[59]

Another way that different substantive rules may come to be applied to the same dispute in litigation and in ICA is if the tribunal applies non-national rules of law, rather than the law of some jurisdiction. Tribunals are more likely than courts to apply international commercial law conventions such as the CISG. More importantly, in theory if not in practice, international arbitral tribunals may apply general principles of international private law, either as free-floating principles identified by the tribunal or by reference to codifications like the UNIDROIT Principles. Arbitral tribunals will enforce choice of law agreements that select rules of law, whereas national courts will only enforce choices of some national law. In addition, arbitral tribunals may apply general principles notwithstanding a choice of national law or of an international commercial law instrument.

Finally, merits determinations in ICA are often guided by non-legal rules of decision. In some cases, the parties will direct the tribunal to consider equity or trade usages in addition to or notwithstanding the applicable law, while in other cases the parties will direct the tribunal to decide on its own sense of equity without applying any legal rules whatsoever (amiable composition or *ex aequo et bono*). Properly speaking, both of these scenarios require the express approval of the parties. However, with respect to trade usages at least, express terms in the parties' arbitration agreement may not be required, since most arbitral rules of procedure require tribunals to apply trade usages.[60]

The second category of rules concerns the ascertainment of the content of the governing law. Very few national laws or arbitral rules of procedure mention the ascertainment of the content of the governing law, and those that do are permissive rather than restrictive—they do not actually constrain arbitrators' discretion, but rather permit tribunals to determine the content of the governing law as they see fit, so long as they do not exceed the scope of the submission to arbitration,[61] respect due process, and adhere to all relevant mandatory laws.

[59] Whichever of these three possibilities applies in a given arbitration probably does not make much difference to the outcome; most choice of law rules require the tribunal to apply the law most closely connected to the contract (although they differ as to the criteria used to determine the closest connection). When tribunals make a direct choice of law, they typically choose according to something like the closest connection principle. Several interviewees concurred on this point.

[60] See Chapter 4, Section III.2.

[61] The importance of the phrasing of the submission to arbitration was highlighted by a recent case involving an insurance contract concluded between Brazilian parties. The contract stated that: 'Any dispute arising under, out or in connection with this Policy shall be subject to the exclusive jurisdiction of the courts of Brazil.' However, it also provided that: 'In case the Insured and the Insurer(s) fail to agree as to the amount to be paid under this Policy through mediation ... such dispute shall then be referred to arbitration under ARIAS Arbitration Rules.... The seat of the arbitration shall

Restricting the award to the issues submitted to the tribunal, respecting due process, and adhering to mandatory laws are vitally important because each of these constitutes a ground on which an award may be set aside or refused enforcement.

Taken together, the ICA-specific rules on the interpretation of the substantive law impose no significant constraints on arbitral decision-making beyond those related to ensuring the enforceability of the award. Each of the rules opens up areas for party or tribunal choice that may not exist in national court litigation, but none of them prevents the application of any set of substantive law rules or prohibits any means of ascertaining the content of those rules.[62]

The only restrictions that bind ICA tribunals, but not national courts, derive from the tribunal's duty to render an award that national courts will enforce. First, to the extent that the arbitration agreement limits a tribunal's authority to deciding particular legal issues, the tribunal must not exceed this limitation; national courts, on the other hand, have a more general jurisdiction. Second, ICA tribunals may need to take additional steps to protect due process beyond what national laws require (at least in jurisdictions that recognize the *iura novit curia* principle).[63] Third, national courts in general must adhere to the public policy and mandatory laws of their own state, while ICA tribunals must take into account the mandatory laws of the seat of arbitration and of any states where enforcement of the award is likely to be sought.

In short, the applicable laws and rules constrain the decision-making of international arbitrators on substantive law matters minimally, if at all. It is therefore unlikely that the applicable substantive rules can explain differences in outcomes between ICA and national court litigation, except when an ICA tribunal applies non-national rules of law or decides under amiable composition.

1. Substantive law rules and international arbitration culture

This limited nature of the constraints imposed by the ICA rules pertaining to substantive law demonstrates the insufficiency of traditional doctrinal analysis to account for outcomes in ICA. The case studies presented in the following two chapters reinforce this point; the applicable rules of law are on their own insufficient to explain arbitral decision-making and must be supplemented with a non-doctrinal analytical model such as the cultural theory of arbitral decision-making presented in Part I. Before turning to the case studies, however, it is worth exploring the extent to which the rules themselves are a function of ICA culture.

Rules of law are often crystallizations of social norms.[64] Social preferences for particular modes of conduct create pressure to impose legal sanctions to enforce that conduct,

be London, England.' Cross-motions in Brazil and London led to the English courts enjoining court proceedings in Brazil and the Brazilian courts enjoining arbitration proceedings in London. See the decision of the English Court of Appeal upholding the anti-suit injunction *Sulamerica CIA Nacional De Seguros SA v Enesa Engenharia SA* [2012] EWCA Civ 638 and Pendell 2012.

[62] Of course, unlike national courts, the substantive law determinations of ICA tribunals are not subject to appellate review.

[63] Cf art 16 of the Swiss Private International Law Act: 'The contents of the foreign law shall be established by the authority on its own motion. For this purpose the cooperation of the parties *may* be requested' (emphasis added).

[64] See, eg, the discussion of the Berkeley, California dog ordinances in Chapter 2, Section II.

and the result is a legal rule that embodies a social norm. The procedural and substantive laws and rules that govern the ICA system both evolved into their modern forms under the influence of ICA culture.

Most obviously and most importantly, ICA rules pertaining to substantive law are designed to subordinate default rules to party autonomy. In ICA, parties have almost total freedom to select the governing law, to select rules of law that are unavailable in national court litigation, or to have their dispute decided without reference to legal rules. The parties may choose whichever rules of decision they prefer; the rules oblige arbitrators to apply the rules (if any) chosen by the parties and national arbitration laws empower courts to set aside or refuse to enforce awards if tribunals exceed the scope of submission to arbitration.

If the parties do not choose a governing law, tribunals have very wide discretion but generally seek to choose the same laws that the parties might have chosen had they concluded a choice of law agreement.[65] Competitive forces reinforce these tendencies. Competition for appointments 'gives arbitrators a stronger incentive than public court judges to enforce the provisions of the parties' contract, including the parties' contractual choice of law'.[66] Benson acknowledges that parties' primary motivations for choosing arbitration are procedural, but argues that, in addition, 'arbitration may also provide a mechanism for assuring that the contracting parties' preferred substantive law is applied'.[67]

The availability in ICA of non-national rules of law and non-legal rules of decision can also be explained on the basis of ICA culture. If parties want to avoid the application of national substantive laws, ICA rules require tribunals to defer to the parties' choice. Moreover, such non-national rules are seen as more responsive to the specific needs of international commerce than national laws and more neutral as between the parties. Rules that expand the availability of rules of law in ICA, and that prevent national courts from refusing to enforce awards on the basis that they apply rules of law, therefore serve the norms of neutrality, internationalism, and service of business.[68] The close relationship between general principles and trade usages (service of business) and between general principles and comparative law (internationalism) highlight the social normative character of substantive law rules that permit the application of non-national rules of law.

The rules and practices that govern the ascertainment of the content of the governing law are similarly explicable on the basis of ICA culture. The fact that few such rules exist is telling in itself; it exemplifies the ICA system's flexibility, a flexibility that commercial parties prize because it permits them to tailor the dispute resolution process to their needs and to the particularities of their dispute. The very absence of rules, therefore, serves business interests.

To the extent that rules do exist regarding the ascertainment of the content of the governing law, they do not limit this flexibility. Instead, they give tribunals access to assistance in understanding the governing law (as in Denmark and the Netherlands) or require tribunals to consult with parties and to give them adequate opportunities to plead their cases (as in England and under Swiss case law). They prevent unpleasant surprises in the form of decisions that turn on legal issues or authorities on which the

[65] See Section II.1 of this chapter. [66] Drahozal 2005, 524. [67] Benson 1999, 92.

[68] Or at least they are intended to serve those interests. Parties may prefer more predictable governing law. See Chapter 4, Section IV.2.

parties had no chance to comment. They empower arbitrators to take the steps necessary to make a legally correct decision without requiring them to take steps that would unduly multiply the cost and unpredictability of the arbitration.[69] The rules give the parties maximum control over the process of substantive law determinations, limited only by tribunals' duty to render an enforceable award.

[69] For example, if the parties' submissions do not mention an important legal issue or a binding authority, the tribunal has the power to raise it with the parties, but does not have the power to require the parties to prepare extensive written submissions on the issue. Cf Park 2011 and Park 2007.

6

Case Study 1: Suspension of Performance

Consider the following ethical proposition: If you do not fulfil your promise, I shall not fulfil mine. Although this proposition is intuitively supported by simplicity and fairness, the question remains: When will it be warranted in law?[1]

I. Introduction

When confronted with a breach of contract, a lawyer's first reaction may be to file a suit. A business person's instinct would probably be simply to refuse to perform his own obligations. Withholding performance and litigating later has advantages over performing and later seeking to recover losses due to the other party's breach. It requires no advance planning and is simple and intuitive; parties that withhold performance may not think of their actions as a legal remedy. Common sense dictates that it is better to hold on to one's money, and later possibly have to pay, than to pay now and try to recoup the loss. Such action not only mitigates losses, but also impels the non-performing party to perform. All legal systems recognize 'the principle that performance of an obligation may be withheld if the other party has itself failed to perform', although they differ as to the scope or basis of that principle.[2]

On the other hand, excessive withholding of performance can create a windfall for the withholding party or work an injustice on the party in breach:

> It is in society's interest to accord each party to a contract reasonable security for the protection of that party's justified expectations. But it is not in society's interest to permit a party to abuse this protection by using an insignificant breach as a pretext for evading its contractual obligations.[3]

Consequently, the right to withhold performance has been limited in a variety of ways. Civil law jurisdictions accomplish this by operation of the *exceptio non adimpleti contractus* ('the *exceptio*'), which is a specific doctrine only pleaded in cases of suspended performance. Under the common law, on the other hand, generally applicable rules pertaining to contractual conditions indirectly determine the availability of suspension. Despite diversity of doctrine, different legal systems all seek to balance the interests of an aggrieved party to suspend performance against the right of a breaching party not to be forced to compensate the creditor for more than the consequences of its own breach.

Doctrines governing suspension of performance are well developed in most national legal systems. This chapter examines the decisions of international commercial arbitrators in cases where a party has suspended performance. Because of the small number of published awards, the conclusions drawn here are necessarily tentative.[4] Nevertheless, the available data suggest that, when it comes to deciding cases of suspension of

[1] Nyer 2006, 30. [2] Crawford and Olleson 2001, 55. [3] Farnsworth 1999, 580.

[4] These limitations are discussed below. See Section IV.4 of this chapter.

performance, arbitrators tend to make decisions in a different way than the courts of any country, and to reach results that are more consistent with each other than with the provisions of any national law. In other words, in this discrete and well-settled area of contract law, the outcomes reached in arbitration and in national court litigation diverge, even when the same national law applies. As will be seen, this divergence is not explicable on the basis of the substantive law rules specific ICA, but can be explained at least in part by the social norms prevailing in ICA.

This chapter begins with an overview of the remedy of suspension of performance, including an assessment of the universality of right to suspend performance. Next, it places the remedy in context by comparing the law on suspension of performance in five states that supply a large number of international arbitrators and host a large number of international arbitrations: three civil law jurisdictions (Germany, Switzerland, and France) and two common law jurisdictions (England and the United States). It also considers suspension under the major international contract law instruments. Finally, it assesses the published arbitral awards that consider suspended performance.

II. The Remedy of Suspension of Performance

The central question is this: when one party breaches a contract, what courses of action other than filing a lawsuit are available to the injured party? Specifically, may the injured party temporarily suspend its own performance until the breaching party performs its remaining obligations, or must the injured party declare the contract at an end, thereby discharging both parties' unperformed obligations?

Remedies that permit an innocent party to withhold its own performance temporarily are labelled here as 'suspension of performance', in contrast to remedies that bring an end to the contractual relationship, all of which are labelled here as 'termination'. The distinct characteristic of suspension is that it paralyses the contract but does not kill it. Suspension is 'a dilatory plea which ... entitles the injured party *for the time being* to refuse to perform his part'.[5] The party suspending performance need not immediately decide whether to terminate the contract; instead, suspension forces the breaching party to choose whether to cure the breach. Conversely, termination brings an end to both parties' obligations; it may give the injured party a right to damages and to the recovery of such performance as it has already rendered, but will not obligate the breaching party to complete performance. A claim for specific performance, therefore, is compatible with suspension but not with termination.

This chapter adopts the civil law terminology of 'creditors' and 'debtors'. These are clearer and more precise than the traditional common law labels of 'breaching' and 'aggrieved'[6] or 'injured' parties and are more elegant than 'obligor' and 'obligee'. Here, the debtor will always be the party that first breached the contract and the creditor will be the party that seeks to suspend its own performance in response to the debtor's breach.

When a creditor suspends performance, the debtor is faced with a choice of whether to remain in breach or to perform. If the debtor does cure its breach, then the creditor must perform its own suspended obligations as quickly as is practicable. In effect, therefore, the suspension postpones the time of performance under the contract. If, on

[5] Treitel 1988, 310–11 (emphasis in original).

[6] Some American scholars, in particular those writing about self-help remedies, use the label PFB for 'party facing breach'.

the other hand, the debtor remains in breach, then the creditor may declare the contract terminated according to the normal rules regarding termination. Damages payable after termination are, similarly, calculated in the normal way.

Suspension of performance has 'been recognized to some extent as an operative principle in international judicial and arbitral decisions'.[7] Consequently, some arbitrators have pronounced the right to suspend performance to be a general principle of international private law. If suspension does constitute a general principle, then arbitral tribunals may be justified in applying it as a part of the *lex mercatoria*. Indeed, several commentators claim that suspension constitutes a general principle.[8] Such a position is supported by suspension's association with the *exceptio*, a maxim of long standing and general acceptance in the civil law world. A good example is this unequivocal statement:

> With respect to contracts for sale ... it is clear that the right of a party not to perform in the face of non-performance by the other party to an international contract is a part of the *lex mercatoria*. With respect to construction, distribution, or technical assistance contracts ... there is little doubt about the adoption of the *exceptio* by the international trade practice.[9]

Arbitral case law may also support the proposition that the *exceptio*, or suspension of performance more generally, constitutes a general principle of international law. For example, in *Azurix v Argentina*, the tribunal held 'This exception is not unknown to Argentine law and to legal systems generally as it is a reflection of the principle of good faith.'[10]

However, claims of the universality of the principle embodied by the *exceptio* are overblown. No common law system provides a general right of creditors to suspend performance. Even among civil law and mixed jurisdictions, the doctrines operate inconsistently. The codes of the Germanic legal systems explicitly enshrine the *exceptio* as a broadly applicable principle of contract law, while the codes of the Romanistic legal systems, exemplified by France, include the *exceptio* but do not enshrine it as a general principle.

The French *Code civil* does not contain one all-encompassing provision for cases where the *exceptio* might be invoked, but rather includes it in provisions dealing with the obligations of the parties in certain nominate contracts. Nevertheless, in a variety of cases spanning more than a century, the *Cour de cassation* has declared the *exceptio* to be a general principle applicable in all bilateral contracts,[11] a position that has been supported by commentators.[12]

[7] Crawford and Olleson 2001, 56.

[8] Debate also exists as to whether the *exceptio* forms a general principle of *public* international law. Arguably, art 60 of the VCLT and art 22 of the International Law Commission's Draft Articles on State Responsibility incorporate the *exceptio* principle. See generally Crawford and Olleson 2001.

[9] Draetta et al 1992, 163. See also O'Neill and Salam 1993.

[10] *Azurix Corp v The Argentine Republic* (ICSID Case No ARB/01/12, award of 14 July 2006), para 260, available at <http://icsid.worldbank.org/ICSID/FrontServlet?requestType=GenCaseDtlsRH&actionVal=ListConcluded> accessed 28 July 28, 2012. An ad hoc tribunal later rejected Argentina's application for annulment of the *Azurix* award. However, it criticized the original tribunal for failing to pay sufficient attention to the particularities of Argentine law expressing the *exceptio* principle, especially its inapplicability to matters governed by administrative law (a principle derived from French law). *Azurix Corp v The Argentine Republic* (ICSID Case No ARB/01/12, decision on application for annulment 1 September 2009), available at <http://icsid.worldbank.org/ICSID/FrontServlet?requestType=GenCaseDtlsRH&actionVal=ListConcluded> accessed 28 July 2012.

[11] See, eg, Req, 28 April 1862, D 1863.I.250; Req, 17 May 1938, DH 1938.419; Civ 1re, 20 June 1995 [1995] 1361 Revue de Jurisprudence de Droit des Affaires.

[12] Most notably Cassin, Pillebout, and Raynaud.

The international contract law instruments promulgated by various non-governmental and intergovernmental organizations provide a mixed picture. The UNIDROIT Principles, which are frequently invoked as a 'codification' or 'expression' of the general principles of international law,[13] state a general right to suspend performance,[14] as does the PECL.[15] However, the CISG, which is the premier uniform contract law instrument and is frequently applied in international contracts of sale, does not espouse suspension of performance as a general principle. Indeed, there is reason to doubt that the CISG ever permits a creditor to suspend performance.[16]

An international consensus that creditors have a right to suspend performance therefore cannot be said to exist. However, even if it did, suspension still would not constitute a general principle of international law because there is no consensus on the contours of this putative right—different jurisdictions employ different terminology and reasoning. Despite this variation, however, the doctrines applicable to suspension of performance in different jurisdictions all consider the same set of factors when determining whether a suspension of performance is justifiable.

III. Suspension of Performance in Comparative Context

In civil law countries, suspension of performance is governed by the *exceptio*, which is found in some form in the laws of every civil law jurisdiction, either explicitly named (as in Germany and Switzerland) or as a rule or set of rules pertaining to particular nominate contracts (as in France). The *exceptio* is unknown in the common law world, except for those jurisdictions (eg South Africa and Scotland) that are part of the English legal family but have a civil law heritage.

In common law jurisdictions 'analogies can be drawn [to the *exceptio*], though they are far from precise'.[17] While the same result will frequently be reached in similar cases before common law and civil law courts, the reasoning and terminology used to justify non-performance is often entirely different.

Treitel suggests two explanations for the absence of the *exceptio* as a singular legal convention in common law countries.[18] First, there is not as elaborate a taxonomy of bilateral contracts as in the civil law systems, where such contracts are divided into nominate subgroups. Second, civil law systems tend to conceive of suspension (under the *exceptio*) and termination as separate remedies, while common law systems lump the two together, applying the same rules for their invocation and in some cases using the same term, 'rescission', for both (although this term is falling into disfavour).[19]

In England and the United States, the rights to suspension of performance and termination are both determined according to the rules on 'conditions'. This term is used in a variety of senses in Anglo-American contract law, but in this context, conditions can be defined as events upon which the parties' obligations are conditioned. This meaning of condition is further subdivided into promissory and contingent conditions.[20] If one or both parties are not bound to perform unless an external event not under either party's

[13] See, eg, Marella 2003, 1142; Farnsworth 1997, 2; Berger 1997, 945; ICC Case No 10422 of 2001 [2003] JDI 1142; ICC Case No 8365 of 1996 [1997] JDI 1078 (obs J-J Arnaldez); ICC Case No 8873 of 1997 [1998] JDI 1017.

[14] Article 7.1.3. See Section III.3 of this chapter.

[15] Article 9:201. See Section III.3 of this chapter.

[16] See Section III.3 of this chapter.

[17] Treitel 1988, 306.

[18] Ibid.

[19] Cheshire, Fifoot, and Furmston 2001, 604.

[20] Treitel 2003, 762.

control occurs, then that event is a contingent condition.[21] If, on the other hand, the contract is immediately binding on both parties, but party A is not obliged to perform or to tender performance until party B has performed certain of its obligations, then party B's performance is a promissory condition of party A's performance.[22] Promissory conditions (which are the type of interest here) are subdivided into precedent, concurrent, and subsequent promissory conditions, depending upon whether the condition arises before, simultaneously with, or after the obligation to which it pertains.[23] The classic example of a contract containing concurrent conditions is the contract of sale, in which the obligations of delivery and payment are contingent upon each other and (unless otherwise agreed) are owed simultaneously.[24]

The importance of concurrent conditions to suspension of performance is that non-performance by the debtor does not lead to the creditor's performance being excused; rather, the creditor's obligation never becomes due without the performance (or at least tender of performance) by the debtor.[25] This characterization of conditions in the common law systems provides the conceptual link to the *exceptio* as an 'exception' in the civil law sense. Under such a theory, just as the *exceptio metus* might be pleaded to assert that a contractual obligation agreed to under duress never actually existed as a binding obligation, the *exceptio non adimpleti contractus* is pleaded to assert that the creditor's obligation never came into existence because of non-performance by the debtor.

Strictly construed, the *exceptio* is a defence: the creditor suspends its performance, the debtor sues, contending that the suspension constituted a breach of contract, and the creditor defends, citing the *exceptio*. In practice, though, suspension of performance is used most frequently as a form of self-help, deployed to coerce the debtor to complete performance rather than as a defence to a suit by the debtor.[26]

The common law is comfortable with the idea of self-help. For example, the American UCC expressly recognizes 'self-help' as a 'remedy' available to an aggrieved party.[27] In contrast, civil law countries are loath to acknowledge the coercive use of suspension, especially France, where the maxim '*nul ne peut se faire justice à soi-même*' (equivalent to the English expression that no one may take the law into his own hands) remains 'exceedingly influential'.[28] Nevertheless, the value of permitting self-help in some circumstances is undeniable and civil law commentators acknowledge it. Draetta describes the *exceptio* as 'the most notable' permissible form of self-help in the civil law.[29] In addition, permitting suspension of performance conforms to the civil law's preference for solutions that preserve the contractual relationship.[30]

The different rules relating to suspension of performance, regardless of the jurisdiction that promulgated them, all consider four essential factors. Therefore, the laws of states and the decisions of arbitrators can be compared according to the ways that they address those factors. First, the contracts in question must make the obligations of the creditor contingent in some manner. Second, the contract must provide that the parties perform simultaneously or that the debtor perform before the creditor. Third, breaches must meet some minimum standard of severity to justify suspension. Fourth, since 'the wider the gap between the withdrawn performance and the defective one, the more effective a weapon the [*exceptio*] will prove',[31] courts typically examine the creditor's

[21] Ibid. [22] Ibid. [23] Ibid, 762–4.

[24] The presumption of concurrent conditions in sales contracts has been codified. In England, Sale of Goods Act 1979, s 28; in the US, Uniform Commercial Code (UCC), ss 2-507(1), 2-511(1).

[25] Crawford and Olleson 2001, 67. [26] Nicholas 1992, 213–14.

[27] UCC, ss 2–706, 2–712. [28] Treitel 1988, 2; Beguin 1966. [29] Draetta et al 1992, 160.

[30] Jukier 2005, 807–8. [31] Legrand 1988, 1028, citing Cassin 1914, 633.

response. (The neutral term 'quality' will be used to describe the different ways in which the creditor's conduct in suspending performance may be evaluated.)

1. Civil law jurisdictions

Throughout the civil law world, suspension of performance is governed by operation of the *exceptio*. This principle is relatively modern, in that it has no roots in Roman law. The *exceptio* and the wider maxim *inadimplenti non est adimplendum* were extrapolated by the medieval glossators from a variety of Roman law principles applicable to specific instances, such as the *exceptio mercis non traditae*, and from the general principle of good faith.[32]

The *exceptio* must be understood within the range of remedies available to a creditor. Of these, three are worth mentioning. The first is retention, which is roughly comparable to a vendor's lien in the common law and permits a seller or depositee (similar to a bailee) who receives insufficient payment to hold back the goods or thing deposited. Retention overlaps the *exceptio* in that both put pressure on a debtor by withholding performance.[33] However, retention applies only to tangible things (not money)[34] and thus is generally available only to sellers and depositees of goods. In addition, retention is available in unilateral contracts, where one party's promise is exchanged for the other party's performance.[35]

The *exceptio* also works alongside the remedy of price reduction. It allows a buyer faced with incomplete delivery or defective goods to reduce the price unilaterally. In common law jurisdictions, a buyer would have to pay the full price then later sue for damages or under a theory of unjust enrichment.[36] Price reduction is distinguished from suspension of performance in two ways; there is no equivalent remedy for sellers (eg, 'goods reduction' or 'services reduction'), while suspension is available to all contracting parties. In addition, price reduction amounts to a unilateral amendment to the contract, while suspension insists on performance of the contract without amendment.

Most importantly, suspension must be examined together with termination. Unlike common law jurisdictions, civil law countries distinguish sharply between suspension of performance and termination of a contract. In all of the civil law nations discussed here, termination requires a more serious breach than does suspension of performance. In addition, in some civil law countries, most notably France, court intervention is required to terminate a contract. Pleading the *exceptio*, on the other hand, is a wholly private action; the court's only role is to decide after the fact whether the creditor's suspension was justified.

Since French law regulates termination so much more strictly than German or Swiss law, one might expect that French law would compensate by making the *exceptio* available for a wider range of breaches. However, the severity of breach required for suspension is closer to that for termination in France than in Germany or Switzerland. The latter two nations regulate use of the *exceptio* primarily according to the creditor's

[32] Zimmerman 1996, 801. [33] Nyer 2006, 46 fn 42.

[34] The Franco-Roman systems contain this limitation. German law recognizes a wider right of retention, which also includes retention of all types of rights under bilateral contracts. Treitel 1988, 249.

[35] Ibid.

[36] Müller-Chen 2005, 596; Lookofsky 1989, 42–3. In England, under regulations introduced in 2002, consumers may require a seller to reduce the purchase price on defective goods. Sale and Supply of Goods to Consumers Regulations 2002, S1 2002/3045.

conduct, while in France, a debtor's breach must be 'sufficiently serious' to justify suspension of performance. Either way, however, the focus is on the creditor's conduct. If the performance suspended is substantially greater than the debtor's non-performance, civil law courts will hold the suspension unjustified.

Germany

Suspension doctrine in Germany is characterized by clarity and simplicity. It is expressed in BGB (German Civil Code), section 320, entitled *Enrede des nicht erfüllten Vertrags* ('defence of unperformed contract'). Section 320 states:

> (1) A person who is a party to a reciprocal contract may refuse his part of the performance until the other party renders consideration, unless he is obliged to perform in advance....
>
> (2) If one party has performed in part, consideration may not be refused to the extent that refusal ... would be bad faith.[37]

BGB, section 320(1) restricts the application of the *exceptio* to true synallagmatic contracts ('reciprocal' in the official translation), meaning contracts where the parties not only exchange promises, but also where those promises are mutually contingent upon each other.[38] Moreover, the obligation suspended by the creditor must be related synallagmatically to the obligation breached by the debtor.[39] German law also assumes, absent contrary intent of the parties, that performance in a synallagmatic contract is simultaneous.[40] If the contract specifies a particular order of performance or belongs to a class of nominate contracts in which sequential performance is the rule, then the party that performs first may not suspend its performance under section 320. German law thus resolves the two issues of order and contingency of performance in one step by limiting the *exceptio* to synallagmatic contracts.

Restricting the *exceptio* to cases of true synallagmatic contracts means that suspension of performance is available in a smaller range of contractual disputes than in other countries. However, the *exceptio* must be seen in the context of the range of remedies available to creditors; under German law, the right of retention (*Zurückbehaltungsrecht*) is available in a wider set of circumstances than in other civil law systems, so the difference between Germany and other civil law countries is not as great as it would appear from looking at the *exceptio* alone.[41]

German law requires merely that the debtor's breach be 'not trivial',[42] so any nonperformance may entitle the creditor to raise the *exceptio*, subject only to the principle *de minimis non curat lex*.[43] In the Germanic family of legal systems generally, the extent of the debtor's breach is immaterial to the availability of suspension. This rule exemplifies

[37] Official English translation by the Langenscheidt Translation Service for the Justice Ministry of Germany <http://www.gesetze-im-internet.de/englisch_bgb/englisch_bgb.html#p1118> accessed 20 July 2012.

[38] In a synallagmatic contract, such as any contract for the sale of goods, the parties' obligations are exchanged for each other and are contingent upon each other. Delivery of goods is contingent upon payment of the price and vice versa. In a bilateral but non-synallagmatic contract, each party takes on obligations but the two performances are not exchanged for each other. The classic example of a bilateral but non-synallagmatic contract is one where an agent has a duty to act and the principal has a duty to reimburse the agent for her expenses. The agent has a contractual duty to act but this duty is not contingent upon reimbursement of her expenses, while the principal's duty to reimburse expenses is not contingent upon the agent successfully completing her performance. Treitel 1988, 249.

[39] Ibid, 287. [40] Ibid. [41] Ibid. [42] Ibid, 304. [43] Christie 2001, 468.

the doctrinal simplicity of German law with respect to suspension of performance, as it avoids the problem of defining what constitutes a fundamental breach.[44]

Instead, German law focuses on the creditor's conduct. Specifically, BGB, section 320(2) provides that the creditor may not refuse to perform if the refusal 'would be bad faith'. Practically speaking, however, the good faith test involves an assessment of the extent of the debtor's breach. The rule is one of proportionality: if the performance suspended by the creditor is substantially greater than the breach committed by the debtor, courts may give effect to the *exceptio* only to the extent of the debtor's breach. Moreover, if the breach is not *de minimis* but still relatively minor, courts may not permit the creditor to invoke the *exceptio* at all.[45] German law, therefore, focuses on whether the creditor's suspension of performance was proportionate; the extent of the breach is relevant to this determination but is not decisive.

Switzerland

The Swiss approach to suspension of performance is similar to the German. In fact, article 82 of the Swiss Code of Obligations (CO) was based on BGB, section 320. There are only two differences of note. First, Swiss law permits invocation of the *exceptio* in all bilateral contracts, not just synallagmatic ones. Second, CO, article 82 does not specifically provide for good faith or proportionality with regard to the conduct of the suspending party. However, Swiss courts and commentators agree that the creditor's conduct is bound by the general good faith provision in Swiss private law, article 2 of the Swiss Civil Code. Thus, Switzerland, like Germany, requires suspension of performance to have been undertaken in good faith and may limit the protections of the *exceptio* to the extent of the debtor's breach.[46]

France

The use of the *exceptio* in French law cannot be understood except in the context of the rules regarding termination of the contract (*résolution*). The right to terminate exists in all bilateral contracts under *Code civil*, article 1184, but a party cannot simply give notice that it is terminating a contract, as in other legal systems. Rather, a creditor must first serve upon the debtor a *mise en demeure*, which is a formal notification of the delinquency, then launch an *action en résolution*. Termination of a contract does not occur until a court orders it. There are only two exceptions to this lengthy and occasionally expensive process: the inclusion in the contract of a termination clause or conduct by the debtor in such bad faith that continuing the contractual relationship would be impossible or unconscionable.[47]

Although the *exceptio* technically may be invoked only by a creditor in defence of a claim launched by the debtor, it may be relied on without judicial process. If a debtor does sue the creditor for breach of the contract, the court must give effect to the *exceptio* if the circumstances are such as to justify the creditor's refusal to perform. Thus, invocation of the *exceptio* is a particularly attractive option in France; it is frequently relied on even in cases of a breach severe enough to warrant *résolution*.[48]

[44] Coester-Waltjen 2005, 141. [45] Treitel 1988, 303. [46] Ibid, 304.

[47] Laithier 2005, 118. The *Cour de cassation* has upheld the right of a creditor to terminate unilaterally if the breaching party's conduct is egregious, but has cautioned that such unilateral action is at the terminating party's risk. Civ 1ère, 28 october 1998, *Bull* I, n° 211.

[48] Treitel 1988, 311.

The *exceptio* is not expressed in the French *Code civil* as a general principle of contractual relationships. Instead, sections of the *Code civil* that deal with certain nominate contracts contain separate expressions of the *exceptio* applicable only to that type of contract. The *exceptio* appears in provisions relating to sales contracts (articles 1612 and 1653), *échanges* (article 1704; an *échange* is in essence a barter contract, where one physical thing is exchanged for another), and *dépôts* (article 1948; a *dépôt* is a deposit contract, where the subject matter of the contract is kept by one party and later returned in kind).

Each of these articles states the relevant principle but provides little detail. For example, article 1612, pertaining to sales, reads in full: 'The seller is not obliged to deliver the thing where the buyer does not pay the price of it unless the seller has granted him time for the payment.'[49] As a result, specific rules limiting use of the *exceptio* have been developed by the courts and by commentators.

The contract must be bilateral but need not be synallagmatic: 'While French law requires that the obligations should arise out of the same contractual relationship, this will of itself generally satisfy the requirement for interdependence.'[50] With respect to order of performance, it is presumed that performance in bilateral contracts is simultaneous, although this can be overridden by express contractual terms or standard industry usages.[51] For nominate contracts, order of performance may be determined statutorily. Thus, under the *Code civil*, article 1612, performance in sales contracts is simultaneous unless the goods are bought on credit or under an arrangement where payment is not due until a later date. In such cases, the seller must perform first.

In France and the jurisdictions influenced by it, the severity ('*gravité*') of the breach is an important factor; the breach must be '*suffisament grave*'.[52] Under the *Code civil*, whether a breach involves partial or defective performance is less important than the effect of the breach on the creditor. One common formulation is that the breach must be such that 'if the aggrieved party had known of it, he would not have entered into the contract'.[53] A frequently cited application of this principle is that a tenant cannot refuse to pay rent solely on the grounds that the landlord has failed to maintain the premises unless the want of repair is so great as to make enjoyment of the premises impossible.[54] Opinion is divided on whether the *exceptio* is available to a buyer in case of defects that give rise only to a type of liability in French law called guarantee liability,[55] but French commentators agree on the whole that the *exceptio* should only be available in cases of severe defects.[56]

As in Germany and Switzerland, creditors suspending performance must do so in good faith. However, French courts place greater emphasis on the proportionality of the suspension—as a measure of good faith—than do German or Swiss courts.[57] In particular, the majority view is that: 'In a [bilateral] contract, the non-performance by one of the parties of some of his obligations does not necessarily release the other from all of his obligations.'[58]

[49] Official English translation <http://www.legifrance.gouv.fr> accessed 20 July 2012.

[50] Marsh 1994, 325. [51] Treitel 1988, 286–8.

[52] Cass 1e civ, 19 October 1999, RJDA N° 1290; see also Ghestin et al 2001, 441.

[53] Nyer 2006, 51. [54] Treitel 1988, 302–3.

[55] The common law has no concept precisely equivalent to guarantee liability. It is similar to strict products liability in American law or, more generally, to liability arising from breach of an implied warranty of merchantability.

[56] Treitel 1988, 302. [57] Marsh 1994, 324.

[58] Cass soc, 21 October 1954, JCP 1955, II, 8563, obs P Ourliac and M de Juglart (cited and translated in Legrand 1988, 1029). Some cases do go the other way. See, eg, Cass req, 20 April 1921, DP 1922,

The requirement of proportionality can also subsume the requirement of a sufficiently serious breach. For example, the *Cour de cassation* has held that a lessee of defective computer disks could not suspend performance. Although the disks did not perform as well as advertised, they were viable for the lessee's purposes. Where the debtor's breach results in no real harm to the creditor, suspension of *any* performance by the creditor is unjustifiably disproportionate.[59] Indeed, some commentators describe the requirement of a serious breach to be an aspect of the general rule of good faith; it would be bad faith for a creditor to suspend performance in response to a relatively minor breach.[60]

Finally, French law includes a public policy exception to the applicability of the *exceptio*. Under French administrative law doctrine, the *exceptio* is unavailable to parties involved in government contracts, a result justified by the overriding state interest in uninterrupted provision of public services.[61]

2. Common law jurisdictions

At about the same time that the doctrine of the *exceptio* was developing among the canonists of continental Europe, actions for assumpsit and wholly executory bilateral contracts came to be recognized in England.[62] (Previously, the only action available was for debt.[63]) It came to be understood that contracts could involve an exchange of one promise for another, but the promises were held to be independent. Thus, if one party failed to perform, the other had no choice but to perform and later sue for damages.[64]

It was not until *Kingston v Preston* in 1773 that there arose the notion that promises in a bilateral contract may be conditional upon one another.[65] In *Kingston*, a silk merchant had promised to sell his business to his apprentice. The price was to be paid in monthly instalments over several years, the apprentice to provide 'good and sufficient security' for the payments before the business was conveyed to him. When the apprentice failed to arrange security, the Court of King's Bench excused the seller, holding that requiring performance would be the 'greatest injustice'.[66] Although Lord Mansfield allowed that promises in bilateral contracts could be independent of one another, here the master's promise to convey the business depended on the apprentice's promise to provide security; the buyer's obligation was a 'precedent condition' of the seller's.

The common law rules on suspension of performance continue to be expressed in terms of 'conditions'. Indeed, in both the United States and England, suspension of performance as a remedy can only be understood in the context of conditions. Whether expressly stated in a contract or implied by law, conditions 'may determine not only the *content* of a party's obligations but also the *consequences of their non-performance*'.[67] Here, the existence of a condition means that a party's obligation is contingent on the occurrence of a particular event, in this case the other party's performance. The primary difference between the United States and England is that American courts presume that obligations

I, 181, where the court held that a tenant was justified in withholding rent in its entirety after the owner refused to make repairs.

59 Cass com, 30 January 1979, DS 1979, Inf rap 317.
60 March 1994, 324.
61 Cons d'Etat, 28 November 1890, Rec Lebon 1890, 881; Cons d'Etat, 19 March 1930, Rec Lebon 1930, 311.
62 Baker 2002, 333–4.
63 Ibid, 329.
64 Farnsworth 1999, 553–4.
65 (1773), 99 Eng Rep 437 (KB).
66 Ibid.
67 Treitel 1988, 257 (emphasis in original).

in bilateral contracts are mutual conditions, while in England, a party seeking to justify suspension of performance has the onus to prove the existence of mutual conditions.

Order of performance is generally considered to be as important in common law systems as under the civil law; a party that must perform first cannot suspend performance. However, in both England and the United States, there is a trend towards recognition of concurrent conditions as the default position. The *Restatement (Second) of Contracts* embodies this trend; where the parties' performances 'can be rendered simultaneously, they are to that extent due simultaneously, unless the language or the circumstances indicate the contrary'.[68]

An important aspect of the holding in *Kingston v Preston*—one that continues to influence common law doctrines of non-performance—is that Lord Mansfield made no distinction between a non-occurrence of a condition precedent that would justify suspension of performance and one that would justify termination of the contract. To this day, no common law legal system distinguishes explicitly between termination and suspension, lumping them both under the heading of 'rescission'.

A consequence of this conflation of the standards applicable to termination and suspension is that, under the common law, a creditor may not suspend performance unless the debtor's breach is serious. Although neither England nor the United States recognizes a distinct remedy of suspension, both limit the ability of creditors to suspend performance primarily according to the extent of the breach; the conduct of the creditor is irrelevant. In particular: 'no requirement of proportionality between the breach and the suspension of performance has been advocated in common law jurisdictions'.[69] Instead, the creditor's conduct is regulated by the doctrine of unjust enrichment; courts will award damages in equity to a debtor if the suspension of performance unjustly enriched the creditor.[70]

England

Mustill cites a 1976 ICC arbitration award to the effect that, under English law, an aggrieved party faced with a serious breach may terminate the contract but may not suspend performance.[71] Such a position may still be operative under English law. In 1992, the Court of Appeal stated: 'there is not yet any established doctrine of English law that [a creditor] may suspend performance, keeping the contract alive'.[72] Nevertheless, English courts do permit suspension of performance in certain circumstances.

England provides the counterpoint to Germany's doctrinal simplicity; the legal issues are clouded by overlapping terms and a lack of consensus on the tests to be applied. Treitel writes: 'discussions of this problem are often widely scattered in the books, with the result that very different solutions are proposed for problems which appear to be basically similar'.[73] Despite the confusion, English doctrine on suspension of performance is streamlined in one sense: issues of order of performance, conditionality of performance, and extent of breach are essentially coterminous. To understand the current state of affairs, a historical perspective is required.

[68] Restatement (2d) of Contracts, s 234. This section also provides that, where one party's performance requires a period of time to complete, that party must perform first.

[69] Nyer 2006, 61.

[70] Treitel 1988, 291.

[71] Mustill 1988, 112 fn 96, citing ICC Case No 2583 of 1976 [1977] JDI 950.

[72] *Channel Tunnel Group Ltd v Balfour Beatty Construction Ltd* [1992] 749 QB 656.

[73] Treitel 1967, 139.

In the landmark case of *Boone v Eyre*,[74] Lord Mansfield elaborated on the doctrine he laid down in *Kingston v Preston*. *Boone* involved a contract for the sale of a plantation, including the slaves who lived and worked on it. The buyer refused to pay, justifying his refusal on the basis that the seller did not own all of the slaves and consequently could not transfer title to them. The court held that the obligation at issue—to deliver title to the slaves—did not go to the heart of the bargain and therefore that the buyer could not avoid his obligation to pay the purchase price. Setting out the rule, Lord Mansfield wrote: 'where mutual covenants go to the whole of the consideration on both sides, they are mutual conditions, the one precedent to the other. But where they go only to a part, where a breach may be paid for in damages, there the defendant has a remedy on his covenant, and shall not plead it as a condition precedent'.[75]

Later cases extended this concept to recognize the existence of concurrent conditions (also called interdependent conditions), which exist when the parties are to perform simultaneously.[76] Thus, with respect to order of performance: 'Where the obligations are concurrent or the breached obligation is a condition precedent of the other party's obligation', the breach may justify suspension of performance.[77]

In the Victorian era, courts came to categorize contractual obligations as either 'conditions' or 'warranties'. The breach of a 'condition' would allow the aggrieved party to terminate the contract, while the breach of a 'warranty' would give rise only to a claim for damages. This terminology was codified in the Sale of Goods Act 1893.

Whether English courts spoke of conditions versus warranties or (following the terminology in *Kingston*) dependent versus independent obligations, the main factor by which suspension was regulated was the importance of the contractual term breached by the debtor. The conditionality and importance of a contractual obligation are notionally independent. However, English courts reasoned that, if an obligation is important, then the other party's performance must be conditioned upon fulfillment of that obligation. Accordingly, an obligation would be characterized as a warranty if it was collateral or relatively unimportant, while obligations that went to the heart of the benefit the creditor expected to receive were characterized as conditions.[78]

In determining whether an obligation constitutes a condition, English courts look first for evidence of the parties' intent, in particular for any terms designated 'of the essence'. Absent such evidence, English courts have tended to rely on characterizations adopted by previous case law in relation to specific types of contracts. In this manner, English law has come to resemble the civil law distinctions between different nominate contracts. For example, under an employment or building contract, the carrying out of work by the employee or builder is regarded as a condition precedent to payment. However, a builder may not suspend work for missed payments unless this is expressly provided in the contract.[79]

The focus on the importance of the term breached persisted until the 1962 Court of Appeal judgment in *Hong Kong Fir Shipping Co v Kawasaki Kisen Kaisha*.[80] This case involved a charterparty in which the ship's owner covenanted to maintain the ship in 'seaworthy' condition. The charterer withheld payment, alleging breach of the seaworthiness term for missing equipment and lack of a competent crew. Lord Diplock swept away the distinction between conditions and warranties, observing that complex obligations such as ensuring seaworthiness, which are endemic in modern contracts, cannot

[74] (1777), 126 Eng Rep 160 (KB). [75] Ibid. [76] Treitel 1988, 281.
[77] Marsh 1994, 325. [78] Treitel 1988, 283.
[79] Ogus 1989, 244–5, citing *Sumpter v Hedges* [1898] 1 QB 673.
[80] [1962] 2 QB 26 (CA).

be cleanly divided into the two categories. Instead, he set out a standard that focuses on the effect of the breach on the creditor, not the centrality of the term breached:

> ... the judge had to ... look at the events which had occurred as a result of the breach ... and to decide whether the occurrence of those events deprived the charterers of substantially the whole benefit which it was the intention of the parties as expressed in the charterparty that the charterers should obtain.[81]

Since *Hong Kong Fir Shipping*, contractual terms have been considered innominate, ie, neither conditions nor warranties, unless the contract says otherwise. Whether performance may be suspended depends on the seriousness of the breach and its consequences for the creditor, not on the character of the term breached. Indeed, where terms can be innominate, it makes no sense to insist upon the condition/warranty dichotomy. Instead, *Hong Kong Fir Shipping* places English law on a course familiar to civil lawyers, where the consequences of the breach for the creditor is a key factor.

Despite this holding, the law remains unsettled. The test set forth by Lord Diplock in *Hong Kong Fir Shipping* is cited as the controlling one under British law by the official comment to article 9:201 of the PECL. However, some English courts and commentators continue to look to the importance of the term breached or continue to use the terminology of independent versus dependent conditions or of conditions versus warranties. For example, the Sale of Goods Act 1979 contains a section entitled 'when condition to be treated as warranty'[82] and specifically designates as conditions certain implied terms, such as those describing the goods[83] or requiring them to be of a particular quality.[84]

Since English courts do not recognize a right to suspend performance and keep the contract alive, no distinction is made in England between breaches that justify termination of a contract and those that only justify suspension. This, combined with the absence of a general duty of good faith in English law, means that little attention is paid to the quality of the creditor's conduct. Proportionality only enters into the question in one sense: if the obligation breached by the debtor is severable, its breach justifies suspension of only the equivalent aspects of the creditor's obligations that remain unperformed.[85] This most frequently occurs in long-term relationships like distributorships or construction contracts, where performance is in stages or instalments.

The United States

In the United States, there is less linguistic confusion than in England—on this subject at least. The non-occurrence of any precedent or concurrent condition will entitle a party to withhold performance, regardless of whether that condition is contingent or promissory. In addition, performance is presumed to be conditional and simultaneous in all bilateral contracts, under the doctrine of 'constructive conditions of exchange'.[86] Unlike in England, therefore, a party usually has little difficulty in demonstrating that its obligation is conditional upon the other party's performance. Thus, the Restatement (Second) provides:

> Performances are to be exchanged under an exchange of promises if each promise is at least part of the consideration for the other and the performance of each promise is to be exchanged at least in part for the performance of the other....[87]

[81] Ibid, 72. [82] Sale of Goods Act 1979, s 11. [83] Ibid, s 12.
[84] Ibid, s 14. [85] See Treitel 1988, 596–601.
[86] Restatement (2d) of Contracts, s 259; see also Farnsworth 1999, 561–5.
[87] Restatement (2d) of Contracts, s 231.

It is a condition of each party's remaining duties to render performances to be exchanged under an exchange of promises that there be no uncured material failure by the other party to render any such performance due at an earlier time.[88]

Summing up the jurisprudence, Farnsworth states: 'only by the clearest language can the parties make a promise to which the concept of constructive conditions does not apply … the judicial preference for constructive conditions of exchange and the self-help remedies that they afford the injured party is overwhelming'.[89]

Thus, proving the conditionality of its obligations is seldom problematic for an American creditor seeking to justify suspension of performance. Furthermore, absent circumstances that indicate a particular order of performance, US courts will generally construe all bilateral contracts to require simultaneous performance.[90] In keeping with its more permissive attitude towards self-help, American law applies the doctrines relating to suspension of performance in all bilateral contracts.

Balancing these presumptions, which favour creditors, are strict rules relating to the severity of the breach required to justify suspension, namely the doctrine of material breach.[91] Only a material breach by the debtor justifies suspension or termination. Under section 241 of the Second Restatement, five factors 'are significant' in determining whether a breach is material:

(a) the extent to which the injured party will be deprived of the benefit which he reasonably expected;
(b) the extent to which the injured party can be adequately compensated for the part of that benefit of which he will be deprived;
(c) the extent to which the party failing to perform or to offer to perform will suffer forfeiture;
(d) the likelihood that the party failing to perform or to offer to perform will cure his failure, taking account of all the circumstances including any reasonable assurances;
(e) the extent to which the behavior of the party failing to perform or to offer to perform comports with standards of good faith and fair dealing.

In contrast to the traditional approach in English law, factors (a), (b), and (d) relate to the effects of the breach upon the creditor, rather than to the importance of the term breached. Under American law, therefore, the threshold determination for the availability of remedies other than damages is more like the civil law standard than the English law standard. However, as with English law, US law does not distinguish between different levels of breach to justify suspension and termination. Instead, a material breach 'triggers several possible legal responses. They include the power to suspend performance, the power to abandon a contract and find substitute performance, and the power to rescind a contract and recover in restitution for performance already rendered.'[92]

Despite this, US courts may in fact permit suspension in some circumstances and termination in others, depending on whether the breach is curable and on the parties' conduct after the breach. Factor (d) of the five factors set out above in section 241 for determining whether a breach is material is: 'the likelihood that the party failing to perform … will cure his failure'. Section 237 states that it is a condition of a party's remaining performance that there be no '*uncured* material failure' of the other party's performance (emphasis added). Finally, section 242 states that, when determining how

[88] Ibid, s 237. [89] Farnsworth 1999, 556. [90] Ibid, 565.
[91] Gergen 2005, 76. [92] Gergen 2005, 76.

long a creditor must wait before its obligations are discharged, the factors in section 241 are relevant, as well as 'the extent to which it reasonably appears to the inured party that delay may prevent or hinder him in making reasonable substitute arrangements'.

It thus appears that, if a material breach is incurable or if a delay in performance would prevent the creditor from concluding a substitute transaction, the creditor may treat the material breach as 'total' and terminate the contract immediately.[93] On the other hand, where a material breach may be cured within a reasonable period of time, 'such a breach would justify only *suspension* of performance by the injured party: he is only discharged if the breach is not cured within the time allowed by law'.[94]

This doctrine performs the same dilatory function as the *exceptio*.[95] It is also sensible—suspension cannot last indefinitely. American courts share continental European courts' preference for 'keeping the deal together' to some degree, but will do so only as long as it does not 'seriously disappoint' the justifiable expectations of the parties.[96] The means by which American courts achieve this balance is the delay factor, permitting suspension of performance for material breaches, but termination only after an appropriate length of time has passed.

In all cases involving discharge from contractual obligations, US law dwells little on the creditor's conduct. Despite some notable exceptions, American courts will permit a party: 'to refuse nonconforming performance to avoid suffering an uncompensated loss even though the refusal imposes a disproportionate loss on the defaulter'.[97] As in England, the relevant jurisprudence deals primarily with contracts that involve severable obligations. Thus, a breach with respect to one instalment will justify withholding only the performance to that instalment. A creditor will only be permitted to withhold the entirety of its performance if 'a breach with respect to one or more instalments substantially impairs the value of the whole contract'.[98]

3. International contract law instruments

The four international contract law instruments considered here all contain similar provisions with respect to termination, to the point of using the same terminology. They all distinguish between ordinary and fundamental breaches of contract and limit termination to cases of fundamental breach, differing only in whether they define fundamental breach according to 'general interpretive guidelines' (the CISG and ULIS) or lists of factors relevant to such a determination (the UNIDROIT Principles and PECL).[99] They also all contain provisions governing instalment contracts, which state that a fundamental breach of one instalment can only lead to termination with respect to that instalment, unless the breach gives rise to a legitimate concern that a fundamental breach will recur in future instalments.[100]

With respect to suspending performance, however, they differ. Most importantly, the UNIDROIT Principles and PECL state a general right to suspend performance, while the CISG and ULIS permit suspension only in limited circumstances, if at all.

[93] The UCC also contemplates a period between suspension and termination, during which the debtor may cure its breach and thus prevent termination. See UCC, s 2-508.

[94] Treitel 1988, 313 (emphasis in original).

[95] Farnsworth 1999, 525.

[96] Ibid, 580.

[97] Gergen 2005, 84. The two well-known exceptions are *Jacob and Youngs v Kent*, 230 NY 239, 129 NE 889 (1921) and *Plante v Jacobs*, 10 Wis 2d 567, 103 NW 2d 296 (1960).

[98] UCC, s 2-612(3). The English Sale of Goods Act 1979 s 31(2) contains a similar rule.

[99] Liu 2005, 124.

[100] See, eg, CISG, art 73(2); UNIDROIT Principles, art 7.3.1(2)(d).

The UNIDROIT Principles and PECL

In both the UNIDROIT Principles and the PECL, suspension of performance is governed primarily by a single provision. UNIDROIT Principles, article 7.1.3 states:

> (1) Where the parties are to perform simultaneously, either party may withhold performance until the other party tenders its performance.
> (2) Where the parties are to perform consecutively, the party that is to perform later may withhold its performance until the first party has performed.

Article 7.1.3 deals with suspension in a single step. Article 6.1.4 sets up a presumption of simultaneous performance where simultaneity is possible; if one party's performance is to be rendered over time, that party must perform first. The conditionality of the creditor's obligations is regulated implicitly, in that contracts are presumed to be bilateral and no requirement of synallagma is expressed. In addition, the UNIDROIT Principles follow the Germanic position in that any non-trivial breach by the debtor suffices. Finally, while the quality of the creditor's conduct is not addressed in the text of article 7.1.3, the official comment makes clear that the creditor must conform to the overriding requirement of good faith and fair dealing stated in article 1.7.

The PECL's suspension of performance regime is similar. Article 9:201(1) states:

> A party who is to perform simultaneously with or after the other party may withhold performance until the other has tendered performance or has performed. The first party may withhold the whole of its performance or a part of it as may be reasonable in the circumstances.

Performance is presumed to be simultaneous unless 'circumstances indicate otherwise'.[101] Thus, the only significant difference from the UNIDROIT Principles is that the requirement of reasonableness on the part of the creditor is express. The official comment to article 9:201 makes the matter even clearer: the debtor's breach need not be 'fundamental', but the performance suspended must not be 'wholly disproportionate' to the obligation breached.

The CISG and ULIS

The CISG and ULIS deal only with contracts for the sale of goods, which are by nature bilateral and synallagmatic. They both presume that performance is to be simultaneous, and permit the parties to agree otherwise. For example, CISG, article 58(1) provides that, unless the parties agree otherwise, the buyer must pay the price when the seller places the goods or documents of title at the buyer's disposal. In other words, 'the goods are exchanged for the price'.[102] Similarly, ULIS, article 71 states: 'delivery of the goods and payment of the price shall be concurrent conditions'. However, the ULIS does not spell out the consequences if a concurrent condition is not fulfilled.

Whether, under the CISG, a creditor may suspend performance for non-performance by the debtor is a matter of debate. The only CISG provision that has ever been held to permit suspension is article 71, which is entitled 'suspension of performance':

> (1) A party may suspend the performance of his obligations if, after the conclusion of the contract, it becomes apparent that the other party will not perform a substantial part of his obligations as a result of:
> (a) a serious deficiency in his ability to perform or in his creditworthiness; or
> (b) his conduct in preparing to perform or in performing the contract.

[101] PECL, art 7:104. [102] Honnold 1999, 364.

Notwithstanding its title, article 71 does not create a right to suspend performance. It may only be invoked before performance is due and thus before any breach could have occurred.[103] In other words, article 71 is available only for cases of 'prospective failure of performance'.[104] As suspension is to termination, article 71 is to anticipatory repudiation. The difference between suspension of performance and the remedy described in article 71 is underlined by legislative history; it was designed to address such situations as when goods are purchased on credit, but the buyer becomes insolvent prior to delivery.[105]

Nevertheless, at least two courts have applied article 71 to find a right of suspension in cases where breach has already occurred.[106] Therefore, some discussion of the circumstances under which article 71 would permit suspension is warranted. Here, too, there is disagreement. Article 71 states that the prospective non-performance must constitute a 'substantial part' of the debtor's obligations, a standard that is not defined and appears only in one other article of the CISG.[107] On the other hand, fundamental breach is explicitly defined in article 25 and appears in several articles. The legislative history of article 71 provides no guidance; debate on its wording focused on the degree of certainty with which the prospective non-performance must be foreseeable.[108]

Heuzé argues that, to define 'substantial' in article 71, we should analogize to CISG, article 46, which permits a buyer to demand cure only if the seller's breach is fundamental; therefore, a requirement of prospective fundamental breach is implied by article 71.[109] However, one could as reasonably analogize to the remedy of price reduction under CISG, article 50, which does not require fundamental breach.[110] More importantly, article 71 does not use the term 'fundamental', while article 72, which deals with anticipatory repudiation, refers specifically to prospective fundamental breaches. Thus, whatever 'substantial' means, it must be something less than 'fundamental'.[111]

When it comes to regulating the creditor's conduct, nothing in the text of article 71 states the extent to which performance may be suspended; there is no mention of proportionality. The CISG does not even contain a general provision requiring the parties to act in good faith.[112] Schlechtriem maintains, in line with CISG, article 50, that prospective suspension of performance under article 71 must: 'correspond with the disadvantage caused by the nonconformity'.[113]

The relevant rules under the ULIS are essentially identical to the CISG. The ULIS does not create a general right of suspension of performance but does include, in article 73, an analogue of CISG, article 71. Also like the CISG, the ULIS contains a buyer's right to reduce the purchase price; however, as noted above, this should not be construed as a specific instance of suspension of performance.

[103] CISG Explanatory Note [33]. [104] Honnold 1999, 428.

[105] Ibid, 426. Cf Hornung 2005.

[106] The Austrian Supreme Court, OGH 12 Feb 1998, 2 Ob 328/97t, and a district commercial court in Hasselt, Belgium, *JPS BVBA v Kabri Mode BV*, AR 3641/94, Rechtbank van Koophandel (Hasselt) 1 March 1995.

[107] Article 3(1), which deals with the CISG's applicability to mixed manufacturing and sales contracts.

[108] Honnold 1999, 428–30.

[109] Heuzé 1992, 158.

[110] Schlechtriem 2004, s II, 5(c)(aa). Article 50 should not be taken as granting a specific right of suspension; the *travaux* make clear that art 50 is derived from the remedy of price reduction, not from the *exceptio*.

[111] Bennett 1987, 518.

[112] CISG, art 7(1) states merely that good faith is to be regarded in the interpretation of the convention.

[113] Schlechtriem 2004, s II, 5(c)(aa).

IV. Suspension of Performance in International Commercial Arbitration

Substantive law determinations involve both choice of the governing law and interpretation of that law. Therefore, in contrasting the approaches of ICA tribunals and courts on cases of suspended performance, one must consider not only to how ICA tribunals apply the law, but also to how they determine which substantive law applies.

As discussed in Chapter 5, arbitral tribunals are generally bound by the parties' choice of law; if the parties do not make a choice, tribunals may select a choice of law rule or select the governing law directly (depending on the rules of procedure). They may also apply non-national rules of law or, if the parties expressly so provide, sit as *amiables compositeurs*.

National courts, on the other hand, must follow the choice of law rules prescribed by their states' private international laws. National choice of law regimes may also prohibit courts from applying transnational rules of law, even if the parties invoke such rules in their contracts. Arbitrators have greater latitude to determine the applicable law than national court judges possess. Accordingly, the laws that arbitrators choose when the contract does not contain a choice of law provide insight into arbitrators' mindset and priorities.

Once the applicable law is determined, state courts can be expected to take the approach consistent with their national legal traditions, and will rely on domestic statutes, precedents, and practices as sources of law. Thus, for example, a French judge confronted with a case of suspended performance can be expected to determine first whether a breach is sufficiently serious to permit suspension by the creditor and then to examine whether the creditor's response was proportionate. A German judge might focus first on whether the contract was synallagmatic and then go directly to a determination of whether the suspension was in good faith. An American judge might hold that a party that suspended performance thereby terminated the contract. Only occasionally will courts reach outside their domestic law; for example, a judge might reinforce an interpretation by noting that courts of other states have reached the same conclusion.

By contrast, after determining that a particular law applies, ICA tribunals frequently refer to general principles of law and employ patterns of reasoning and terminology associated with other jurisdictions. This is so regardless of the country of origin of the arbitrators and regardless of which national law or international contract law instrument is applied. Thus, for example, an arbitrator considering a contract under American law might make reference to the *exceptio*, and an arbitrator applying German law might consider whether the debtor breached an important term of the contract.

In any award that reaches a decision on the merits, ICA tribunals can take one of four courses of action:

- state that a particular national law or international instrument governs, then apply that law closely, using terminology and reasoning associated with the state or instrument and turning to authorities associated with the state or instrument;
- state that a particular law governs, but also appeal to general principles or utilize terminology or reasoning associated with a different jurisdiction;
- apply general principles, either because the contract calls for their application or because the tribunal decides to apply them; or
- apply no legal principles whatsoever, when sitting as *amiable compositeur*.

The following are examinations of twelve publicly available arbitral awards that deal with cases of suspension of performance.[114] Where the nationality of the parties or of the arbitrators is stated in the published version of the award, these are supplied. Cases that deal with termination of contracts are more numerous, but they are included here only insofar as they also consider suspension. Although the number of awards is small, each of the first three possible courses of action is represented. There were two awards decided under amiable composition, but in both cases the tribunal decided to apply general principles of law. As will be seen, the outcomes reached are not explicable solely on the basis of the governing law; however, they can be explained by reference to the international arbitral culture described in Part I.

1. Awards involving straightforward application of the governing law

The first category of cases is the least surprising or controversial. It involves the straightforward application of the governing law (whether national or non-national), using terminology, sources of authority and modes of reasoning that are associated with the governing law and (if appropriate) the state from which it derives. One would expect this category to account for most of the awards; however, tribunals followed this approach in only five of the twelve cases.

In ICC Case No 4629 of 1989,[115] the claimants were to construct a hotel for the respondent, a Middle Eastern hotel developer. The claimants were to supply all materials and equipment and to complete the work before a deadline. In addition to paying the purchase price, the respondent was to obtain the necessary import licences and regulatory authorizations and to satisfy various credit requirements set by the claimants' bank. The claimants began work, but soon suspended performance on the ground that the respondent had failed to fulfil its obligations. When the respondent drew down the performance bond that the claimants' bank had issued, the claimants initiated arbitration.

The contract contained an express choice of Swiss law. The tribunal did as a court would and applied Swiss law; where a contract contains a clear and valid choice of law clause invoking a particular national law, there is little leeway for a court or an ICA tribunal to apply a different law.

This case is also paradigmatic of an arbitration tribunal following the approach of a national court in applying the law to the facts: the tribunal decided the suspension of performance issue in accordance with article 82 of the Swiss Code of Obligations (CO), which it specifically cited, and referred only to Swiss authorities to interpret article 82.

The tribunal held that the respondent had breached its obligations, so it 'could not reasonably insist' that the contractors finish by the deadline. It analysed the propriety

[114] Arbitral awards considering suspension as a principle of public international law (including investment law) are not included in this comparison. For example, the award in *Azurix v Argentina* is not considered here because the tribunal's discussion of the *exceptio* is part of its decision regarding breach of the fair and equitable treatment standard in international investment law, rather than breach of contract. *Azurix Corp v The Argentine Republic* (ICSID Case No ARB/01/12, award of 14 July 2006) available at <http://icsid.worldbank.org/ICSID/FrontServlet?requestType=GenCaseDtlsRH&actionVal=ListConcluded> accessed 28 July 28, 2012. Chamber of Arbitration of Milan award of 22 February 2008 (unpublished, available at <http://www.kluwerarbitration.com>) also mentions the *exceptio*. However, it appears to have been a case of termination, not suspension, so it is also excluded from this analysis.

[115] (1993) XVIII Ybk Comm Arb 11.

of the claimants' suspension under CO, article 82, which it characterized as embodying the *exceptio*, and which it found to apply when the parties are to perform simultaneously. The tribunal further cited the Swiss Federal Court to the effect that article 82 is inapplicable to breaches of collateral obligations, but found that the obligations breached by the respondent were not collateral. Finally, the tribunal held that, under CO, article 108(1), the claimants would have been entitled to terminate the contract as soon as the respondent refused to remedy its non-performance, so the claimants 'were *a fortiori* justified in suspending their work'. Such a ruling is consistent with the Swiss approach, which requires a more severe breach to justify termination than suspension of performance.

Zurich Chamber of Commerce Case No 273/95 of 31 May 1996[116] concerned a series of contracts involving multiple parties. The Russian respondent was to supply materials to Claimant 1, a Hungarian enterprise, and Claimant 2, an Argentine conglomerate. The respondent also took a 15 per cent ownership in Claimant 1 and a 20 per cent share in Claimant 2. At the time of contracting, the respondent was a government entity, but was privatized in December 1994. After the respondent's new owners took control in early 1995, the respondent ceased delivery. The claimants initiated arbitration, seeking specific performance. The respondent argued that its cessation of delivery was justified by prior fundamental breaches of the claimants; it alleged that the claimants had not paid for certain instalments and that they had fraudulently induced the respondent to purchase an ownership interest in them.

The dispute was decided by an arbitral tribunal convened by the Zurich Chamber of Commerce, and was composed of three Swiss lawyers. The tribunal applied the choice of law rule contained in Switzerland's Private International Law statute (which was required by the Zurich Chamber of Commerce Rules). The statute provides that, if the parties do not make a choice of law, the law of the seller's domicile governs. The seller's domicile was Russia, so the tribunal applied Russian law to the entire group of contracts. Since Russia had ratified the CISG, and the parties all came from different CISG signatory countries, application of Russian law led to application of the CISG to the sales of goods between the parties. The tribunal applied Russian domestic laws to the other contracts.

The tribunal's approach to the choice of law was similar to one a Swiss court would have taken. It began by applying the Swiss choice of law rules. These called for the seller's law. The tribunal then determined which Russian law would apply to which aspects of the relationship. Finally, the tribunal applied the CISG only to its area of applicability—the sales contracts—which is the narrow approach that a national court would likely have taken.

The tribunal found that no provision of the CISG permits suspension of performance. The respondent asserted that the claimants' failure to pay for certain previous instalments amounted to fundamental breach. The tribunal analysed the respondent's actions according to the CISG's provisions regarding termination, in particular article 73. This article permits termination of an entire instalment contract only if a breach as to one instalment gives the creditor 'good grounds to believe' that a fundamental breach will occur with respect to future instalments as well. However, the tribunal found that no such grounds existed and, in any event, that article 73 deals with termination of instalment contracts, not with the suspension of performance. In sum, the

[116] (1998) XXIII Ybk Comm Arb 128.

tribunal found that the CISG governed and interpreted it without reference to general principles or exogenous terminology.

In ICC Case No 9448 of 1999,[117] a Swiss manufacturer of roller bearings, and the respondent, an American distributor, entered into an exclusive distribution contract. The contract contained a choice of Swiss law. Switzerland and the United States had ratified the CISG and the tribunal characterized the contract as 'successive sales and deliveries of bearings to be manufactured by Claimants and delivered to Respondent, while granting Respondent exclusive representation in the USA'. Therefore, the contract was governed by the CISG according to CISG, article 3. The tribunal did not state whether it considered the sales aspects of the contract to be predominant, but did assert that 'all preconditions for the application of the CISG to the [contract] are fulfilled'. A national court is likely to have made the same determination.

After two years, the respondent refused to pay for future instalments on the grounds that some prior instalments had arrived late and that there were shortfalls in the number of bearings in other shipments. The claimant initiated arbitration to recover the missing payments. The respondent claimed the right to suspend performance based on the claimant's alleged breaches, citing CISG, article 71.

The tribunal stated that it did not need to determine whether the breaches alleged by the respondent had actually occurred. The respondent's allegations, even if true, could not justify suspension of performance under article 71, since that provision gives a party the right only 'to withhold its performance corresponding to a future anticipated breach'. Thus, since the respondent had already received the allegedly late and incomplete deliveries, it had to pay for the amount received and could assert separate claims relating to the allegedly late and incomplete deliveries. Moreover, if the late or incomplete deliveries had constituted a fundamental breach of contract, the respondent would had the right to terminate the contract with respect to those deliveries under CISG, article 73(1); however, the respondent had not alleged fundamental breach, nor had it purported to terminate the contract.

The tribunal's analysis of the relevant CISG provisions stays close to the wording of those provisions. For interpretive guidance, the tribunal cited two well-known treatises (those edited by Schlechtriem and by Bianca and Bonell). As to the interest rate (which, under the CISG, is governed by domestic law), the tribunal cited a decision of the Swiss federal court. A national court would likely have followed the same approach and reached the same conclusions.

In Cairo Regional Centre for International Commercial Arbitration Case No 142/1999,[118] a tribunal composed of three Egyptian arbitrators considered a contract for the claimant to construct, install, and operate a plant for the respondent, the Ministry of Defence of an African state. The claimant was also to train the respondent's personnel in the use and maintenance of the plant's machinery and to supply raw materials and spare parts for ten years, after which the claimant was to turn the plant over to the respondent in good condition. The respondent undertook to purchase from the claimant an agreed quantum of products over the course of the ten years, and also to provide the plant with free water and electricity.

[117] Available at <www.unilex.info> accessed 10 December 2012.

[118] *An African enterprises company v The Ministry of Defence of an African state*, Final award of 29 January 2000, reprinted in MEI Alam Eldin (ed), *Arbitral Awards of the Cairo Regional Centre for International Commercial Arbitration II, 1997–2000* (Kluwer Law International, The Hague 2003) 85.

The claimant alleged that the respondent had breached its obligation to purchase the agreed quantum of products and claimed damages on the basis of the shortfall plus consequential losses. The claimant had not delivered the land and the plant, but had declared itself ready to deliver them if it received the moneys it claimed. The respondent, among other arguments, averred that the contract was an administrative contract governed by public law, and that it therefore had the right to reduce the quantities it needed for its armed forces.

The tribunal found that, although the contract related to a public utility (ie the country's military), it could not be classified as an administrative contract, so the respondent could not unilaterally reduce the agreed upon quantities. The tribunal found that the contract was innominate and that the respondent had breached it.

The respondent counterclaimed on the ground that the claimant had failed to deliver the plant to the respondent at the end of the ten-year period. The claimant raised the *exceptio* as a defence to this counterclaim, and cited moreover article 161 of the Egyptian Civil Code, which codifies the *exceptio* principle. The tribunal found against the claimant on the ground that the *exceptio* 'cannot be raised against a public authority in the matters of public utilities because the jurisprudence and the doctrine are unanimous upon the rule of continuance of public utility without any interruption'. The Egyptian civil code is based on that of France, which provides that the *exceptio* cannot be pleaded against public bodies, regardless of the category of the contract or its subject matter.[119] Therefore, the tribunal appears to have followed the approach that an Egyptian court would have taken.

The final case in this first category is *Aucoven v Venezuela*.[120] The dispute arose out of a concession agreement concluded between Aucoven and Venezuela's Ministry of Infrastructure for the construction of two major highways. The concession agreement was governed by Venezuelan law.

Aucoven alleged that Venezuela had breached various obligations under the concession agreement, including obligations to issue a guarantee and to pay Aucoven a minimum guaranteed income from the highways. The tribunal found that Venezuela was liable for various breaches of the concession agreement, and that Aucoven had validly terminated the agreement, but also found that Aucoven had committed various breaches. The tribunal then turned to the question of whether Aucoven could recover for its lost profits.

Aucoven acknowledged the existence and applicability of the *exceptio*, as reflected in article 168 of the Venezuelan Civil Code. The tribunal held that, in principle, therefore, breaches by Aucoven might bar recovery of lost profits. However, the tribunal held further that any such breaches would have to be material in order for the *exceptio* principle to apply.[121] Since the tribunal found that Aucoven had not materially breached the concession agreement, it considered the matter no further. This approach to the *exceptio* appears to be consistent with the approach a Venezuelan court would take.

[119] See Section III.1 of this chapter.

[120] *Autopista Concesionada de Venezuela CA (Aucoven) v Bolivarian Republic of Venezuela (Venezuela)*, ICSID Case No ARB/00/5, award of 23 September 2003, available at <http://icsid.worldbank.org/ICSID/FrontServlet?requestType=GenCaseDtlsRH&actionVal=ListConcluded> accessed 31 July 2012.

[121] The tribunal cited no authority for this proposition. However, this may be because the parties agreed that only material breaches would suffice to bar a recovery of lost profits, so there was no need to seek any further legal support.

2. Awards relying on principles or sources external to the governing law

The second category of awards includes those where the tribunal applied a particular law (national or otherwise) but also referred to general principles, or otherwise applied doctrines or modes of reasoning that are extrinsic to the applicable law. There were five such awards. Some may be characterized as involving simple oversights or errors of law, but others are notable for the particular ways in which the tribunal departed from the applicable law.

In *Klöckner v Cameroon*,[122] Klöckner had entered into several contracts in the 1970s with the government of Cameroon to supply the materials for and construct a fertilizer plant, and to provide technical and commercial management for the plant. The contracts contained no choice of law clause.

The arbitration was conducted under the auspices of ICSID. Under the ICSID Convention,[123] absent a choice of law by the parties, the law of the party which is a contracting state to the ICSID Convention will apply. Klöckner did not contest the application of Cameroonian law. However, Cameroon has a dual judicial heritage, different parts of the country having been colonies of France and the United Kingdom. The two systems of law remain; disputes between parties from the same region are decided under the law historically in force in that region. Since the fertilizer plant was located and the contracts negotiated in eastern Cameroon, where the law is French, the tribunal applied French-derived Cameroonian law. This appears to be the approach that a Cameroonian court would have taken.

After nineteen months of 'unprofitable and technically inadequate operation', the plant shut down. Klöckner instituted arbitration for the outstanding balance of the price for constructing the plant. Cameroon claimed that it was justified in withholding the purchase price because of Klöckner's various breaches. The tribunal decided the *exceptio* issue under French law. However, since the parties had disagreed as to the applicable law, the tribunal noted that the outcome would have same under English law and international law.

The tribunal (composed of Uruguayan, American, and French arbitrators), found the *exceptio* to embody a general principle of 'French, English and international law'. To find the *exceptio* in French law, it cited various French commentators and court decisions.

As to English law, the tribunal cited a single ICC arbitration award,[124] in which the sole (English) arbitrator had held that, given the 'mutuality' inherent in all contracts, 'if the seller does not [perform], the buyer may release himself from his obligation to pay'. The tribunal cited no English statute or case law to the effect that the *exceptio* constitutes a general principle under English law. Had an English court decided the issue, it is unlikely to have made such a statement, since the necessary 'mutuality' is not presumed under English law. Instead, an English court would likely have inquired first (following *Hong Kong Fir Shipping*) whether the debtor's breach substantially deprived

[122] *Klöckner Industrie-Anlagen GmbH (FR Germany) v United Republic of Cameroon*, ICSID Case No ARB/81/2, award of 21 October 1983, 2 ICSID Rep 95 (1994) (original decision, English tr); ICSID Case No ARB/81/2, decision on annulment (of 3 May 1985 (1986) XI Ybk Comm Arb 162 (annulment decision, English tr).

[123] Convention on the Settlement of Investment Disputes between States and Nationals of Other States (18 March 1965), 575 UNTS 159.

[124] The *Fertilizer Corporation of India* case, published as an annex to Paulsson 1987.

the creditor of the benefit it expected to receive under the contract or (according to the older formulation) whether the debtor's obligation was a condition of the creditor's performance.

The tribunal cited an opinion of the PCIJ in the *Diversion of Water from the Meuse* case,[125] which stated that the general principle of *inadimplenti non est adimplendum* constitutes a general principle of international law. This citation is dubious. First, the *Klöckner* tribunal did not address the distinction between general principles of public and of private international law; the *Meuse* case dealt with the treaty obligations of states, not the contractual obligations of private parties. Second, it failed to note that the opinion cited, that of Judge Anzilotti, was a dissent. Third, it did not distinguish between the wider maxim of *inadimplenti non est adimplendum* and the more specific *exceptio non adimpleti contractus*.

Satisfied that it could recognize the *exceptio* in principle, the tribunal turned to the circumstances in which it might apply. Citing French commentaries and judgments, the tribunal held that the debtor's breach must be of more than 'slight importance', that partial non-performance by the debtor does not justify suspension of the entirety of the creditor's performance, and that the tribunal must 'measure the relative effect of the refusal to perform against the seriousness of the faulty performance'. This approach corresponds to what a French (or Cameroonian) court would likely do.

However, the tribunal also found that, given Klöckner's defective performance, it was not entitled to any more payment than it had already received; that is, Klöckner's breaches partially discharged Cameroon's obligations. The tribunal cited no authority for this proposition, and indeed a French court is unlikely to have reached the same conclusion. As discussed above, the *exceptio* is a dilatory plea. It permits a creditor temporarily to withhold payment but cannot by itself lead to the discharge of any party's obligations.

Klöckner v Cameroon is remembered primarily because it involved the first application for annulment of an ICSID award. The ad hoc annulment committee (composed of Swiss, Egyptian, and Austrian arbitrators), annulled the award in its entirety on several grounds, including its treatment of the *exceptio*. (The dispute was later resubmitted to ICSID.) It declined to consider whether the award correctly construed the requirements for invocation of the *exceptio*, so it is unclear whether the annulment committee agreed that the *exceptio* constitutes a general principle of French, English, or international law. However, the annulment committee did find that the tribunal failed adequately to support its holding as to the effects of the *exceptio*:

> It looks as if the Arbitral Tribunal considered the *exceptio non adimpleti contractus* as giving rise to the *extinction* of obligations under French law, a conclusion which, on any reading of the citations used in the Award itself, does not necessarily follow and, moreover, does not appear consistent with what the *ad hoc* Committee knows about this area of law.

The annulment committee was heavily criticized in the academic literature for re-examining the merits of the original tribunal's decision and thereby 'improperly crossing the line between annulment and appeal'.[126] However, no one appears to have doubted the correctness of the annulment committee's findings on French substantive law. There was also a second annulment application, and a second, different annulment

[125] [1937] PCIJ (ser A/B), No 70, 4, 50.

[126] Schreuer 2004, 18. Schreuer characterizes the annulment decision in *Klöckner* as having aroused 'much concern'. Ibid, 17.

committee was formed ('*Klöckner II*'). The application was rejected but the opinion has not been published, so little of the substance of the application or the reasons for its rejection are publicly known. However, Schreuer comments that the decision in *Klöckner II* helped to 'alleviate concerns' generated by the first annulment decision,[127] so the second annulment committee presumably declined to consider the merits of the original tribunal's substantive legal determinations.

A second case in this category, ICC Case No 11849 of 2003,[128] involved an exclusive distributorship agreement between the respondent, an Italian fashion house, and the claimant, an American retailer. The agreement provided that the goods were to be delivered in seasonal instalments; payment was also to be in instalments, by way of letters of credit opened prior to each shipment.

The agreement contained a choice of law clause directing the sole arbitrator to 'apply the [CISG] for what is not expressly or implicitly provided for under the contract. Letters of credit shall be governed by the [ICC] Uniform Customs and Practices for Documentary Credits'. However, the claimant took the position that the CISG should apply only to the sales aspects of the contract, and not to the obligations related to the buyer's exclusive distributorship rights.

The sole arbitrator rejected this argument and applied the CISG to the entirety of the contract. This may have been the correct result under CISG, article 3, which provides that the CISG applies to the entirety of a mixed contract so long as the sales aspects of the contract predominate and are not severable. Here, the contract was non-severable, but it is unclear whether the sales aspects predominated because the award does not touch on this issue. Indeed, the arbitrator did not refer to article 3 at all; instead, he applied the CISG based on his view of the parties' motivations for selecting it: 'the parties have clearly indicated their intention to avoid their respective internal law rules, and to resort to neutral solutions'. A court may have reached the same conclusion, but is unlikely to have reasoned from an apparent preference of the parties for non-national rules, rather than the text of the convention.

After a few deliveries, the respondent demanded higher prices on the remaining instalments. The claimant refused to open a new letter of credit at either the original or the new price. After unsuccessful negotiations, the respondent set a deadline for the claimant to open a letter of credit, after which the respondent stated that it would consider the agreement terminated. When this deadline passed, the claimant did open a letter of credit, but the respondent declared the contract to be terminated.

The claimant initiated arbitration, claiming that the respondent's attempt to terminate the contract was unjustified. The respondent defended on the grounds that termination was justified by the claimant's failure to open the letter of credit before the deadline the respondent had set. In turn, the claimant asserted that the respondent's attempt unilaterally to increase the price justified the claimant's having suspended payment. It is this action—the claimant's refusal to open the letter of credit at the higher price—that the claimant characterized as suspension.

The claimant invoked the *exceptio*. The arbitrator found that under the CISG, the *exceptio* is expressed in article 71, but held that article 71 permits only prospective suspension of performance. However, the arbitrator did not rule against the claimant on the grounds that the CISG does not permit suspension for prior non-performance. Instead, he ruled that the claimant's suspension of performance was improper because

[127] Ibid, 18. [128] (2006) XXXI Ybk Comm Arb 148.

it was 'excessive and disproportionate'. Under CISG, article 54, a refusal to open a letter of credit is tantamount to a total refusal to pay the purchase price, while the disagreement related to '10 or 15% only of the prices'. Except for the reference to article 54, there was no analysis of the claimant's actions under the CISG, nor did the arbitrator cite any authority for the 'excessive and disproportionate' standard. The tribunal thus applied the CISG to the non-sales aspects of the parties' relationship according to a theory of party intent that international instruments should prevail over national ones (rather than according to the relevant CISG provisions), then into the CISG principles (ie, the *exceptio*) not found anywhere in its text.

In ICC Case No 8547 of 1999,[129] the claimant, a Bulgarian seller of goods, and the respondent, a Greek importer, concluded a contract through a series of telexes for the delivery of goods in a series of instalments. One telex sent by the claimant stated that the contract was to be 'governed by, constructed and interpreted in accordance with the Uniform Law for the international sale of corporal movables'. The tribunal held the contract to be governed by the ULIS.

ULIS, article 4 provides that it applies where the parties have chosen it as the governing law of a contract, regardless of whether the states in which they are domiciled have ratified it. The tribunal praised this interpretation of article 4 as being 'in accordance with the principle of party autonomy'. This may or may not be a correct interpretation; national courts have divided on the question of whether the ULIS can apply simply because the parties have chosen it. For example, the German *Bundesgerichtshof* (federal supreme court) applied the ULIS in such a situation[130] but a US District Court in New York refused to do so.[131]

After delivery commenced, the respondent alleged that the goods were of poor quality. The claimant admitted this but took no action to remedy the non-conformity. In response, the respondent suspended payment for subsequent deliveries, specifically citing the *exceptio* in its communications with the claimant. Asserting that the respondent's suspension breached the contract, the claimant initiated arbitration.

The tribunal found that the respondent had the right: 'to stop payment because of the nonconformity of the goods'. It noted that the order of performance under the contract was such that the payment was to occur after delivery, then concluded: 'It would amount to a curtailment of the rights of the buyer if he had to continue payment ... without knowing what will happen in regard to the nonconformity.' Finally, the tribunal found 'the degree of nonconformity is ... irrelevant in regard to [the] right to suspend payment'. It therefore held that the respondent was justified in suspending performance.

This may well be a sensible result, but it has no basis in the governing law. The tribunal acknowledged as much, noting that a right to suspend performance 'is not expressly stated in ULIS'. The tribunal found that the *exceptio* is a general principle of international law, incorporated into the ULIS by its article 17, which states that gaps in the may be filled by reference to general principles. The tribunal cited UNIDROIT Principles, article 7.1.3 as authority for the proposition that the *exceptio* is a general principle of international law. It justified the reference to the UNIDROIT Principles on the basis of 'the internationality of the relations between the parties'. The tribunal thus evidenced a preference for general principles of international law, even when these conflict with the law chosen by the parties.

129 (2003) XXVIII Ybk Comm Arb 27.
130 Bundesgerichtshof, case VIII ZR 185/92 (9 March 1994).
131 *Tarbert Trading, Ltd v Cometals, Inc*, 663 FSupp 561, 566 fn 9 (SDNY 1987).

If a court had decided this case, it would not likely have found a right to suspend of performance since such a right is not granted by the ULIS. In particular, the mere fact that the parties came from different countries would be an insufficient basis on which apply the UNIDROIT Principles.

ICC Case No 7645 of 1995[132] involved a contract for the sale and delivery of goods from a Slovak seller (the claimant) and a Korean buyer (the respondent). The seller initiated arbitration over non-payment of the purchase price. The contract contained a choice of Austrian law, which the tribunal held led to application of the CISG by virtue of CISG, article 1(1)(b). A court is likely to have made the same determination.

The tribunal found that the seller had breached the contract by failing to load the cargo by the date required and by delivering non-conforming shipping documents. Accordingly, the tribunal found that the buyer was justified in terminating the contract under article 49 of the CISG. Therefore, the claimant had no right to demand the purchase price.

In discussing whether the buyer had properly terminated the contract according to the requirements of the CISG, the tribunal noted that even if the avoidance was unjustified or ineffective, the claimant still could not win because: 'According to a basic rule of the law on contracts, the *exceptio non adimpleti contractus*, the purchaser is not bound to pay the purchase price as long as the seller has not performed or at least adequately tendered correct performance.' The tribunal stated that the *exceptio* principle could be derived from article 58(1) of the CISG. This provision states only that if a date for payment of the purchase price is not set in the contract, the price is due when the seller places either the goods or the documents controlling their disposition at the buyer's disposal. The tribunal did not explain how it derived the *exceptio* from article 58(1), and there does not seem to be adequate support for its reasoning.

Duke Energy Electroquil v Ecuador[133] is another investment arbitration that included a contractual claim of justified suspension of performance. In 1995, Electroquil, the first private power generator in Ecuador, entered into a power purchase agreement (PPA) with INECEL, a state-owned power company. Under the PPA, Electroquil would construct and operate a power plant in Ecuador and sell the electricity to INECEL. A second PPA was entered into in 1996, after which Duke acquired a controlling interest in Electroquil. Both PPAs were governed by Ecuadorian law. The Ecuadorian civil code is based on the Chilean, which in turn is based on the French (Napoleonic) civil code, at least with respect to the law of obligations.[134]

Payments from INECEL to Electroquil under the PPA were to be made through a set of 'payment trusts', which the PPA required INECEL to establish before the plants commenced commercial operations. There were delays in the establishment of the trusts, and therefore delays in payment. Electroquil also experienced delays in its own performance, and INECEL imposed various fines that were provided for in the PPA.

The tribunal (composed of Swiss, Columbian, and Dutch arbitrators) considered the question of whether INECEL was justified in imposing the fines. Electroquil claimed, inter alia, that its delays in performance were justified under the *exceptio* principle

132 (2001) XXVI Ybk Comm Arb 130.

133 *Duke Energy Electroquil Partners and Electroquil SA v Republic of Ecuador*, ICSID Case No ARB/04/19, award of 18 August 2008, available at <http://icsid.worldbank.org/ICSID/FrontServlet?requestType=GenCaseDtlsRH&actionVal=ListConcluded> accessed 28 July 2012.

134 Murillo 2001, 170–2.

because INECEL had been late in making its payments under the PPA. The tribunal rejected this defence on two grounds.

First, the tribunal held that Electroquil could not invoke the *exceptio* because its obligation to commence operation of the power plants was not conditional on INECEL's payment for the energy provided. However, the Ecuadorian law expressing the *exceptio* does not appear to require that the debtor's breached obligation be a condition of the creditor's suspended obligation, and indeed the tribunal did not cite any authority for this proposition. The tribunal also noted that the PPA did not permit Electroquil to withhold performance if payments from INECEL were delayed.

Second, the tribunal held that there was no evidence that Electroquil had not commenced operation of the power plants because of the delay in payment. Accordingly, the tribunal reasoned, there was no chain of causation between INECEL's failure to establish the payment trusts and Electroquil's failure to commence operations at the power plants. This lack of causation meant that Electroquil could not invoke the *exceptio*. The tribunal provided no explanation for this limitation on Electroquil's right to invoke *exceptio*, and it is not mentioned in article 1568 of the Ecuadorian civil code.[135] It may well be justified under broader principles of good faith or of synallagmatic contractual relationships, but the tribunal did not refer to such arguments. The tribunal's decision, therefore, appears motivated at least as much by its sense of the general operation of the *exceptio* as by the text of the Ecuadorian civil code.

3. Awards involving direct application of general principles

There are only two awards in this category, both of which were decided under amiable composition. The first is ICC Case No 3540 of 3 October 1980.[136] The claimant, a French construction company, contracted with a Yugoslav subcontractor (the respondent) to build a project in the USSR for a Soviet principal. The contract contained no choice of law clause and empowered the tribunal to act as *amiable compositeur*. The tribunal, composed of Swiss, Yugoslav, and French arbitrators, was constituted in Switzerland under the ICC rules.

The parties disagreed on the applicable substantive law, the respondent pleading for French law, the claimant for Swiss law. The tribunal determined that ICA tribunals in general, including when acting as *amiables compositeurs*, may avoid the choice of law process by taking the 'direct approach' (*voie directe*) and selecting a substantive law. The tribunal decided it should apply *lex mercatoria* and not any national law.

Under the contract, payment was to be in monthly instalments. A dispute arose and the claimant refused to pay some of the instalments. The respondent raised a counterclaim seeking an interim award for the monthly payments that the claimant had withheld. In its defence, the claimant invoked the *exceptio* and, subsidiarily, a set-off to the extent of the breaches that it claimed against the respondent.

The tribunal held that the *exceptio*: 'must be considered as belonging to the general principles of law forming the *lex mercatoria* applicable here'. It gave no authority or justification for this conclusion but did note that both Swiss and French law—the laws pleaded by the parties—recognize the *exceptio*. The tribunal went on to state a familiar

[135] Article 1568 provides only that the principle applies in bilateral contracts: '*En los contratos bilaterales ninguno de los contratantes está en mora, dejando de cumplir lo pactado, mientras el otro no lo cumple por su parte, o no se allana a cumplirlo en la forma y tiempo debidos.*'

[136] [1981] JDI 914 (in French; all translations are the author's).

description of the remedy as: 'by nature dilatory ... it momentarily paralyses the action for execution of the creditor's obligations'.

In any event, the tribunal decided that it was 'more expedient' to resolve the dispute on the basis of the claimant's alternative argument for a set-off. It therefore made no determination as to whether the claimant's invocation of the *exceptio* was proper, nor did it address the content of the rights granted to a creditor by the *exceptio*. A common law lawyer might say that the tribunal's characterization of suspension of performance as a general principle of international law was mere obiter.

The second case in this category is ICC Case No 3267 of 1979,[137] which was also decided under amiable composition. The respondent, a Belgian building contractor, was part of a consortium that was to construct developments in two Saudi Arabian cities. It subcontracted part of this project to the claimant. The tribunal found that, since it was appointed as *amiable compositeur*, it need not 'decide which specific law governs the contractual relationship between the parties'. Instead, it applied 'general principles of international commercial law ... with no specific reference to a particular system of law'.

The contract called for a fixed price, subject only to limited circumstances that could justify modification. The respondent was to pay in instalments, after the claimant reached specified contractual milestones. The respondent made the first five payments, but deducted certain sums from the sixth and seventh payments because of alleged failures by the claimant to reach the milestones. In response, the claimant terminated the contract.

The tribunal characterized the respondent's deductions as suspensions of performance. Since the contract mandated a particular procedure for withholding payments 'specifically devised for this kind of contingency', and the respondent did not follow this procedure, the payment deductions were not justified. Importantly, the tribunal held that the existence of a particular contractual term on-point means that: 'The argument that such ... deduction was made in "accordance with ... international trade usages", does not carry any weight.' In other words, the tribunal declined to state whether suspension of performance constituted a general principle of law consonant with 'international trade usages' because the agreement of the parties supersedes any such principles.

4. Analysis of the published awards

Given the small sample of just twelve awards in this case study, firm conclusions cannot be made about international arbitrators' approaches to suspension of performance. However, certain patterns may be discerned.

Throughout the awards, international arbitral tribunals' preference for transnational law is evidenced in their choice of law analyses and their reasoning. In seven of the twelve awards, the tribunal applied an international instrument or general principles, sometimes over the objection of one or both parties. Anecdotally, at least, this is a far higher rate than one might see in national court litigation, even looking only at cross-border commercial disputes. Case No 11849 is particularly noteworthy in this regard. There, the tribunal applied the CISG to parts of the contractual relationship that were not sales on the grounds that the contract's references to the CISG and to the

137 (1982) VII Ybk Comm Arb 96.

ICC Uniform Customs and Practices for Documentary Credits evinced an intent to avoid their respective national laws and seek 'neutral solutions'.

In five awards, general principles of international law were expressly invoked by the tribunal and were decisive in the tribunal's decision on the propriety of a party's suspension of performance.[138] In one award, ICC Case No 8547, general principles were applied that were contrary to the explicit language of the ULIS, which is itself an international instrument. In both awards involving amiable composition—where there was no obligation to cite any legal standard whatsoever—the tribunals applied general principles.[139]

In *Electroquil v Ecuador*, the tribunal did not expressly state that it was relying on general principles, but applied a particular version of the *exceptio* for which it cited no Ecuadorian authority (that only the obligations of the creditor conditioned on the unperformed obligations of the debtor may be suspended, and that the suspension must have occurred in response to the creditor's delay in performance). The tribunal's interpretation may well be justified under Ecuadorian law, and it is possible that the relevant authority was considered by the tribunal but not mentioned in the award. However, it seems more likely that the tribunal was reasoning from what it saw as the general operation of the suspension principle around the world. The same may well have occurred in the two cases in which the tribunal erroneously held that the CISG permits suspension of performance.[140]

Perhaps the most striking pattern that arises from the awards in this case study is the readiness with which tribunals declared that a general principle of international law permits contractual parties to suspend performance. This occurred in five awards, nearly half of the published awards involving suspension.[141] (Moreover, there was not one case in which the tribunal expressly stated that there is *no* general right to suspend performance.) As discussed above, such a conclusion is dubious; even if there is general agreement that some right to suspend performance exists, there is no international consensus on when or how such a right may be exercised.[142]

Now that a few published awards include such declarations, they may become self-fulfilling prophecies.[143] While the decision of one ICA tribunal cannot bind another in the sense of *stare decisis*, very few arbitral awards are published and tribunals cite published awards on points of substantive law. This is especially so in cases dealing with transnational law. The awards discussed here are consistent with the propositions that arbitrators promote the application of general principles of international law and that suspension of performance constitutes such a general principle. Moreover, they do so regardless of whether there is an applicable law, or whether the applicable law is silent on the question, or even whether the applicable law provides a right to suspend performance.

[138] *Klöckner v Cameroon* and ICC Cases Nos 8547, 7645, 3540, and 3267.

[139] ICC Cases Nos 3540 and 3267.

[140] ICC Cases Nos 11849 and 76458.

[141] *Klöckner v Cameroon*, *Aucoven v Venezuela*, and ICC Cases Nos 8547, 7645, and 3540. The tribunal in ICC Case No 3267 declined to decide whether suspension of performance constitutes a general principle of international law because this determination was not necessary to the result.

[142] In each of the awards that found that suspension of performance constitutes a general principle, where the nationality of the arbitrators is known, the tribunals were composed of civil lawyers (except for one American arbitrator who signed the original *Klöckner* award). This may account for the readiness of the tribunals to invoke the *exceptio* by name and to declare it to be universally accepted.

[143] Cf Oliver Wendell Holmes's characterization of the law as 'the prophecies of what the courts will do in fact'. Holmes 1897, 461.

Among the tribunals that discussed the circumstances under which a creditor may suspend performance, there was little disagreement. In all of the cases, the contracts were bilateral and no tribunal imposed a requirement that the contract be synallagmatic. Order of performance was discussed only in ICC Cases Nos 4629 and 8547, and there the creditor was to perform simultaneously with or after the debtor. The only award that addressed the severity of the breach was *Aucoven v Venezuela*, where the tribunal held that the debtor's breach must be material. The award in ICC Case No 4629 implicitly addresses the proportionality of the creditor's conduct—since the breach was serious enough to justify termination, the lesser response of suspension was '*a fortiori*' acceptable. In ICC Case No 11849, decided under the CISG, the tribunal held that the creditor's response was unjustifiable because it was 'excessive and disproportionate'; however, no source was cited for this standard.

In sum, the tribunals that address suspension of performance seem to prefer a rule that does not require a serious breach but does contain a requirement of proportionality on the part of the creditor. This formula is clearly influenced by the *exceptio non adimpleti contractus*, and in particular the Germanic formulation of the *exceptio*. Taking into account the UNIDROIT Principles and the PECL—the most recently-enacted major international contract law instruments—which also adopt a Germanic approach to suspension of performance, this version of the remedy will likely be the dominant one in future characterizations of the general principles of international law.

V. Conclusion

Doctrines relating to suspension of performance present a clear divergence between common law and civil law approaches. Civil law jurisdictions recognize the *exceptio non adimpleti contractus*, whereby contracting parties may defend a claim of breach of performance by pleading a prior breach by the other party. In common law jurisdictions, on the other hand, parties facing a breach generally have only two choices: perform their own obligations and seek damages, or withhold performance and terminate the contract. In the United States, the law does not expressly permit suspension; however, the interrelationship between various provisions of the Restatement that deal with material breaches has the effect of permitting a creditor to suspend in cases where the debtor's breach is curable within a reasonable period of time.

The various international contract law instruments are similarly divided. The older instruments—the ULIS and the CISG—make no specific provision for suspension of performance. The more recently-enacted instruments—the PECL and UNIDROIT Principles—adopt a Germanic version of the *exceptio*, whereby any non-*de minimis* breach can justify suspension of performance, but the party suspending performance must do so in good faith, which is generally measured according to whether the obligation suspended was proportional to the obligation breached.

There is no single general principle of international law relating to suspension of performance, nor is there even a convergence among national legal systems. None of the published cases involving a claim of justified suspension was governed by the law of a common law jurisdiction, perhaps because parties from common law jurisdictions do not typically attempt to suspend performance in the manner permitted by the *exceptio*. It is therefore impossible to make a full comparison of the outcomes in national courts and in ICA. However, the fact that the ULIS and CISG, properly construed, do not permit suspension of performance means that one can compare the approaches of international arbitral tribunals in situations where the governing law does and does not permit suspension.

In this light, the pattern in the published awards is clear: international arbitrators tend to permit parties to suspend performance in the face of a breach by the other party. No tribunal acting under the law of a civil law jurisdiction found a suspension to be unjustified, except on the basis of well-recognized exceptions in the governing law. In Cairo Regional Center for International Commercial Arbitration Case No 142/1999 the tribunal held that the *exceptio* is unavailable in contracts with public authorities, and in *Aucoven v Venezuela* the tribunal held that Venezuela had no right to suspend performance because Aucoven's breach was not material. On the other hand, there were three cases governed by the CISG and one governed by the ULIS where the tribunal held that a party was justified in suspending performance. Moreover, as noted above, several tribunals made the dubious assertion that the *exceptio*, or suspension of performance more generally, is a general principle of international law.

1. Suspension of Performance and International Arbitration Culture

As one might expect, tribunals appear to reach different outcomes depending on which substantive law applies. For example, the awards in this case study that apply national laws do seem to have approached those laws in the same manner as courts in the relevant jurisdictions would have done, although the *Klöckner* arbitration is a possible exception.

However, the substantive law rules specific to ICA cannot account for much of these findings. Awards involving straightforward application of the governing law were in the minority. Most of the awards refer to general principles and, when they do, invariably declare the right to suspend performance to be a general principle. The fact that general principles are available in ICA, and uncertainty about the extent of those principles, do not explain this result, nor do the different means by which the content of governing laws are ascertained in litigation and ICA (again, with the possible exception of *Klöckner v Cameroon*). Similarly, the fact that arbitral tribunals may act as *amiables compositeurs* does not explain the fact that, in the two awards decided under amiable composition, the tribunals exercised their powers first to apply general principles and second to declare that a right to suspend performance is a general principle. Finally, no international arbitral practice appears relevant, nor indeed did any of the awards in this case study cite one.

The outcomes seen in this case study are better explained on the basis of the ICA culture described in Part I. In particular, the awards show the influence of the norms of internationalism, neutrality, and service of business.

The impact of the internationalism and neutrality norms is evident in the large number of tribunals that referred to general principles of international law. Tribunals referred to general principles when the governing law provided the same result,[144] and in some cases to justify outcomes not supported by the governing law.[145]

A preference for international and substantively neutral laws also explains the choice of law made in ICC Case No 11849. There, the tribunal applied the CISG to the entirety of the contractual relationship, contrary to both the terms of the contract and

[144] This occurred in *Klöckner v Cameroon* and *Electroquil v Ecuador*.

[145] This occurred in ICC Cases Nos 11849, 8547, and 7645 and in the CAM award of 22 February 2008.

the text of the CISG, because the parties had 'indicated their intention to avoid their respective internal law rules, and to resort to neutral solutions'. Similarly, the award in ICC Case No 8547 held that gaps in the governing law (the ULIS) should be filled by reference to the UNIDROIT Principles. The applicable rules did not require this, but the tribunal held that its course of action was justified because of party autonomy to choose non-national rules of law and because of 'the internationality of the relations between the parties'.

Klöckner v Cameroon is such a clear example of the trends discussed above that it is worthy of separate consideration. At one level, it was simply wrongly decided, or at least relied on insufficient legal reasoning. As Paulsson notes in his comment on the award: 'The discussion of *exceptio non adimpleti contractus* ... contains the only passages in the award that include an analysis of French case law and commentary.'[146] However, for present purposes the correctness or incorrectness of the *Klöckner* tribunal's treatment of the *exceptio* issue is beside the point; what matters is the way that the tribunal diverged from an orthodox treatment of the governing French-influenced Cameroonian law.

First, the tribunal analysed the *exceptio* not only in terms of French law, but also under English and international law. As noted above, arbitral tribunals will often take the extra, legally unnecessary step of explaining that the outcome would be the same if a different law applied; this may be motivated by a desire to maintain neutrality or an internationalist ethos. Similarly, the tribunal argued that the *exceptio* constitutes a general principle of international law, another example of arbitral internationalism in action.

Finally, it may be argued that the tribunal's treatment of the *exceptio* issue was motivated by a commercial mentality or, alternatively, is an example of arbitral 'lawlessness'. As the annulment committee pointed out, the original tribunal, when deciding on the applicability of the *exceptio*, shifted back and forth between Klöckner's obligation to deliver the factory and its obligation to manage the factory: 'This may be explained from an industrial or economic perspective but does not always facilitate legal analysis.'[147]

The service of business norm also explains the near unanimity with which the tribunals held that a party suspending performance was justified in doing so, and that a right to suspend performance constitutes a general principle of international law. Suspending performance is an intuitive course of action and is probably the first instinct of most business people who are faced with a breach of contract. More generally, expanding the range of available self-help remedies is in the interests of commercial parties; after all, self-help is more efficient than resorting to (uncertain, slow, expensive) litigation.[148]

The same preference for remedies that are intuitive and economically efficient also accounts for the apparent preference in the awards in this case study toward a Germanic version of the *exceptio*. French-influenced jurisdictions require that the debtor's breach be material before a creditor can suspend performance. It is often difficult to determine at the moment a breach occurs whether it is a material breach; creditors therefore take the risk that, if they suspend performance, they will later be held to have wrongly repudiated the contract. The rule of proportionality that is the focus of the Germanic *exceptio* is easier and more certain for commercial parties to put into practice—it does not take legal training to see whether one obligation is roughly proportional to another. The

146 Paulsson 1984.

147 Paragraph 136 of the decision on annulment.

148 Self-help remedies as a whole are considered to be economically efficient, so long as the do not lead to windfalls for the party engaging in self-help. See, eg, Gergen 2009, 1430–9.

Germanic *exceptio* therefore accords better with commercial expectations and exposes commercial parties to fewer risks. Arbitral tribunals' inclination toward it is predictable based on the cultural theory of arbitral decision-making advanced here.

The results of this case study have implications for both contract drafting and advocacy. Given the frequency with which ICA tribunals referred to general principles and the uncertainty inherent in such determinations, contract drafters would be well advised to expressly provide for the conditions in which parties may suspend performance. If the contract contains a choice of law that calls for general principles or *lex mercatoria*, or directs the tribunal to rule on the basis of trade usages or amiable composition, they should expect that a tribunal will likely apply a Germanic version of the *exceptio* to cases of suspended performance. Accordingly, if counsel are consulted after a breach occurs, they should in most cases feel confident advising their clients to suspend performance but should ensure that any performance suspended is proportionate to the breach. It would be advisable to give notice to the breaching party stating that performance is being suspended in response to an equivalent breach.

When the issue of suspended performance arises in an arbitration, counsel should keep in mind that arbitrators are most likely to be convinced by arguments related to proportionality, especially if the governing law contains a general duty of good faith. Thus, counsel who represent the party that suspended performance would likely be best served by arguments that highlight the proportionality of their client's conduct rather than arguments that highlight the severity of the breach or the bad faith of the breaching party. Such arguments may be couched in terms of the *exceptio*, since arbitrators appear likely to be amenable to the notion that the *exceptio* constitutes a general principle of international law. Conversely, counsel for the party that was the first to breach the contract should emphasize the disproportionate character of the suspending party's conduct.

7

Case Study 2: The Interpretation of Contracts

I. Introduction

'A horse! a horse! my kingdom for a horse!' Poor King Richard. What did he mean by his famous cry? Was he saying that in his extremity on Bosworth field he was willing to give up his kingdom if only he could have a horse? Or was this a despairing recognition that for loss of a mere horse he was losing his very kingdom? Sir William Catesby may have thought the former. Certainly he urged the king to withdraw, saying he would help him to a horse. But that was not Richard's meaning: 'Slave, I have set my life upon a cast, and I will stand the hazard of the die'.[1]

As Lord Nicholls relates, this episode from Shakespeare's *Richard III* illustrates a fundamental truth: language is 'an inherently imperfect means of communication', so 'the law must find some way to ascribe to language when used as the source of legal right or obligation a certainty of meaning it inherently lacks'.[2] The indeterminacy of language, combined with the fact that parties negotiating a contract may not contemplate matters that later prove to be relevant, means that interpretation is necessary whenever the parties disagree as to the obligations a contract creates.[3] Disagreements over the content of a contract are frequently characterized as disputes over the 'law of the contract' (obligations created by the terms of the contract) as opposed to 'contract law' (obligations created by the law governing the contract).[4]

Before a court can interpret the applicable contract law, it must find the sources of that law: statute, case law, and perhaps academic commentary. Similarly, before the 'law of the contract' can be interpreted, the adjudicator must first find that law. It is the sources of the law of the contract that form the subject of this case study: how do adjudicators determine what Farnsworth called 'the subject matter to be interpreted'?[5] In particular, what evidence extrinsic to the text of the contract itself will an adjudicator consider? When adjudicators consider that evidence, from what perspective do they proceed?

A gulf separates the common law and civilian models. As a general rule, the common law focuses on the 'plain meaning' of the final agreement between the parties. A set of exclusionary rules work to shut out evidence extrinsic to the contract itself: evidence of the parties' communications and actions before, contemporaneous with, and subsequent to the conclusion of the contract and of their subjective intent or understanding of what the contract meant. Because the exclusionary rules can have unjust or absurd effects in some cases, a number of exceptions have been developed and the result is a complex set of overlapping rules and exceptions. The civil law has no counterpart to these rules. It seeks the 'true intention' of the parties, and therefore admits all relevant extrinsic evidence. It then expects the adjudicator to assign evidence more or less weight, depending on its reliability and relevance.

[1] Nicholls 2005, 1. [2] Ibid. [3] Zweigert and Kötz 1998, 400.
[4] Farnsworth 1999, 426. [5] Ibid, 427.

The exceptions to the common law exclusionary rules narrow the gap somewhat, and in any given case civil law and common law courts may ultimately reach the same interpretation.[6] However, the underlying doctrines remain irreconcilable. After accounting for the various exceptions, there are three classes of evidence that, generally speaking, the civil law admits and the common law excludes: statements of the parties prior to and contemporaneous with the conclusion of the contract (although England is more friendly to the introduction of such evidence than is the United States), evidence of one party's subjective intent, and conduct or statements of either party subsequent to the contract's conclusion.

This chapter considers the approach of international arbitrators when they are called upon to interpret a contract. Arbitration is an alternative to litigation in national courts and contractual interpretation is a matter of substantive contract law, so it is necessary first to understand what courts would do in similar situations. As with the previous case study, this one proceeds by putting the issue of contractual interpretation into comparative context, first considering the opposing perspectives that underlie the different interpretive doctrines, then comparing the rules in some of the most commercially important common law and civil law jurisdictions and the major international contract law instruments. Next, it assesses fifty-three published arbitral awards where the tribunal engaged in the interpretation of a contract.

In many contractual disputes, the disagreement is over whether a valid, binding agreement ever came into force. Where the existence of a contract itself is disputed, the court has no choice but to consider extrinsic evidence of what the parties agreed to. Such situations include allegations of lack of consideration, failure of a condition precedent, a defect of consent (eg fraud, duress, mistake, or incapacity), and formal invalidity (eg, cases under the common law statutes of frauds or similar writing requirements for some types of contracts in the civil law). All legal systems therefore agree that extrinsic evidence is widely admissible to resolve such differences, and there is little difference between the common law and civil law approaches.

The same principle applies to cases involving alleged amendments to a contract or actions for rectification—all legal systems admit extrinsic evidence to prove or disprove an amendment or to rectify a contract. These types of disputes are therefore not fruitful ground for an investigation such as the present one, and are excluded. In addition, disputes over the existence of an excuse (eg, *force majeure* or unconscionability) or over the type of remedy or extent of damages available are outside the scope of this case study, which considers only the obligations created by contracts, not the effects of those obligations.

II. Contractual Interpretation in Comparative Context

Both the common and civil law theories of contract analyse contracts in terms of a free agreement of autonomous wills—in common law terms, a 'meeting of the minds'.[7] However, there are doctrinal differences in addition to the differences in practice. The

[6] One interviewee, an experienced arbitrator with both common law and civil law training, observed: 'Very often, in my experience, whatever approach you adopt, you get the same contractual interpretation. The results aren't that different, although the approach is. I think for common law lawyers, looking at some of the evidence that is admitted or used in a civil law approach can be discomfiting, but at the end of the day, I don't see the result as that different.'

[7] Nicholas 1992, 35.

common law and civil law models begin from two opposed perspectives, neither of which is found in its pure form in modern practice:

> On one [civilian] view, it is the *intention* of the promisor which counts; this is justified by the principle of private autonomy which treats the free will of legal persons as the source and measure of legal consequences.... On the other [common law] view, priority is given to the external phenomenon of *expression* ... the internal will of the promisor is treated as significant only in so far as it coincides with the normal objective meaning that a reasonable man would attribute to its expression.[8]

In other words, the common law focuses on the 'meeting', while the civil law focuses on the 'minds'.

The two perspectives have yielded philosophically incompatible methods of interpretation. For common law judges 'the inquiry is objective: the question is what reasonable persons, circumstanced as the actual parties were, would have had in mind'.[9] Or, in Corbin's phrasing, a contract's 'legal operation must ... be in accordance with the meaning that the words convey to the court, not the meaning that the parties intended to convey'.[10] The opposing view is exemplified by article 133 of the German BGB: 'it is necessary to ascertain the true intention rather than adhering to the literal meaning of the declaration'.

Of course, all interpretation is objective in the colloquial sense, since no one can know with certainty the thoughts of another. Adjudicators can only work on the basis of 'external phenomena'—the parties' written contract, their other communications, and their conduct.[11] However, from the civil law viewpoint, such external phenomena are used as tools to ascertain what the parties themselves actually intended, and not what a reasonable person in the position of the parties would have intended. According to article 1156 of the French *Code civil*, the primary role of interpretation is to discover the 'common intention of the parties' (*commune intention des parties*).[12] Where such cannot be ascertained 'the judge is supposed to ascertain the "hypothetical" intention of the parties or to adopt the interpretation which in all the circumstances, objective and subjective, must be regarded as the one the parties would reasonably have intended'.[13]

This contrasts sharply with the objective method, set out by Lord Hoffman in one of the leading cases, *Investors Compensation Scheme v West Bromwich Building Society*: 'Interpretation is the ascertainment of the meaning which the document would convey to a reasonable person having all the background knowledge which would reasonably have been available to the parties in the situation in which they were at the time of the contract.'[14] The objective method may sacrifice equity in a given case but promotes certainty and predictability:

> Commercial stability requires of any developed system of contract that the terms of the agreement should normally be binding in the sense in which they would reasonably be understood, even though one of the parties, Humpty-Dumpty like, was using the language in a private sense of his or her own.[15]

[8] Zweigert and Kötz 1998, 401 (emphases in original).

[9] *Mannai Investments Co Ltd v Eagle Star Life Assurance Co Ltd* [1997] 1 AC 749, 778 (HL).

[10] Corbin 1964, 161. [11] Zweigert and Kötz 1998, 406.

[12] The full article states: 'One must in agreements seek what the common intention of the contracting parties was, rather than pay attention to the literal meaning of the terms' ('*On doit dans les conventions rechercher quelle a été la commune intention des parties contractantes, plutôt que de s'arrêter au sens littéral des termes*'). Official translation available online: <http://www.legifrance.gouv.fr/content/download/1950/13681/version/3/file/Code_22.pdf> accessed 20 July 2012.

[13] Zweigert and Kötz 1998, 402. [14] [1998] 1 WLR 896 (HL).

[15] Hoffman 1997, 666.

In practice, the common law approach is distinguished not only by its emphasis on objectivity, but also by 'the intellectual rigour with which the analysis is carried through to detailed consequences'.[16] The common law rules governing extrinsic evidence are significantly more complicated than their civil law equivalents, and contractual interpretation in common law courts is also frequently a complex affair. Judges must rule on objections to the introduction of extrinsic evidence as they arise (excusing the jury each time) and separate briefs and oral arguments are usually required. Even documentary evidence must usually be introduced by testimony, so witnesses must be instructed to avoid injecting extrinsic evidence into the record. Civil law procedure is more streamlined, with its emphasis on documentary evidence and the investigatory powers of the judge.

Another difference in perspective, which is not frequently mentioned, is that the civil law sees contracts as the legal expressions of ongoing relationships between parties—the cumulation of a series of individual acts of will—while the common law sees contracts as crystallizing at a particular, identifiable moment.[17] This difference in perspective has implications beyond the admissibility of extrinsic evidence. For example, the civil law provides broader scope than does the common law for precontractual liability; it also prioritizes remedies, like specific performance, that keep the contractual relationship alive. Consequently, common law interpretive doctrine asks the adjudicator to focus on the contract itself and the circumstances immediately surrounding its conclusion, while the civil law directs the adjudicator to consider the whole arc of the parties' relationship.

Finally, the common law and civil law differ on whether the rules which govern the use of extrinsic evidence are substantive or procedural. This issue is of vital importance when considering arbitral awards, because arbitral tribunals perform a choice of law analysis to determine the substantive law that governs the contract, but follow the procedural rules determined by or in accordance with the agreement to arbitrate.

Under the common law, the matter is settled: although the exclusionary rules deal with the admissibility of evidence, the rules themselves are substantive law. As Farnsworth notes, evidentiary rules 'bar some methods of proof to show a fact but permit that fact to be shown in a different way', while the rules that exclude extrinsic evidence bar 'a showing of the fact itself—the fact that the terms of the agreement are other than those in the writing'.[18] The substantive nature of the exclusionary rules in the common law is borne out in their application. For example, an objection based on an exclusionary rule (a point of substantive law) is not lost by failure to raise it at trial, while an objection to a leading question during direct examination or to the admission of hearsay evidence (points of procedural law) must be made at trial to preserve the issue for appeal.[19] In addition, when US federal courts sit under diversity jurisdiction (in which situation they apply federal procedural law but state substantive law), they apply the rules governing extrinsic evidence of the state whose substantive law governs the dispute.[20]

Under the civil law, the matter is equally settled: all rules governing the admissibility of evidence, for whatever purpose, are procedural. Indeed, while there are no direct equivalents in the civil law to the common law exclusionary rules, such guidance on the admission of extrinsic evidence as does exist is found in codes of procedure

[16] Nicholas 1992, 35. [17] McMeel 2003, 272.

[18] Farnsworth 1999, 428. [19] Ibid, 429.

[20] Restatement (2d) of Conflict of Laws, s 140. See also, eg, *Betz Laboratories v Hines*, 647 F2d 402 (3d Cir 1981): 'The parol evidence rule is substantive rather than evidentiary, so we apply state law.'

and evidence, rather than in civil codes and codes of obligations (except for provisions requiring certain contracts to be proved by a writing).

1. Common law jurisdictions

Contractual interpretation in the common law is characterized by a series of rules that exclude different types of extrinsic evidence, with exceptions that allow certain types of extrinsic evidence in certain cases. During the 20th century, the strictness of these rules was loosened to a great degree, especially in England, where courts now regularly admit extrinsic evidence that is part of the context or surrounding circumstances of the contract.

However, the rules as a whole continue to apply and the rationales behind them continue to be influential. The broadest and most basic exclusionary rule is the one most closely derived from the requirement of objectivity: extrinsic evidence can only be admissible if it is evidence of objective facts known to both parties, rather than evidence of the intentions of either party.[21] Summing up recent English case law, McMeel writes that, although English judges are increasingly willing to admit some extrinsic evidence as part of the circumstances surrounding the conclusion the contract, 'there appears to be little appetite ... for the regular admissibility of the parties' opinions as to what the contract meant'.[22] For this reason, admissible extrinsic evidence must concern matters that both parties knew (or ought to have known). Evidence of one party's unilateral expectations is not admissible in any form.[23]

The rules governing extrinsic evidence seem to be thought of as practical, nuts-and-bolts law—matters for students and advocates but not for scholars. The article by Patterson cited below even contains something of a disclaimer: 'Mindful of the beginning law student, to whom much of the writing in law reviews seems esoteric, the Editors are pleased to publish this article on a fundamental aspect of the law of contracts.'[24] All general contract law treatises address the rules governing extrinsic evidence, but the only available book-length treatments of these issues under English law are those by Lewison and McMeel, both of which were written by active barristers and aimed primarily at practitioners.[25] Few pertinent academic articles are available, and most of these are jeremiads against the parol evidence rule.[26] Furthermore, many of the articles that do exist were written by sitting judges, whose daily work involves frequent exercises in contractual interpretation.[27]

Interpretation in a common law court traditionally begins by application of the 'plain meaning rule', which requires the judge to read the contract according to the 'natural and ordinary' meaning of the words used.[28] Only if the words of the contract are vague or ambiguous, 'capable in some context of bearing another meaning, perhaps less natural but not so as to amount to a misuse of language,' then extrinsic evidence

[21] Lewison 2004, 85, citing *Rabin v Gerson Berger Assoc Ltd* [1986] 1 WLR 526; *Barlee Marine Corp v Mountain* [1987] 1 Lloyd's Rep 471.

[22] McMeel 2003, 274; see also McLauchlan 1999, 182.

[23] McMeel 2003, 293.

[24] Patterson 1964, 1.

[25] Lewison 2004; McMeel 2003.

[26] Such attacks seem to be launched anew by each generation of contract scholars. A classic example is Sweet 1968.

[27] For example, those cited herein by Lords Nicholls and Hoffman and by Judges Staughton and Steyn.

[28] On the plain meaning rule generally, see Farnsworth 1999, s 7.12.

may be introduced to resolve the ambiguity, but not to contradict the written terms.[29] If, on the other hand:

the utterance could be given a different meaning only on the basis that the parties had made a mistake or adopted an idiosyncratic usage, evidence of background to show that this must have been the case is inadmissible unless the natural meaning, when applied to the real world, would produce an impossibility or absurdity.[30]

The controversies surrounding the plain meaning rule have focused on the breadth of the context within which the words of the contract must be read. American courts have traditionally adhered to the strictest version of the plain meaning rule, often called the 'four corners rule', which restricts a judge to reading the literal terms of the contract itself, and only the terms of the contract, in order to determine whether an ambiguity exists that might permit the introduction of extrinsic evidence. While the four corners rule has fallen into disfavour in England and among academics generally, many American states maintain it.[31] This divergence may be explained by the continued use of juries for civil trials in the United States:

If the jury is directed to bring a general verdict (*i.e.*, for the plaintiff or for the defendant), it may in so doing exercise its views of jury equity and thus impair the reliability of written instruments. This possibility may account for the reluctance of courts to admit parol evidence and other extrinsic aids to interpretation, and for their adherence to the 'plain meaning' of the contract.[32]

The more common modern practice, sometimes called the 'context rule', admits evidence of the circumstances surrounding the conclusion of the contract 'in all cases to place the contract in its correct setting, even where there is no ambiguity apparent on the face of the document'.[33] The cases that set off this round of liberalization are *Prenn v Simmonds*[34] and *Reardon Smith Line Ltd v Yngvar Hansen-Tangen*.[35] In the former, Lord Wilberforce introduced an influential concept, the 'matrix of facts' surrounding the conclusion of contracts:

The time has long since passed when agreements, even those under seal, were isolated from the matrix of facts in which they were set and interpreted purely on internal linguistic considerations.... We must ... inquire beyond the language and see what the circumstances were with reference to which the words were used, and the object appearing from those circumstances, which the person using them had in view.[36]

In *Reardon*, Lord Wilberforce reiterated this point: 'what the court must do must be to place itself in thought in the same factual matrix as that in which the parties were'.[37]

[29] Hoffman 1997, 670. [30] Ibid.

[31] Including the commercially important jurisdictions of New York and Delaware. A characteristic expression of this principle can be found in *Treemont, Inc v Hawley*, 886 P2d 589 (Wyo 1994): '[When] the provisions are clear and unambiguous, our examination is confined to the "four corners" of the document.'

[32] Patterson 1964, 837. Another aspect of the American adherence to traditionally strict evidentiary rules may be explained by the role of juries in American trials. England began only recently to admit hearsay evidence, with the proviso that the judge must consider the context in which the statement was made when considering the reliability of the evidence and the weight to give it. Civil Evidence Act 1995, s 4. Largely because jurors are not trusted to weigh the strength of evidence with the same care that judges are presumed to use, the US Federal Rules of Civil Procedure and those of every state maintain the ban on hearsay evidence.

[33] Lewison 2004, 82. [34] [1971] 1 WLR 1381 (HL).

[35] [1976] 1 WLR 989 (HL). [36] [1971] 1 WLR 1381 (HL), 1383–4.

[37] [1976] 1 WLR 989 (HL), 997.

The effect of these decisions was to set off a series of judgments relaxing the exclusionary rules that had previously bound contractual interpretation in England.

This liberalization was extended by more recent courts, especially in the speeches of Lord Hoffman in a pair of cases, *Investors Compensation Scheme v West Bromwich Building Society*[38] and *BCCI v Ali*.[39] In the former, Lord Hoffman stated:

> The meaning of words is a matter of dictionaries and grammars; the meaning of the document is what the parties using those words against the relevant background would reasonably have been understood to mean. The background may not merely enable the reasonable man to choose between the possible meanings of words which are ambiguous but even (as occasionally happens in ordinary life) to conclude that the parties, for whatever reason, have used the wrong words or syntax....
>
> The 'rule' that words should be given their 'natural and ordinary meaning' reflects the commonsense proposition that we do not easily accept that people have made linguistic mistakes, particularly in formal documents. On the other hand, if one would nevertheless conclude from the background that something must have gone wrong with the language, the law does not require judges to attribute to the parties an intention which they plainly could not have had.[40]

Despite some resistance from traditionally minded judges, the modern doctrine in England is characterized by 'a liberal approach to the relevance of surrounding circumstances in favouring one interpretation over another'.[41] In the United States, the trend is in the same direction, but adherence to the four corners rule and the plain meaning rule continues in many jurisdictions. Whatever the attitude of the court to the surrounding circumstances, however, evidence of the surrounding circumstances still cannot be used to contradict the 'natural meaning' of the contract's words. If background evidence contradictory to the written contract is admitted, that would amount to a court impermissibly determining that the parties really meant something different from what it objectively interpreted the contract to say.[42] As Judge Learned Hand famously wrote: 'there is a critical breaking point ... beyond which no language can be forced'.[43] This breaking point marks the boundary beyond which even admissible extrinsic evidence cannot survive.

The best-known common law exclusionary rule is the parol evidence rule, which, although unloved by many, continues to be in force in all common law jurisdictions. A classic formulation of the parol evidence rule is found in *Goss v Lord Nugent*:

> If there be a contract which has been reduced to writing, verbal evidence is not allowed to be given of what passed between the parties, either before the written instrument was made, or during the time that it was in a state of preparation so as to add or to subtract from, or in any manner to vary or qualify the written contract.[44]

Although, as this quotation suggests, the rule originally applied only to exclude oral evidence, it has evolved to exclude all prior and contemporaneous extrinsic evidence from cases where the parties have concluded a contract that represents the entirety of their agreement.

The first step in applying the parol evidence rule is to determine whether the written contract constitutes the final agreement of the parties. If so, 'the agreement is said to be "integrated", [but] if the parties had no such intention, the agreement is said to be

[38] [1998] 1 WLR 896 (HL). [39] [2002] 1 AC 251 (HL). [40] [1998] 1 WLR 896, 897.
[41] McMeel 2003, 272.
[42] *The Melanesian Mission Trust Board v Australian Mutual Provident Society* [1997] 2 EGLR 128.
[43] *Eustis Mining Co v Beer*, 239 Fed 976, 982 (SDNY 1917). [44] (1833), 110 Eng Rep 713.

"unintegrated" and the parol evidence rule does not apply'.[45] In the United States, contracts may also be entirely or partially integrated. In the latter case, the written contract constitutes the final agreement of the parties on all or only some of the obligations to which they intended to bind themselves.[46] For example, when a written sales contract specifies the price and quantity terms but reserves the date or manner of delivery to be agreed upon at a later time, then the contract is integrated with respect to price and quantity only.

The degree of integration of an agreement is determined according to the actual intent of the parties. Evidence relating to all the circumstances, including statements and conduct that would be inadmissible under the parol evidence rule, is admissible to determine whether the parties intended the agreement to be integrated.[47] In other words, the applicability of the parol evidence rule is determined by reference to parol evidence. This is an exception that arguably swallows the rule, and led the Law Commission to describe the parol evidence rule as circular.[48] However, as Lewison notes, a presumption applies that written contracts constitute the whole of the parties' agreement; thus, a party seeking to introduce extrinsic evidence of an antecedent non-written agreement has the burden of proving that this agreement was intended to continue in force together with the eventual written contract.[49]

Frequently, parties will include in their written contracts a term to the effect that the contract constitutes the entire agreement of the parties. In the United States, such terms are often called 'merger clauses' because they are said to merge the parties' negotiations and other prior statements into the final written instrument. Outside the United States, such terms are more commonly referred to as 'entire agreement' or 'integration' clauses.[50] The presence of an entire agreement clause is not on its own determinative that the parties intended the agreement to be fully integrated,[51] but it is strong evidence of such intent and usually precludes admission of parol evidence.[52]

If an entirely or partially integrated written agreement exists, then the parol evidence rule applies to exclude any evidence of the parties' prior or contemporaneous statements or actions. A typical example of the rule's operation is *Gianni v R Russell & Co.* Gianni held a lease to run a sales kiosk in the lobby of an office building. After the landlord granted a soda concession to another sales kiosk, Gianni sued on the ground that the owner had orally agreed to give Gianni the exclusive right to sell soda in the building. The lease contained no exclusivity provision, and the Pennsylvania Supreme Court held that it was error to admit testimony relating to the oral agreement: 'As the written lease is the complete contract of the parties and since it embraces the field of

45 Farnsworth 1999, 431. The integrated agreement may also be oral, or contained in an exchange of correspondence; what matters is the intent of the parties that the agreement be integrated. *Patton v Mid-Continent Systems*, 841 F2d 742 (7th Cir 1988). See also Restatement (2d) of Contracts, s 209 cmt *b*.

46 Farnsworth 1999, 432–3.

47 Restatement (2d) of Contracts, s 209(3). The Restatement sets up a presumption that contracts appearing to be complete are integrated unless evidence establishes the contrary.

48 Law Commission 1986 [2.89].

49 Lewison 2004, 71, citing *Gillespie v Cheney Egar & Co* [1896] 2 QB 59.

50 CISG-AC Opinion No 3 [4].

51 For example, Restatement (2d) of Contracts, s 209 cmt *b* warns that: 'such a declaration may not be conclusive'. Courts have tended toward the same view. *Sierra Diesel Injection Services v Burroughs Corp*, 874 F2d 653 (9th Cir 1989).

52 Farnsworth 1999, 436, citing *Tapper Chevrolet Co v Hansen*, 510 P2d 1091 (Idaho 1973). See also *McGrath v Shah* (1987) 57 P & CR 452, holding that an entire agreement clause constitutes an 'insuperable hurdle'.

the alleged oral contract, evidence of the latter is inadmissible under the parol evidence rule.'[53]

In the phrasing of the Restatement, the effect of a determination that an agreement is integrated is that 'evidence of prior or contemporaneous agreements or negotiations is not admissible to contradict a term' of the integrated agreement.[54] If the agreement is partially integrated, evidence of prior agreements or negotiations is admissible to supplement the agreement, but not to contradict it.[55] If, on the other hand, the agreement is completely integrated (for example, if it contains a merger clause), then even 'consistent additional terms' may not be admitted to explain or supplement the final agreement.[56]

In England, the distinction is not generally made between partially and fully integrated agreements. If an agreement is held to be integrated, then extrinsic evidence may not be admitted to contradict any part of it. In *Investors Compensation Scheme*, Lord Hoffman stated : 'The law excludes from the admissible background the previous negotiations of the parties.'[57] In 2009, in *Chartbrook v Persimmon Homes*, the House of Lords reaffirmed the ban on consideration of prior negotiations as evidence of what the parties understood the contract to mean, except for purposes of rectification or estoppel by convention. This was so even though the contractual term at issue in *Chartbrook*, if interpreted 'in accordance with ordinary rules of syntax, makes no commercial sense'.[58] On the other hand, to the extent that objective facts are communicated in the course of the parties' negotiations, those facts may be admitted as part of the factual matrix forming the necessary background for the parties' agreements.[59]

A common type of excluded parol evidence is drafts of a contract.[60] Parties are particularly apt to introduce such evidence, especially when the contract was concluded by an exchange of drafts. When both parties argue that their own, different, standard conditions of business were incorporated into the contract (a 'battle of the forms'), the accepted approach is to admit evidence of the negotiations and assess them according to the traditional rules respecting offers, counter-offers, and acceptance.[61]

As a specific application of this principle, English courts traditionally held that sentences struck by hand from the final version of a contract could not be considered

[53] 126 A 791, 792 (Pa 1924). See *Mellon Bank Corp v First Union Real Estate Equity & Mortgage Investments*, 951 F2d 1399 (3d Cir 1991): 'Pennsylvania courts still rely upon *Gianni*'s definitive statement of Pennsylvania's parol evidence rule'. Pennsylvania's common law parol evidence rule is typical of those prevailing in most US states. Farnsworth 1999, 427.

[54] Restatement (2d) of Contracts, s 215. The language in UCC, s 2-202 is similar: 'may not be contradicted by evidence of any prior agreement'.

[55] Restatement (2d) of Contracts, s 210(2). In this situation, UCC, s 2-202 reaches the same result with oppositely phrased language: 'consistent additional terms ... may be proved unless the court finds that the writing was intended by both parties as a complete and exclusive statement of all the terms'.

[56] Restatement (2d) of Contracts, s 216(1). Once again, the UCC is similar. Fully integrated contracts may not be 'explained or supplemented ... by evidence of conditional additional terms', s 2–202.

[57] [1998] 1 WLR 896 (HL). See also Lewison 2004, 59.

[58] *Chartbrook Ltd v Persimmon Homes Ltd* [2009] UKHL 38 [16] (speech of Lord Hoffman).

[59] This is so even with respect to 'without prejudice' negotiations toward a settlement agreement. *Oceanbulk Shipping and Trading SA v TMT Asia Ltd* [2010] UKSC 44 [40].

[60] Lewison 2004, 56.

[61] Ibid, 76, citing *Butler Machine Tool Co Ltd v Ex-Cell-O Corp (England) Ltd* [1979] 1 WLR 401 (CA); *Gibson v Manchester City Council* [1979] 1 WLR 294 (HL). But see Lord Denning's dissenting opinion in *Butler Machine Tool*, which argued that both parties' standard conditions are to be construed together, and either reconciled if they are harmonious or ignored if they are mutually contradictory.

in construing the contract.[62] As the rule evolved, the admissibility of deleted words became dependent upon whether the words were deleted from a standard form (admissible) or from a contract specifically negotiated between the parties (inadmissible).[63] Today, however, English courts tend to consider deleted terms as part of the admissible background of a contract, regardless of whether the contract was made from standard terms or was a one-off.[64]

Like the plain meaning rule, the parol evidence rule has come in for a great deal of criticism, not least for the large number of exceptions to it. Only those exceptions most relevant to international disputes will be detailed here.

The parol evidence rule does not exclude evidence of documents or statements that are referred to in the written contract. Expressly or impliedly incorporated terms cannot truly be said to be extrinsic to the contract and are admissible. The most common example of this 'exception' is terms which expressly incorporate an extrinsic term or document. In international commerce, it is common for contracts to incorporate form contracts or standard terms, such as the INCOTERMS promulgated by the International Chamber of Commerce or the sets of standard terms promulgated by a variety of industry trade groups.

Extrinsic evidence is also admissible to prove industry customs or practices established between the parties by a course of conduct. However, such evidence cannot be introduced if it contradicts the written terms of the contract.[65] Like incorporated terms, usages, if established, become a part of the contract and must be interpreted in the same way as the rest of the written contract.[66] Usages are facts that must be proven, and the required standard is high: 'Custom, or usage, must be notorious, certain and reasonable, and in effect such as is regarded as binding in the trade in question. Mere trade practice is insufficient.'[67]

Criticism of the parol evidence rule has been fierce. Sweet called for 'diagnosis and treatment of a sick rule',[68] while Honnold went so far as to say that the parol evidence rule: 'has been an embarrassment for the administration of modern transactions'.[69] The critics' point of view was summed up well by the Law Commission in a 1976 working paper: 'It is a technical rule of uncertain ambit which, at best, adds to the complications of litigation without affecting the outcome and, at worst, prevents the courts getting at the truth'.[70]

Criticisms generally fall into two categories: that the rule is needlessly complicated and that it often leads to unreasonable or unjust results. The many exceptions to the exclusionary rules are indeed a source of confusion and may detract from the

[62] *Sassoon (MA) & Sons Ltd v International Banking Corp* [1927] AC 711 (HL): 'Their Lordships take it to be settled ... that the effect is the same as if the deleted words had never formed part of the print at all.' (speech of Viscount Sumner). See also *Inglis v Buttery* (1878), 3 AC 552, 571 (HL).

[63] Lewison 2004, 58, citing *National Bank of Australasia v Falkingham & Sons* [1902] 1 AC 585 (PC).

[64] *Team Services plc v Kier Management and Design Ltd* (1993), 63 BLR 76, noting that one-off contracts 'are often composed of ready-made clauses taken from one or more sources, together with *ad hoc* clauses drafted afresh for the purpose of the particular contract'.

[65] *Baker v Black Sea & Baltic General Insurance Co Ltd* [1998] 1 WLR 974 (HL).

[66] Lewison 2004, 172.

[67] Staughton 1999, 311. See also *McCutcheon v Macbrayne (David) Ltd* [1964] 1 WLR 125, 138 (HL): 'It is the consistency of a course of conduct which gives rise to the implication that in similar circumstances a similar contractual result will follow. Where the conduct is not consistent, there is no reason why it should still produce an invariable contractual result.'

[68] Sweet 1968. [69] Honnold 1999, 121. [70] Law Commission 1976 [43].

predictability of results in a given case.[71] More importantly, the line between inadmissible parol evidence and admissible background is far from clear. Lawyers unsurprisingly will dress one up as the other, according to the interests of their clients, and judges frequently reach the result they think most just and then admit or exclude evidence as consistent with that result. As Sweet observed: 'New and unique methods of avoiding the parol evidence rule continually appear.'[72]

In addition, because contractual interpretation is considered an issue of law, not of fact, determinations of the admissibility of extrinsic evidence may be appealed and are reviewable *de novo*. Since perceptions of ambiguity and the scope of the surrounding circumstances may differ from one judge to the next, the result is a degree of unpredictability. In fact, statistics bear out the notion that 'there is a substantial chance of a reversal of trial court decisions'.[73] In the United States, juries determine the facts in many civil suits, so the characterization of interpretation as an issue of law has been justified by 'the judge's superior equipment—his education and legal experience—to interpret written instruments and give them reliability'.[74]

With respect to perverse results, Hoffman rightly points out that the exclusionary rules are designed 'to prevent the court from giving effect to the meaning which, as a matter of probability, it thinks the parties actually intended to convey by the words which they used in the instrument'.[75] From the common law's objective point of view, 'the legal certainty produced by the parol evidence rule is more important than the true intention of the parties'.[76]

Legal certainty is only one of several rationales that have been advanced in defence of the exclusionary rules. Originally, the parol evidence rule was justified on purely evidentiary grounds—oral evidence was seen as less reliable than documents.[77] Now, however, this view has fallen from favour.[78] A variety of rationales are now advanced in support of the exclusionary rules. In a much-quoted passage from his speech in *Prenn v Simmonds*, Lord Wilberforce explained that extrinsic evidence can simply be a distraction:

> The reason for not admitting evidence of these exchanges is not a technical one or even mainly of convenience.... It is simply that such evidence is unhelpful. By the nature of things, where negotiations are difficult, the parties' positions, with each passing letter are changing and until the final agreement, though converging, still different. It is only the final document which records a consensus. If the previous documents use different expressions, how does construction of those expressions, itself a doubtful process, help on the construction of the contractual words? If the same expressions are used, nothing is gained by looking back.[79]

[71] See *Zell v Am Seating Co*, 138 F2d 641, 643–4 (2d Cir 1943), rev'd 322 US 709 (1944).
[72] Sweet 1968, 1042. [73] Ibid, 1047. [74] Patterson 1964, 837.
[75] Hoffman 1997, 670. [76] Zweigert and Kötz 1998, 407.
[77] In the *Countess of Rutland's Case* (1604), 77 Eng Rep 89 (KB), the first recorded judgment to articulate the parol evidence rule, the rationale given was evidentiary: 'It would seem inconvenient, that matters in writing made by advice and on consideration, and which finally import the certain truth of the agreement of the parties should be controlled by averment of the parties to be proved by the uncertain testimony of slippery memory.' For an American case expressing the same rationale, see *GL Webster Co v Trinidad Bean & Elevator Co*, 92 F2d 177 (4th Cir 1937).
[78] Farnsworth 1999, 429.
[79] *Prenn v Simmonds* [1971] 1 WLR 1381 (HL) (speech of Lord Wilberforce). See also *The Rio Assu (No 2)* [1999] 1 Lloyd's Rep 115, 124 (CA): 'The negotiations of a contract can often be a compromise. It is dangerous to make the assumption that one party intended to have something else supplied or provided by the contract' (opinion of Waller LJ).

Lord Hoffman reached a similar conclusion:

> [E]xperience shows that such evidence seldom makes any difference. It usually tends most to show that the parties adopted a form of words which, if things went well, might not have to be examined too closely but which each hoped, in the last resort, would be interpreted favourably to him- or herself.[80]

This rationale is similar to the dominant one in American law, that the exclusionary rules, and in particular the parol evidence rule, promote certainty and protect the expectations of parties that intended their written contract to be a final agreement.[81]

Another compelling rationale for the exclusionary rules is that interpretation of a contract, combined with the rules of *stare decisis* and *res judicata*, can establish a meaning for contractual terms beyond the (possibly idiosyncratic) meaning given to them by the two parties. Most directly, this might occur in the case of a contract that affects a large number of people, such as a standard form contract or a collective labour agreement. Moreover, in modern commerce, 'many projects, whether construction, trading or banking, involve a network or other complex structure of contractual relations'.[82] Third parties whose interests are affected by a contract are not likely to have been present for its negotiation, so they are not likely to be familiar with much beyond the text of the contract and its immediate surrounding circumstances. They can only base their decisions on the contract as it is written, according to a reasonable understanding of its terms. It would be unjust to alter the rights of third parties based on factors of which they could have no knowledge.

Many commentators have also remarked upon the efficiency provided by exclusionary rules. When extrinsic evidence is admitted, the work of the court increases, and so does the length of trials and the concomitant costs. As Staughton said of Lord Hoffman's speech in *Investors Compensation Scheme*, which increased the range of evidence that may be admitted as part of the surrounding circumstances: 'It is hard to imagine a ruling more calculated to perpetuate the vast cost of commercial litigation.'[83] Conversely, as Gilmore argues in *The Death of Contract*, if 'we can restrict ourselves to the "externals" [ie objective evidence of facts known to both parties] then the factual inquiry will be much simplified'.[84]

Finally, there is what McMeel calls the 'disciplinary' rationale for the exclusionary rules.[85] Excluding evidence of the true intent of the parties and emphasizing the natural meaning of the terms of the contract encourages 'contracting parties to embody their agreement in a clearly written, comprehensive document'.[86] This rationale may make particular sense in the United States, as the exclusionary rules reduce the role of the jury by shifting the trial's centre of gravity from issues of fact to issues of law: 'Parties to contracts may prefer, *ex ante* (that is, when negotiating the contract ...), to avoid the expense and uncertainty of having a jury resolve a dispute between them, even at the cost of some inflexibility in interpretation.'[87] This rationale is borne out by the

[80] Hoffman 1997, 668.

[81] See, eg, Corbin 1944, 607–8. This rationale underlies the Restatement's version of the parol evidence rule, which states that a final agreement 'discharges' any previous understandings. Restatement (2d) of Contracts, s 213. See also *United States v Clementon Sewerage Authority*, 365 F2d 609 (3d Cir 1966).

[82] McMeel 2003, 296.

[83] Staughton 1999, 307.

[84] Gilmore 1974, 42.

[85] McMeel 2003, 290.

[86] R Posner 1998, 210. See also Sweet 1968, 1036, citing *Jones v Guilford Mortgage Co*, 120 SW2d 1081 (Tex Civ App 1938).

[87] *Federal Deposit Insurance Co v WR Grace & Co*, 877 F2d 614, 621 (7th Cir 1989).

common law style of drafting. Contracts written by common lawyers are notorious for their tendency to 'provide expressly for the resolution of every dispute that might conceivably arise'.[88]

There are a few routes by which direct evidence of a party's subjective intent may enter the record. These involve either allegations of misrepresentation (or another defect of consent) or an action for what is called rectification in England and reformation in the United States. Rectification is called for when the 'erroneous belief' of the parties 'that the writing expresses their agreement can be characterized as a mistake as to expression ... one that goes to the contents or effect of the writing intended to express their agreement'.[89] In such cases, the court may, in its discretion, 'rectify' or 'reform' the contract to express the agreement that was actually reached by the parties. To so do, the court cannot help but examine extrinsic evidence.

Rectification is often described as an exception to the exclusionary rules, but it is not. As Lord Hoffman explains: 'In the case of rectification, the text of the contract is not being construed; it is being amended by reference to another text, namely the prior agreement or understanding of the parties.'[90] In theory, when subjective evidence of party intent is admitted to help settle a question of rectification or misrepresentation, the court must then ignore this evidence if it is thereafter called upon to interpret the rectified agreement.[91] In practice, however, such neat intellectual segregation is difficult. For this reason, it has become common practice to plead rectification for the sole purpose of introducing extrinsic evidence that would otherwise be excluded, in the hope that the evidence will influence the judge when she interprets the contract.

Despite relaxation of the exclusionary rules in common law jurisdictions, evidence of the parties' conduct subsequent to the conclusion of the contract remains broadly inadmissible in both the United States and England.[92] A frequently cited rationale for excluding evidence of subsequent conduct is similar to that given for the parol evidence rule: the promotion of certainty and reliability. As Lord Reid put it in *James Miller and Partners Ltd v Whitworth Street Estates (Manchester) Ltd*, if evidence of subsequent conduct is admitted, 'one might have the result that a contract meant one thing the day it was signed, but by reason of subsequent events meant something different a month or a year later'.[93]

The one exception to the exclusion of subsequent conduct evidence applies when a party's subsequent conduct might give rise to an estoppel by convention.[94] It should be noted, though, that, as with rectification, estoppel by convention is not really an exception to the normal rule because it avoids interpretation of the contract. A successful estoppel claim has no effect on the content of the contract in question. Rather, it prevents a party from enforcing rights created by the contract where the party's actions make it inequitable for it to do so.[95]

[88] Farnsworth 1999, 426.

[89] A definitive American formulation of this notion can be found in *Wiener v Eastern Ark. Planting Co*, 975 F2d 1350 (8th Cir 1992), where the court held that reformation lies where 'the language used in the contract is not an accurate rendition of what the parties actually meant'.

[90] Hoffman 1997, 667.

[91] *Arrale v Costain Civil Engineering Ltd* [1976] 1 Lloyd's Rep 98.

[92] In England, if an agreement is unintegrated, subsequent conduct evidence may be admitted in order to determine the full terms of the contract. *Wilson v Maynard Shipbuilding Consultants AG Ltd* [1978] QB 665.

[93] [1970] AC 583.

[94] Ibid.

[95] Hoffman 1997, 667.

2. Civil law jurisdictions

In comparison with the common law doctrines, civilian rules on contractual interpretation are simple. There are no counterparts to the common law exclusionary rules because extrinsic evidence is not excluded. Instead, extrinsic evidence is broadly admitted and then considered by the adjudicator together with the rest of the evidence. The extrinsic evidence may be of little weight in the face of a clearly drafted contract, but it will be admitted nonetheless. In sharp contrast to the common law's approach, the admissibility of extrinsic evidence extends even to purely unilateral intentions of a single party. As Zweigert and Kötz relate, the German BGB 'rejects as "unacceptable" the perfectly reasonable view that in contracts what matters is not what real intention lay behind what one contractor said but what the other contractor must in the circumstances have understood him to mean'.[96]

Interpretation in the civil law is subjective: the purpose of interpretation is to define the true intention of the parties, even if this contradicts the apparent meaning of the contractual terms. This is emphatically so in France,[97] Germany,[98] and Switzerland.[99]

The seriousness with which the civil law takes subjective interpretation is exemplified by a 1980 decision of the Swiss Federal Court. The court was called upon to interpret a 1973 employment agreement that provided for consultations between management and trade unions over individual dismissals but had no provisions regarding layoffs as a result of downsizing. During the recession of 1978, the company closed several of its factories and the trade unions sued for compensation. The Swiss Federal Court found for the unions on the ground that the employment agreement had a 'gap' because, at that time, the economy was strong and the parties did not consider the possibility of factory closures. The court reasoned that there was 'no doubt' that the unions had 'expressed their desire for a comprehensive protection of the employees and that the employers could not misunderstand them'.[100]

In practice, the civil law's dedication to subjective interpretation is not unconditional, and all judges will begin by looking at the words of the contract in their ordinary and natural sense. Indeed, since judges rarely have definitive evidence of the parties' true intentions, they have no choice but to focus on the natural meaning of the contract's words and any relevant usages or practices. Nevertheless, decisions must be justified on the basis of the parties' subjective intent. Of course, the judge remains 'perfectly free to come to his conclusion on the basis of objective considerations and call it the [common intention of the parties] when he comes to write his judgment'.[101]

[96] Zweigert and Kötz 1998, 403 (quotation omitted).

[97] *Code civil*, art 1156: 'One must in agreements seek what the common intention of the contracting parties was, rather than pay attention to the literal meaning of the terms.' Official translation available online: <http://www.legifrance.gouv.fr/content/download/1950/13681/version/3/file/Code_22.pdf> accessed 20 July 2012.

[98] BGB, s 133: 'When a declaration of intent is interpreted, it is necessary to ascertain the true intention rather than adhering to the literal meaning of the declaration.' Official translation available online: <http://www.gesetze-im-internet.de/englisch_bgb/> accessed 20 July 2012.

[99] CO, art 18: 'When assessing the form and terms of a contract, the true and common intention of the parties must be ascertained without dwelling on any inexact expressions or designations they may have used.' Official translation available online at <http://www.admin.ch/ch/e/rs/2/220.en.pdf> accessed 20 July 2012.

[100] Hermann 1983, 11, quoting (and translating) Einigungsamt Baselland, 'Chemical Workers' Union and other v Firestone', *Neue Zurcher Zeitung*, 1 February 1980.

[101] Zweigert and Kötz 1998, 402.

The civil law has a rough counterpart to the plain meaning rule, in the form of the brocard *in claris non fit interpretatio* (what is clear needs no interpretation), and code provisions expressing this concept. Danneman's formulation is typical: 'If the declarations by the parties are ambiguous in wording or intent, interpretation is required to find out if, and what, the parties have agreed.'[102] As Zweigert and Kötz note, such a doctrine is nonsensical: all terms must be interpreted, if only to determine that they are clear.[103] However, the doctrine remains influential and is 'effective in constraining any undue tendency on the part of courts to overly subjective constructions'.[104]

Thus, in cases where a term of the contract appears to be clear on its face (in French, a *clause claire et précise*), the court will not generally request the production of extrinsic evidence or give it any weight. However, to discount evidence is not the same thing as to exclude it, and if a party seeks to introduce such evidence, the court will admit it into the record, even if only to assign it little weight and disregard it.

Where common law interpretation begins by asking: 'To what terms did the parties agree?', a civilian asks: 'Into what type of contract did the parties enter?'[105] This is because the interpretive starting point in civil law is that 'the incidents of a contract are fixed by law, subject to the parties' power to vary them'.[106] Thus, a court must first 'qualify' (characterize) the agreement before it as belonging to one of the categories of nominate contracts.[107] Even if the contract is innominate, the obligations created by it 'will often be determined by reference to the one (or more) of the special contracts to which it is most analogous'.[108]

Once the contract is characterized, its terms will be determined largely according to the mandatory (*ius cogens/zwigend/lois imperatives*) and supplementary (*ius dispositivum/nachgiebig/lois supplétives*) rules pertaining to that type of contract.[109] The mandatory rules apply as a matter of course and the supplementary rules apply unless the parties specifically derogate from them. Similarly binding are any relevant practices established by the parties or usages prevailing in the industry. Thus, the French *Code civil* provides that: 'Agreements are binding not only as to what is therein expressed, but also as to all the consequences which equity, usage or statute give to the obligation according to its nature.'[110] Scholarly treatments of 'contractual interpretation' are generally restricted to the proper application of these rules.[111] Of course, the common law contains similar concepts, but they form only a part of the doctrines relating to the interpretation of contracts.[112]

Rules analogous to the common law exclusionary rules apply to certain nominate contracts. The most important example is the requirement, similar to the common law statutes of frauds, that certain contracts be made in writing, be notarized, or comply with other formalities. In cases involving contracts which must be in writing, oral evidence is frequently inadmissible to contradict the written terms. For example, article 1341 of the French *Code civil* provides:

> An instrument before notaries or under private signature must be executed in all matters exceeding a sum or value fixed by decree, even for voluntary deposits, and no proof by witnesses is

[102] Danneman 1993, 14. [103] Zweigert and Kötz 1998, 403. [104] Ibid.
[105] Nicholas 1992, 49–50. [106] Ibid, 49. [107] Markesinis et al 1997, 34.
[108] Nicholas 1992, 49. [109] Markesinis et al 1997, 28.
[110] Article 1135. [111] Nicholas 1992, 34.
[112] The two types of rules are not separately labelled in the common law; both are subsumed under the heading of contractual terms implied by law, and such terms may be either mandatory or derogable (in which case they may be characterized as presumptions as to the intent of the parties).

allowed against or beyond the contents of instruments, or as to what is alleged to have been said before, at the time of, or after the instruments, although it is a question of a lesser sum or value.

Since most international arbitrations occur between incorporated entities, it should be noted that contracts between merchants are often governed (in France and Germany but not in Switzerland) by a separate commercial code. The restrictions that apply to methods of proof in contracts governed by the civil codes (such as contracts between merchants, on the one hand, and consumers, on the other) may not apply to contracts between merchants. As with the civil codes, the commercial codes delineate types of nominate contracts, some of which must follow written formalities. However, for contracts between merchants, even if a writing is required, such contracts are nevertheless provable by any means.[113]

While the civil law permits adjudicators freely to go beyond the text of the contract, it insists that the text is where the process of interpretation must begin. Civilian jurisdictions tend to 'accept the probative force of a writing on the assumption that when there is no indication of the existence of a vice of consent ... [then] the instrument is an accurate mirror of the entire agreement of the parties'.[114] For example, under German law, the good faith principle of *Treu und Glauben*[115] has been interpreted to mean that, unless there is evidence of a defect of consent, a rebuttable presumption exists that written agreements correctly reflect the intent of the parties.[116]

Another fundamental difference between the common law and civil law perspectives is that, under the civil law, interpretation of contracts is a matter of fact, not of law. The most important consequence of this is that determination of the facts is within the sole jurisdiction of the trial judge, and cannot be reviewed on appeal.[117] The subjective method of interpretation and the restriction of contractual interpretation to the trial level mean that 'in a world of standard form contracts each court is free to interpret each contract as if it were unique. There are standard terms but, strictly speaking, no standard interpretation'.[118] For the sake of loyalty to the parties' intentions, the civil law thus sacrifices some of the standardization and stability prized by the common law.

The only substantial limitation on the 'sovereign power' of trial courts over contractual interpretation is that, in France, they may not 'denature' contractual provisions that are *clauses claires et précises*.[119] In other words, where there is no ambiguity in a contractual term, the issue becomes one of law and the appeal courts may intervene to overturn lower courts' interpretations. Such intervention is justified according to two premises. First, under article 1134 of the *Code civil*, a contract constitutes law between the parties. Second, clear contractual provisions are deemed to need no interpretation. Therefore, any attempt by a trial court to interpret a *clause claire et précise* would not be a ruling on the facts, but rather a contravention of the law that may be appealed.[120] However, since the rule stands in opposition to the general civilian method

[113] See, eg, the French *Code de Commerce*, art L110-3, official English translation available online: <http://www.legifrance.gouv.fr/content/download/1951/13685/version/5/file/Code_32.pdf> accessed 20 July 2012.

[114] Zuppi 2007, 258. [115] BGB, s 157. [116] Zweigert and Kötz 1998, 404.

[117] Nicholas 1992, 47. Perhaps due in part to the fact that there is no appeal from the decision of an arbitral tribunal on the merits, none of the arbitral awards discussed below mentions the issue of whether contractual interpretation is an issue of fact or of law.

[118] Ibid, 48. [119] Ibid, 49.

[120] Zweigert and Kötz 1998, 403, citing Civ 14 December 1942, D 1944, 112; Civ 23 April 1945, D 1945, 261, obs Lerebours-Pigeonnière.

of interpretation, it is perhaps not surprising that the *Cour de cassation* has only rarely used its power to enforce the terms of *clauses claires et précises*.[121]

The common law's focus on the written terms has led drafters to craft lengthy, detailed contracts, while civil law courts' interpretive practices have shaped the terser style of civilian contracts:

> The [civilian] judge begins by qualifying the contract before him, so also the draftsman begins by asking himself the same question and then proceeds in the knowledge that the main incidents of the contract are provided for and that he need concentrate only on those points which are of particular concern to the parties.[122]

In the end, these two systems are self-reinforcing. The common law judge knows that commercial contracts were probably negotiated in great detail, so a strict textual interpretation is likely to reflect the true intention of the parties and is unlikely to lead to injustice. The civil law judge knows that commercial parties rely on the relevant mandatory and supplementary rules and the force of business custom when they draft their agreements, so a written contract is unlikely to express the entire agreement between the parties.

3. International contract law instruments

All of the major international contract law instruments except the ULIS contain clauses which specify the method of interpretation and the admissibility of extrinsic evidence. All these instruments employ concepts from both the civil law and the common law. They direct a tribunal to look at the unilateral subjective intent of each party but, if this cannot be determined or if the other party could not have been aware of this subjective intent, then objective interpretation must lie to determine the contract's content. The CISG rules exemplify this trend. CISG, article 8 directs the adjudicator to a two-stage approach, first subjective, then objective:

> (1) ... statements made by and other conduct of a party are to be interpreted according to his intent where the other party knew or could not have been unaware what that intent was.
>
> (2) If the preceding paragraph is not applicable, statements made by and other conduct of a party are to be interpreted according to the understanding that a reasonable person of the same kind as the other party would have had in the same circumstances.

The CISG thus inhabits an area in between the civil law and the common law. It admits direct evidence of parties' subjective intentions, but disregards evidence of unexpressed or undeclared intentions. Instead, for one party's subjective understanding of the contract to govern, the other party must either know or ought to know of that intention. If no subjective intention was made known, then the contract must be interpreted objectively.

With respect to extrinsic evidence, the CISG is widely inclusive. Article 8 continues:

> (3) In determining the intent of a party or the understanding a reasonable person would have had, due consideration is to be given to all relevant circumstances of the case including the negotiations, any practices which the parties have established between themselves, usages and any subsequent conduct of the parties.

[121] Nicholas 1992, 49. [122] Ibid, 57.

The CISG therefore contains no version of the plain meaning rule or the parol evidence rule.[123] Indeed, at the Vienna diplomatic conference the Canadian delegation attempted to introduce into the convention a version of the parol evidence rule, but a majority rejected the proposal.[124] Thus, where a federal trial court in Florida refused to abandon Florida's parol evidence rule in a case governed by the CISG, the 11th Circuit Court of Appeals overruled and held that CISG, article 8(3) governs the admissibility of parol evidence and is 'a clear instruction to courts to admit and consider all evidence that could reveal the parties' true intent'.[125]

The CISG makes no mention of entire agreement clauses, but courts applying the convention have consistently given force to them.[126] However, in determining the effect of an entire agreement clause (eg, whether the clause bars evidence of trade usages), all of the relevant circumstances, including the parties' conduct, must be taken into account.[127]

The UNIDROIT Principles enunciate a rubric for interpretation that is essentially identical to the CISG's. Article 4.2 contains the same two-stage subjective and objective method of interpretation, and article 4.3 contains a similar list of types of extrinsic evidence that must be admitted. While the UNIDROIT Principles do not include any version of the parol evidence rule, they do explicitly direct adjudicators to give effect to entire agreement clauses. Article 2.17, states that if a contract contains 'a clause indicating that the writing completely embodies the terms on which the parties have agreed', then the written contract 'cannot be contradicted or supplemented by evidence of prior statements or agreements'.

The PECL set out a similar but not identical three-stage interpretive rubric:

> (1) A contract is to be interpreted according to the common intention of the parties even if this differs from the literal meaning of the words.
>
> (2) If it is established that one party intended the contract to have a particular meaning, and at the time of the conclusion of the contract the other party could not have been unaware of the first party's intention, the contract is to be interpreted in the way intended by the first party.
>
> (3) If an intention cannot be established according to (1) or (2), the contract is to be interpreted according to the meaning that reasonable persons of the same kind as the parties would give to it in the same circumstances.[128]

As with the CISG and the UNIDROIT Principles, PECL, article 5:102 lists various types of extrinsic evidence, declaring them all to be admissible. PECL, article 2:105 explicitly states that 'prior statements may be used to interpret the contract', unless the contract includes an 'individually negotiated' entire agreement clause. If the contract does contain such a clause, adjudicators are to give it effect. If the contract contains an entire agreement clause, but it was not individually negotiated (such as when it appears in one party's standard terms), then 'it will only establish a presumption that the parties intended that their prior statements, undertakings or agreements were not to form part of the contract'.

[123] This conclusion has been affirmed by the CISG Advisory Council, a private body of academic experts. CISG-AC Opinion No 3. On the nature and role of the CISG Advisory Council, see Karton and de Germiny 2009.

[124] United Nations Conference on Contracts for the International Sale of Goods, Official Records, UN Doc A/Conf/97/19, UN Sales No E.81.IV.3, 90 (1981), reprinted in Honnold 1989, 662.

[125] *MCC-Marble Ceramic Center Inc v Ceramica Nuova d'Agostino SpA*, 144 F3d 1384, 1389 (11th Cir 1998).

[126] Schmidt-Kessel Art 8 2010, 163; see also CISG-AC Opinion No 3 [4.5].

[127] Ibid.

[128] PECL, art 5:101.

In addition to the international contract law instruments, tribunals have also looked to the Vienna Convention on the Law of Treaties (VCLT)[129] for rules for the interpretation of contracts. This convention does not purport govern the interpretation of private contracts. It is a law of 'treaties', which the VCLT defines as 'international agreement[s] concluded between States'.[130] Nevertheless, it may be applied by agreement of the parties or as indicative of general principles on the interpretation of agreements in international law. After all, both treaties and contracts are consensual, binding agreements between autonomous parties. As Crawford has noted in another context, the two may be different things: 'But they are not clean different things, in the sense of inhabiting different worlds.'[131]

In the *Eurotunnel* arbitration,[132] the tribunal was called upon to interpret both a contract and a treaty. The dispute arose from operation of the fixed rail link passing through the Channel Tunnel between France and the United Kingdom. The concessionaires who operated the fixed link alleged various violations by the two governments of both the Concession Agreement in force between the governments and the concessionaires and a treaty between the two governments (the Treaty of Canterbury).[133] The tribunal considered in detail the 'principles of interpretation' that would apply to the Concession Agreement. The parties agreed that, although the Concession Agreement was not a treaty, it was an 'international contract' governed by 'international law'.[134] The tribunal therefore agreed that: 'international law principles of interpretation are to be applied'.[135] The parties further agreed that application of 'international law principles' meant that the VCLT applied to both the Treaty of Canterbury and the Concession Agreement.[136]

The general rule of interpretation under the VCLT is stated in article 31; interpretation should be 'in accordance with the ordinary meaning to be given to the terms of the treaty in their context and in light of its object and purpose'. If the ordinary meaning, context, and purpose of the text do not resolve an ambiguity or obscurity, or if they lead to an absurd or unconscionable result, '[r]ecourse may be had to supplementary means of interpretation, including preparatory work of the treaty and circumstances of its conclusion'.[137]

In summary, the international contract law instruments (the CISG, UNIDROIT Principles, and PECL) and the VCLT all direct adjudicators to discern the parties' subjective intention via a two-stage interpretive method. The international contract law instruments instruct the adjudicator to begin by assessing the parties' common subjective intention and, only if this cannot be discerned, to interpret the contract objectively. On the other hand, the VCLT directs adjudicators to take a textual approach, beginning with the 'ordinary meaning' of the words of the agreement, in context and in light of the agreement's 'object and purpose'. The VCLT and the international instruments all agree that extrinsic evidence should be used. The difference is that the Vienna Convention declares the examination of such materials to be 'subsidiary', ie to be used only when the objective interpretation fails to produce a reasonable result, while the

[129] Vienna Convention on the Law of Treaties (adopted 23 May 1969, entered into force 27 January 1980) 1155 UNTS 331.

[130] Article 2(1)(a). [131] Crawford 2008, 21.

[132] Permanent Court of Arbitration Case 2003–06, Partial Award of 30 January 2007.

[133] France–United Kingdom, Treaty concerning the Construction and Operation by Private Concessionaires of a Channel Fixed Link, Canterbury (adopted 12 February 1986) 1497 UNTS 334.

[134] *Eurotunnel* [92]. [135] Ibid. [136] Ibid. [137] Article 32.

international instruments direct adjudicators to consider all relevant extrinsic evidence from the outset.

III. Contractual Interpretation in International Commercial Arbitration

A review of the published arbitral awards identified fifty-three awards whose published extracts included interpretations of contracts. Not included are instances where the breaching party pleaded an excuse, such as *force majeure*, unconscionability, or changed circumstances (*rebus sic stantibus*), because the pleading of an excuse requires a concession that a breach of contract occurred. In such cases (unless excuse is pleaded in the alternative), there is no disagreement as to the contract's content. Also excluded are cases where the existence or validity of a contract was challenged, unless this challenge was rejected and the parties proceeded to dispute the content of the contract. Finally, cases are excluded where the contractual term being interpreted is a dispute resolution agreement, in particular an arbitration clause. Under the well-established separability principle, an arbitration clause need not be governed by the same substantive law as the remainder of the contract,[138] so interpretations of arbitration clauses cannot be directly compared to interpretations of substantive contractual provisions.

Given this case study's small sample size (fifty-three awards) and the fact that most arbitrators do not state their interpretive agenda or their reasons for considering or failing to consider extrinsic evidence, no firm statement can be made about the 'preferences' of international arbitrators.

In theory, the available awards ought to be neatly divisible into four distinct categories, based on the applicable law. Awards governed by common law would begin with an objective interpretation of the plain meaning of the contract and exclude extrinsic evidence. Awards governed by civil law would employ subjective interpretation of contractual terms and liberally admit extrinsic evidence. The same would be true of awards governed by an international contract law instrument. Awards adjudicated under amiable composition or governed by general principles of international law will not necessarily employ the same interpretive methods because tribunals may differ as to the fair result in a given case or as to the content of the relevant general principles.

The awards are indeed largely divisible in this manner, as detailed below. However, before turning to the awards themselves, two additional factors must be considered: first, confusion over whether the rules governing extrinsic evidence are substantive or procedural, and second, a bias among international tribunals toward admission into the record of whatever evidence the parties submit (party autonomy).

1. The substance/procedure dichotomy and rules of evidence

With an eye to efficient resolution of disputes and informality in the arbitral proceedings, tribunals often conduct hearings and draft awards with a minimum of investigation into the requirements of substantive law. Many disputes are resolved 'by arbitral tribunals with no more than a passing reference to the law. They turn on matters of fact: what was said and what was not said; what was promised and what was not promised;

[138] Redfern and Hunter 2004, 193–5.

what was done and what was not done'.[139] This assertion, though undoubtedly true, is striking: every legal system has rules that govern the admissibility of evidence. Thus, a decision without reference to law ought to be possible only in cases of amiable composition. Nevertheless, arbitrators often consider questions of the admissibility of evidence without reference to any rules of law, a tendency that the purported judicialization of ICA has not diminished.[140]

For example, in ICC Case No 6281 of 1989,[141] the parties concluded a contract for delivery of steel in instalments. After the market price of steel increased, the claimant exercised an option to purchase additional instalments at the same price. The respondent refused to send the additional instalments and the claimant initiated arbitration. Among other arguments, the respondent justified its refusal to sell the additional steel on the ground that the claimant had not opened a letter of credit to pay for the order (which it was required to do prior to delivery). The sole arbitrator rejected this argument without referring to the terms of the contract; he found for the claimant, reasoning that it would be irrational to require a buyer to open a letter of credit for goods that it is not certain the seller will provide. In other words, the arbitrator interpreted the contract according to his sense of what the parties must have intended, without reference to rules of admissibility.

Tribunals tend not to set out their reasoning on questions of the admission of evidence. Only seventeen of the fifty-three published awards canvassed in this case study explicitly discuss the admissibility of extrinsic evidence. The others do or do not consider such evidence, but in either case do so without discussing its admissibility. This makes it difficult to determine why most of the tribunals decided as they did.

In ICA, substance and procedure will normally be governed by different sources of law. In general, the applicable evidentiary rules will be those promulgated by an arbitral institution or those chosen by the parties to govern an ad hoc arbitration.[142] However, arbitral rules typically leave questions of evidence (and of the conduct of hearings generally) up to the discretion of the tribunal and the agreement of the parties. Of the major arbitral rules, only those of the London Court of International Arbitration (LCIA) even address the weight or admissibility of evidence, and these rules say only that the tribunal has the additional powers:

> to decide whether or not to apply any strict rules of evidence (or any other rules) as to the admissibility, relevance or weight of any material tendered by a party on any matter of fact or expert opinion; and to determine the time, manner and form in which such material should be exchanged between the parties and presented to the Arbitral Tribunal. . . .[143]

As discussed above, the common law exclusionary rules are undoubtedly substantive; although they deal with evidence, they are not evidentiary rules. The latter regulate the means by which facts may be proved, while the exclusionary rules regulate what facts may be proved, regardless of the means. By contrast, such civil law rules excluding evidence as do exist are clearly procedural in character. Examples of these include rules permitting contracts between merchants to be proved by any type of evidence[144] or

[139] Ibid, 89. [140] See Chapter 4, Section II.4. [141] (1990) XV Ybk Comm Arb 96.

[142] Parties sometimes agree to the application of a set of evidentiary rules drafted by a committee of the International Bar Association. See Section III.2 of this chapter.

[143] Article 22(f).

[144] For example, *Code de commerce* (France), art L110-3 ('*A l'égard des commerçants, les actes de commerce peuvent se prouver par tous moyens à moins qu'il n'en soit autrement disposé par la loi.*'). Official English translation available at <http://www.legifrance.gouv.fr/content/download/1951/13685/version/5/file/Code_32.pdf> accessed 20 July 2012.

rules prohibiting oral testimony to contradict a written agreement for those nominate contracts that must be in writing to be enforceable.[145]

Thus, it might seem that a tribunal may be drawn into an absurd result. If the tribunal finds that the national law of a common law jurisdiction applies to the substance of the dispute, then the way forward is clear: the national law will apply to exclude extrinsic evidence and the arbitral rules will govern all procedural issues. If, on the other hand, the tribunal finds that the national law of a civil law jurisdiction applies to the substance of the dispute, then questions of extrinsic evidence will not be settled by the governing substantive law. However, the only applicable procedural rules—the institutional or ad hoc rules of procedure and the national arbitration law of the seat of arbitration—are silent on the question of extrinsic evidence, and indeed on contractual interpretation generally. The tribunal seems to be left with no rules to apply.

This apparent dead end is illusory. Although the few civil law rules that do exist to exclude extrinsic evidence are procedural, rules governing the interpretation of contracts—including those enshrining the subjective method of interpretation—are substantive. The different perspectives from which the two systems operate dictate at least some of the types of extrinsic evidence they include or exclude. The objective method requires adjudicators to exclude direct evidence of the parties' intentions, while the subjective method requires adjudicators to consider such evidence. In other words, the role of extrinsic evidence in the interpretation of a contract is determined by substantive law; rules on the admissibility of such evidence must be classified as substantive, even if they are contained in codes of civil procedure. It would be nonsensical to characterize common law rules that exclude extrinsic evidence as substantive and civil law rules that admit extrinsic evidence as procedural. This conclusion is supported by the fact that the international contract law instruments, which include only rules of substantive contract law and draw from both the common law and civil law, contain provisions on interpretation of contracts that address both the method of interpretation and the admissibility of extrinsic evidence.

Of the published arbitral awards that discuss the admissibility of extrinsic evidence, only one held expressly that rules governing admissibility are procedural.[146] In that case, an Indian claimant and an Austrian respondent entered into negotiations regarding the construction of a chemical plant in India. These led to a 'draft contract' and a 'supplemental agreement', both of which were initialled by the two parties but not signed. When the respondent commenced work on the project with a different Indian partner, the claimant initiated arbitration, citing 'understandings of exclusivity' in the two agreements.

The respondent alleged that no binding contract existed. It sought to introduce the diaries of two of its employees who were present at the discussions with the claimant. They each kept a daily notebook in German, to which they referred when giving evidence at an oral hearing. The tribunal requested and was provided with English translations of the diaries. The claimant objected to their admission, citing exclusionary rules in Indian law, which the parties agreed was the governing law. Under Indian law, the diaries should actually have been admitted. India is a common law jurisdiction and, under the common law, extrinsic evidence is admissible to prove the existence of a

145 For example, *Code civil* (France), art 1341.

146 ICC Case No 7626 of 1995 (1997) XXII Ybk Comm Arb 132. This award is not discussed in detail below because it deals with the existence of a contract, rather than interpretation of a contract.

contract. However, the tribunal did not apply Indian law to determine the admissibility of extrinsic evidence. Instead, it held that the admission of the diaries was a question of procedure. Noting that the ICC Rules give tribunals discretion over what evidence may be considered, the tribunal admitted the diaries without further comment.

The outcome was the same as it would have been in an English or Indian court, but the tribunal ought to have held that the applicable Indian substantive law governed the admissibility of extrinsic evidence. In the other cases where tribunals explicitly discussed the admissibility of extrinsic evidence in cases governed by a national substantive law or the CISG, they applied that substantive law to determine admissibility. Therefore, it is fair to conclude that, when tribunals do consider the issue, they find that extrinsic evidence is a matter of substantive law.

2. General principles of evidence in international law

Since the majority of the awards did not discuss the admissibility of extrinsic evidence, it is impossible to say with certainty whether those tribunals would have concluded that substantive law applied to determine the issue. However, all these tribunals either admitted or excluded extrinsic evidence, and such decisions must have been guided by some identifiable—even if inchoate—interpretive or evidentiary model. Such a model could not have come from the arbitral rules of procedure (since these are silent as to interpretation of contracts). This leaves either the applicable substantive law or some other principles of interpretation, which in practice means the tribunals' understanding of standard practices in ICA or general principles of international law. It is therefore necessary to investigate whether there exist such standard practices or general principles relating to extrinsic evidence and, if so, what these might be.

With respect to rules of evidence generally, current arbitral practice resembles—and in fact owes much to—the practices established by public international law tribunals, principally the ICJ and its predecessor, the PCIJ. These international tribunals have traditionally 'taken the view that they should hear and consider everything that each party has to say concerning the dispute. The tribunal itself determines the relevance, materiality and probative value of all evidence submitted by the parties, and does not need to hear argument from the parties concerning these matters'.[147]

For example, in 1925, when the PCIJ amended its rules of procedure, Judge Huber (Switzerland) wrote that, under the established practices of the court as codified in the amended rules: 'The Parties may present any proof that they judge useful, and the Court is entirely free to take the evidence into account to the extent that it deems pertinent.'[148] Such practices have been maintained by the ICJ, as evidenced by this statement of ICJ President Spender (Australia) in ruling on an objection to the admission of testimonial evidence during proceedings on the *South-West Africa* cases (Second Phase):

> The evidence will remain on the record; the Court is quite able to evaluate evidence.... This court is not bound by the strict rules of evidence applicable in municipal courts and if the evidence established by the witness does not sufficiently convey that the evidence is reliable in point of fact, then the Court, of course, deals with it accordingly when it comes to its deliberation.[149]

These doctrines, although developed in a public international law context, are relevant to ICA. The PCIJ was itself a 'product of the arbitral process'.[150] Its rules, and

[147] Pietrowski 2006, 378. [148] Huber 1926, 250.
[149] [1966] ICJ Rep, Pleadings, vol 10, 122; vol 11, 460.
[150] Pietrowski 2006, 373 fn 2.

by derivation those of the ICJ, came out of the Hague Peace Conferences of 1899 and 1907, which also established the Permanent Court of Arbitration. More importantly, as Reisman notes: 'All contemporary international judicial institutions, whether named courts, tribunals, panels or commissions are arbitral, in that at least the formal contingency for their authority in specific cases emanates from the joint will of the litigating parties.'[151] The common link is the principle of party autonomy; international tribunals, whether nominally arbitral or judicial, derive their jurisdiction from the consent of disputing parties.

Over time, the inclusionary bias among international tribunals has solidified into a standard practice—arguably, a principle of customary public international law. There have been two main avenues for such a process of solidification: first, express agreement by the parties in arbitral *compromis*, terms of reference or bilateral treaties, or second, codification in conventions, model laws, and the rules of international organizations.[152] Such rules are evidentiary in that they pertain only to means of proof, not to the admissibility of extrinsic evidence. They also exhibit the mixture of common and civil law traditions that is typical of international procedure. For example, the common law restrictive rules concerning competence, relevance, and materiality of evidence, which were developed primarily in the context of jury trials, are seldom applied in international proceedings.[153] In addition, international tribunals have developed a preference for—and tend to place greater weight on—documentary evidence, another civil law trait.[154] Conversely, most international institutions permit witnesses to be examined by counsel and cross-examined by opposing counsel—a practice derived from the common law—but for evidence in chief (also called direct evidence), they tend to rely on written witness statements—a product of the civil law tradition.[155]

Many of these procedures have been codified in such international instruments as the UNCITRAL Arbitration Rules and the rules of procedure of the various international courts and arbitral institutions. However, as noted above, such documents tend to deal only minimally with the conduct of proceedings, including rules of evidence.

The International Bar Association (IBA) has promulgated a set of Rules on the Taking of Evidence in International Commercial Arbitration.[156] However, the IBA Rules contain no provision relating to the interpretation of contracts. With respect to admissibility of evidence, the IBA Rules state only: 'The arbitral tribunal shall determine the admissibility, relevance, materiality and weight of the evidence.'[157]

Since all of these rules are procedural, they should not govern the admissibility of extrinsic evidence. General principles of evidence in international law or practice seem to go no further than the concept that tribunals ought to consider whatever evidence the parties think relevant. However, even if such procedural principles were universally accepted in arbitration, they still would not yield any substantive principle of contractual interpretation. Only such a substantive principle could govern the

[151] Reisman 1971, 66. [152] Pietrowski 2006, 374.
[153] See generally Brown 2007, 90–2. [154] Sandifer 1975, 197.
[155] Pietrowski 2006, 375.
[156] <http://www.ibanet.org/Publications/publications_IBA_guides_and_free_materials.aspx> accessed 20 July 2012. The IBA Rules were intended to be applied directly by arbitrators as a codification of general principles or to be incorporated into arbitration agreements. However, despite the urging of the IBA and various prominent commentators (many of whom were involved in drafting the rules), they are only infrequently applied in practice. Salomon 2004, 117.
[157] Article 9(1).

admissibility of extrinsic evidence. Nevertheless, DiMatteo's statement that international tribunals are 'freed of the limitations of the parol evidence rule' represents a widespread attitude.[158] Arbitral procedure continues to be determined on a case-by-case basis, shaped by the choice of the parties and (in the absence of such choice) by the arbitrators' preferences.[159] Therefore, tribunals will generally admit all evidence the parties submit.

Furthermore, most arbitral rules of procedure empower tribunals to require the parties to produce additional evidence.[160] However, tribunals tend not to exercise this power; as can be seen in the cases reviewed below, tribunals seldom inquire beyond what the parties place in front of them. Such a trend is striking in light of the fact that most arbitral rules enshrine inquisitorial powers derived from the civil law tradition. However, this does not necessarily mean that arbitrators take their lead from the common law model of the judge's role as a neutral umpire. Tribunals' reticence to demand additional potentially relevant evidence is better explained by deference to party autonomy. Similarly, regardless of the governing law, a tribunal is unlikely to exclude extrinsic evidence on its own motion, and sometimes not even if a party seeks to have it excluded.

3. Analysis of the published awards

Fifty-three published awards include a discussion of the meaning of contractual terms.[161] Care must be taken not to read too much into the results, given the small sample size and the fact that, in many awards, the tribunal's use of evidence is not explicitly discussed. For example, if the award focuses solely on the language of the contract, it is impossible to tell whether extrinsic evidence was excluded on legal grounds, or was never introduced by the parties, or was presented in an unconvincing manner and discounted, or was unnecessary because the answer seemed clear from the text of the contract. Moreover, most of the awards are published in summary or redacted form. It is possible that relevant discussions were excluded from the published extract. Despite these caveats, certain patterns can be observed.

Awards applying the law of common law jurisdictions

Of the fifty-three published awards, eight involved cases where the applicable substantive law was that of a common law jurisdiction. One of these was ICC Case No 7626, discussed above, in which the tribunal characterized questions of the admissibility of extrinsic evidence as procedural and declined to apply the applicable (Indian) substantive law. Therefore, the tribunal did not purport to apply any substantive law to this issue, so its reasoning will not be discussed here. Table 7.1 summarizes the way in which the contracts were interpreted in the remaining seven cases:

[158] DiMatteo 1997, 71. [159] Strong and Dries 2005, 301.

[160] See, eg, ICC Rules, art 25(5); ICDR Rules, art 19(3); UNCITRAL Rules, art 27(3).

[161] There is no discussion of the tribunals' choice of law in the analysis that follows. None of the forty-three awards contained a choice of law analysis, in most cases because the parties agreed as to the applicable law.

Table 7.1

Award	Applicable Law[162]	Method of Interpretation and Treatment of Extrinsic Evidence
ICC Case No 4555 of 1985[163]	Not stated, but apparently the law of a US state. Sole American arbitrator.	Declared that it would proceed by an objective method of interpretation. Applied the parol evidence rule, citing an exception thereto in order to admit evidence of a usage. However, also admitted other extrinsic evidence of one party's subjective understanding of a term of the contract.
ICC Case No 4975 of 1988[164]	English law. Three English barristers.	Declared that it would proceed by an objective method of interpretation. Citing relevant English case law, ruled that evidence of preliminary negotiations could only be considered as part of the surrounding circumstances of the contract.
ICC Case No 5946 of 1990[165]	New York law (applies the UCC).	Applied an objective method of interpretation. Began by interpreting 'plain meaning' of the disputed contractual term. Also admitted a wide range of extrinsic evidence, noting that such evidence led to the same interpretation as the plain meaning. Did not discuss admissibility.
ICC Case No 6955 of 1993[166]	Illinois law (applies the UCC).	Applied an objective method of interpretation. Excluded extrinsic evidence, citing UCC, s 2-202, which expresses the parol evidence rule. Admitted evidence of a trade usage under s 202(a), which permits admission of evidence of usages so long as these do not contradict the plain meaning of the contract.
ICC Case No 7722 of 1999[167]	Law of an unidentified Middle Eastern country, apparently influenced by common law traditions.	Applied a subjective method of interpretation. Began with the plain meaning of the text, referring to case law that gives priority to the written text. Considered witness testimony as to the intention of the parties, as well as negotiations and other correspondence between the parties.
ICC Case No 8694 of 1996[168]	New Hampshire law (applies the UCC).	Declared that it would proceed by an objective method of interpretation and would apply the plain meaning rule. Excluded extrinsic evidence and interpreted the contract by reference to its text alone.
ICC Case No 12172 of 2003[169]	English law.	Declared that it would proceed by an objective method of interpretation, giving primacy to the 'clear and unambiguous text' of the contractual term at issue. Admitted and held to be decisive evidence of a witness who participated in the contract negotiations.

[162] If the extract discloses the number of arbitrators or their nationality, that information is also included in this column.

[163] (1986) XI Ybk Comm Arb 140.

[164] (1989) XIV Ybk Comm Arb 122.

[165] (1991) XVI Ybk Comm Arb 97.

[166] (1999) XXIVa Ybk Comm Arb 107.

[167] (2007) XXXII Ybk Comm Arb 13.

[168] [1997] JDI 1056 (published in French translation; unpublished original in English).

[169] (2007) XXXII Ybk Comm Arb 85.

The picture presented by these seven awards is not consistent. In three,[170] the tribunal proceeded according to the letter of the applicable substantive law, following an objective method of interpretation and treating evidence in accordance with the applicable rules. In the others,[171] the tribunal considered extrinsic evidence of the parties' subjective intent.

The three awards in the first category are unremarkable; the tribunals applied substantive law in the same way that courts in England or the United States would have. In ICC Cases Nos 4975 and 6955, the tribunals expressly cited appropriate authorities for the exclusionary rules they then applied—in the former, the two then-leading English cases on the use of extrinsic evidence,[172] and in the latter, the relevant provisions of the UCC.[173] In ICC Case No 8694, the tribunal cited no legal rule to support its interpretation of the contract but did explicate a mode of interpretation consistent with the applicable New Hampshire law:

> It is mutually agreed that the tribunal is to determine the ordinary and evident intent of the parties in the words used in the written contract. The tribunal may not in any case divine the intention of the parties or substitute their presumed intention for their expressed intention. In determining the intention of the parties, [the tribunal] will consider the documents that comprise the contract and will attempt to interpret in a coherent manner the various clauses of the contract so long as it is not impossible to give to one clause a meaning compatible with the other clauses of the contract. To the extent that the terms used are clear and unambiguous, they must be interpreted according to their plain meaning.

ICC Case No 7722 is difficult to characterize because the applicable law was that of an unidentified Middle Eastern country. However, citations in the award to case law from several common law jurisdictions make it likely that the unstated country is itself a common law jurisdiction. The tribunal did not declare its adherence to any particular method of interpretation, but did cite a statute of the unidentified country that directs adjudicators to consider all the circumstances surrounding the conclusion of the contract, including the parties' correspondence. On the other hand, the tribunal also cited case law from the unidentified country that gives priority to the written text of the contract; if the text has an identifiable clear meaning, that meaning will be applied. It is therefore possible that the unidentified country's rules on contractual interpretation differ from traditional common law methods.

In the other three cases, the tribunals declared their adherence to common law methods of interpretation but then proceeded to admit evidence that a common law court would likely have excluded.

In ICC Case No 5946, the sole arbitrator stated that New York law would apply to interpret the contract. He held that the plain meaning of the disputed term was both clear and decisive, but then considered extrinsic evidence of the parties' negotiations without explaining why it was admissible. The arbitrator found that the extrinsic evidence did not change the result, but a New York court is not likely to have admitted it.

In ICC Case No 4555, the dispute centred on the meaning of the word 'unconditional' in the contract. The arbitrator stated that he would 'place substantial weight on the objective, commonly understood meaning of the contract language actually employed, and to give less weight to unarticulated and undocumented understandings'.

[170] ICC Case Nos 4975, 6955, and 8694.

[171] ICC Case Nos 4555, 5946, 7722, and 12172.

[172] *Prenn v Simmonds* and *Reardon Smith Line v Hansen-Tangen*. See Section II.1 of this chapter.

[173] UCC, s 2-202, which sets out the parol evidence rule, and s 1-205, which sets out rules for the pleading and proof of trade usages. See Section II.1 of this chapter.

The arbitrator allowed that: 'This meaning of the term could be overridden by persuasive evidence of standard commercial usage or the clear intent of the parties' (quoting a well-known, if dated, American treatise, *Williston on Contracts*).

Thus far, the arbitrator had followed the approach that an American court would likely have followed. However, he then admitted testimony to the effect that the claimant believed that the letter of credit it had opened conformed to the requirements of the contract, thus allowing into the record subjective, extrinsic evidence that a court would likely have excluded. The arbitrator did eventually find that evidence of the parties' express agreement held more weight than evidence of one party's subjective intent, but an American court is unlikely to have admitted such direct evidence of party intent at all.

Finally, in ICC Case No 12172, the applicable law was English. However, at the hearing, the sole arbitrator considered the testimony of a witness 'directly responsible for negotiating the contract with the Respondent'. This witness gave evidence on his impressions of what was agreed during the parties' negotiations. Describing the witness as 'credible', the arbitrator accepted his evidence as decisive on one of the points of dispute between the parties. The arbitrator also considered elements of the parties' correspondence that an English court would likely have held to be inadmissible parol evidence.

Awards applying the law of civil law jurisdictions

The largest group of the published awards, twenty-three of the fifty-three, involved application of the substantive law of a civil law jurisdiction. Table 7.2 summarizes the way that the contracts were interpreted in these cases.

Table 7.2

Award	Applicable Law	Mode of Interpretation and Treatment of Extrinsic Evidence
ICC Case No 1250 of 1964[174]	Lebanese law (based on French law). French, Lebanese, and Swedish arbitrators	Decided based on text of the contract alone. No reasoning given in the extract.
ICC Case No 1434 of 1975[175]	French law.	Cited the *Code civil* for principles of interpretation, admitted extrinsic evidence, but found that the evidence did not prove either side's interpretation of the contract. Applied a third interpretation which it found in the text of the contract.
ICC Case No 2708 of 1976[176]	French law.	Found written contract to be clear but also admitted extrinsic evidence. Ultimately found both the terms of the contract and the extrinsic evidence insufficient to derogate from an applicable trade usage.
ICC Case No 3055 of 1980[177]	Swiss law.	Decided based on text of the contract alone. Did not discuss admissibility of extrinsic evidence.

[174] (1980) V Ybk Comm Arb 168. [175] [1976] JDI 978.
[176] [1977] JDI 943. [177] [1981] JDI 937.

Award	Applicable Law	Mode of Interpretation and Treatment of Extrinsic Evidence
ICC Case No 3130 of 1980[178]	French law. Sole French arbitrator.	Decided based on text of the contract alone, including expressly incorporated INCOTERM. Did not discuss admissibility of extrinsic evidence.
ICC Case No 3894 of 1981[179]	West German law.	Decided based on text of the contract alone, including expressly incorporated INCOTERM. Did not discuss admissibility of extrinsic evidence.
ICC Case No 4131 of 1982[180]	French law. Dutch and two French arbitrators.	Admitted a variety of extrinsic evidence, basing its decision largely on the parties' negotiations and their subsequent conduct. Did not discuss admissibility of extrinsic evidence.
ICC Case No 5080 of 1985[181]	Swiss law. Sole Swiss arbitrator.	Admitted extrinsic evidence of the parties' negotiations, which was dispositive of their intent. Did not discuss admissibility of extrinsic evidence.
ICC Case No 5485 of 1987[182]	Spanish law. French and two Spanish arbitrators.	Found the disputed contractual term to be clear and admitted extrinsic evidence. Cited the maxim *in claris not fit interpretatio* as a general principle, and also cited the Spanish civil code provision that embodies this principle. Interpreted the disputed term according to its ordinary meaning and disregarded the extrinsic evidence.
ICC Case No 5505 of 1987[183]	Swiss law. Sole Swiss arbitrator.	Declared its intention to seek the parties' true intention by beginning with the ordinary meaning of the contract's terms but admitted extrinsic evidence. Found the disputed term and the extrinsic evidence insufficient to establish the parties' intent, so interpreted the clause objectively.
ICC Cases Nos 6515 and 6516 (joined) of 1994[184]	Greek law.	Decided based on text of the contract alone. Neither party adduced any extrinsic evidence, nor did the tribunal request its production.
ICC Case No 6527 of 1991[185]	Turkish law (based on Swiss law).	Declared its intention to follow Swiss rules of interpretation. Held that the disputed term was vague and that extrinsic evidence did not clarify it, then imposed a term implied by international trade usages.
ICC Case No 6653 of 1993[186]	French law.	Admitted extrinsic evidence of parties' negotiations, which was decisive.
ICC Case No 6673 of 1992[187]	French law.	Decided based on text of the contract alone. Unclear whether extrinsic evidence was considered.

178 [1981] JDI 932. 179 [1982] JDI 987. 180 [1983] JDI 899.
181 (1987) XII Ybk Comm Arb 124. 182 (1989) XIV Ybk Comm Arb 156.
183 (1988) XIII Ybk Comm Arb 110. 184 (1999) XXIVa Ybk Comm Arb 80.
185 (1993) XVIII Ybk Comm Arb 44. 186 [1993] JDI 1040.
187 [1992] JDI 992.

Award	Applicable Law	Mode of Interpretation and Treatment of Extrinsic Evidence
ICC Case No 7518 of 1994[188]	Portuguese law.	Declared it would proceed by a subjective method of interpretation. Admitted extrinsic evidence of one party's undeclared subjective intent, the parties' negotiations and their subsequent conduct. Did not discuss admissibility of extrinsic evidence.
ICC Case No 7792 of 1994[189]	Spanish law.	Analysed the terms of the contract but found that extrinsic evidence of the parties' negotiations was decisive. Did not discuss admissibility of extrinsic evidence.
ICC Case No 9443 of 1998[190]	French law.	Found that the plain meaning of the contract could not be enforced, as contrary to general principles of French law and international commerce. Did not discuss admissibility of extrinsic evidence.
ICC Case No 10188 of 1999[191]	German law.	Declared that it would follow German methods of interpretation, citing BGB, s 133. Found that the contract contained a gap. Admitted extrinsic evidence of prior dealings and negotiations to fill the gap.
ICC Case No 11440 of 2003[192]	German law.	Declared that it would follow German methods of interpretation, citing BGB, ss 133 and 157. Did not consider extrinsic evidence, stating that it could determine the parties' intent from the available materials.
ICC Case No 11776 of 2002[193]	French law.	Decided based on text of the contract alone. Unclear whether extrinsic evidence was considered.
ICC Case No 12745[194]	French law.	Declared that it would follow French methods of interpretation. Began with the plain meaning of the contract language, including consideration of expert witness testimony of the correct literal translation of Italian phrases in the contract. Admitted extrinsic evidence of the negotiators' understandings of the meaning of the text.
ICC Case No 13278[195]	Spanish law.	Declared that it would follow Spanish methods of interpretation, citing Spanish Civil Code, arts 1281, 1282, and 1285 and decision of the Spanish Supreme Court. Considered extrinsic evidence of the parties' negotiations, negotiation of ancillary contracts, and correspondence subsequent to the conclusion of the contract.
Netherlands Arbitration Institute, Partial Award of 17 May 2005, Final Award of 5 July 2005[196]	Dutch law.	Interpreted the plain meaning of the text to arrive at a 'provisional' interpretation, which it 'corroborated' with extrinsic evidence of negotiations and related contractual documents. Did not discuss admissibility.

188 [1998] JDI 1034. 189 [1995] JDI 993. 190 [2002] JDI 1106.
191 (2003) XXVIII Ybk Comm Arb 68. 192 (2006) XXXI Ybk Comm Arb 127.
193 [2006] JDI 1460. 194 (2010) XXXV Ybk Comm Arb 40.
195 (2008) XXXIII Ybk Comm Arb 118. 196 (2006) XXXI Ybk Comm Arb 172.

There was little discussion of the rules of admissibility in the awards applying national civil laws. This is to be expected; civil law systems generally do not possess rules that specifically regulate the admission of extrinsic evidence. In no case was extrinsic evidence excluded, and all of the tribunals appear to have followed a subjective method of interpretation. In less than half the awards (ten), the tribunals did not discuss any extrinsic evidence; this may because in each those cases the contract was clear on its face.[197]

In three awards, the tribunal admitted and considered extrinsic evidence but declined to rely upon such evidence because the contract was clear.[198] In these cases, the parties either declined to introduce any extrinsic evidence or the tribunal found the evidence proffered to be insufficient to overcome the ordinary meaning of a clearly drafted contractual term.

In several awards, the tribunals appear to have discounted extrinsic evidence because the contract was clear. This approach appears to be taken for granted—all but two of the tribunals that adopted it did so without separate justification. The only tribunals to cite a legal basis for this textualist approach were those in ICC Case Nos 5485 and 13278. The contracts in both cases were governed by Spanish law, and both tribunals cited the same provisions of the Spanish Civil Code that, if a contractual term is clear and leaves no doubt as to the intention of the parties, it should be interpreted literally. Such an approach is consistent with that which a Spanish court would have taken: admitting extrinsic evidence but discounting it when it conflicts with the plain meaning of a clear contractual term.

This pattern—first looking at whether the written contract, in its context, is unambiguous, and then if necessary examining extrinsic evidence—also marks the remaining awards. ICC Cases Nos 5505 and 10188 are exemplary. In the former, the tribunal found the relevant contractual term to be ambiguous, while in the latter, the tribunal found the written contract to be silent on the issue in dispute. In both cases, the tribunal went on to consider evidence of the parties' negotiations. Such reasoning is not controversial—in both common law and civil law jurisdictions, extrinsic evidence may be admitted to clarify an ambiguity or to fill a gap.

More distinctly civilian in their approach are cases where the tribunal considered extrinsic evidence regardless of the clarity or completeness of the written contract. In every case applying a national civil law in which extrinsic evidence was admitted, the tribunal considered evidence of the parties' subjective intentions, ranging from draft contracts and other negotiation correspondence,[199] to witness testimony about the negotiators' understandings,[200] to internal memoranda of one party,[201] to ancillary contracts concluded between the parties.[202] In four awards, the tribunal considered evidence of one or both parties' subsequent conduct.[203]

Taken together, these awards tend to show that, when applying the law of civil law countries, tribunals will not hesitate to consider any extrinsic evidence that may be helpful in determining the intent of the parties. However, none of the tribunals sought out such evidence on their own motion.

Tribunals were similarly consistent in expressing their fidelity to the principle of subjective interpretation. In eight awards, the tribunal expressly declared its intention

[197] ICC Case Nos 1250, 3055, 3130, 3894, 5485, 6515/6516, 6673, 9443, 11440, and 11776.

[198] ICC Case Nos 2708, 6515/6516, and 11440.

[199] ICC Case Nos 1434, 4131, 5080, 5485, 5505, 6527, 6653, 7518, 10188, and 13278, and the Netherlands Arbitration Institute award.

[200] ICC Case No 12745. [201] ICC Case No 7518. [202] ICC Case No 13278.

[203] ICC Case Nos 4131, 6527, 7518, and 13278.

to seek the 'true intention' of the parties or otherwise indicated that it would proceed by a subjective interpretive method.[204] In some of these cases, the tribunal cited the articles of the relevant civil code that express the principle of subjectivity.

There were two exceptions; in both, the tribunal found that there was insufficient evidence to determine the parties' true intent.[205] In civil law jurisdictions, when the true intent of the parties cannot be determined, even with the help of relevant usages, implied terms, and extrinsic evidence, courts will determine the parties' 'hypothetical' intention by application of a reasonableness standard—in other words, objective interpretation. The tribunals proceeded in a manner consistent with that of a domestic court applying civil law principles.

Awards applying international contract law instruments

Eight of the fifty-three published awards involved the application of an international contract law instrument as the substantive law of the contract. Table 7.3 summarizes the way that the contracts were interpreted in these cases.

Table 7.3

Award	Applicable Law	Mode of Interpretation and Treatment of Extrinsic Evidence
ICC Case No 6309 of 1991[206]	The ULIS, via West German private international law.	Did not refer to lack of interpretive guidance from the ULIS. Admitted extrinsic evidence of the parties' negotiations and of other, related contractual documents. Did not discuss admissibility of extrinsic evidence.
ICC Case No 7585 of 1994[207]	The CISG, as express choice of the parties.	Decided based on text of the contract alone, which it characterized as clear. Unclear whether either party sought to introduce extrinsic evidence.
ICC Case No 7645 of 1995[208]	The CISG, via Austrian private international law.	Declared that it would proceed by the methods contained in CISG, art 8, but resolved dispute without reference to extrinsic evidence.
ICC Case No 8324 of 1995[209]	The CISG, via French private international law.	Declared that it would proceed by the methods contained in CISG, art 8. Considered the plain meaning of the contract, but also admitted a variety of extrinsic evidence. Did not discuss admissibility.
ICC Case No 8782 of 1997[210]	The CISG, via Danish private international law.	Admitted extrinsic evidence of negotiations and subsequent conduct. Did not discuss admissibility.
ICC Case No 8817 of 1997[211]	The CISG, via Spanish private international law.	Admitted extrinsic evidence of the parties' negotiations and subsequent conduct. Did not discuss admissibility.

[204] ICC Case Nos 1434, 5505, 6527, 7518, 10188, 11440, 12745, and 13278.
[205] ICC Case Nos 1434 and 5505.
[206] [1991] JDI 1046.
[207] [1995] JDI 1015.
[208] (2001) XXVI Ybk Comm Arb 130.
[209] [1996] JDI 1019.
[210] (2003) XXVIII Ybk Comm Arb 39.
[211] (2000) XXV Ybk Comm Arb 355.

Award	Applicable Law	Mode of Interpretation and Treatment of Extrinsic Evidence
ICC Case No 10377 of 2002[212]	The CISG, as express choice of the parties.	Decided based on text of the contract and evidence of a trade usage, proved by testimony from an expert appointed by the tribunal.
ICC Case No 12173[213]	The CISG, via Swiss law.	Cited expert report on contractual interpretation under the CISG. On the basis of this report, started with the text of the contract, then considered extrinsic evidence of the parties' negotiations.

The treatment of extrinsic evidence is consistent in these awards. In every case, extrinsic evidence was admitted; it was specifically mentioned in six of the eight awards. In the other two, the tribunals admitted extrinsic evidence but did not rely on it to reach a decision because the contract was 'clear'.[214] The other awards applying the CISG follow its rules closely.[215]

The award in ICC Case No 6309, where the ULIS was the applicable law, is of interest because the ULIS contains no provision relating to the interpretation of contracts or to the admissibility of extrinsic evidence. The claimant contracted to sell to the respondent a lift system for an office building. The claimant had attached to its offer a copy of the General Conditions of the Association of German Mechanical Construction Firms ('the VDMA Conditions'). However, these were not attached to the 'order confirmation' that the claimant sent after receiving the respondent's acceptance. The respondent argued that the VDMA Conditions had not been incorporated into the contract. The sole arbitrator admitted extrinsic evidence, and held that the respondent must have been aware of the VDMA Conditions because of their attachment to the claimant's offer. Its failure to object to the VDMA Conditions meant that they became binding obligations of the contract. The published version of the award does not address the admissibility of this evidence.

Awards applying general principles or stating no applicable substantive law

Six of the fifty-three published awards involved application of general principles of international law to the substance of the contract. For the purposes of this analysis, these have been placed in the same category as the eight awards that contained no discussion of substantive law. In the absence of any reference to substantive law, the tribunal must have drawn its interpretive method from what it saw as the general principles of international commercial law. Table 7.4 summarizes the tribunals' approaches to interpretation.

[212] (2006) XXXI Ybk Comm Arb 72.

[213] (2009) XXXIV Ybk Comm Arb 111.

[214] ICC Case Nos 7585 and 7645.

[215] ICC Case Nos 8324, 8782, 8817, 10377, and 12173.

Table 7.4

Award	Applicable Law	Mode of Interpretation and Treatment of Extrinsic Evidence
ICC Case No 2103 of 1972[216]	No applicable law stated.	Admitted extrinsic evidence of parties' negotiations but found the contract to be 'clear and explicit' so interpreted according to its plain meaning.
ICC Case No 2291 of 1975[217]	No applicable law stated. Some reference to general principles.	Decided based on extrinsic evidence of negotiations; justified this conclusion because contract was concluded by exchange of correspondence.
ICC Case No 2478 of 1974[218]	No applicable law stated.	Decided based on text of contract alone.
ICC Case No 3267, Partial Award of 1979[219]	Amiable composition. Swiss and two French arbitrators.	Detailed 'Anglo-American' style contract, interpreted without reference to extrinsic evidence. Classified the contract as a lump sum contract for a fixed price and implied terms accordingly.
ICC Case No 3267, Final Award of 1984[220]	See above.	Addressing issues unresolved in the previous award, continued to interpret text of contract alone. Neither party argued for admission of extrinsic evidence. Declined to use equitable powers of *amiable compositeur* to vary the terms of the contract.
ICC Case No 3820 of 1981[221]	No applicable law stated. Sole Dutch arbitrator.	Declined to apply literal reading of the contract because it conflicted with rules on documentary credits incorporated into the contract. Noted that result reached would be 'understandable and acceptable' in international trade.
ICC Case No 5953 of 1989[222]	'Common usages of international commerce, also called *lex mercatoria*.' Sole arbitrator.	Analysed text of the contract according to its ordinary meaning and the type of contract. Considered extrinsic evidence of parties' negotiations and prior course of dealing. Did not address admissibility of extrinsic evidence.
ICC Case No 6281 of 1989[223]	No applicable law stated.	Decided based on 'reasonableness' without reference to the text of the contract or extrinsic evidence.
ICC Case No 6378 of 1991[224]	No applicable law stated.	Admitted extrinsic evidence of parties' negotiations. Did not address admissibility.
ICC Case No 8035 of 1995[225]	No applicable law stated.	Admitted extrinsic evidence of parties' negotiations and of trade usages. Did not address admissibility.

216 (1978) III Ybk Comm Arb 218. 217 [1976] JDI 989.
218 (1978) III Ybk Comm Arb 222. 219 (1982) VII Ybk Comm Arb 96.
220 (1987) XII Ybk Comm Arb 87. 221 (1982) VII Ybk Comm Arb 134.
222 [1990] JDI 1056. 223 (1990) XV Ybk Comm Arb 96.
224 [1993] JDI 1018. 225 [1997] JDI 1040.

Award	Applicable Law	Mode of Interpretation and Treatment of Extrinsic Evidence
ICC Case No 12127 of 2003[226]	No applicable law stated; some references to French law.	Began with analysis of a 'combination of various provisions of the contract' to find the subjective intention of parties. Considered extrinsic evidence of parties' negotiations. Did not address admissibility.
ICC Case No 12421/MS of 2005[227]	No applicable law stated; some references to English law.	Began with analysis of the text of the contract. Held to be decisive according to witness testimony of parties' understandings of the contract's meaning. Did not discuss admissibility.
ICC Case No 13129[228]	'General principles of international commercial law.'	Declared that it would proceed by a subjective method of interpretation because a 'strict, legalistic approach' would be 'inappropriate'. Considered extrinsic evidence of parties' pre- and post-contract correspondence.
Permanent Court of Arbitration, *Eurotunnel* Partial Award of 2007[229]	'International law principles of interpretation', specifically the VCLT.	Interpreted by 'ordinary meaning' of the text; admitted extrinsic evidence of negotiations by analogy to admission of treaty *travaux* permissible under the VCLT. Stated that extrinsic evidence would be considered with 'due caution'.

Cases involving the application of general principles of substantive international law—especially those involving amiable composition—provide the clearest evidence of the thought processes of international commercial tribunals; these principles give tribunals the greatest latitude to apply whatever rules they consider appropriate. However, only in ICC Case No 13129 and the *Eurotunnel* arbitration did the tribunal discuss explicitly what rules it would apply with respect to the interpretation of the contract and the use of extrinsic evidence.

The *Eurotunnel* award is worthy of separate attention, partly because so few awards applying general principles of international law discuss their mode of interpretation, and partly because it involved interpretation of both a contract and a treaty under the rules of the VCLT.[230]

The five-member tribunal, convened under the auspices of the Permanent Court of Arbitration, was composed of prominent arbitrators from both civilian and common law backgrounds.[231] It hewed closely to the principles set out in the VCLT, beginning with the ordinary meaning of the contract, viewed in its context, and then making a 'supplementary interpretation' based on extrinsic evidence. Both parties sought to introduce extrinsic evidence of their negotiations, which the tribunal admitted with the caveat that it would consider this evidence with 'due caution'.[232] The award does

226 (2008) XXXIII Ybk Comm Arb 82.

227 (2008) XXXIII Ybk Comm Arb 102.

228 (2009) XXXIV Ybk Comm Arb 231.

229 Permanent Court of Arbitration Case No 2003–06, Partial Award of 30 January 2007.

230 The background of the *Eurotunnel* award is discussed above in Section II.3 of this chapter.

231 An Australian chair, with one English, two French, and one French-Canadian co-arbitrators.

232 *Eurotunnel* [94].

not explain what the tribunal meant by due caution, but it presumably refers to the unreliability of testimonial evidence and to the fact that evidence of negotiations should not be allowed to contradict the clearly expressed agreement of the parties.

There were two claims asserted by the claimants, only one of which potentially involved extrinsic evidence. The concessionaires who operated the fixed rail link under the English Channel claimed that the French government had improperly given assistance to SeaFrance, a company operating a ferry service between France and England. The dispute focused on clause 34.3 of the contract, which stated that: 'The Principals [France and the UK] agree that throughout the Concession Period no link shall be financed with the support of public funds, either directly or by the provision of government guarantees of a financial or commercial nature.'[233] The claimants argued that the assistance to SeaFrance constituted financing of another 'link' between the United Kingdom and France.

The tribunal embarked on a close textual analysis of the contract, noting that while 'link' could refer to a ferry service, the equivalent word in the equally authoritative French version of the contract, '*ouvrage*', could not refer to a ferry. Reading the term in its 'context', the tribunal concluded that there was no evidence that the parties had intended to prohibit assistance to any trans-channel operator, but only to potential competitors in the operation of a fixed link, in the manner of a railroad or motorway.[234] Finally, the tribunal stated that accepting the claimant's interpretation of 'link' to include ferry services would lead to absurd results: air cargo flights between Paris and London would also qualify as a link.[235]

Finally, the tribunal considered the claimants' argument that the Invitation to Promoters, a document by which the two governments had initially publicized the concession opportunity, stated that the governments would ensure that the concessionaires would not be 'subject to any inequality of treatment likely to distort free competition between types of international transport, including maritime and air transport'.[236] The claimants alleged that this clause, and other broad protectionist language in the Invitation to Promoters, created a 'legitimate expectation' of protection from competition from ferry operators. However, no clause similar to that paragraph of the Invitation existed in the contract. The tribunal characterized the contract, and not the Invitation, as determining the parties 'legal relationship'. Thus, if expectations were raised by the Invitation, this 'would have been a reason to insist on their inclusion in the Concession Agreement. But it is not a reason for reading into that Agreement stipulations which are notably absent from it'.[237] This reasoning is reminiscent of the common law perspective of a contractual relationship, that it crystallizes with the signing of the written contract. At the same time, however, a common law court probably would not have admitted such evidence of the parties' negotiations.

In ICC Case No 13129, the sole arbitrator expressed 'reservations as to the real existence of anything that can be described as lex mercatoria'. Nevertheless, he applied general principles because he could not find any reason to apply any national law. However, he noted that application of English law—the only national law plausibly connected to the contract—would likely have led to the same outcome.

The arbitrator decided that a 'strict, legalistic' approach to interpretation was inappropriate. This was justified by the 'common sense' nature of general principles and by two factors specific to the contract: it was negotiated between traders and without the

233 Ibid [280].
234 Ibid [374]–[375].
235 Ibid [376].
236 Ibid [378].
237 Ibid [384].

assistance of lawyers, and it was concluded in English between negotiators whose native languages were not English. Accordingly, the arbitrator explained: 'What is necessary is to read the contract [including] the parties' negotiations as a whole, with a view to ascertaining the parties' true intentions.'

The lack of reasoning in the published extracts of the other awards applying general principles leaves the reader with no choice but to attempt to divine the tribunals' approaches from the results reached in their awards, much as a civil law court attempts to divine the parties' true intentions from their outward expressions of intent. Taking the fourteen awards as a group, six generalizations can be made:

- Tribunals see their primary interpretive task as to discern the true common intention of the parties.[238]
- Tribunals begin by examining the natural and ordinary meaning of the contractual terms in dispute.[239]
- Tribunals faced with an apparently clear contractual term are unlikely to allow extrinsic evidence of the parties' intentions to overtake the natural meaning.[240]
- In contrast to their treatment of subjective extrinsic evidence, tribunals will broadly enforce practices established between the parties and trade usages that may contradict the apparent meaning of the contract; tribunals are particularly likely to take such an approach with 'codified' usages like the INCOTERMS or widely adopted standard contractual terms.[241]
- Tribunals which are free to choose the applicable law (in particular those acting as *amiables compositeurs*) do not prohibit parties from introducing whatever extrinsic evidence the parties may think relevant, including direct evidence of subjective intent and evidence of subsequent conduct.[242]
- Although tribunals acting under all major arbitral rules have the power to request the production of extrinsic evidence, they rarely exercise this power.

IV. Conclusion

Derains writes: 'The interpretation of contracts is one of the areas in which international commercial arbitrators are most inclined to disengage from national laws in order to resort to general principles of law.'[243] The results of this survey indicate that arbitrators are indeed quick to refer to generally accepted maxims or canons of construction, such as *in claris non fit interpretatio*, *contra proferentem*, and good faith, but when it comes to contractual interpretation, international arbitrators tend to stick to the rules of the applicable national law. More importantly, in the cases where arbitrators do not follow the applicable rules precisely, or where no national substantive law applies, they tend to

[238] Most of the tribunals, including one applying the law of a common law jurisdiction, either declared this to be their goal or cited national law statutory or case law expressing this core principle of subjective interpretation.

[239] This occurred in all of the awards.

[240] ICC Cases Nos 2103, 2478, and 3267 and *Eurotunnel*.

[241] ICC Case Nos 3267, 3820, 5963, 7722, 8035, and 13129.

[242] This did not occur in any of the awards where the applicable law was not stated, where the tribunal applied general principles or *lex mercatoria*, or where the tribunal acted as *amiable compositeur*.

[243] ICC Case No 2291 of 1975 [1976] JDI 989, obs Y Derains.

interpret contracts according to an approach that is consistent with other arbitrators, but not identical to any given national law.

In thirty-nine awards, the applicable law was a national law or codified international contract law instrument (usually, the CISG). In all but three of those cases, the tribunal employed an interpretive method consistent with the applicable law. It therefore seems that the great majority of international arbitral tribunals faithfully follow the rules of contractual interpretation contained in the applicable law. However, looking at the overall number obscures an important point. In all cases where the applicable law was an international contract law instrument or the law of a civil law jurisdiction, the tribunal accurately applied the prescribed method of interpretation. However, the same was not true of the awards applying the law of a common law jurisdiction; in three out of seven such awards, the tribunal interpreted the contract subjectively and admitted extrinsic evidence that a common law court would likely have excluded.[244]

Despite the small sample size, it seems fair to conclude that a civil law perspective on contractual interpretation is becoming dominant in international commercial law. Notwithstanding the governing law—common law, civil law, or international law—arbitral tribunals seek the true intention of the parties and consider a range of extrinsic evidence. This observation is reinforced by two additional factors. First, the ULIS, promulgated in 1964, has no rules on the interpretation of contracts, but all of the more recently drafted international contract law instruments call for subjective interpretation and admit a wide range of extrinsic evidence.[245]

Second—and more important, because it provides direct evidence of the preferences of international commercial arbitrators—all of the tribunals acting under general principles or amiable composition were receptive to the subjective method of interpretation and the admission of extrinsic evidence. It is not surprising that these should go together; subjective interpretation necessitates the admission of evidence of the parties' subjective intentions. Nevertheless, pure subjectivity does not reign; these tribunals tended to give primacy to the written text of a contract, but admitted extrinsic evidence in all cases where it was submitted.[246]

In general, tribunals seem to have disregarded extrinsic evidence only in those cases where they were able to reach a satisfactory interpretation based on the words of the contract alone. Conversely, when the contractual term at issue was vague or ambiguous, the tribunals did consider extrinsic evidence. If a party sought to introduce extrinsic evidence that contradicted the plain language of a clear term in the contract, most tribunals gave little weight to the extrinsic evidence. Thus, the tribunals did not exclude extrinsic evidence, but considered it to be decisive only when the contract was unclear or incomplete.

What is more, with one exception, tribunals did not actively seek out extrinsic evidence, even when the disputed term was vague or ambiguous. The exception is trade usages, evidence of which several tribunals sought out on their own motion. For

[244] ICC Case Nos 4555, 5946, and 12172.

[245] It should also be noted that, beginning in the 1970s, the common law jurisdictions have themselves shifted toward greater acceptance of extrinsic evidence, although they still stop short of permitting evidence of the parties' subjective understandings of the contract.

[246] In one case decided under common law where extrinsic evidence was admitted, the sole American arbitrator seems to have subscribed to this methodology. The award states that 'unarticulated and undocumented understandings' can be considered, but should be given 'less weight than the objective … meaning of the contract language'. ICC Case No 4555 of 1985 (1986) XI Ybk Comm Arb 140.

example, in ICC Case No 10377, the tribunal appointed its own expert to testify as to the content of a trade usage.[247]

Taken together, these trends indicate that international arbitral tribunals are primarily concerned with discerning the true (subjective) common intention of the parties, and will restrict themselves to objective interpretation only when the applicable law is that of a common law jurisdiction (and even then, not always). Tribunals tend to see the written contract as the best evidence of the parties' true intent, and consider extrinsic evidence only if they think it necessary to determine that intent.

1. Contractual interpretation and international arbitration culture

These outcomes cannot be explained by differences in the rules applicable to substantive law in ICA and in national court litigation. The choice of law rules specific to ICA should have no bearing on the way that tribunals apply the chosen law. Similarly, the fact that arbitrators may apply general principles or act as *amiables compositeurs* should have no effect on cases where a national law governs. Moreover, the fact that general principles may be relied upon does not require tribunals to rely upon them. Finally, the rules of contractual interpretation are well settled in national jurisdictions and under the major international contract law instruments, so differences in the way that courts and arbitral tribunals ascertain the content of the applicable law should yield no differences in outcome.

On the other hand, the results of this case study are explained by the cultural theory of ICA decision-making set out in Part I. In particular, they can be attributed largely to tribunals' respect for party autonomy and their sense of serving business interests.

Commercial parties tend to neither like nor understand technical legal rules such as the parol evidence rule, nor do they act with those rules in mind. An attunement to business interests and an internalization of the commercial mentality should also lead international arbitrators to disfavour such rules. ICA was developed apart from national legal systems and was designed to serve its clientele rather than to rule them, so one would expect the substantive law of international arbitration to develop in line with business practices, rather than the other way around. The service of business norm therefore helps to explain international arbitrators' apparent preference for subjective interpretation and reluctance to apply the common law exclusionary rules.

In accordance with the party autonomy norm, international commercial arbitrators are likely to let the parties take the lead in building the evidentiary record. A broad allegiance to party autonomy therefore encourages tribunals to consider whatever evidence the parties seek to introduce (a characteristic of the civil law) and also to refrain from searching beyond that evidence (a characteristic of the common law). The awards surveyed in this chapter are not in themselves evidence that international arbitrators prefer subjective interpretation over objective interpretation, but they do indicate that arbitrators prefer to let the parties decide for themselves what facts ought to be introduced in order to interpret the contract.

When given the opportunity, parties are likely to introduce whatever evidence they see as helpful to their cause, including extrinsic evidence of their subjective intentions. Once evidence of the parties' actual intentions is in the record, judges cannot help but be influenced by such evidence, notwithstanding that the governing law calls for

[247] (2006) XXXI Ybk Comm Arb 72 at [47].

objective interpretation. Thus, when tribunals allow the parties to develop the evidentiary record, subjective interpretation follows as a near-inevitable consequence. The trend in the published awards toward subjective interpretation is thus explicable in terms of a norm favouring party autonomy and business perspectives.

At the same time, attention to the arbitral context and the differing constraints on judges and arbitrators helps to explain why, when not applying the law of a common law jurisdiction, arbitrators tend to admit all relevant extrinsic evidence. The exclusionary rules evolved largely to keep unreliable evidence away from unreliable lay juries, an issue that does not arise in arbitration. Another rationale for the exclusionary rules is that, by prioritizing the objective meaning of the written terms of a contract, they help to give similar terms in different contracts a uniform meaning; this promotes predictability and protects third parties who may have already drafted contracts according to the apparently settled meaning of terms.

Arbitrators are not institutionally concerned with issues of general applicability that arise from individual cases, but rather with giving expression to the intentions of the parties that selected those arbitrators to resolve their dispute. After all, most arbitral awards are only read by the parties and, even if published, cannot bind future tribunals. In addition, arbitrators are not likely to hear from third parties whose interests may be affected by interpretation of the contract in dispute.[248]

As with the previous case study, the patterns in arbitral decision-making identified in this chapter have implications for both contract drafting and advocacy before tribunals. Contract drafters, especially those trained in common law jurisdictions, should be aware that international arbitral tribunals are likely to consider all materials that may help to reveal the subjective understandings of the parties, even where the applicable law is that of a common law jurisdiction. Accordingly, if a party wants to ensure that draft contracts or other such extrinsic evidence do not carry weight in an eventual dispute, it should insist on an entire agreement clause, even to the point of expressly stating that prior drafts and negotiations are subsumed under the final written agreement. In addition, contract negotiators should be directed to maintain copies of any contemporaneous notes and correspondence from the beginning of the negotiations through the performance of the contract. Notes, in particular, may help to prove the party's subjective intention at the time of contracting and increase the credibility of witness evidence.

When a dispute arises, counsel appearing in international arbitrations should similarly be aware that international arbitral tribunals (including some applying the substantive law of common law jurisdictions) are unlikely to respond positively to arguments that extrinsic evidence must be excluded from the record. Counsel should therefore be willing to make use of any materials that support their preferred interpretation of the contract—indeed, they should introduce and seek production of such evidence, because tribunals are unlikely to do so on their own motion. Even when the governing law is that of a common law jurisdiction, counsel should be prepared to respond to arguments that rely on extrinsic evidence. Merely objecting to the admissibility of such evidence is unlikely to succeed. Therefore, if a party will benefit from a literal interpretation of the contract's text, it would most likely be served by an argument that the plain meaning of the text is the best evidence of the true intention of the parties, and that therefore any contradictory extrinsic evidence should be given little weight.

[248] Note, however, that this may change as arbitral awards are published in greater numbers (and therefore are more likely to have precedential value) and as third parties increasingly find their way into arbitral proceedings.

8

The Future of Contract Law

> ... it is easy to put too much weight on harmonization projects, model laws, and the like. They are surely less causal than their advocates think. Convergence and voluntary actions of private parties are no doubt more fundamental in building a global legal order than drafting and enacting.[1]

> The more you resolve international cases and the more you get used to applying different laws, the clearer it gets that there is a process of uniformizing the law and disregarding idiosyncrasies of specific national laws in international arbitration.[2]

The modern international arbitral order was born on 10 June 1958, when the New York Convention was opened for ratification. States that ratified this convention pledged to enforce international arbitration agreements and foreign arbitral awards. Without this pledge, arbitration could not have become an important venue for the resolution of cross-border commercial disputes.

Perhaps more importantly, the states that ratified the New York Convention also agreed that their courts would scrutinize arbitral awards only on procedural matters. The architects of the ICA system probably believed that they were creating only a distinct procedure for the resolution of international commercial disputes. Certainly, commentators on ICA have focused on its procedural characteristics. However, when states agreed that their courts would not supervise arbitral tribunals' determinations of substantive law, they acquiesced to the creation of a system of substantive commercial law separate from the law of any state.

The literature on international uniform laws frequently cautions that, without appellate courts to enforce uniformity of interpretation, judicial interpretations of the same laws will eventually diverge: 'Uniform application of the agreed rules is by no means guaranteed, as in practice, different countries almost inevitably come to put different interpretations upon the same enacted words.'[3] This perspective is too narrow. After all, arbitration has already evolved a coherent set of procedural rules. As Rogers observes: 'Even in the absence of a formal system of *stare decisis*, and despite the confidential and "private" nature of international arbitration, arbitration proceedings generate procedural rules and practices, and to a lesser extent substantive rules, that serve as precedent for future arbitrations and beyond.'[4]

[1] Friedman 1996, 77. [2] A leading Swiss arbitrator, interviewed for this book.

[3] Munday 1978, 450. Harmonization advocates often lament that it is 'insufficient to merely create and enact uniform instruments'. Ferrari 2005, 233. See also Andersen 2005, 162; Ryan 1995, 117; Honnold 1988, 207.

[4] Rogers 2005, 999–1000.

Consistent (albeit not entirely uniform) decision-making can be achieved without a hierarchy of courts or binding legislation, so long as the decision-makers share a common set of legal and social norms. If those norms guide a sufficiently broad range of conduct within a definable community, they constitute a culture. For this reason, one need not believe that ICA constitutes an autonomous legal system to conclude that an autonomous substantive law will evolve—and is evolving. It is sufficient that ICA possesses a distinct culture.

Culture produces reflexive behaviour in members of a community. It both shapes and is shaped by their interactions. Culture is distinguished from other factors that shape behaviour, such as economic self-interest or the threat of punishment; culture causes members of a community to act reflexively in accordance with its norms. The culture of ICA is defined according to the legal and social norms that comprise it; these are, in turn, described by the rules of law that bind international arbitrators, the institutional structure of the ICA system, and the values that international arbitrators share. The norms that emerged from the grounded theory research conducted for this book are as follows.

The institutional structure of ICA yields one set of norms. ICA is a party-centred system. Although the cooperation of national laws and courts is essential, arbitral tribunals are called into being by the parties' agreement and arbitrators are selected and paid by the parties. Once it issues a final award, a tribunal ceases to exist. Arbitration is also characterized by close relationships and fluid shifting of roles within a relatively small community. International arbitrators and leading counsel tend to know each other personally and work together regularly; one may appear as counsel in front of the other, and then in a subsequent arbitration the roles are reversed. Arbitration practitioners publish in academic and trade journals and converse frequently at conferences and through online discussion groups. The ICA system is also characterized by intense competition in a market-driven environment. Individual arbitrators and arbitral venues compete with each other to provide the best service to the parties, and the ICA community as a whole collaborates to promote arbitration over other forms of international commercial dispute resolution.

The values shared by international arbitrators, counsel, and parties yield a second set of norms. Party autonomy is a central value in ICA, and arbitrators defer to the parties, subject only to ensuring that an eventual award will be enforceable. Arbitrators see their role as providing a service to the parties, and conceive of that service as being commercial rather than judicial in character. They strive to provide a cost-effective process that is tailored to the particularities of each dispute, and cultivate a commercial mentality that contrasts with the legal formalism that tends to predominate in national judiciaries.

Neutrality is an important characteristic of the ICA system—one of the main reasons that parties choose to arbitrate their disputes is out of fear that each other's national court systems will not treat them fairly. Accordingly, arbitrators foster an ethic of scrupulous neutrality between the parties, which affects both the procedures and the governing laws that they choose. Finally, arbitrators are a cosmopolitan, globalized community that reveres internationally minded ways of thinking and rejects national perspectives which they consider narrow and parochial.

These norms constitute the cultural context within which international commercial arbitrators make decisions. As the case studies in Chapters 6 and 7 show, the applicable rules are insufficient in themselves to explain the substantive law determinations in international arbitral awards. Arbitrators do not always stay within the dictates of the applicable law, and when they depart from that law they do so in ways that are consistent with ICA social norms.[5] The cultural theory of ICA explains how arbitrators choose and apply existing laws, why new rules of law are likely to develop in ICA, and what those new rules are likely to be.

***

Choice of law in ICA is determined first according to party autonomy. If the parties choose a particular law, whether national or transnational, the tribunal will apply it. When the parties do not make a choice of law, the tribunal will normally choose a law in accordance with what it sees as the parties' intentions. This will usually mean a national law that is closely connected to the transaction, but will usually not be the national law of one of the parties (which would be non-neutral), unless it is clear that the parties negotiated the contract in contemplation of that law.

Arbitrators are likely to apply national laws in accordance with what they see as modern international standards. This is most visible in cases where the tribunal declares that it will refer to transnational principles because the governing national law has gaps or leads to commercially unreasonable results.[6] However, tribunals also diverge from national courts' interpretations of national laws in more subtle ways that they do not always acknowledge. In particular, they tend to interpret those laws so as to diminish the laws' idiosyncrasies and to achieve commercially reasonable results. This tendency is visible in the case studies. Regardless of the applicable law, tribunals protected parties' right to suspend performance so long as the suspending party acted proportionately, and also interpreted contracts according to the parties' true intentions, as revealed in both their written contracts and contemporaneous extrinsic evidence. Such outcomes are predictable based on the party-centric nature of the arbitral system and arbitrators' dedication to the values of party autonomy, the service of business, neutrality, and internationalism.

When tribunals refer to transnational rules of law, whether to supplement a national law chosen by the parties or because the contract is governed by transnational rules, those rules are unlikely to take the form of *lex mercatoria*. Contrary to the apparent expectations of many arbitrators of the older generation, consumers of ICA services—businesses engaged in cross-border commerce—have shown that they do not want their contracts to be governed by '*lex mercatoria*' or 'general principles'. Only a tiny and shrinking fraction of contracts choose these. In particular, it appears that parties reject free-floating transnational principles because of their unpredictability.

Accordingly, arbitrators are not likely to be as ambitious as tribunals of the 1970s and 80s in declaring new general principles of international law. However, tribunals can reconcile their preference for neutral and international rules with the parties' interests by applying codified instruments that embody general principles.

Today, arbitrators seldom call for the application of *lex mercatoria* or general principles under those labels. However, they do frequently apply codified instruments that embody the very same transnational principles, like the CISG and UNIDROIT Principles.[7] The increased predictability that comes with codification seems to have

[5] This is not to say that ICA legal norms are irrelevant to substantive law determinations. However, as discussed in Chapter 5, the ICA legal norms that pertain to substantive law are permissive rather than determinative, so they cannot on their own explain the outcomes reached in ICA.

[6] The clearest example is arbitrators' derogation from national rules that specify a rate of interest. See Chapter 4, Section V.1.

[7] This can be seen in the way that arbitrators characterize the UNIDROIT Principles as part of, or an expression of, the *lex mercatoria*. See, eg, Brower and Sharpe 2004, 210, arguing that the

satisfied commercial parties, which prefer the codified to the uncodified versions of transnational rules. In one survey, a majority of corporate counsel reported that they never conclude choice of law agreements that refer to 'general principles of law, commercial practices or fairness and equity', but only a minority never refer to codifications like the UNIDROIT Principles or INCOTERMS.[8]

Accordingly, the number of awards that expressly apply general principles or *lex mercatoria* is likely to continue to dwindle, but awards applying these principles in codified instruments are likely to become more numerous. At the same time, arbitrators are likely to continue to justify references to a given instrument on the basis that it expresses an international legal consensus or international trade usages. Since the arbitral institutions share many of the priorities of arbitrators—in particular, competition with other forms of dispute resolution—awards that apply transnational law should continue to account for a disproportionate share of the published awards. In turn, published awards that apply international contract law instruments will be more likely to be cited by subsequent tribunals.

Among the international contract law instruments, arbitrators are most likely to prefer the UNIDROIT Principles, which are the most 'universal' of the existing instruments. The CISG, which deals only with sale of goods contracts, is limited in scope, and the PECL, which claim only to be pan-European, are geographically limited. The UNIDROIT Principles therefore best exemplify internationalism. They are is also the least likely to require gap-filling and are easier to update than the CISG, which can only be amended or replaced by a diplomatic convention.[9]

***

The culture of ICA also explains why we should expect a consistent body of new transnational law to emerge from ICA. Admittedly, there are good reasons to be sceptical of this proposition. International arbitrators have largely disavowed the *lex mercatoria* and apply transnational law only in codified forms. Moreover, the ICA community is heterogeneous. The at-best slow and halting pace of convergence among distinct national legal cultures in transnational arenas such as the European Union testifies to the durability of culture and the difficulties inherent in developing a global legal order.[10]

However, ICA is different from state-centric transnational harmonizing projects like the European Union. In many ways, it is the ideal incubator for a new commercial law that is not merely transnational (crossing national borders) but truly global. To borrow a phrase from criminal prosecutions, ICA culture gives international arbitrators the motive, means, and opportunity to create a global commercial law.

First, the opportunity for a new global law to arise in ICA exists because many of the factors that inhibit convergence between national legal cultures are not relevant in ICA. Unlike criminal and family law, commercial law does not implicate religious and moral values; unlike constitutional and administrative law, it is not shaped by concepts of the roles and responsibilities of governments; unlike consumer protection law, it is

UNIDROIT Principles have altered the perception of the *lex mercatoria*, so that they are seen simply as general principles in codified form.

[8] W&C/QMUL 2010, 15.

[9] One might also expect to see increasing numbers of scholarly publications by arbitrators about the international contract law instruments, as a by-product of arbitrators' internationalism and competition for business.

[10] See generally Legrand 1996.

not guided by the need to compensate for power imbalances. State sovereignty is rarely at stake in commercial disputes, even those that involve government entities.

In addition, no unified administrative apparatus is necessary to make a new global commercial law effective. Separate arbitral tribunals can apply the same substantive legal principles even as they are convened by different arbitral institutions or are called into being directly by the parties, as in ad hoc international arbitrations. Indeed, variety in procedural rules and administrative styles is itself a virtue of the ICA system, since it permits parties to choose the most appropriate procedure from a range of available options. Therefore, a space exists that is largely free from national interference and largely independent of national jurisdiction, which provides the opportunity for a global commercial law to develop.

Second, international arbitrators possess the means to develop a new global commercial law. National legislatures have largely agreed—at the instigation of the commercial and ICA lobbies—to restrict their own supervision of international arbitral awards on matters of substantive law. The only remaining significant tool of substantive national court control of ICA awards is the public policy exception, and there, too, arbitrators are working to reduce the impact of diverse national legal systems and traditions.

Therefore, international arbitrators may recognize new, non-national principles of substantive law in their awards, largely without fear of sanction. The widespread dissemination of new substantive law principles is hindered by the confidentiality of arbitral awards. However, international arbitrators do cite prior tribunals on points of law, including on matters of substance.[11] More importantly, substantive law principles diffuse throughout the ICA community as arbitrators work with each other in different venues, including arbitrations, publications, conferences, and discussion fora.

Moreover, it is arbitrators themselves who determine policy development within ICA. Arbitrators and arbitration counsel populate the boards of directors of the various arbitral institutions that determine the rules of procedure and appoint many sole arbitrators and tribunal chairs. They also make up the IBA and ILA committees that are tasked with identifying and codifying international arbitral practices. Finally, national arbitration laws are passed by legislatures, but are drafted largely by members of the ICA community. Arbitrators thus possess a number of means by which they can promote the adoption of coherent and consistent global legal principles.

Third, the social norms of ICA culture motivate international arbitrators to develop a uniform (or at least coherent) global commercial law. Differences in national substantive laws impose costs on cross-border commercial relationships, so the more that existing national substantive laws fail to harmonize with each other, the greater the demand for a unified commercial law. Globalization of commerce has led to 'an urgent need for a corresponding legislative policy' that is globally consistent and independent of national legal systems.[12] Due to the institutional structure of ICA and the service of business norm, arbitrators' interests are aligned with those of the parties. In addition, international arbitrators are apt to prefer rules that are international and that are neutral as between the parties.

In sum, international commercial arbitrators have an ideological and a material incentive to aid in the development of a global commercial law. As one tribunal put it: 'Arbitral awards gradually develop a body of case law that reflects economic realities and complies with the needs of international trade.'[13]

[11] The development of international investment law through arbitral case law testifies to the fact that new, global substantive law can emerge within ICA.

[12] Ferrari 1999, 895.

[13] ICC Case No 4131 of 1982 [1983] JDI 899 (author's translation).

There is also a purely practical reason to expect the development of new global rules of law within ICA. In each arbitration, arbitrators are faced with parties of different nationalities, and often members of the tribunal are of different nationalities. In their deliberations, they seek to reach decisions that are unanimous and acceptable to both parties. Of necessity, this involves making compromises, partly in how the award is drafted but also in the application of law to facts. The inevitable result is to encourage the evolution of legal doctrines that draw from multiple national traditions and are distinct from the laws of any one state.

***

The cultural theory of arbitral decision-making not only explains the emergence of new procedural and substantive rules of law within ICA, but also provides a basis on which to predict what those new rules will be and how transnational legal instruments will change over time.

Procedural harmonization has already occurred in ICA. This book focuses on the effects of ICA culture on arbitrators' substantive law determinations, but it is worth noting that the procedural standards that have emerged in ICA are also explained by the cultural theory of arbitral decision-making. Correspondences between those procedures and the social norms of ICA can be seen, for example, in the IBA's Rules on the Taking of Evidence in International Arbitration.[14] The IBA Rules are flexible, leaving significant scope for the parties to structure hearings according to their own agreement (the norms of party autonomy and service of business).[15] They draw from both common law and civil law sources to create an autonomous set of evidentiary rules that are specific to ICA (the norms of neutrality and internationalism).[16] They are intended to make the process of taking evidence quick and therefore cheap (service of business).[17] The Rules apply only when the parties agree to adopt them (party autonomy).[18] They were drafted by a working party composed of prominent arbitrators and counsel who competed to be selected to this visible and prestigious IBA committee (competition, arbitrators' multiple roles).

ICA procedures have harmonized toward a position of maximum flexibility. In the areas that the parties can control, they are likely to want flexible rules that give them the greatest possible choice. Deference to party autonomy and a desire to serve their clientele leads arbitrators to defer to the parties' chosen procedures. If the parties do not choose, arbitrators are likely to adopt procedures consistent with ICA norms, such as efficient conduct of hearings and confidentiality.

However, where party autonomy cannot be allowed to intrude—application of the substantive law to the facts of the dispute—commercial parties are likely to prefer rules

[14] While debate persists as to whether evidentiary rules are substantive or procedural, in ICA they are treated as procedure.

[15] IBA Rules, art 2: 'The Arbitral Tribunal shall consult the Parties at the earliest appropriate time in the proceedings and invite them to consult each other.'

[16] For example, the IBA Rules chart a middle path between the restrictive and expansive document production regimes associated, respectively, with the civil and common law systems (art 3). They permit cross-examination of witnesses (art 8, a common law tradition) but encourage reliance on documentary evidence (art 4, a civil law tradition). See generally Elsing and Townsend 2002.

[17] The IBA Rules admonish the tribunal to establish, in consultation with the parties, an 'efficient, economical and fair process' (art 2). They also encourage the wide use of witness statements in order to reduce the need for live witness testimony and thereby shorten hearings (art 4).

[18] IBA Rules, art 1.

that lead to predictable outcomes. These permit the parties to plan and price their conduct more accurately and, when disputes arise, to settle them more efficiently.

In the absence of a system of appellate review, predictability can be achieved in one of two ways: through bright-line (non-discretionary) rules or through rules that enforce the expectations of commercial parties, such as adjudication according to trade usages or good faith. To the extent that bright-line rules are developed, they are likely to be derogable and to be derived from commercial practice.[19] More generally, arbitrators are likely to be swayed by industry-specific and transaction-specific arguments. Such rules are contextual, and therefore may appear to be unpredictable. However, they are predictable to the constituency that matters—the parties—because they are rooted in the context within which those parties operate.

As a general matter, the contract law doctrines that develop in ICA will likely be flexible and derogable in deference to party autonomy, neutral both culturally and as between the parties, and consistent with commercial reasonableness and commercial expectations. Applying the norms of ICA culture, one can make predictions about the full range of contract law doctrines, from contract formation to remedies for breach.

Arbitrators are unlikely to prefer technical rules of contract formation and validity, such as were traditionally observed in the common law. Instead, they are likely to find that contractual liability arises whenever one party has induced reasonable expectations of performance in the other party. Disputes over offer and acceptance seldom arise in ICA, given the fact that a valid arbitration agreement is a precondition to arbitral jurisdiction. However, parties may argue that preliminary negotiations never crystallized into a contract. Arbitrators are unlikely to be receptive to such arguments if one or both of the parties has commenced performance; commercial parties do not perform if they have no expectation of remuneration.

For the same reasons, international arbitrators will likely downplay the writing requirements and other rules of formal validity that are prevalent in civil law systems, or will find that formal requirements in the applicable law have been satisfied. Even if the applicable law is the law of a common law jurisdiction, arbitrators are unlikely to hold that a contractual amendment is unenforceable for lack of consideration, or that a contract is unenforceable for lack of privity. More broadly, the commercial law that develops in ICA is likely to contain few and narrow grounds on which an obligation may be declared unenforceable.

When arbitrators interpret contracts, they seek to enforce the true common intention of the parties—subjective interpretation. However, this does not mean that the text of the contracts will be subordinated to other evidence. International arbitrators tend to focus tightly on the text of the contract and a few contemporaneous documents, even to the exclusion of requirements of the applicable law, because they see the written contract as the best evidence of the parties' intentions.

Arbitrators' identification with business attitudes and interests—the service of business norm—means that trade usages will likely play a prominent role in ICA's global contract law, both to determine the meaning of express contractual terms and to fill gaps. Arbitrators will adopt interpretive rules that promote trade usages, although deference to party autonomy would suggest that, if express contractual terms exclude the application of usages, arbitrators will respect those terms. In the same vein, tribunals are unlikely to set high standards of proof if a party seeks to rely on a business custom

[19] This development is akin to what has been called the 'incorporation strategy' pursued by the drafters of the UCC, art 2. Bernstein 1999, 710.

or course of dealing. Where they exist, arbitrators will likely refer to instruments that purport to codify international trade usages, such as the Hague-Visby Rules[20] for shipping or the UCP for documentary credits, even if the parties have not raised them.[21]

Arbitral attention to the commercial context of transactions is likely to lead to an increased particularization of trade usage determinations. This may lead to increased formal or informal specialization within ICA, with different standard practices in different types of arbitrations. An existing example of this phenomenon is the prevalence of *ex aequo et bono* determination in contract disputes administered by the Court of Arbitration for Sport.[22] ICA may therefore fragment according to the subject matter of disputes, in the same manner as public international law is said to have done.[23]

When a breach occurs, arbitrators are likely to prefer rules that permit parties to engage in a wide range of self-help remedies without prejudicing their rights to sue under the contract. Self-help remedies, such as price reduction and suspension of performance, are simple and intuitive and are often economically efficient; businesses tend to prefer them, so arbitrators are likely to promote them. Along the same lines, complex or lengthy procedures to terminate contracts, such as the *mise en demeure* and *action en résolution* process in France, are unlikely to find their way into a future global commercial law.

If a contract contains a liquidated damages provision, arbitral tribunals are likely to enforce it unless it seems grossly disproportionate to the risk that the party held liable took on. For example, arbitrators are likely to balk at enforcing a liquidated damages provision that would drive a party out of business. For the same reason, arbitrators are likely to take a liberal approach to a *force majeure* defence.

***

ICA has already generated a set of harmonized, autonomous procedural rules that enjoy general acceptance. The same is not true with respect to substantive law. However, the cultural forces within ICA that created the one are now creating the other. Informally, haltingly, incompletely, but inexorably, international arbitrators are establishing a set of contract law principles of global applicability. They are doing so without the need for diplomatic conferences or scholarly drafting parties. And they are doing so along patterns that are predictable according to the social norms that make up the nascent culture of international commercial arbitration.

[20] International Convention for the Unification of Certain Rules of Law relating to Bills of Lading (1924) as amended in 1968. The Hague-Visby Rules are a set of international rules for the carriage of goods by sea. They have been incorporated into various national statutes but are most commonly incorporated by reference into carriage contracts.

[21] See Friedman 2001, 356–7. Friedman argues that sets of contractual provisions with quasi-legal power, like the Hague-Visby Rules and the UCP, do not on their own constitute autonomous norms created within the international economy: 'In the end all such customs and practices have to be validated somehow by national courts applying what they consider to be national law or rules that national law recognizes—or, as is often the case, the law that the parties to a contract may have stipulated.' ICA can also perform the validating function that Friedman assigns to national courts.

[22] One interviewee, an experienced London-based arbitrator, said that he had only ever encountered amiable composition or ex aequo et bono provisions in sport-related contracts.

[23] The so-called fragmentation of international law has been a source of much scholarly attention since at least the beginning of the 21st century. Fragmentation is usually taken to encompass two related phenomena: the expansion of international law to govern new areas of conduct and the diversification of international law to distinct sub-fields, many of which have their own separate tribunals. See, eg, ILC Fragmentation Report 2006.

APPENDIX I

Semi-Structured Interview Template

This is the template used in each of the interviews conducted for this book. It is only a template. Not all of these questions were asked in every interview, nor were they necessarily phrased the same way in each interview or asked in the same order.

- Personal background
  - Where did you grow up?
  - What languages do you currently speak at a level high enough to do at least some work in those languages? Do you speak any other languages at a conversational level?
  - Were you raised in a multilingual environment? When did you learn any languages other than your native language? Did you learn any of those languages for professional motivations?
- Legal education and training
  - Would you describe yourself primarily as having been trained in a common law tradition, a civil law tradition, or some other tradition?
  - In what countries and at what universities or other training institutions did you study law?
  - Would you say that your career has been primarily as a practitioner, primarily as an academic, a mix of the two, or something else?
- Current work
  - About what percentage of your current work focuses on international arbitrations, including commercial, investment, and state-state disputes?
  - Do you currently work primarily as an arbitrator, counsel, consultant/expert witness, academic, officer of an arbitral institution, or in some other role?
- Adjudicative philosophy
  - In general, how do you see your role as an arbitrator, vis-à-vis the parties, counsel and the other arbitrators?
  - Would this vary depending on whether the you were appointed by one of the parties?
  - Do you see your role or practice in deciding the merits of commercial disputes as roughly the same or different from the role or practice of national courts with which you are familiar? In what ways?
  - When acting as an arbitrator, do you encourage the parties to settle their dispute? If so, what techniques do you use to encourage a settlement?
  - How would you characterize your interactions with other members of the tribunal? Does the character of your interactions change over the course of an arbitration, from determinations of early procedural issues like scheduling up to deliberations over an award?
- Decisions on matters of substantive law
  - Suppose that a dispute has arisen over what law is applicable to the merits of the dispute. There is no choice of law provision in the contract, and the parties disagree. How would you go about determining the applicable substantive law?
  - Suppose that the applicable law is not in dispute, and it is the law of some state. Please explain your thought process as to how you would go about ascertaining the content of the relevant law.
  - Have you ever participated in an arbitration where the tribunal applied *lex mercatoria* or general principles as the governing substantive law? If so, as far as you know, how did the tribunal go about determining the content of those principles?

    - Have you ever participated in an arbitration where the tribunal acted under amiable composition powers? If so, as far as you know, can you walk me through the tribunal's process in reaching its decision on the merits?
- Assorted matters pertaining to international commercial arbitration generally
    - What does delocalization mean to you? To what extent do you think international commercial arbitration is or should be delocalized?
    - What, in your experience, are the most important reasons why commercial parties choose to arbitrate their disputes?
    - What characteristics do you see as necessary to be effective as an international arbitrator?
        - Do you see any of these as different from the qualities necessary to be an effective judge?
        - What about arbitration counsel? Do you see any specific qualities necessary for them to be effective?
    - Are there any characteristics, separate from being a good arbitrator, that you think are necessary or helpful to garner appointments as an arbitrator?

Bibliography

Abel, RL, *English Lawyers Between Market and State* (OUP, Oxford 2003)

Abel, RL, 'Transnational Law Practice' (1994) 44 Case Western Reserve L R 737

Afilalo, A, 'Meaning, Ambiguity and Legitimacy: Judicial (Re-) Construction of NAFTA Chapter 11' (2005) 25 Nw J Int'l L & Bus 279

Ahdieh, RB, 'Between Dialogue and Decree: International Review of National Courts' (2004) 79 NYU L R 2029

Alford, RP, 'The American Influence on International Arbitration' (2003) 19 Ohio St J on Disp Resol 69

Alaggia, R, E Lambert, and C Regehr, 'Where is the Justice? Parental Experiences of the Canadian Justice System in Cases of Child Sexual Abuse' (2009) 47 Family Court R 634

American Law Institute, *Restatement of the Law Second, Contracts* (ALI, Philadelphia 1981)

American Law Institute, *Restatement of the Law Second, Conflict of Laws* (ALI, Philadelphia 1971)

Amstutz, M, 'Global (Non-)Law: The Perspective of Evolutionary Jurisprudence' (2008) 9 German L J 465

Ancel, B, 'The *Tronc Commun* Doctrine: Logic and Experience in International Arbitration' (1990) 7(3) J Int'l Arb 3

Andersen, CB, 'The Global Jurisconsultorium of the CISG Revisited' (2009) 13(1) Vindobona J Int'l Comm L & Arb 43

Andersen, CB, 'The Uniform International Sales Law and the Global Jurisconsultorium' (2005) 24 J L & Comm 159

Annells, M, 'Grounded theory method—Philosophical Perspectives, Paradigms of Inquiry, and Postmodernism' (1996) 6(3) Qualitative Health Research 379

Arold, N, *The Legal Culture of the European Court of Human Rights* (Martinus Nijhoff, Leiden 2007)

Arthurs, HW, 'The Role of Global Law Firms in Constructing or Obstructing a Transitional Regime of Labour Law' in RP Appelbaum and others (eds), *Rules and Networks: The Legal Culture of Global Business Transactions* (Hart, Oxford 2001)

Arthurs, HW, 'Globalization of the Mind: Canadian Elites and the Restructuring of Legal Fields' (1997) 12 Can J L & Soc'y 219

Atiyah, PS and RS Summers, *Form and Substance in Anglo-American Law: A Comparative Study of Legal Reasoning, Legal Theory and Legal Institutions* (OUP, Oxford 1979)

Bachand, F, '*Kompetenz-Kompetenz*, Canadian Style' (2009) 25(3) Arb Int'l 431

Baker, JH, *An Introduction to English Legal History* (4th edn Butterworths, London 2002)

Bales, RA and M Eviston, 'The Federal Arbitration Act Needs a Due Process Protocol' (2010) 29(7) Banking & Financial Services Pol'y Report 9

Balthasar, S, 'Kingsbridge Capital Advisors v AlixPartners: What Confidentiality in Arbitration?' (*Kluwer Arbitration Blog* 2012) <http://kluwerarbitrationblog.com/blog/2012/02/03/kingsbridge-capital-advisors-v-alixpartners-what-confidentiality-in-arbitration> accessed 5 August February 2012

Bantekas, I, 'The Proper Law of the Arbitration Clause: A Challenge to the Prevailing Orthodoxy' (2010) 27(1) J Int'l Arb 1

Barnes, WR, 'Contemplating a Civil Law Paradigm for a Future International Commercial Code' (2005) 65 La L R 677

Battersby, L, L Greaves, and R Hunt, 'Legal Redress and Institutional Sexual Abuse: A Study of the Experiences of Deaf and Hard of Hearing Survivors' (2008) 10 Fla Coastal L R 67

Baudoin, J-L and P-G Jobin, *Les Obligations* (6th edn Yvon Blais, Paris 2005)

Beale, H, *Remedies for Breach of Contract* (Sweet & Maxwell, London 1980)

Béguin, J, 'Rapport sur L'adage "Nul ne peut faire justice à soi-même en droit français"' (1966) 18 Trav Ass H Capitant 41

Bell, J, *Judiciaries Within Europe* (CUP, Cambridge 2006)

Bell, J, *French Legal Cultures* (Butterworths, London 2001)

Benjamin, PI, 'The Developing Nations and Certain Legislative Obstacles in the Field of International Commercial Arbitration' in P Sanders (ed), *International Arbitration: Liber Amicorum for Martin Domke* (Martinus Nijhoff, The Hague 1967)

Bennett, T, 'Article 71' in C Bianca and MJ Bonell, *Commentary on the International Sales Law* (Giuffrè, Milan 1987)

Benson, BL, 'To Arbitrate or Litigate: That is the Question' (1999) 8 Eur J L & Econ 91

Benson, BL, 'The Spontaneous Evolution of Commercial Law' (1989) 55 So Econ J 644

Berger, KP, 'Evidentiary Privileges: Best Practice Standards versus/and Arbitral Discretion' (2006) 22(4) J Int'l Arb 501

Berger, KP, *The Creeping Codification of the New Lex Mercatoria* (2nd edn Kluwer, The Hague 2010)

Berger, KP, 'International Arbitral Practice and the UNIDROIT Principles of International Commercial Contracts' (1998) 46 Am J Comp L 129

Berger, KP, 'The Lex Mercatoria Doctrine and the UNIDROIT Principles of International Commercial Contracts' (1997) 28 Law & Pol'y in Int'l Bus 943

Berger, KP, *International Economic Arbitration* (Kluwer, Deventer 1993)

Berger, KP and others, 'The CENTRAL Enquiry on the Use of Transnational Law in International Contract Law and Arbitration' in KP Berger (ed), *The Practice of Transnational Law* (Kluwer, The Hague 2001)

Berman, HJ and C Kaufman, 'The Law of International Transactions (Lex Mercatoria)' (1978) 19 Harv Int'l LJ 221

Bermann, GA, 'Domesticating the New York Convention: the Impact of the Federal Arbitration Act, (2011a) 2(2) J Int'l Disp Settlement 317

Bermann, GA, 'Mandatory rules of law in international arbitration' in F Ferrari and S Kröll (eds), *Conflict of Laws in International Arbitration* (Sellier, Munich 2011b)

Bermann, GA, 'Ascertaining the Parties' Intentions in Arbitral Design' (2009) 113 Penn St L R 1013

Bermann, GA, 'Introduction: Mandatory Rules of Law in International Arbitration' (2007) 18 Am R Int'l Arb 1

Bermann, GA and L Mistelis (eds), *Mandatory Rules in International Arbitration* (Juris, Huntington, NY 2011b)

Bernardini, P, 'International Arbitration and A-National Rules of Law' (2004a) 15(1) ICC Bull 58

Bernardini, P, 'The Role of the International Arbitrator' (2004b) 20(2) Arb Int'l 113

Bernstein, L, 'The Questionable Basis of Article 2's Incorporation Strategy' (1999) 66 U Chicago L R 710

Bersani, MD, 'The Enforcement of Arbitration Awards in China' (1993) 10(2) J Int'l Arb 47

Bidwell, M, 'Do Peripheral Workers do Peripheral Work? Comparing the Use of Highly Skilled Contractors and Regular Employees' (2009) 62 Industrial & Lab Relations R 200

Bingham, T, 'Reasons and Reasons for Reasons' (1988) 4 Arb Int'l 141

Birks, P, 'Rights, Wrongs and Remedies' (2000) 20 OJLS 1

Bishop, D, 'Drafting Arbitration Agreements in the International Arena' (2003) 25 The Advocate (Texas) 32

Bisom-Rapp, S, 'Exceeding our Boundaries: Transnational Employment Law Practice and the Export of American Lawyering Styles to the Global Worksite' (2004) 25 Comp Lab L & Pol'y J 257

Bjorklund, AK, 'The Emerging Civilization of Investment Arbitration' (2009) 113 Penn St L R 1269

Bjorklund, AK, 'Investment Treaty Arbitral Decisions as Jurisprudence Constante' in CB Picker, ID Bunn, and DW Arner (eds), *International Economic Law: The State and Future of the Discipline* (Hart, Oxford 2008)

Blackstone, A, C Uggen, and H McLaughlin, 'Legal Consciousness and Responses to Sexual Harassment' (2009) 43 L & Soc'y R 631

Blanke, G, 'International Arbitration in EC Merger Control: A "Supranational Lesson to Be Learnt"' (2006) 27 Eur Competition L R 324

Blankenburg, E, 'Patterns of Legal Culture: The Netherlands Compared to Neighboring Germany' (1998) 46 Am J Comp L 1

Blessing, M, 'Choice of Substantive Law in International Arbitration' (1997) 14(2) J Int'l Arb 39

Böckstiegel, K-H, 'The Role of Arbitration within Today's Challenges to the World Community and to International Law' (2006) 22(2) Arb Int'l 165

Böckstiegel, K-H, 'Case Management by Arbitrators: Experiences and Suggestions' in G Aksen and others (eds), *Global Reflections on International Law, Commerce and Dispute Resolution: Liber Americorum for Robert Briner* (ICC, Paris 2005)

Böckstiegel, K-H, 'The Role of Party Autonomy in International Arbitration' (1997) 62(SUM) Disp Resol J 24

Bond, SR, 'Expert Report of Stephen Bond Esq in *Esso/BHP v Plowman*' (1995) 11(3) Arb Int'l 273

Bond, SR, 'How to Draft an Arbitration Clause (Revisited)' [1990] ICC Bull 14

Bonell, MJ, 'Die UNIDROIT-Prinzipien der internationalen Handelsvertrage: Eine neue Lex Mercatoria?' [1996] Zeitschrift für Rechtsvergleichung 152

Borchers, PJ, 'Categorical Exceptions to Party Autonomy in Private International Law' (2008) 82 Tulane L R 1645

Born, GB, *International Commercial Arbitration: Commentary and Materials* (2nd edn Kluwer, The Hague 2009)

Borris, C, 'The Reconciliation of Conflicts between Common Law and Civil Law Principles in the Arbitration Process' in SN Frommel and BAK Rider (eds), *Conflicting Legal Cultures in Commercial Arbitration* (Kluwer, London 1999)

Terdiman (tr), P Bourdieu, 'The Force of Law: Toward a Sociology of the Juridical Field' (1987) 38 Hastings L J 805

Bourdieu, P and LJD Wacquant, *An Invitation to Reflexive Sociology* (U Chicago P, Chicago 1992)

Bourdieu, P and LJD Wacquant, 'Epilogue: On the Possibility of a Field of World Sociology' in P Bourdieu and JL Coleman (eds), *Social Theory for a Changing Society* (Westview, Boulder 1991)

Brekoulakis, S, 'The Relevance of the Interests of Third Parties in Arbitration: Taking a Closer Look at the Elephant in the Room' (2009) 113 Penn St L R 1165

Brennan, T, L Epstein and N Staudt, 'The Political Economy of Judging' (2009) 93 Minn L R 1503

Bridge, M, 'Uniformity and Diversity in the Law of International Sales' (2003) 15 Pace Int'l L R 55

Briggs, A, *Agreements on Jurisdiction and Choice of Law* (OUP, Oxford 2008)

Briggs, A, *The Conflict of Laws* (1st edn OUP, Oxford 2002)

Briner, R, 'Globalization and the Future of Courts of Arbitration' (2000) 2 Eur J L Reform 439

Brower, CN and JK Sharpe, 'The Creeping Codification of Transnational Commercial Law: An Arbitrator's Perspective' (2004) 35 Va J Int'l L 199

Brown, C, *A Common Law of International Adjudication* (OUP, Oxford 2007)

Brown, AC, 'Presumption Meets Reality: An Exploration of the Confidentiality Obligation in International Commercial Arbitration' (2001) 16 Am U Int'l L R 969

Brubaker, JR, 'The Judge Who Knew too Much: Issue Conflicts in International Adjudication' (2008) 26 Berkeley J Int'l L 111

Brubaker, JR and MW Kulikowsky, 'A Sporting Chance? The Court of Arbitration for Sport Regulates Arbitrator-Counsel Role Switching' (2010) 10 Va Sports and Entertainment L J 1

Bruinsma, F and D Nelken (eds), *Explorations in Legal Cultures* (Elsevier, The Hague 2007)

Bühring-Uhle, C, *Arbitration and Mediation in International Business* (1st edn Kluwer, The Hague 1996)

Bühring-Uhle, C and others, 'The Arbitrator as Mediator: Some Recent Empirical Insights' (2003) 20(1) J Int'l Arb 81

Burkhart, AM, 'Real Estate Practice in the Twenty-First Century' (2008) 72 Missouri L R 1031

Buys, C, 'The Tensions between Confidentiality and Transparency in International Arbitration' (2003) 14 Am R Int'l Arb 121

Calliess, G-P, 'The Making of Transnational Contract Law' (2007) 14 Indiana J Global Leg Stud 469

Calliess, G-P and HB Hoffmann, 'Judicial Services for Global Governance—Made in Germany?' (2009) 10 German L J 115

Calliess, G-P and M Renner, 'Transnationalizing Private Law: The Public and Private Dimensions of Transnational Commercial Law' (2009) 10 German L J 1341

Cappelletti, M, JK Merryman, and JM Perillo, *The Italian Legal System: An Introduction* (Stanford UP, Stanford 1967)

Carbonneau, TE, 'Judicial Approbation in the Building of the Civilization of Arbitration' (2009a) 113 Penn St L R 1343

Carbonneau, TE, 'Arguments in Favor of the Triumph of Arbitration' (2009b) 10 Cardozo J Conflict Resol 395

Carbonneau, TE, 'Arbitral Law-Making' (2004) 25 Mich J Int'l L 1183

Carbonneau, TE, 'Arbitral Adjudication: A Comparative Assessment of Its Remedial and Substantive Status in Transnational Commerce' (1984) 19 Tex Int'l L J 33

Carbonneau, TE and F Janson, 'Cartesian Logic and Frontier Politics: French and American Concepts of Arbitrability' (1994) 2 Tulane J Int'l & Comp L 193

Carducci, G, 'The Arbitration Reform in France: Domestic and International Arbitration Law' (2012) 28(1) Arb Int'l 125

Carlston, KS, 'Psychological and Sociological Aspects of the Judicial and Arbitration Process' in P Sanders (ed), *Liber Amicorum for Martin Domke* (Martinus Nijhoff, The Hague 1967)

Carter, JH, 'Improving Life with the Party-Appointed Arbitrator: Clearer Conduct Guidelines for Nonneutrals' (2000) 11 Am R Int'l Arb 295

Carter, JH, 'Rights and Obligations of the Arbitrator' (1997) 52(JAN) Disp Resol J 56

Cassin, R, *De l'exception tirée de l'inexécution dans les rapports synallagmatiques (exception non adimpleti contractus) et de ses relations avec le droit de retention, la compensation et la resolution* (Thèse, Paris 1914)

Chamberlin, BF and others, 'Searching for Patterns in the Laws Governing Access to Records and Meetings in the Fifty States by Using Multiple Research Tools' (2007) 18 U Fla J L & Pub Pol'y 415

Chartered Institute of Arbitrators, 'CIArb Costs of International Arbitration Survey 2011' (2011) <http://www.ciarb.org/conferences/costs/2011/09/28/CIArb%20costs%20of%20International%20Arbitration%20Survey%202011.pdf>

Chatterjee, C, 'The Reality of the Party Autonomy Rule in International Arbitration' (2003) 20(6) J Int'l Arb 539

Cheng, T-H, 'Precedent and Control in Investment Treaty Arbitration' (2007) 20 Fordham Int'l L J 1014

Furmston, MP, *Cheshire, Fifoot & Furmston's Law of Contract* (14th edn Butterworths, London 2001)

Chimni, BS, 'International Institutions Today: An Imperial Global State in the Making' (2004) 15 EJIL 1

Christie, RH, *The Law of Contract in South Africa* (Butterworths, Durban 2001)

Coe Jr, JJ, *International Commercial Arbitration: American Principles and Practice in a Global Context* (Transnational Publishers, Irvington 1997)

Coester-Waltjen, D, 'The New Approach to Breach of Contract in German Law' in N Cohen and E McKendrick (eds), *Comparative Remedies for Breach of Contract* (Hart, Oxford 2005)

Cohen, L and others, *Research Methods in Education* (6th edn Routledge, London 2007)

Cohen, N, 'Introduction' in N Cohen and E McKendrick (eds), *Comparative Remedies for Breach of Contract* (Hart, Oxford 2005)

Cole, T, 'Commercial Arbitration in Japan: Contributions to the Debate on "Japanese Non-Litigiousness"' (2007) 40 NYU J Int'l L & Politics 29

Coleman, JL, *The Practice of Principle: In Defence of a Pragmatist Approach to Legal Theory* (OUP, Oxford 2001)

Collins, A, 'Sprechen Sie Englisch?' (2010) 97 Eur Lawyer 16

Collins, H, *Regulating Contracts* (OUP, Oxford 1999)

Collins, L (ed), *Dicey and Morris on The Conflict of Laws* (14th edn Sweet & Maxwell, London 2000)

Collins, M, 'Do International Arbitral Tribunals Have Any Obligations to Encourage Settlement of the Disputes Before Them' (2003) 19(3) Arb Int'l 333

Commission of the European Communities, *Proposal for a Regulation of the European Parliament and the Council on the law applicable to contractual relations (Rome I)* (2005/0621 (COD))

Commission, JP, 'Precedents in Investment Treaty Arbitration: a Citation Analysis of a Developing Jurisprudence' (2007) 24 J Int'l Arb 129

Conlin, Jan M and Thomas C Mahlum, 'Trial Tactics in International Arbitration' (2012) 9(1) Executive Counsel, <http://www.ecounselmag.com/i44/trial-tactics-in-international-arbitrations/>

Connolly, DA, HM Gordon, and HL Price, 'Judging the Credibility of Historic Child Sexual Abuse Complainants: How Judges Describe their Decisions' (2009) 15 Psychology, Pub Pol'y & L 102

Cooper, JM, 'Competing Legal Cultures and Legal Reform: The Battle of Chile' (2008) 29 Mich J Int'l L 501

Cooter, RD, 'Three Effects of Social Norms on Law: Expression, Deterrence, and Internalization' (2000) 79 Oregon L R 1

Corbin, AL, 'The Interpretation of Words and the Parol Evidence Rule' (1964) 50 Cornell L Q 161

Corbin, AL, *Contracts* (2nd edn West Publishing, St Paul 1963)

Corbin, AL, 'The Parol Evidence Rule' (1944) 53 Yale L J 603

Corbin, J and AL Strauss, *Basics of Qualitative Research: Techniques and Procedures for Developing Grounded Theory* (3rd edn Sage, Los Angeles 2008)

Cotterrell, R, 'The Concept of Legal Culture' in D Nelken (ed), *Comparing Legal Cultures* (Dartmouth, Aldershot 1997)

Cotterrell, R, *The Sociology of Law: An Introduction* (Butterworths, London 1992)

Craig, WL, 'Uses and Abuses of Appeal from Awards' (1988) 4(3) Arb Int'l 174

Craig, WL, WW Park, and J Paulsson, *International Chamber of Commerce Arbitration* (3rd edn OUP, Oxford 2001)

Crawford, J, 'Treaty and Contract in Investment Arbitration' (2008) 24(3) Arb Int'l 351

Crawford, J and S Olleson, 'The Exception of Non-Performance: Links between the Law of Treaties and the Law of State Responsibility' (2001) 21 Australian Ybk Int'l L 55

Cremades, BM, 'Overcoming the Clash of Legal Cultures: The Role of Interactive Arbitration' in SN Frommel and BAK Rider (eds), *Conflicting Legal Cultures in International Arbitration* (Kluwer, London 1999)

Crowter, HS and AGV Tobin, 'Ensuring that Arbitration Remains a Preferred Option for International Dispute Resolution' (2002) 19(4) J Int'l Arb 301

Cuniberti, G, 'Beyond Contract—The Case for Default Arbitration in International Commercial Disputes' (2009) 32 Fordham Int'l L R 417

Curran, VG, 'The Interpretive Challenge to Uniformity' (1995) 15 J L & Comm 175

Daly, MP, 'Come One, Come All: The New and Developing World of Nonsignatory Arbitration and Class Arbitration' (2007) 62 U Miami L R 95

Dammann, J and H Hansmann, 'Globalizing Commercial Litigation' (2008) 94 Cornell L R 1

Danneman, G, *An Introduction to German Civil and Commercial Law* (British Institute for International and Commercial Law, London 1993)

Dasser, F, 'Mouse or Monster? Some Facts and Figures on the Lex Mercatoria' in R Zimmermann (ed), *Globalisierung und Entstaatlichung des Rechts* (Mohr Siebeck, Tübingen 2008)

David, R, 'L'avenir de l'arbitrage' in P Sanders (ed), *Liber Amicorum for Martin Domke* (Martinus Nijhoff, The Hague 1967)

David, R, *Le Droit français I: Les Données fondamentales du droit français* (Librairie générale de droit et de jurisprudence, Paris 1960)

Davis, KR, 'Unconventional Wisdom: A New Look at Articles V and VII of the Convention on the Recognition and Enforcement of Foreign Arbitral Awards' (2002) 37 Tex Int'l L J 43

de Boer, TM, 'The Missing Link: Some Thoughts on the Relationship Between Private International Law and Comparative Law' in K Boele-Woelki and others (eds), *Comparability and Evaluation: Essays on Comparative Law, Private International Law and International Commercial Arbitration in Honour of Dimitra Kokkini-Latridou* (TMC Asser Institut, The Hague 1994)

De Ly, F, 'Judicial Review of the Substance of Arbitral Awards' in K Boele-Woelki and others (eds), *Comparability and Evaluation: Essays on Comparative Law, Private International Law and International Commercial Arbitration in Honour of Dimitra Kokkini-Latridou* (TMC Asser Institut, The Hague 1994)

de Vera, C, 'Arbitrating Harmony: "Med-Arb" and the Confluence of Culture and Rule of Law in the Resolution of International Commercial Disputes in China' (2004) 18 Columbia J Asian L 149

Delaney, J and DB Magraw, 'Procedural Transparency' in Peter Muchlinski and others (eds), *The Oxford Handbook of International Investment Law* (OUP, Oxford 2008)

Delaume, GR, 'Comparative Analysis as a Basis of Law in State Contracts: The Myth of Lex Mercatoria' (1989) 63 Tulane L R 575

Delaume, GR, *Law and Practice of Transnational Contracts* (Oceana, New York 1988)

Del Duca, LF, 'Developing Global Transnational Harmonization Procedures for the Twenty-First Century: The Accelerating Pace of Common and Civil Law Convergence' (2007) 42 Tex Int'l L J 625

Della Noce, DJ, 'The Beaten Path to Mediator Quality Assurance: The Emerging Narrative of Consensus and its Institutional Functions' (2004) 19 Ohio St J on Disp Resol 937

Derains, Y, 'Jurisprudence of International Commercial Arbitrators Concerning the Determination of the Proper Law of the Contract' [1996] Int'l Bus L J 514

Derains, Y and E Schwartz, *A Guide to the New ICC Rules of Arbitration* (1st edn Kluwer, The Hague 1998)

Dey, I, *Grounding Grounded Theory: Guidelines for qualitative inquiry* (Academic Press, San Diego 1999)

Dezalay, Y, 'From a Symbolic Boom to a Marketing Bust: Genesis and Reconstruction of a Field of Legal and Political Expertise at the Crossroads of a Europe Opening to the Atlantic' (2007) 32 Law & Soc Inquiry 161

Dezalay, Y and BG Garth, *Dealing in Virtue: International Commercial Arbitration and the Construction of a Transnational Legal Order* (U Chicago P, Chicago 1996)

Dezalay, Y and BG Garth, 'Merchants of Law as Moral Entrepreneurs: Constructing International Justice from the Competition for Transnational Business Disputes' (1995) 29 Law & Soc'y R 27

Dibadj, R, 'Panglossian Transnationalism' (2008) 44 Stanford J Int'l L 253

DiMatteo, LA, 'An International Contract Law Formula: The Informality of International Business Transactions Plus the Internationalization of Contract Law Equals Unexpected Contractual Liability' (1997) 23 Syracuse J Int'l L 67

Domke, M, *Commercial Arbitration* (Prentice-Hall, Englewood Cliffs 1965)

Donahey, MS, 'The Independence and Neutrality of Arbitrators' (1992) 9(4) J Int'l Arb 31

Draetta, U, RB Lake, and VP Nanda, *Breach and Adaption in International Contracts: An Introduction to Lex Mercatoria* (Butterworths, Salem 1992)

Drahozal, CR, 'Why Arbitrate? Substantive Versus Procedural Theories of Private Judging' (2011) 22 Am R Int'l Arb 163

Drahozal, CR, 'Private Ordering and International Commercial Arbitration' (2009a) 113 Penn St L R 1031

Drahozal, CR, 'Business Courts and the Future of Arbitration' (2009b) 10 Cardozo J Conflict Resol 491

Drahozal, CR, 'Arbitration by the Numbers: The State of Empirical Research on International Commercial Arbitration' (2006a) 22(2) Arb Int'l 291

Drahozal, CR, 'New Experiences of International Arbitration in the United States' (2006b) 54 Am J Comp L 233

Drahozal, CR, 'Contracting out of National Law: An Empirical Look at the New Law Merchant' (2005) 80 Notre Dame L R 523

Drahozal, CR, 'Of Rabbits and Rhinoceri: A Survey of Empirical Research on International Commercial Arbitration' (2003) 20(1) J Int'l Arb 23

Drahozal, CR, 'The Effect of Competition Among Arbitral Venues on Choice of Situs in ICC Arbitration Proceedings', Annual Meeting of the Canadian Law & Economics Association (Toronto 27 September 2002) <http://www.chass.utoronto.ca/clea/Drahozal.pdf> accessed 28 November 2010

Drahozal, CR, 'Commercial Norms, Commercial Codes, and International Commercial Arbitration' (2000) 33 Vanderbilt J Transnat'l L 79

Drahozal, CR and SJ Ware, 'Why Do Businesses Use (or not Use) Arbitration Clauses?' (2010) 25 Ohio St J on Disp Resol 433

Drahozal, CR and S Zyontz, 'Private Regulation of Consumer Arbitration' (2012) 49 Tennessee L R 289

Halls, WD (tr), E Durkheim, *The Rules of Sociological Method and Selected Texts on Sociology and its Method* (Macmillan, London 1988)

Epstein, L and others, 'Ideological Drift Among Supreme Court Justices: Who, When, and How Important?' (2007) 101 Nw U L R 1383

Ellickson, Robert C, 'The Market for Social Norms' (2001) 3(1) Am L & Econ R 1

Ellickson, Robert C, 'Law and Economics Discovers Social Norms' (1998) 27 J Leg Stud 537

Elsing, SH and JM Townsend, 'Bridging the Common Law—Civil Law Divide in International Arbitration, (2002) 18(1) Arb Int'l 59

Epstein, L and J Knight, *The Choices Justices Make* (CQ Press, Washington 1998)

Erbe, N, 'The Global Popularity and Promise of Facilitative ADR' (2004) 18 Temple Int'l & Comp L J 343

Etienne, M, 'The Declining Utility of the Right to Counsel in Federal Criminal Courts: An Empirical Study on the Diminished Role of Defense Attorney Advocacy under the Sentencing Guidelines' (2004) 92 Cal L R 425

Farnsworth, EA, *Contracts* (3rd edn Aspen Law and Business, New York 1999)

Farnsworth, EA, 'An International Restatement: The UNIDROIT Principles of International Commercial Contracts' (1997) 26(1) U Baltimore L R 1

Faulconbridge, JR and D Muzio, 'Legal Education, Globalization, and Cultures of Professional Practice' (2009) 22 Georgetown J Leg Ethics 1335

Fauchald, Ole Kristian, 'The Legal Reasoning of ICSID Tribunals: An Empirical Analysis' (2008) 19(2) Eur J Int'l L 301

Fellas, J, 'A Fair and Efficient International Arbitration Process' (2004) 59(APR) Disp Resol J 78

Ferguson, RB, 'The Adjudication of Commercial Disputes and the Legal System in Modern England' (1980) 7 British J L & Soc 141

Ferrari, F, 'The CISG's Uniform Interpretation by Courts—An Update' (2005) 9 Vindobona J Int'l Comm L & Arb 233

Ferrari, F, 'The International Sphere of Application of the 1988 Ottawa Convention on International Factoring' (1999) 8 Int'l Bus L J 895

Feutrill, M and N Rubins, 'The Preparation of Expert Evidence in International Commercial Arbitration: Practical Aspects' [2009] Int'l Bus L J 307

Flood, J, 'Lawyers, Law Firms and the Stabilization of Transnational Business' (2008) 28 Northwestern J Int'l L & Bus 489

Flood, J, 'Lawyers as Sanctifiers: The Role of Elite Law Firms in International Business Transactions' (2007) 14 Indiana J Global Leg Stud 35

Flood, J, 'Megalawyering in the Global Order: the cultural, social and economic transformation of global legal practice' (1996) 3(1/2) Int'l J Leg Profession 169

Fortier, LY, 'The New, New *Lex Mercatoria*, or, Back to the Future' (2001) 17(2) Arb Int'l 121

Foxall, G, 'What Judges Maximize: Toward an Economic Psychology of the Judicial Utility Function' (2005) 25 Liverpool L R 177

Franck, SD, 'Empirically Evaluating ICSID' (2011) 51(4) Va J Int'l L 977

Franck, SD, 'Development and Outcomes of Investment Treaty Arbitration' (2009) 50 Harv Int'l L R 435

Franck, SD, 'An Empirical Analysis of Investment Treaty Awards' (2007) 101 Am Soc'y Int'l L Proc 214

Franck, SD, 'The Role of International Arbitrators' (2006) 12 ILSA J Int'l & Comp L 499

Franck, SD, 'The Legitimacy Crisis in Investment Treaty Arbitration: Privatizing Public International Law Through Inconsistent Decisions' (2005) 73 Fordham L R 1521

Franck, SD, 'The Liability of International Arbitrators: A Comparative Analysis and Proposal for Qualified Immunity' (2000) 20 NY Law School J Int'l & Comp L 1

Frederickson, DG and HG Frederickson, *Measuring the Performance of the Hollow State* (Georgetown UP, Washington DC 2006)

Friedman, LM, 'Erewhon: The Coming Global Legal Order' (2001) 37 Stan J Int'l L 347

Friedman, LM, 'The Concept of Legal Culture: A Reply' in D Nelken (ed), *Comparing Legal Cultures* (Dartmouth, Aldershot 1997)

Friedman, LM, 'Borders: On the Emerging Sociology of Transnational Law' (1996) 32 Stanford J Int'l L 65

Friedman, LM, *The Republic of Choice* (Harvard UP, Cambridge 1990)

Friedmann, D, 'Rights and Remedies' in N Cohen and E McKendrick (eds), *Comparative Remedies for Breach of Contract* (Hart, Oxford 2005)

Fry, J, 'The New ICC Rules of Arbitration', *6th Annual Fordham Conference of International Arbitration and Mediation* (New York, 13 June 2011)

Gaillard, E, *Legal Theory of International Arbitration* (Martinus Nijhoff, Leiden 2010a)

Gaillard, E, 'The Representations of International Arbitration' (2010b) 1(2) J Int'l Disp Settlement 271

Gaillard, E, 'Transnational Law: A Legal System or Method of Decision Making?' (2001) 17(1) Arb Int'l 59.

Gaillard, E, 'Enforcement of Awards Set Aside in the Country of Origin: The French Experience' in AJ van den Berg (ed), *Improving the Efficiency of Arbitration Agreements and Awards: 40 Years of Application of the New York Convention* (1st edn Kluwer, The Hague 1999)

Gaillard, E and J Savage (eds), *Fouchard Gaillard Goldman on International Commercial Arbitration* (1st English edn Kluwer, The Hague 1999)

Galanter, M, 'The Vanishing Trial: An Examination of Trials and Related Matters in Federal and State Court' (2004) 1 J Empirical Leg Stud 459

Garapon, A, 'French Legal Culture and the Shock of Globalisation' (1995) 4 Soc & Leg Stud 493

Garro, AM, 'The Gap-Filling Role of the UNIDROIT Principles in International Sales Law: Some Comments on the Interplay Between the Principles and the CISG' (1995) 69 Tulane L R 1149

Garro, AM, 'Reconciliation of Legal Traditions in the UN Convention on Contracts for the International Sale of Goods' (1989) 23 Int'l Lawyer 443

Garth, BG, 'Tilting the Justice System: From ADR as Idealistic Movement to a Segmented Market in Dispute Resolution' (2002) 18 Georgia St U L R 927

Garth, BG, 'How to Become an International Commercial Arbitrator' (1997) 8 World Arb & Med Rep 10

Gaubatz, KT and M MacArthur, 'How International is "International" Law?' (2001) 22 Mich J Int'l L 239

Gearing, M, 'Jivraj v Hashwani: A Pro-Choice, Corrective Ruling from the Supreme Court' (*Kluwer Arbitration Blog* 2011) <http://kluwerarbitrationblog.com/blog/2011/09/22/jivraj-v-hashwani-a-pro-choice-corrective-ruling-from-the-supreme-court/> accessed 31 August 2012

Gélinas, F, 'Arbitration and the Challenge of Globalisation' (2000) 17(4) J Int'l Arb 117

Gergen, MP, 'A Theory of Self-Help Remedies in Contract' (2009) 89 Boston U L R 1397

Gergen, MP, 'The Law's Response to Exit and Loyalty in Contract Disputes' in N Cohen and E McKendrick (eds), *Comparative Remedies for Breach of Contract* (Hart, Oxford 2005)

Gessner, V, A Hoeland, and C Varga (eds), *European Legal Cultures* (Dartmouth, Aldershot 1996)

Ghestin, J, C Jamin and M Billiau, *Traité de droit civil—Les effets du contrat—vol 5—les obligations* (3rd edn Librairie générale de droit et de jurisprudence, Paris 2001)

Gibson, CS, 'Arbitration, Civilization and Public Policy: Seeking Counterpoise Between Arbitral Autonomy and the Public Policy Defense in View of Foreign Mandatory Public Law' (2009) 113 Penn St L R 1227

Gilmore, G, *The Death of Contract* (1st edn Ohio St U P, Columbus 1974)

Ginsburg, T, 'The Culture of Arbitration' (2003) 39 Vanderbilt J Transnat'l L 1335

Giovannini, T, 'Qui contrôle les pouvoirs des arbitres: les parties, l'arbitre ou la cour d'arbitrage?', Société de législation comparée: Les arbitres internationaux (Paris, 4 February 2005)

Giovannini, T, 'The Psychological Aspects of Dispute Resolution: Commentary' in AJ van den Berg (ed), *International Commercial Arbitration: Important Contemporary Questions* (Kluwer, The Hague 2003)

Glaser, BG, *Basics of Grounded Theory Analysis: Emergence vs. Forcing* (Sociology Press, Mill Valley 1998)

Glaser, BG and AL Strauss, *The Discovery of Grounded Theory: Strategies for Qualitative Research* (Aldine, Chicago 1967)

Glenn, HP, 'Comparative Law and Legal Practice: On Removing the Borders' (2001) 75 Tulane L R 977

Glenn, HP, 'Globalization and Dispute Resolution' (2000) 19(APR) Civil Justice Q 136

Goldman, B, *La lex mercatoria dans les contrats et l'arbitrage internationaux* (Clunet, Paris 1979)

Goldstajn, A, 'The New Law Merchant' [1961] J Bus L 12

Gotanda, JY, 'Settling Arbitrators' Fees: An International Survey' (2000) 33 Vanderbilt J Transnat'l L 779

Graffi, LD, 'Securing Harmonized Effects of Arbitration Agreements under the New York Convention' (2006) 28 Houston J Int'l L 663

Greene, E, K Hayman, and M Motyl, '"Shouldn't We Consider?" Jury Discussions of Forbidden Topics and Effects on Damage Awards' (2008) 14 Psychology, Pub Pol'y & L 194

Greig, DW, 'Reciprocity, Proportionality and the Law of Treaties' (1994) 34 Va J Int'l L 275

Griffin, PR, 'Recent Trends on the Conduct of International Arbitration, Discovery Procedures and Witness Hearings' (2000) 17(2) J Int'l Arb 19

Grigera Naón, HA, 'Latin American Arbitration Culture and the ICC Arbitration System' in SN Frommel and BAK Rider (eds), *Conflicting Legal Cultures in Commercial Arbitration* (Kluwer, London 1999)

Grizel, F, 'Control of Awards and Re-Centralisation of International Commercial Arbitration' (2006) 25(APR) Civil Justice Q 166

Grosheide, FW, 'Legal Borrowing and Drafting International Commercial Contracts: Some Methodological Reflections' in K Boele-Woelki and others (eds), *Comparability and Evaluation: Essays on Comparative Law, Private International Law and International Commercial Arbitration in Honour of Dimitra Kokkini-Latridou* (TMC Asser Institut, The Hague 1994)

Gruner, DM, 'Accounting for the Public Interest in International Arbitration: The Need for Procedural and Structural Reform' (2003) 41 Colum J Transnat'l L 923

Gu, W, 'Confidentiality Revisited: Blessing or Curse in International Arbitration?' (2004), 15 Am Rev Int'l Arb 607

Gunz, HP and SP Gunz, 'The Lawyer's Response to Organizational Professional Conflict: An Empirical Study of the Ethical Decision Making of In-House Counsel' (2002) 39 Am Bus L J 241

Gutteridge, HC, *Comparative Law, An Introduction to the Comparative Method of Legal Study and Research* (2nd edn CUP, Cambridge 1949)

Haarhuis, CK and B Niemeijer, 'Vanishing or Increasing Trials in the Netherlands?' [2006] J Disp Resol 71

Hacking, D, 'Ethics, Elitism, Eligibility: A Response' (1998) 15(4) J Int'l Arb 73

Hacking, D, 'International Commercial Arbitrations—Recent Developments in London, Paris and Stockholm,' Society of Maritime Arbitrators, New York, 20 February 1979

Haines, CG, 'General Observations on the Effects of Personal, Political, and Economic Influences in the Decisions of Judges' (1922) 17 Illinois L R 96

Hamilton, CA and C Maestre de Robles, 'Madrid Update: Confidentiality in Arbitration, An Issue for Personal Privacy' (2009) 24(5) Mealey's Int'l Arb Rep 18

Hanotiau, B, 'Consent to Arbitration: Do We Share a Common Vision?' (2011) 27(4) Arb Int'l 539

Hansen, PI, 'Judicialization and Globalization in the North American Free Trade Agreement' (2003) 38 Texas Int'l L J 489

Harris, A, 'Diverting and Abdicating Judicial Discretion: Cultural, Political, and Procedural Dynamics in California Juvenile Justice' (2007) 41 Law & Soc'y R 387

Harris, PR and RT Moran, *Managing Cultural Differences* (3rd edn Gulf Publishing, Houston 1991)

Hartkamp, AS, 'The UNIDROIT Principles for International Commercial Contracts and the United Nations Convention on Contracts for the International Sale of Goods' in K

Boele-Woelki and others (eds), *Comparability and Evaluation: Essays on Comparative Law, Private International Law and International Commercial Arbitration in Honour of Dimitra Kokkini-Latridou* (TMC Asser Institut, The Hague 1994)

Haskell, PG, *Why Lawyers Behave As They Do* (Westview, Boulder 1998)

Havel, B, 'The Constitution in an Era of Supranational Adjudication' (2000) 78 NC L R 257

Haydn-Williams, J, 'International Commercial Arbitration in Barbados' (2011) 77(2) Arbitration 184.

Heldrich, A and GM Rehm, 'Modernisation of the German Law of Obligations: Harmonisation of Civil Law and Common Law in the Recent Reform of the German Civil Code' in N Cohen and E McKendrick (eds), *Comparative Remedies for Breach of Contract* (Hart, Oxford 2005)

Helmer, EV, 'International Commercial Arbitration: Americanized, "Civilized", or Harmonized?' (2003) 19 Ohio St J on Disp Resol 35

Herber, R, 'Article 3' in P Schlechtriem and I Schwenzer (eds), *Commentary on the UN Convention on Contracts for the International Sale of Goods (CISG)* (2nd English edn OUP, Oxford 2005)

Hermann, AH, *Judges, Law and Businessmen* (Kluwer, Deventer 1983)

Hermida, J, 'Convergence of Civil Law and Common Law Contracts in the Space Field' (2004) 34 HK L J 339

Heuzé, V, *La vente internationale de marchandises: droit uniforme* (Joly Éditions, Paris 1992)

Hirsch, M, 'The Sociology of International Economic Law: Sociological Analysis of the Regulation of Regional Agreements in the World Trading System' (2008) 19 EJIL 277

Hirsch, M, 'The Sociology of International Law: Invitation to Study International Rules in their Social Context' (2005) 55 U Toronto L J 891

Lord Hoffman, 'The Intolerable Wrestle with Words and Meanings' (1997) 114 South African L J 656

Holmes, OW, 'The Path of the Law' (1897) 10 Harv L R 457

Hondius, EH, 'The Judiciary: An Obstacle to the Harmonisation of Civil and Common Law?' in K Boele-Woelki and others (eds), *Comparability and Evaluation: Essays on Comparative Law, Private International Law and International Commercial Arbitration in Honour of Dimitra Kokkini-Latridou* (TMC Asser Institut, The Hague 1994)

Honnold, JO, *Uniform Law for International Sales* (3rd edn Kluwer, The Hague 1999)

Honnold, JO (ed), *Documentary History of the Uniform Law for International Sales* (Kluwer, Deventer 1989)

Honnold, JO, 'The Sales Convention in Action—Uniform International Words: Uniform Application?' (1988) 8 J L & Comm 207

Hornung, R, 'Article 71' in P Schlechtriem and I Schwenzer (eds), *Commentary on the UN Convention on Contracts for the International Sale of Goods (CISG)* (2nd English edn OUP, Oxford 2005)

Huber, M, *Acts and Documents Concerning the Organization of the Court*, PCIJ Series D, Addendum to No 2, *Revision of the Rules of Court* (1926)

International Chamber of Commerce, '2007 Annual Statistical Report' (2008) 19(1) ICC Bull 5

International Chamber of Commerce Commission on Arbitration, 'Techniques for Controlling Time and Costs in Arbitration' (2007) <http://www.iccwbo.org/uploadedFiles/TimeCost_E.pdf> accessed 28 November 2010

International Council for Commercial Arbitration, *ICCA's Guide to the Interpretation of the 1958 New York Convention: A Handbook for Judges*, available at <http://www.arbitration-icca.org/publications/NYC_Guide.html> accessed 31 August 2012

International Law Association, International Commercial Arbitration Committee, 'Report and Recommendations—Ascertaining the Contents of the Applicable Law in International Commercial Arbitration', 2008, LG Radicati di Brozolo and M Friedman, rapporteurs, published in (2010) 26(2) Arb Int'l, 193

International Law Association, International Commercial Arbitration Committee, 'Report on Public Policy as A Bar to Enforcement of International Arbitral Awards', 2002, P Mayer and A Sheppard, rapporteurs, published in (2003) 19(2) Arb Int'l 249

International Law Association, 'Adoption of a Resolution on Transnational Rules', 65th International Law Association Conference (Cairo, 26 April 1992) published in E Gaillard (ed), *Transnational Rules in International Commercial Arbitration* (ICC, Paris 1992)

International Law Association, 'Discussion of the ILA Resolution on Transnational Rules', 65th International Law Association Conference (Cairo, 26 April 1992) published in E Gaillard (ed), *Transnational Rules in International Commercial Arbitration* (ICC, Paris 1992)

International Law Association, *Resolution on Public Policy*, ILA Resolution 2002/2, available at <http://www.newyorkconvention.org/publications/full-text-publications/general/ila-resolution-on-public-policy-2002> accessed 10 December 2012

International Law Commission, 'Conclusions of the work of the Study Group on the Fragmentation of International Law: Difficulties arising from the Diversification and Expansion of International Law', 2006, Report of the Study Group of the International Law Commission, UN Doc A/CN4/L682, 13 April 2006

Isele, T, 'The Principle Iura Novit Curia in International Commercial Arbitration' (2010) 13(1) Int'l Arb L R 14

Ivkovic, SK and VP Hans, 'Jurors' Evaluations of Expert Testimony: Judging the Messenger and the Message' (2003) 28 L & Soc Inquiry 441

Jessup, PC, *Transnational Law* (Yale UP, New Haven 1956)

Jacquet, Jean-Michel, 'Avons-nous besoin d'une jurisprudence arbitrale?' [2010] *Revue de l'Arbitrage* 445

Jolivet, E, 'Access to Information and Awards' (2006) 22(2) Arb Int'l 265

Jones, D, 'Acquisition of Skills and Accreditation in International Arbitration' (2006) 22(2) Arb Int'l 275

Jukier, R, 'Where Law and Pedagogy Meet in the Transsystemic Contracts Classroom' (2005) 50 McGill L J 789

Kaczmarek, CB, 'Public Law Deserves Public Justice: Why Public Law Arbitrators Should be Required to Issue Written, Publishable Opinions' (2000) 4 Employee Rights & Employment Policy J 285

Karton, J, 'A Conflict of Interests—Seeking a Way Forward on Publication of International Arbitral Awards' (2012) 27(3) Arb Int'l 441

Karton, J and L de Germiny, 'Has the CISG Advisory Council Come of Age?' (2009) 27 Berkeley J Int'l L 448

Katz, AW, 'On the Use of Practitioner Surveys in Commercial Law Research' (2000) 98 Mich L R 2760

Kaufmann-Kohler, G, 'Soft Law in International Arbitration: Codification and Normativity' (2010) 1(2) J Int'l Disp Settlement 283

Kaufmann-Kohler, G, 'Arbitral Precedent: Dream, Necessity or Excuse?' (2007) 23(3) Arb Int'l 357

Kaufmann-Kohler, G, '"The Governing Law—Fact or Law?"—A Transnational Rule on Establishing its Contents' in M Wirth (ed), *Best Practices in International Arbitration* (ASA Special Series No 26, July 2006)

Kaufmann-Kohler, G, 'The Arbitrator and the Law: Does He/She Know It? Apply It? How? And a Few More Questions' (2005) 21(4) Arb Int'l 631

Kaufmann-Kohler, G, 'Beyond Gadgetry—Substantive New Concepts to Improve Arbitral Efficiency' (2004a) 5(1) J World Invs & Trade 60

Kaufmann-Kohler, G, '"Iura Novit Arbiter" Est-ce bien raisonnable?' in Anne Héritier Lachat and Laurent Hirsch (eds), *De Lege Ferenda: Réflexions sur le droit désirable en l'honneur du professeur Alain Hirsch* (Éditions Slatkine, Geneva 2004b)

Kaufmann-Kohler, G, 'Le contrat et son droit devant l'arbitre' in F Belanger et al (eds), *Le contrat dans tous ses états* (Stämpfli, Bern 2004c)

Kaufmann-Kohler, G, 'Globalization of Arbitration Procedure' (2003) 36 Vanderbilt J Transnat'l L 1313

Kaushal, A, 'Reconciling the Public Interest: Third-Party Participation, Confidentiality and Privacy in NAFTA Chapter 11 Arbitrations' (2006) 9(6) Int'l Arb L R 172

Keer, SE and RW Naimark, 'Arbitrators do not "Split the Baby"—Empirical Evidence from International Business Arbitration' (2001) 18(5) J Int'l Arb 573

Kelle, U, '"Emergence" vs. "Forcing" of Empirical Data? A Crucial Problem of "Grounded Theory" Reconsidered' (2005) 6(2) Forum Qualitative Sozialforschung/Forum: Qualitative Social Research art 27 <http://www.qualitative-research.net/index.php/fqs/article/view/467/1001> accessed 28 November 2010

Kennedy, D, 'New Approaches to Comparative Law: Comparativism and International Governance' [1997] Utah L R 545

Kerr, M, 'Concord and Conflict in International Arbitration' (1997) 13(2) Arb Int'l 121

Kerr, M, 'Arbitration and the Court: The UNCITRAL Model Law' (1985) 34 ICLQ 1

Kilian, M, 'CISG and the Problem with Common Law Jurisdictions' (2001) 10 J Transnat'l L & Pol'y 217

Kitagawa, T, 'Contractual Autonomy in International Arbitration, Including a Japanese Perspective' in P Sanders (ed), *International Arbitration: Liber Amicorum for Martin Domke* (Martinus Nijhoff, The Hague 1967)

Klimas, T, *Comparative Contract Law: A Transsystemic Approach with an Emphasis on the Continental Law* (Carolina Academic P, Durham 2006)

Koch Jr, C, 'Envisioning a Global Legal Culture' (2003) 25 Mich J Int'l L 1

Koopmans, T, 'The Birth of European Law at the Crossroads of Legal Tradition' (1991) 39 Am J Comp L 493

Kroeber, AL and C Kluckhohn, *Culture: A Critical Review of Concepts and Definitions* (U Chicago Press, Chicago 1952)

Kull, A, 'Restitution as Remedy for Breach' (1994) 67 So Cal L R 1465

Kurkchiyan, M, 'Russian Legal Culture: Analysis of an Adaptive Response to an Institutional Transplant' (2009) 34 Law & Soc Inquiry 337

Laithier, Y-M, 'Rights and Remedies' in N Cohen and E McKendrick (eds), *Comparative Remedies for Breach of Contract* (Hart, Oxford 2005)

Lalive, P, 'Transnational (or Truly International) Public Policy in International Arbitration' in P Sanders (ed), *ICCA Congress Series No. 3, Comparative Arbitration Practice and Public Policy in Arbitration* (Kluwer, the Hague 1987)

Lalive, P, 'International Arbitration—Teaching and Research' in JDM Lew (ed), *Contemporary Problems in International Arbitration* (Martinus Nijhoff, Dordrecht 1986)

Lalive, P, 'Enforcing Awards' in International Chamber of Commerce (ed), *60 Years of ICC Arbitration: A Look at the Future* (ICC Press, Paris 1984)

Lalive, P, 'Les regles de conflit de lois appliqués au fond du litige par l'arbitre international siègient en Suisse' [1976] *Revue de l'arbitrage* 155

Lando, O, 'The Law Applicable to the Merits of the Dispute' in P Šarčević (ed), *Essays on International Commercial Arbitration* (Martinus Nijhoff, The Hague 1989)

Landolt, P, 'Arbitrators' Initiatives to Obtain Factual and Legal Evidence' (2012) 28(2) Arb Int'l 173

Langer, M, 'The Rise of Managerial Judging in International Criminal Law' (2005) 53 Am J Comp L 835

Law Commission, 'Law of Contract: The Parol Evidence Rule' (Law Com No 154 Cmnd 9700, 1986)

Law Commission, 'Consultation Paper, Law of Contract: The Parol Evidence Rule' (Law Com No 70, 1976)

Lawson, FH, *A Common Lawyer Looks at the Civil Law* (U Mich P, Ann Arbor 1955)

Lazareff, S, 'International Arbitration: Towards a Common Procedural Approach' in SN Frommel and BAK Rider (eds), *Conflicting Legal Cultures in Commercial Arbitration* (Kluwer, London 1999)

Leahy, ER and CJ Bianchi, 'The Changing Face of International Arbitration' (2000) 17(4) J Int'l Arb 19

Legrand, P, *Fragments on Law-as-Culture* (WEJ Ejeenk Willink, Deventer 1999)

Legrand, P, 'European Legal Systems Are Not Converging' (1996) 45 ICLQ 52

Legrand, P, 'Judicial Revision of Contracts in French Law: A Case-Study' (1988) 62 Tulane L R 963

Lew, JDM, 'Does National Court Involvement Undermine the International Arbitration Process' (2009) 24 Am R Int'l Arb 489

Lew, JDM, 'Achieving the Dream: Autonomous Arbitration' (2006) 22(2) Arb Int'l 179

Lew, JDM, 'Proof of Applicable Law in International Commercial Arbitration' in KP Berger and others (eds), *Festschrift für Otto Sandrock zum 70. Geburstag* (Verlag, Heidelberg 2000)

Lew, JDM, *Applicable Law in International Commercial Arbitration* (Oceana, Dobbs Ferry 1978)

Lew, JDM, LA Mistelis and SM Kröll, *Comparative International Commercial Arbitration* (Kluwer, The Hague 2003)

Lewison, K, *The Interpretation of Contracts* (3rd edn Sweet & Maxwell, London 2004)

Lillich, RB and CN Brower (eds), *International Arbitration in the 21st Century: Toward 'Judicialization' and Conformity?* (Transnational Publishers, New York 1994)

Lin, L-W, 'Legal Transplants Through Private Contracting' (2009) 57 Am J Comp L 711

Liu, C, 'The Concept of Fundamental Breach: Perspectives from the CISG, UNIDROIT Principles, PECL and Case Law' (2005) 9 Vindobona J Int'l Comm L & Arb 123

Lo, C-F, 'On a Balanced Mechanism for Publishing Arbitral Awards' (2008) 1(2) Contemporary Asia Arb J 235

Lookofsky, J, 'Digesting CISG Case Law: How Much Regard Should We Have?' (2004) 9 Vindobona J Int'l Comm L & Arb 181

Lookofsky, J, 'Remedies for Breach under the CISG' in CL Knapp (ed), *Commercial Damages: A Guide to Remedies in Business Litigation* (Matthew Bender, New York 1989)

Lord, R and S Salzedo, *Guide to the Arbitration Act of 1996* (Routledge, London 1996)

Luttrell, S and GA Moens, 'The Arbitration Rules of the Australian Centre for International Commercial Arbitration: Distinctive Features' (2009) 75(4) Arbitration 520

Lord Mackay of Clashfern (ed), *Halsbury's Laws of England* (4th edn LexisNexis, London 1998)

Lowenfeld, AF, 'International Arbitration as Omelette: What Goes Into the Mix' in SN Frommel and BAK Rider (eds), *Conflicting Legal Cultures in Commercial Arbitration* (Kluwer, London 1999)

Lowenfeld, AF, 'The Party-Appointed Arbitrator in International Controversies: Some Reflections' (1995) 30 Tex Int'l L J 59

Lowenfeld, AF, 'Review of S Schwebel, *International Arbitration: Three Salient Problems*' (1987) 42(3) Arb J 53.

Loza, E, 'Attorney Competence, Ethical Compliance, and Transnational Practice' (2009) 52(Oct) The Advocate (Ohio) 28.

Lustig, SL and others, 'Inside the Judges' Chambers: Narrative Responses from the National Association of Immigration Judges Stress and Burnout Survey' (2008) 23 Georgetown Immigration L J 57

Madeira, JL, 'When It's So Hard to Relate: Can Legal Systems Mitigate the Trauma of Victim-Offender Relationships?' (2009) 46 Houston L R 401

Malloy, PM, 'Current Issues in International Arbitration' (2002) 15 Transnat'l Lawyer 43

Mann, FA, 'Lex Facit Arbitrum' in P Sanders (ed), *International Arbitration: Liber Amicorum for Martin Domke* (Martinus Nijhoff, The Hague 1967)
Mantakou, AP, 'Arbitrability and Intellectual Property Disputes' in LA Mistelis and SL Brekoulakis (eds), *Arbitrability: International and Comparative Perspectives* (Kluwer, The Hague 2009)
Marella, F, 'Unity and Diversity in International Arbitration: The Case of Maritime Arbitration' (2005) 20 Am U Int'l L R 1055
Marella, F, 'Choice of Law in Third Millennium Arbitrations: The Relevance of the UNIDROIT Principles of International Commercial Contracts' (2003) 36 Vanderbilt J Transnat'l L 1137
Markesinis, BS, W Lorenz, and G Danneman, *The German Law of Obligations—Vol 1, The Law of Contracts and Restitution: A Comparative Introduction* (Clarendon, Oxford 1997)
Marsh, PDV, *Comparative Contract Law: England, France and Germany* (Gower, Aldershot 1994)
Martinez-Fraga, PJ, *The American Influence on International Commercial Arbitration: Doctrinal Developments and Discovery Methods* (CUP, Cambridge 2009)
Mather, H, 'Choice of Law for International Sales Issues Not Resolved by the CISG' (2001) 20 J L & Comm 155
Maveety, N (ed), *The Pioneers of Judicial Behaviour* (U Mich P, Ann Arbor 2003)
Mayer, P, 'L'arbitre internationale et la hierarchie des normes' [2011] Revue de l'Arbitrage 361
Mayer, P, 'The Role of the UNIDROIT Principles in ICC Arbitration Practice' in International Chamber of Commerce (ed), *UNIDROIT Principles of International Commercial Contracts: Reflections on their Use in Arbitration* (ICC, Paris 2002)
Mayer, P, 'Reflections on the International Arbitrator's Duty to Apply the Law' (2001) 17(3) Arb Int'l 235
Mayer, P, 'The Trend Toward Delocalisation in the Last 100 Years' in M Hunter and others (eds), *The Internationalisation of International Arbitration: The LCIA Centenary Conference* (Kluwer, The Hague 1995)
McConnaughay, PJ, 'The Risks and Virtues of Lawlessness: A "Second Look" at International Commercial Arbitration' (1999) 93 Nw L R 453
McGill, S, 'Consumer Arbitration Clause Enforcement: A Balanced Legislative Response' (2010) 47 Am Bus L J 361
McGinnis, JO and ML Movsesian, 'The World Trade Constitution' (2000) 114 Harv L R 511
McLauchlan, D, 'A Contract Contradiction' (1999) 20 Victoria U Wellington L R 175
McMeel, G, 'Prior Negotiations and Subsequent Conduct—The Next Step Forward for Contractual Interpretation' (2003) 119 LQR 272
McNollgast, 'Politics and the Courts: A Positive Theory of Judicial Doctrine and the Rule of Law' (1995) 68 So Cal L R 1631[1]
Menkel-Meadow, C, 'Ethics Issues in Arbitration and Related Dispute Resolution Processes: What's Happening and What's Not' (2002) 56 U Miami L R 949
Menyhart, R, 'Changing Identities and Changing Law: Possibilities for a Global Legal Culture' (2003) 10 Indiana J Global Leg Stud 157
Merry, SE, 'New Legal Realism and the Ethnography of Transnational Law' (2006) 31 L & Soc Inquiry 975
Merryman, JH, *The Civil Law Tradition: An Introduction to the Legal Systems of Western Europe and Latin America* (2nd edn Stanford UP, Stanford 1985)

[1] 'McNollgast' is the collective name used by Matthew McCubbins, Roger Noll, and Barry Weingast when writing together.

Michaels, R, 'Two Paradigms of Jurisdiction' (2006) 27 Mich J Int'l L 1003

Minoli, E and others, 'Introduction' in P Sanders (ed), *International Arbitration: Liber Amicorum for Martin Domke* (Martinus Nijhoff, The Hague 1967)

Mistelis, LA, 'Is Arbitrability a National or an International Law Issue?' in LA Mistelis and SL Brekoulakis (eds), *Arbitrability: International and Comparative Perspectives* (Kluwer, The Hague 2009)

Morse, SC and others, 'Cash Businesses and Tax Evasion' (2009) 20 Stanford L & Pol'y R 37

Mosk, RM, 'The Role of Party-Appointed Arbitrators in International Arbitration: The Experience of the Iran-US Claims Tribunal' (1988) 1 Transnat'l Lawyer 253

Müller-Chen, M, 'Article 50' in P Schlechtriem and I Schwenzer (eds), *Commentary on the UN Convention on Contracts for the International Sale of Goods (CISG)* (2nd English edn OUP, Oxford 2005)

Munday, RJC, 'The Uniform Interpretation of International Conventions' (1978) 27 ICLQ 450

Murillo, MM, 'The Evolution of Codification in the Civil Law Legal Systems: Towards Decodification and Recodification, (2001) 11 J Transnat'l L & Pol'y 163

Mustill, M, 'The 1991 Cedric Barclay Memorial Lecture' [1992] The Arbitrator 159

Mustill, M, 'Arbitration: History and Background' (1989) 6(2) J Int'l Arb 43

Mustill, M, 'The New Lex Mercatoria: The First Twenty-Five Years' (1988) 4(2) Arb Int'l 86

Nabatchi, T and LB Bingham, 'Transformative Mediation in the USPS REDRESSTM Program: Observations of ADR Specialists' (2001) 18 Hofstra Lab & Employment L J 399

Naimark, RW, 'Building a Fact-Based Global Database: The Countdown' (2003) 20(1) J Int'l Arb 105

Naimark, RW and SE Keer, 'International Private Commercial Arbitration: Expectations and Perceptions of Attorneys and Business People' (2002) 30 Int'l Bus Lawyer 203

Naimark, RW and SE Keer, 'Analysis of UNCITRAL Questionnaires on Interim Relief' (2001) 16(3) Mealey's Int'l Arb Rep 23

Needham, CA, 'Practicing Non-US Law in the United States: Multijurisdictional Practice, Foreign Legal Consultants and Other Aspects of Cross-Border Legal Practice' (2007) 15 Mich St J Int'l L 605

Nicholas, B, *The French Law of Contract* (2nd edn OUP, Oxford 1992)

Nicholas, B, 'Introduction to the French Law of Contract' in D Harris and D Tallon (eds), *Contract Law Today: Anglo-French Comparisons* (Clarendon, Oxford 1989)

Lord Nicholls of Birkenhead, 'My Kingdom for a Horse: The Meanings of Words', Chancery Bar Association Annual Lecture (London, 16 March 2005)

Nierobisz, A, 'Wrestling with the New Economy: Judicial Rhetoric in Canadian Wrongful Dismissal Claims' (2010) 35 L & Soc Inquiry 403

Nolan, M and F Sourgens, 'Issues of Proof of General Principles of Law in International Arbitration' (2009) 3(4–5) World Arb and Med R 505

Nyer, D, 'Withholding Performance for Breach in International Transactions: an Exercise in Equations, Proportions or Coercion?' (2006) 18 Pace Int'l L R 30

Ogus, A, 'The Economic Basis of Legal Culture: Networks and Monopolization' (2002) 22 OJLS 419

Ogus, A, 'Remedies: English Report' in D Harris and D Tallon (eds), *Contract Law Today: Anglo-French Comparisons* (Clarendon, Oxford 1989)

O'Neill Jr, PD and N Salam, 'Is the exceptio non adimpleti contractus Part of the New Lex Mercatoria?' in E Gaillard (ed), *Transnational Rules in International Commercial Arbitration* (ICC, Paris 1993)

Ong, CYC, 'Confidentiality of Arbitral Awards and the Advantage for Arbitral Institutions to Maintain a Repository of Awards' (2005) 1(2) Asian Int'l Arb J 169

O'Reilly, M, 'Provisions on Costs and Appeals: An Assessment from an International Perspective' (2010) 76(4) Arbitration 705

Outhwaite, O and others, 'The Pursuit of Grounded Theory in Agricultural and Environmental Regulation: A Suggested Approach to Empirical Legal Study in Biosecurity' (2007) 29(4) L & Pol'y 493

Paik, L, 'Maybe He's Depressed: Mental Illness as a Mitigating Factor for Drug Offender Accountability' (2009) 34 L & Soc Inquiry 569

Pair, LM, 'Cross-Cultural Arbitration: Do the Differences Between Cultures Still Influence International Commercial Arbitration Despite Harmonization?' (2002) 9 ILSA J Int'l & Comp L 57

Palazzolo, J, 'Chief Judge Says NY Courts Must Be "More Hospitable" for Business' (*Wall Street Journal Law Blog* 2012) <http://blogs.wsj.com/law/2012/02/14/chief-judge-says-ny-courts-must-be-more-hospitable-for-business/?mod=WSJBlog> accessed 27 August 2012

Pamboukis, C, 'Thoughts About the Applicable Law on Arbitrability' in LA Mistelis and SL Brekoulakis (eds), *Arbitrability: International and Comparative Perspectives* (Kluwer, The Hague 2009)

Park, WW, 'Rectitude in International Arbitration' (2011) 27(3) Arb Int'l 473

Park, WW, 'Arbitrators and Accuracy' (2010) 1(1) J Int'l Disp Settlement 25

Park, WW, 'Forward' in S Luttrell, *Bias Challenges in International Commercial Arbitration: The Need for a 'Real Danger' Test* (Kluwer, The Hague 2009)

Park, WW, 'Two Faces of Progress: Fairness and Flexibility in Arbitral Procedure' (2007) 23(3) Arb Int'l 499

Park, WW, 'The Specificity of International Arbitration: The Case for FAA Reform' (2003) 36 Vanderbilt J Transnat'l L 1241

Park, WW, 'Income Tax Treaty Arbitration' (2002) 10 George Mason L R 803

Park, WW, 'Neutrality, Predictability and Economic Co-operation (1995) 12(4) J Int'l Arb 99

Park, WW, 'National Law and Commercial Justice: Safeguarding Procedural Integrity in International Arbitration' (1989) 63 Tulane L R 647

Park, WW, 'National Legal Systems and Private Dispute Resolution' (1988) 82 AJIL 616

Park, WW, 'The *Lex Loci Arbitri* and International Commercial Arbitration' (1983) 32 ICLQ 21

Park, WW, 'Judicial Supervision of Transnational Commercial Arbitration' (1980) 21 Harv Int'l L J 87

Patterson, EW, 'The Interpretation and Construction of Contracts' (1964) 64 Columbia L R 833

Paulsson, J (ed), *International Handbook on Commercial Arbitration* (Kluwer, The Hague 2010)

Paulsson, J (ed), 'Unlawful Laws and the Authority of International Tribunals' (2008) 23(2) ICSID Review—Foreign Investment L J 215

Paulsson, J (ed), 'International Arbitration and the Generation of Legal Norms: Treaty Arbitration and International Law' in AJ van den Berg (ed), *ICCA Congress Series No. 13, International Arbitration 2006: Back to Basics?* (Kluwer, The Hague 2007)

Paulsson, J (ed), 'The Timely Arbitrator—Reflections on the Böckstiegel Method' in R Briner and others (eds), *Law of International Business and Dispute Settlement in the 21st Century—Liber Amicorum Karl-Heinz Böckstiegel* (Carl Heymans Verlag, Cologne 2001)

Paulsson, J (ed), 'Enforcing Arbitral Awards Notwithstanding a Local Standard Annulment (LSA)' (1998) 9(1) ICC Bull 14

Paulsson, J (ed), 'Ethics, Elitism, Eligibility' (1997) 14(4) J Int'l Arb 13

Paulsson, J (ed), 'Third World Participation in International Investment Arbitration' (1987) 2 ICSID R 19

Paulsson, J (ed), 'Introduction' (1985) 1(1) Arb Int'l 2

Paulsson, J (ed), 'The ICSID Klöckner v. Cameroon Award: The Duties of Partners in North-South Economic Development Agreements' (1984) 1(2) J Int'l Arb 145

Paulsson, J (ed), 'Delocalisation of International Commercial Arbitration: When and Why it Matters' (1983) 32 ICLQ 53

Paulsson, J (ed), 'Arbitration Unbound: Award Detached from the Law of its Country of Origin' (1981) 30 ICLQ 358

Pearson, N, 'Arbitration and the Business Man' in P Sanders (ed), *International Arbitration: Liber Amicorum for Martin Domke* (Martinus Nijhoff, The Hague 1967)

Peerenboom, R, 'Seek Truth from Facts: An Empirical Study of Enforcement of Arbitral Awards in the PRC' (2001) 49 Am J Comp L 249

Pendell, G, 'The Brazilian dispute with the "close" connection to England & Wales' (*Kluwer Arbitration Blog* 2012) <http://kluwerarbitrationblog.com/blog/2012/08/10/the-brazilian-dispute-with-the-%E2%80%98close%E2%80%99-connection-to-england-wales> accessed 23 August 2012

Petsche, MA, *The Growing Autonomy of International Commercial Arbitration* (QUADIS, Frankfurt am Main 2005)

Picciotto, S, 'Networks in International Economic Integration: Fragmented States and the Dilemmas of Neo-Liberalism' (1997) 17 Nw J Int'l L & Bus 1014

Pietrowski, R, 'Evidence in International Arbitration' (2006) 22(3) J Int'l Arb 373

Pillebout, J-F, *Recherches sur l'exception d'inexécution* (Thèse, Paris 1971)

Pinto, JG, 'Transparency Policy Initiatives in Latin America: Understanding Policy Outcomes from an Institutional Perspective' (2009) 14 Communication L & Pol'y 41

Posner, EA, 'Symbols, Signals, and Social Norms in Politics and the Law' (1998) 27 J Leg Stud 765

Posner, R, *Law and Literature* (2nd edn Harv UP, Cambridge 1998)

Posner, R, 'What Do Judges and Justices Maximize? (The Same Thing Everybody Else Does)' (1993) 3 Supreme Ct Econ R 1

PriceWaterhouse Coopers and Queen Mary, University of London School of International Arbitration, 'International Arbitration: Corporate Attitudes and Practices' (2008) <http://www.pwc.com/be/en/publications/international-arbitration.jhtml> accessed 28 November 2010

Pryles, M, 'Limits to Party Autonomy in Arbitral Procedure' (2007a) 24(3) J Int'l Arb 327

Pryles, M, 'Reflections on Transnational Public Policy' (2007b) 24(1) J Int'l Arb 1

Pryles, M, 'Confidentiality' in LW Newman and RD Hill (eds), *The Leading Arbitrators' Guide to International Arbitration* (1st edn Juris Publishing, Huntington 2004)

Lord Radcliffe, *The Law and its Compass* (Faber and Faber, London 1961)

Ramos, F, 'Judicial Cooperation in the European Courts: Testing Three Models of Judicial Behavior' (2002) 2 Global Jurist Frontiers 1

Rau, AS and EF Sherman, 'Tradition and Innovation in International Commercial Arbitration Procedure' (1995) 30 Tex Int'l L J 89

Raymond, AH, 'Confidentiality in a Forum of Last Resort: Is the Use of Confidential Arbitration a Good Idea for Business and Society?' (2005) 16 Am R Int'l Arb 479

Raynaud, E, *L'exception tirée de l'inexécution dans les contrats synallagmatiques* (Thèse, Paris 1906)

Redfern, A, 'Having Confidence in International Arbitration' (2003) 57(JAN) Disp Resol J 60

Partasides, C, N Blackaby, A Redfern and M Hunter, *Redfern and Hunter on International Arbitration* (5th edn OUP, Oxford 2009)

Redfern, A and others, *Law and Practice of Commercial Arbitration* (4th edn Sweet & Maxwell, London 2004)

Reed, L and J Sutcliffe, 'The "Americanization" of International Arbitration?' (2001) 16(4) Mealey's Int'l Arb Rep 37

Rehnquist, W, 'A Jurist's View of Arbitration' (1977) 32 Arb J 1

Reimann, M, 'The Good, the Bad, and the Ugly: The Reform of the German Law of Obligations' (2009) 83 Tulane L R 877

Reisman, WM, *Nullity and Revision* (Yale UP, London 1971)

Relis, T, '"It's Not About the Money!" A Theory on Misconceptions of Plaintiffs' Litigation Aims' (2007) 68 U Pittsburgh L R 701

Reuben, RC, 'Personal Autonomy and Vacatur after Hall Street' (2009) 113 Penn St L R 1103

Ribstein, LE, 'Choosing Law by Contract' (1993) 18 J Corp L 245

Ridgway, D, 'International Arbitration: The Next Growth Industry' (1999) 54(FEB) Disp Resol J 50

Rigaux, F, 'Souveraineté des etats et arbitrage transnational' in P Fouchard and others (eds), *Le droit des relations economiques internationales: etudes offertes à Berthold Goldman* (Litec, Paris 1982)

Riles, A, 'Global Designs: The Aesthetics of International Legal Practice' (1999) 93 Proc Am Soc'y Int'l L 28

Rivkin, DW, 'Towards a New Paradigm in International Arbitration: The Town Elder Model Revisited' (2008) 24(3) Arb Int'l 375

Rivkin, DW, 'Enforceability of Awards Based on Lex Mercatoria' (1993) 9(1) Arb Int'l 67

Robert, J, 'De la place de la loi dans l'arbitrage' in P Sanders (ed), *International Arbitration: Liber Amicorum for Martin Domke* (Martinus Nijhoff, The Hague 1967)

Rodner, JO, 'International and National Arbitration: A Fading Distinction' (2002) 19(5) J Int'l Arb 491

Roesler, SM, 'The Ethics of Global Justice Lawyering' (2010) 13 Yale Human Rights & Development L J 185

Rogers, CA, 'Lawyers Without Borders' (2009) 30 U Penn J Int'l L 1035

Rogers, CA, 'Transparency in International Commercial Arbitration' (2006) 54 U Kansas L R 1401

Rogers, CA, 'The Vocation of the International Arbitrator' (2005) 20 Am U Int'l L R 957

Rogers, CA, 'Fit and Function in Legal Ethics: Developing a Code of Conduct for International Arbitration' (2002) 23 Mich J Int'l L 341

Rogers, CA, 'Gulliver's Troubled Travels, or, the Conundrum of Comparative Law' (1998) 67 George Washington L R 149

Rowley, J William and Robert Wisner, 'Party Autonomy and its Discontents: The Limits Imposed by Arbitrators and Mandatory Laws' (2011) 5(3) World Arb and Med R 321

Rubino-Sammartano, M, 'Amiable Compositeur (Joint Mandate to Settle) and Ex Bono et Aequo (Discretional Authority to Mitigate Strict Law): Apparent Synonyms Revisited' (1992) 9(1) J Int'l Arb 5.

Rubins, N, '"Manifest Disregard of the Law" and Vacatur of Arbitral Awards in the United States' (2001) 12 Am R Int'l Arb 363

Rutledge, PB, 'Toward a Contractual Approach for Arbitral Immunity' (2004) 39 Georgia L R 151, 195

Rutledge, PB and AW Howard, 'Arbitrating Disputes Between Companies and Individuals: Lessons From Abroad' (2010) 65(APR) Disp Resol J 30

Ryan, LM, 'The Convention on Contracts for the International Sale of Goods: Divergent Interpretations' (1995) 4 Tulane J Int'l & Comp L 99

Salomon, C, 'The Conduct of an International Arbitration: Do the Rules Make a Difference?' (2004) 21(2) J Int'l Arb 103

Sandifer, DV, *Evidence Before International Tribunals* (U Va P, Charlottesville 1975)

Sandrock, O, 'To Continue Nationalizing or to De-Nationalize? That is Now the Question in International Arbitration' (2001) 12 Am R Int'l Arb 301

Sayre, PB, 'Development of Commercial Arbitration Law' (1927) 37 Yale L J 595

Scheuner, U, 'Decisions ex aequo et bono by International Courts and Arbitration Tribunals' in P Sanders (ed), *International Arbitration: Liber Amicorum for Martin Domke* (Martinus Nijhoff, The Hague 1967)

Scherer, M, 'Long-Awaited New French Arbitration Law Revealed' (*Kluwer Arbitration Blog* 2011) (2011a) <http://kluwerarbitrationblog.com/blog/2011/01/15/long-awaited-new-french-arbitration-law-revealed> accessed 5 August 2012

Scherer, M, 'Arbitral Institutions Under Scrutiny' (*Kluwer Arbitration Blog* 2011) (2011b) <http://kluwerarbitrationblog.com/blog/2011/10/05/arbitral-institutions-under-scrutiny> accessed 28 July 2012

Schlechtriem, P, 'Requirements of Application and Sphere of Applicability of the CISG' (2005) 36 Victoria U Wellington L R 781

Koehler, M and A Kritzer (trs), P Schlechtriem, 'Auslegung, Lückenfüllung und Weiterentwicklung', Symposium zu Ehren von Professor Dr, iur Dr, hc Frank Vischer (Basel 11 May 2004) <http://cisgw3.law.pace.edu/cisg/biblio/schlechtriem6.html> accessed 28 November 2010

Schmidt-Kessel, M, 'Article 8' in P Schlechtriem and I Schwenzer (eds), *Commentary on the UN Convention on Contracts for the International Sale of Goods (CISG)* (2nd English edn OUP, Oxford 2005)

Schmidt-Kessel, M, 'Article 9' in I Schwenzer (ed), *Schlechtriem & Schwenzer Commentary on the UN Convention on Contracts for the International Sale of Goods (CISG)* (3rd English edn OUP, Oxford 2010)

Schmitthoff, CM, 'The Codification of the Law of International Trade' [1985] J Bus L 23

Schmitthoff, CM, 'The Reform of the English Law of Arbitration' [1977] J Bus L 305

Schneider, AK, 'Not Quite a World Without Trials: Why International Dispute Resolution is Increasingly Judicialized' [2006] J Disp Resol 119

Schreuer, C, 'Three Generations of ICSID Annulment Proceedings' in E Gaillard and Y Banifatemi (eds), *Annulment of ICSID Awards* (Juris Publishing, Huntington 2004)

Schreuer, C and M Weiniger, 'Conversations Across Cases—Is there a Doctrine of Precedent in Investment Arbitration?' in P Muchlinski, F Ortino and C Schreuer (eds), *The Oxford Handbook on International Investment Law* (OUP, Oxford 2008)

Schultz, T and R Kovacs, 'The Rise of a Third Generation of Arbitrators?—Fifteen Years after Dezalay and Garth' (2012) 28(2) Arb In'l 161

Schwartz, E, 'The Domain of Arbitration and Issues of Arbitrability: The View from the ICC' (1994) 9 ICSID R 17

Secunda, PM, '"Arasoi o mizu ni nagasu" or "Let the dispute flow to water": Pedagogical Methods for Teaching Arbitration law in American and Japanese Law Schools' (2006) 21 Ohio St J on Disp Resol 687

Segal, JA and HJ Spaeth, *The Supreme Court and the Attitudinal Model Revisited* (CUP, Cambridge 2002)

Seidenberg, S, 'International Arbitration Loses Its Grip' ABA Journal (April 2010) <http://www.abajournal.com/magazine/article/international_arbitration_loses_its_grip> accessed 28 November 2010

Sellers, MNS, 'The Doctrine of Precedent in the United States of America' (2006) 54 Am J Comp L 67

Shapiro, M, *Courts: A Comparative and Political Analysis* (U Chicago P, Chicago 1981)

Shapiro, M, 'Political Jurisprudence' (1964) 52 Kentucky L J 294

Shapiro, S, *Legality* (Harv U P, Cambridge 2010)

Sheppard, A, 'Rights of Appeal under s 68 of the Arbitration Act 1996, Case Comment on *Lesotho Highlands Development Authority v Impregilo SpA*' (2005) 8(5) Int'l Arb L R 64

Shilston, AW, 'The Evolution of Modern International Arbitration' (1987) 4(2) J Int'l Arb 45

Shore, L, 'What Lawyers Need to Know About International Arbitration' (2003) 20(1) J Int'l Arb 67
Silberman, L, 'Transnational Litigation: Is there a "Field"?' (2006) 39 Vanderbilt J Transnat'l L 1427
Silberman, L and F Ferrari, 'Getting to the Law Applicable to the Merits in International Arbitration and the Consequences of Getting it Wrong' in F Ferrari and S Kröll (eds), *Conflict of Laws in International Arbitration* (Sellier, Munich 2011)
Silver, C, 'Winners and Losers in the Globalization of Legal Services: Situating the Market for Foreign Lawyers' (2005) 45 Va J Int'l L 897
Singhal, S, 'Independence and Impartiality of Arbitrators' (2008) 11(3) Int'l Arb L R 124
Siqueiros, JL, 'The Arbitral Phase: The Comparative Method of Research and the Evaluation of the Different Issues in Historical Perspective' in AJ van den Berg (ed), *International Arbitration in a Changing World* (Kluwer, The Hague 1993)
Skeat, J and A Perry, 'Grounded Theory as a Method for Research in Speech and Language Therapy' (2008) 43(2) Int'l J Language and Communication Disorders 95
Slate II, WK, 'Paying Attention to "Culture" in International Commercial Arbitration' (2004) 59(OCT) Disp Resol J 96
Slaughter, A-M, 'Judicial Globalization' (2000) 40 Va J Int'l L 1103
Smit, H, 'Contractual Modifications of the Arbitral Process' (2009) 113 Penn St L R 995
Smit, H, 'Breach of Confidentiality as a Ground for Avoidance of the Arbitration Agreement' (2000) 11 Am R Int'l Arb 567
Smit, H, 'A-National Arbitration' (1989) 63 Tulane L R 629
Smit, H, 'The Future of International Commercial Arbitration: A Single Transnational Institution?' (1986) 25 Columbia J Transnat'l L 9
Smits, JM, 'Law Making in the European Union: On Globalization and Contract Law in Divergent Legal Cultures' (2007) 67 La L R 1181
Smureanu, I, *Confidentiality in International Commercial Arbitration* (Kluwer, The Hague 2011)
Sohn, LB, 'Arbitration of International Disputes *ex aequo et bono*' in P Sanders (ed), *International Arbitration: Liber Amicorum for Martin Domke* (Martinus Nijhoff, The Hague 1967)
Sono, K, 'The Rise of Anational Contract Law in the Age of Globalization' (2001) 75 Tulane L R 1185
Sornarajah, M, 'Power and Justice: Third World Resistance in International Law' (2006) 10 Singapore Ybk Int'l L 19
Sourgens, FG, 'Comparative Law as Rhetoric: An Analysis of the Use of Comparative Law in International Arbitration' (2007) 8 Pepperdine Disp Resol L J 1
Spiller, PT and R Gely, 'Congressional Control or Judicial Independence: The Determinants of US Supreme Court Labor-Relations Decisions, 1949–1988' (1992) 23 Rand J Econ 463
Stallard, A, 'Joining the Culture Club: Examining Cultural Context When Implementing International Dispute Resolution' (2002) 17 Ohio St Disp Resol J 463
Staudt, N, L Epstein, and P Wiedenbeck, 'The Ideological Component of Judging in the Taxation Context' (2006) 84 Wash U L R 1797
Staughton, C, 'How Do the Courts Interpret Commercial Contracts?' (1999) 58(2) CLJ 303
Stewart, DP and A Conley, 'E-mail Service on Foreign Defendants: Time for an International Approach?' (2007) 39 Georgetown J Int'l L 755
Steyn, J, 'Written Contracts: To What Extent May Evidence Control Language?' [1988] Current Leg Probs 23
Stipanowich, T, 'Arbitration: The "New Litigation"' [2010] Illinois L R 1
Stoffel, WA, 'Enlightened Decision Making' (2001) 75 Tulane L R 1195
Strauss, AL and J Corbin, *Basics of Qualitative Research: Techniques and Procedures for Developing Grounded Theory* (2nd edn Sage, Thousand Oaks 1998)
Strauss, AL and J Corbin, *Grounded Theory in Practice* (Sage, Thousand Oaks 1997)

Strauss, AL and J Corbin, 'Grounded Theory Methodology: An Overview' in NK Denzin and YS Lincoln (eds), *Handbook of Qualitative Research* (Sage, Thousand Oaks 1994)

Strong, SI and JJ Dries, 'Witness Statements under the IBA Rules of Evidence: What to do about Hearsay?' (2005) 21(3) Arb Int'l 301

Stürner, R, 'Why are Europeans Afraid to Litigate in the United States?' in MJ Bonell (ed), *Conferenze e seminari di Centro di studi e ricerche di diritto comparato e straniero* (Centro di studi e ricerche di diritto comparato e straniero, Rome 2001)

Sunstein, C and others, *Are Judges Political? An Empirical Analysis of the Federal Judiciary* (Brookings Institution P, Washington 2006)

Sussman, E, 'Why Arbitrate? The Benefits and Savings' (2009) 81(OCT) NY St Bar J 20

Swallow, M, 'Smooth as Silks' *The Lawyer* (London 5 April 2004) <http://www.thelawyer.com/smooth-as-silks/109491.article> accessed 28 November 2010

Swallow, M, 'Swedish Appeals Court Upholds AIT Award, Reverses Decision by Stockholm City Court' (1999) 14(4) Mealey's Int'l Arb Rep 3

Sweet, AS and TL Brunell, 'Constructing a Supranational Constitution: Dispute Resolution and Governance in the European Community' (1998) 92 Am Pol Sci R 63

Sweet, J, 'Contract Making and Parol Evidence: Diagnosis and Treatment of a Sick Rule' (1968) 53 Cornell L R 1036

Symeonides, SC, 'Contracts Subject to Non-State Norms' (2006) 54 Am J Comp L 209

Tallon, D, 'Remedies: French Report' in D Harris and D Tallon (eds), *Contract Law Today: Anglo-French Comparisons* (Clarendon, Oxford 1989)

Tamanaha, BZ, 'The Distorting Slant in Quantitative Studies of Judging' (2009) 50 Boston College L R 685

Tashiro, K, 'Quest for a Rational and Proper Method for the Publication of Arbitral Awards' (1992) 9(2) J Int'l Arb 97

Terry, LS, 'The European Commission Project Regarding Competition in Professional Services' (2009) Nw J Int'l L & Bus 1

Terry, LS and others, 'Transnational Legal Practice' (2008) 42 Int'l Lawyer 833

Teubner, G, 'Global Private Regimes: Neo-Spontaneous Law and Dual Constitution of Autonomous Sectors?' in K-H Ladeur (ed), *Public Governance in the Age of Globalization* (Ashgate, Aldershot 2004)

Teubner, G, 'Breaking Frames: The Global Interplay of Legal and Social Systems' (1997) 45 Am J Comp L 149

Teubner, G, 'Autopoeisis in Law and Society: A Rejoinder to Blankenburg' (1984) 18 L & Soc R 291

Thirgood, R, 'International Arbitration: The Justice Business' (2004) 21(4) J Int'l Arb 341

Tieder Jr, JB, 'Factors to Consider in the Choice of Procedural and Substantive Law in International Arbitration' (2003) 20(4) J Int'l Arb 393

Trakman, LE, '"Legal Traditions" and International Commercial Arbitration' (2006) 17 Am R Int'l Arb 1

Treitel, GH, *The Law of Contract* (11th edn Sweet & Maxwell, London 2003)

Treitel, GH, *Remedies for Breach of Contract: A Comparative Account* (Clarendon, Oxford 1988)

Treitel, GH, 'Some Problems of Breach of Contract' (1967) 30 MLR 139

Treibel, V, 'The Choice of Law in Commercial Relations: A German Perspective' (1988) 37 ICLQ 935

Trubek, DM and others, 'Global Restructuring and the Law: Studies of the Internationalization of Legal Fields and the Creation of Transnational Arenas, (1994) 44 Case Western L R 407

Tschanz, P-Y, 'Arbitrage international et sécurité juridique' in P Gilliéron and others (eds), *Mélanges en l'honneur de François Dessemontet* (CEDIDAC, Geneva 2009)

Tschanz, P-Y, 'The Award: How to Structure it, How Detailed? Order and Reasons, Adding Insult to Injury?' in M Wirth (ed), *The Resolution of the Dispute—from Hearing to the Award* (Association Suisse de l'Arbitrage, Geneva 2007)

Ulmer, NC, 'Language, Truth, and Arbitral Accuracy' (2011) 28(4) J Int'l Arb 295
Ulmer, NC, 'A Comment on "The 'Americanization' of International Arbitration?"' (2001) 15(6) Mealey's Int'l Arb Rep 24
UNCITRAL, *Explanatory Note by the UNCITRAL Secretariat on the United Nations Convention on Contracts for the International Sale of Goods* <http://www.uncitral.org/pdf/english/texts/sales/cisg/CISG.pdf> accessed 28 November 2010
UNCITRAL, *Explanatory Note by the UNCITRAL Secretariat on the 1985 Model Law on International Commercial Arbitration as amended in 2006* <http://www.uncitral.org/pdf/english/texts/arbitration/ml-arb/07-86998_Ebook.pdf> accessed 28 November 2010
Vago, S, *Law and Society* (2nd edn Prentice-Hall, Englewood Cliffs 1988)
van den Berg, AJ (ed), *ICCA Congress Series No. 13, International Arbitration 2006: Back to Basics?* (Kluwer, The Hague 2007)
van den Berg, AJ (ed), 'Refusals of Enforcement under the New York Convention of 1958: The Unfortunate Few' (1999) 10 ICC Bull special supplement 75
Van Harten, G and M Loughlin, 'Investment Treaty Arbitration as a Species of Global Administrative Law' (2006) 17(1) EJIL 121
van Hof, J, *Commentary on the UNCITRAL Arbitration Rules: The Application by the Iran-US Claims Tribunal* (Kluwer, The Hague 1991)
van Houtte, H, 'The UNIDROIT Principles of International Commercial Contracts' (1995) 11(4) Arb Int'l 373
van Zelst, B, 'The Proposed New Dutch Arbitration Act' (2012) 15(3) Int'l Arb L R 75.
von Mehren, AT, 'The Rise of Transnational Legal Practice and the Task of Comparative Law' (2001) 75 Tulane L R 1215
Wai, R, 'Transnational Private Law and Private Ordering in a Contested Global Society' (2005) 46 Harv Int'l L J 471
Waibel, M and others (eds), *The Backlash Against Investment Arbitration* (Kluwer, The Hague 2010).
Waincymer, J, 'International Arbitration and the Duty to Know the Law' (2011) 28(3) J Int'l Arb 201
Wallace, IND, 'Control by the Courts: A Plea for More, Not Less' (1990) 6(3) Arb Int'l 253
Wang, SC and L Cao, 'Toward Greater Party Autonomy and Transparency: The CIETAC Introduces its 2005 New Rules' (2005) 8(4) Int'l Arb L R 117
Weber, M, *Economy and Society* (U Cal P, Berkeley 1978)
Shils, E and M Rheinstein (trs), M Weber, *On Law in Economy and Society* (Harv UP, Cambridge 1954)
Webster, TH, 'Party Control in International Arbitration' (2003) 19(2) Arb Int'l 119
Weidemeier, WMC, 'Judging-Lite: How Arbitrators Use and Create Precedent' (2012) 90 N Carolina L R 1091
Weidemeier, WMC, 'Toward a Theory of Precedent in International Arbitration' (2010) 51 William & Mary L R 1895
Weisbord, N, 'Conceptualizing Aggression' (2009) 20 Duke J Comp & Int'l L 1
Weisman, K, 'The Euro-American Court of Arbitration: Can it Compete in the Large Market of International Commercial Arbitration?' (2007) 16(SUM) Currents: Int'l Trade L J 70
White & Case LLP and Queen Mary, University of London School of International Arbitration, '2010 International Arbitration Survey: Choices in International Arbitration' <http://www.arbitrationonline.org/docs/2010_InternationalArbitration SurveyReport.pdf> accessed 28 November 2010
Wilkey, M, 'The Practicalities of Cross-Cultural Arbitration' in SN Frommel and BAK Rider (eds), *Conflicting Legal Cultures in Commercial Arbitration* (Kluwer, London 1999)
Williams, DAR, 'The Further Development of International Arbitration Through the Unidroit Principles of International Commercial Contracts' (1996) 2 NZ Bus L Q 7

Wittinghofer, M, 'Instead of a Foreword: What Arbitration Is About—Or: How to Win the Moot' in P Huber and A Mullis (eds), *The CISG—A New Textbook for Students and Practitioners, Special Edition for Participants of the 15th Willem C. Vis International Commercial Arbitration Moot* (Sellier, Munich 2007), <http://www.cisg.law.pace.edu/cisg/moot/Wittinghofer.pdf>

Wood, DS, 'International Arbitration and Punitive Damages: Delocalization and Mandatory Rules' (2004) 71 Defence Counsel J 402

Xiao, JZ, J Dahya, and Z Lin, 'A Grounded Theory Exposition of the Role of the Supervisory Board in China' (2004) 15 British J Management 53

Yarn, D, 'The Death of ADR: A Cautionary Tale of Isomorphism through Institutionalization' (2004) 108 Penn St L R 929

Yu, H, 'Explore the Void—An Evaluation of Arbitration Theories' (2004) 7(6) Int'l Arb L R 180 (Part 1) and (2005) 8(1) Int'l Arb L R 14 (Part 2)

Yu, H and M Ahmed, 'The New French Arbitration Law: An Analysis' (2012) 15(1) Int'l Arb L R 20.

Ziegel, J, 'The Scope of the Convention: Reaching out to Article One and Beyond' (2005) 25 J L & Comm 59

Zimmerman, R, *The Law of Obligations: Roman Foundations of the Civilian Tradition* (OUP, Oxford 1996)

Zuppi, AL, 'The Parol Evidence Rule: A Comparative Study of the Common Law, the Civil Law Tradition, and Lex Mercatoria' (2007) 35 Georgia J Int'l & Comp L 233

Weir, T (tr), K Zweigert and H Kötz, *Introduction to Comparative Law* (3rd edn Clarendon, Oxford 1998)

Index

The manufacturer's authorised representative in the EU for product safety is Oxford University Press España S.A. of el Parque Empresarial San Fernando de Henares, Avenida de Castilla, 2 – 28830 Madrid (www.oup.es/en or product.safety@oup.com). OUP España S.A. also acts as importer into Spain of products made by the manufacturer.

www.ingramcontent.com/pod-product-compliance
Lightning Source LLC
LaVergne TN
LVHW020057220926
848484LV00002BB/645

* 9 7 8 0 1 9 9 6 5 8 0 0 8 *